"Log College Press has done the church a great service in collecting the reflections of an essential black voice from the Presbyterian and Reformed tradition. I am genuinely excited about this book because Grimké is a hidden gem that has remained buried for far too long. He was a man possessed of great learning and pastoral insight who ministered faithfully and courageously in a time of sweeping national turbulence and racial hostility. We can all benefit from the vision communicated in these pages."

— **Russ Whitfield**, Lead Pastor of Grace Mosaic, Washington, D.C., Visiting Professor at Reformed Theological Seminary, and Director of Cross-Cultural Advancement for Reformed University Fellowship

"How would you like to sit at the feet of a pastor who served a single congregation nearly fifty years, soaking up his wisdom and insight into pastoral ministry? How much would you pay for such an opportunity? Thanks to Log College Press, you have this opportunity and you don't have the break the bank to do it. That's because here you have distilled the pastoral wisdom of Francis Grimké, a hero of mine, who served a Presbyterian pastorate in Washington, D.C., between 1878 and 1928. What you'll find is a feast that will guide you in the Lord's service for his glory!"

— **Dr. Sean Michael Lucas**, Senior Pastor of Independent Presbyterian Church, Memphis, TN, and Chancellor's Professor of Church History, Reformed Theological Seminary

"I am nothing short of thrilled that Log College Press has published Francis Grimké's *Meditations on Preaching*. When Grimké says: 'I have never had any desire to preach what are called great sermons – sermons which display learning or ability, and which are relished particularly by the highly educated members of the congregation; but I have desired and have sought to preach helpful sermons, sermons that meet the real needs of the human heart in the midst of life's trials, struggles, temptations, sorrows…' it makes me want to sit down right there at his feet and learn. Grimké is a Presbyterian hero, but he is a blessing for the whole church. Read and be encouraged, fellow preachers."

— **Dr. J. Ligon Duncan III**, Chancellor and CEO of Reformed Theological Seminary, and John E. Richards Professor of Systematic and Historical Theology

"*Meditations on Preaching* is a helpful reminder of the serious nature of the pulpit ministry. Today it is easy to see preaching as an end in itself. However, Francis Grimké, one of the giants in African American church history, reminds us that the power and genius of preaching is in expounding the Word of God, not in echoing popular ideologies. For all who aspire to fill the pulpit, Francis Grimké's wisdom is indispensable."

— **Dr. Carl Ellis**, Jr., Assistant to the Chancellor, Senior Fellow of the African American Leadership Initiative, and Provost's Professor of Theology and Culture at Reformed Theological Seminary

Meditations On Preaching

Francis James Grimké

Log College Press

www.logcollegepress.com

Meditations on Preaching
By Francis James Grimké

Log College Press
92 Cotton Wood Dr.
Madison, MS 39110
www.logcollegepress.com

Page and cover design by Clay Meyer
Printed in the USA by Color House Graphics, Grand Rapids, MI

ISBN: 978-1-948102-09-4 (Paperback)

ISBN: 978-1-948102-10-0 (ePub)

ISBN: 978-1-948102-11-7 (Mobi)

FOREWORD

I am a pastor in the Presbyterian Church in America, a denomination that formed in 1973 and declared itself to be "A Continuing Presbyterian Church." In this proclamation, the founders were declaring a connection to historic Presbyterianism in America and a belief that it was "preserving what was best from the PCUS [Presbyterian Church in the United States]."[1] This connection and preservation, however, has rarely included any focus on the biblical writings and teachings of Black American men and women within the Presbyterian tradition. The overwhelmingly common experience of those who have pursued theological education in the seminaries that train ministers for biblically conservative Presbyterian denominations is being assigned readings by theologians within the tradition who defended American chattel slavery.

During one of my seminary courses, the professor asked us why we thought there were no Black American Presbyterian denominations. In the history of America, you find the formation of distinctly Black denominations – African Methodist Episcopal Church, African Methodist Episcopal Zion Church, Colored Methodist Episcopal Church, National Baptist Convention, Progressive National Baptist Convention, Church of God in Christ. No Presbyterians. In my ignorance, I believed the answer was found in the racist ideology of Southern Presbyterianism. I thought that this was too much for Blacks to bear and made them unwilling to self-identify as Presbyterian. I was sorely mistaken – not about the racist ideology of Southern Presbyterianism, but about the willingness of Blacks to self-identify as Presbyterian.

Black Presbyterians in American history did not form separate Black Presbyterian denominations because they chose to remain in the majority

---

1. Sean Michael Lucas, *For a Continuing Church* (Phillipsburg, NJ: P&R Publishing Co., 2015), 3.

White Presbyterian denominations, seeking interracial cooperation and integration. In addition, they fought to hold their White brothers accountable to biblical norms of justice and love in the context of shared mission.[2]

All-Black Presbyteries continued well into the 1900s, but they never split off to form a Black Presbyterian Church. The process of learning about Black Presbyterians in American church history has been nothing less than the quenching of a deep thirst with the most refreshing of water. It has always been a struggle for me to step to the microphone and address my fellow presbyters with the standard greeting, "Fathers and brothers." I simply could not bring myself to say the word "Fathers" to a room full of White men. The experience of becoming acquainted with Black Presbyterian Fathers is a balm to my soul.

The Reverend Doctor Francis James Grimké (1850-1937) is one of those fathers. Born into slavery in Charleston, South Carolina, his story is complex and compelling. His White father provided for Grimké's freedom in his will. So at five years of age he became free. When he was ten years old, his older half-brother attempted to re-enslave him. Grimké escaped and served as a valet for a Confederate officer, whom he served for two years. He was captured and sold by his half-brother, serving in bondage until the end of the Civil War. He had opportunity to attend Lincoln University (he was the valedictorian of the class of 1870) and Princeton Theological Seminary (class of 1878). As I read his call to the pastorate at 15th Street Presbyterian Church in Washington, D.C., issued February 7, 1878, my heart was warmed again:

The congregation of 15th Street Presbyterian Church Washington

---

2. Sean Michael Lucas, "Lost Legacies: African American Fathers and Brothers in Presbyterian History," PCA General Assembly Workshop, Greensboro, NC, 2017.

City, being on sufficient grounds, well satisfied of the ministerial qualifications of you, Frank J. Grimké, now of Princeton, N.J.; and having, from our past experience of your labors, good hopes that your ministrations in the gospel will be profitable to our spiritual interests, do earnestly call and desire you to undertake the pastoral office in said congregation, promising you in the discharge of your duty all proper support, encouragement, and obedience in the Lord.[3]

Our churches continue to use similar language in the calling of ministers to their pulpits. I hear my own call in his and am reminded that, although still a minority in the PCA, God has always called Black ministers to labor in White Presbyterian denominations.

What would be the mark of his pastoral labors at 15th Street Presbyterian Church? You will become familiar with that mark as you read his meditations on preaching in the pages of this book. You will hear him reflect after almost forty years of preaching:

I have never had any desire to preach what are called great sermons – sermons which display learning or ability, and which are relished particularly by the highly educated members of the congregation; but I have desired and have sought to preach helpful sermons, sermons that meet the real needs of the human heart in the midst of life's trials, struggles, temptations, sorrows…The function of the pulpit is not to entertain, to amuse, to satisfy an idle curiosity: it is to instruct, to inspire, to fire the heart and mind, to implant within us noble desires and ambitions: and, above all to keep ever before men the one supreme figure in history, the Lord Jesus Christ, and to beget within

---

3. Carter G. Woodson, ed., *The Works of Francis J. Grimké, Volume I: Addresses Mainly Personal and Racial* (Washington, D.C.: The Associated Publishers, Inc., 1942), ix.

them a passion for him, and for a Christly life.

Dr. Grimké labored in ministry to keep presenting to people, in word and by example, the Lord Jesus Christ and their need for his saving power. Because of that he also wrote, "I have always been ready to speak in behalf of the rights of the race, and have never hesitated to condemn, and in the strongest terms, those who are trying to deprive us of our rights as men and as American citizens."

Dr. Grimké rooted the biblical mandate for reconciliation in creation. He preached "that 'God hath made of one blood all nations that dwell upon the face of the earth.' He insisted that since all people were made of one blood they should live as brothers and worship together one God."[4] Carter G. Woodson notes that one of the White ministers who responded to Dr. Grimké's teaching on this point claimed that he was being inconsistent because in the attempt to "uproot the argument in favor of segregation," he failed to quote all of that verse (Acts 17:26). He neglected to include the fact that God "hath appointed to them their metes and bounds."[5] Indeed, this argument was still being made by some Presbyterian ministers in support of the separation of the races when my denomination was founded. The White minister argued that "the Negro was created and placed in Africa, the white man in Europe, and the yellow man in Asia. The church, in segregating the Negro, was doing the will of God."[6] What was Dr. Grimke's response?

If God appointed to each race its metes and bounds, by what right did the white man come from Europe and take possession of the Red Man's land in America? By what right did the white man compel the

---

4. *Ibid.*, xvi.

5. *Ibid.*

6. *Ibid.*

Negro to come to America to labor for him on the plantations and in the mines? By what right can the white man go to Africa today and deprive the natives of their most fertile land and corner them on reserves where they have to starve or leave to labor like slaves in the mines and on the plantations?[7]

I invite you into these meditations on preaching. Hear the thoughts and reflections of a Black Presbyterian minister who, while living under the intolerable weight of American oppression, segregation, and injustice, was captivated by Jesus Christ. Hear from this "father" whose biblical fidelity compelled him to be drawn into the battle for human rights. As Woodson writes, "[A]s a minister he was duty-bound to plead for equality and justice in accordance with the teachings of the Bible."[8] Be encouraged as you hear what commitment to proclaim Christ no matter the cost sounds like. Be blessed to know that God is never without faithful witnesses who will apply his truth to the hearts of people.

Irwyn Ince
Assistant Pastor at Grace DC Presbyterian Church
Director at Grace DC Institute for Cross-Cultural Mission
Washington, D.C.

---

7. *Ibid.*
8. *Ibid.*, xviii.

MEDITATIONS ON PREACHING[1]

Every preaching service on the Sabbath is a feast spread by God, and to it all are invited. But not a great many come, and the excuses given are various. Even professing Christians are found dodging behind excuses of one kind or another, of which they ought to be ashamed – excuses that would not keep them away from business, or pleasure, or anything that they really wanted to do. [1]

In preaching are we seeking to impress the truth or to impress ourselves upon others – to draw men's attention to Jesus Christ or to ourselves? Too often it is of ourselves that we are thinking; and this is one reason why, though we may preach brilliant and eloquent sermons, they are attended with so little results in the development of Christian character, in the building up of those who listen in faith and holiness. The preacher's aims should be to get such a clear conception of the truth, and should be so impressed with its value, its importance, that in his effort to present it, he will not only lose sight of himself, but his hearers also will, in thought of the truth. It is of no importance whatever that our hearers should think of us, but it is important that they should think of the truth of God presented. [3]

Grip your subject, get a firm hold upon it; then plunge into it; go at it

---

1. The following meditations are found in Carter G. Woodson, ed., *The Works of Francis J. Grimké, Volume III: Stray Thoughts and Meditations* (Washington, D.C.: The Associated Publishers, Inc., 1942). The number in brackets at the end of each meditation is the page on which it begins in that volume, available at www.logcollegepress.com/francis-james-grimke. These meditations have been edited in some places to conform to modern spelling and grammar.

as if you meant business. Keep it well in hand; don't lose sight of it for a moment; and don't let anything intrude that will tend to divert your attention, or the attention of your hearers. Let your treatment be fresh, which will always be the case where the subject grips you, where you are really interested in what you are talking about. Where your utterances are merely formal, merely perfunctory, it is impossible to impart life, to give freshness to what you are saying. I listened to a sermon this afternoon (Bordentown, N. J., Aug. 23, 1914), by a Rev. gentleman, which failed of the effect which it might have produced, because, while the matter was good, he did not have it well in hand. It was not sufficiently compact and pointed. He failed to grip the subject, and the subject to grip him. He did not go at it as if he meant business and knew what he was driving at. It was a flat failure. [6]

Help us, O Lord, more and more, as thy servants, to realize that in and of ourselves we can do nothing: we are only instruments in thy hand, and our effectiveness as instruments depends entirely upon whether or whether not the Spirit uses us. From beginning to end, all effective work is due to the presence and power of the Spirit in the preacher and in the people to whom he speaks. The more fully we understand this, and the more fully, after we have made the most careful preparation, we depend upon the Spirit in all that we do or attempt to do, the more certain we may be of results. "Not by might, nor by power, but by my Spirit saith the Lord," is a truth which every minister should lay to heart and carry ever with him in all that he undertakes for the Lord. There is no other guarantee of success. There is no other power that can bring results, that can open blind eyes, unstop deaf ears, soften hard hearts, and bring men to repentance and faith.

When the Holy Spirit is upon you, the truth grips you in a way that it doesn't at other times, and the truth as uttered by you at such times, grips others in a way different from the ordinary preaching of the word. Hence the importance in all our preaching of having the enduement from on high, the unction from the Holy One. [17]

Sometimes we ministers get discouraged at the seemingly little results which flow from our preaching of the gospel; but we should not be. We shall be helped, if we but remember, that we have nothing to do with results. All that is required of us is to be faithful in sowing the good seed. The results are with God. Let us not worry about results. If we worry at all, let it be as to whether we are doing our full duty, whether we are sowing beside all waters, whether we are instant in season and out of season. That is what we need to worry about, if we worry at all. [18]

The greatness of a sermon does not depend upon its literary qualities, or the profoundness of its thought, but upon the extent to which it is used by the Holy Spirit in bringing about spiritual results. Peter's sermon on the day of Pentecost, plain, simple, direct, pointed, dealing with conditions as they really were, judged by the results that followed, was one of the greatest, if not the greatest sermon ever preached. If, as ministers, we find ourselves desirous of preaching great sermons, let them be great as measured by this standard – great in spiritual effects – great in winning souls to Christ, and in building them up in faith and holiness.

The sermon that excites only the admiration of the hearers, that impresses them only with the intellectual ability of the preacher, or with his learning or eloquence, is the clearest proof of its failure. For the aim or purpose of a sermon, if it is really a sermon, is not to impress the hearers with the preacher, but with the truth; is not to win applause for the preacher, but to win the hearers over to a certain course of conduct. The preacher who succeeds in impressing himself only, without producing results in the hearts and minds of the hearers, is not a good but a poor preacher. The end of the sermon should always be the good of the hearers and not to increase the fame or popularity of the preacher. [20]

—

The message which we preachers bring to others, Sabbath after Sabbath, we should be very careful to see that it is enforced by example, that what we exhort others to do, that we ourselves do. Otherwise our preaching will be in vain.

We often deal with matters in the Scriptures of the most serious and solemn import in a way that fails to impress their seriousness upon others. And the reason is because we are not ourselves, as ministers, impressed with their seriousness and far reaching significance. The truths that we present ought first of all to lay hold of our own hearts. It is when we ourselves are fully impressed by them that we are in a condition to present them effectively to others.

My constant prayer to God is that he would help me to preach, not great sermons, but helpful sermons – sermons that will appeal, not mainly to the intellect, but to the heart, sermons that will tend to strengthen and develop the good within us, to inspire us with right desires and that will fortify the will.

Lord Jesus, make me earnest, make me enthusiastic in the work thou hast given me to do. May I love to preach the gospel and love to work for thee. Paul was never so happy as when he was trying to lift thee up before men and to persuade them to come over on thy side. That is the kind of life I want to live. I want to be so thoroughly in love with thee and thy work that I shall delight to speak of thee to others. Simply to do it from a sense of duty doesn't satisfy me; I want to do it because I love to do it. [22]

—

It isn't so much what we say, or how we say it, as the spirit in which we say it, as the extent to which what we say is realized by us, and is a part of our own experience. It is the truth vitalized that is effective. When that which we utter is a part of our own lives, is witnessed to by our own experience, and we come to realize its value as a life-giving and life-saving force that we can speak of it with authority, with a conviction that will at once be recognized. It must be something more than the mere utterance of the lip. Back of it there must be not only a sense of its reality but of its value and importance.

The preaching of the apostles consisted very largely of the simple story of Jesus and his love, culminating in his death upon the cross, his resurrection and ascension, calling attention particularly to the purpose for which he came, and the meaning of his suffering and death, and depending for the effect of their words not upon anything in themselves but upon the presence and power of the Holy Spirit. And it is upon this same power that we must depend if any results are to follow our preaching. When the Spirit gives the message and prepares the heart of the messenger to give it, and the hearts of the people to receive it, then, and only then, may we expect results. The man who is to preach effectively must keep in close touch with God, must be much in the secret place of the Most High. [23]

A discourse, however learned, eloquent, or rhetorically correct in construction is valuable only so far as it is used by the Holy Spirit, and the measure of its worth will depend upon how far it actually helps in bringing men to Christ or in building them up in faith and holiness, in Christian character. It is to be judged entirely by its effect in awakening men to a sense of their need of higher things and in stimulating them to seek after the things that are true, just, pure, lovely and of good report. A sermon, however eloquent, that doesn't awaken in man a desire for better things, is a failure. [25]

~

What the world needs is the Gospel of the grace of God in Christ Jesus and that Gospel preached by men who believe it and who know from personal experience that it has power to save. [26]

~

I have been preaching now for nearly forty years. During all that time, there are certain things that I can truthfully say of myself:

1. I have never been afraid of anybody. I have always spoken fearlessly what I believed to be right whether it agreed with the views of others or not.

2. I have never sought to curry favor with anybody. I have always tried to do my duty and to treat everybody with due consideration, not, however, with a view of reaping some personal benefit because I thought they might do me a good turn someday but because I felt it was the right thing to do.

3. I have never been influenced by the financial or social standing of those with whom I have come in contact. I have never been able to bring myself to think more of a man simply because he had money and lived more expensively than others. I have always made it a rule to estimate people by their moral and spiritual worth rather than by their material possessions. People who live in fine houses and dress in purple and fine linen and live sumptuously every day, unless they have something else to commend them, are no more to me than people who are unable to afford these luxuries. The man to be respected and held in high estimation is not the one whose home is expensively furnished but the one whose soul is arrayed in the beautiful garments of righteousness, however meager his material resources may be. It is the man of upright character, of sterling worth, that is to be respected and honored.

4. I have never, consciously, in all my ministry, sought to impress

myself upon people, to speak with a view of advertising myself, of making what is popularly called a reputation. If I have made a reputation it has been without any desire or design on my part. It has been pleasant, of course, to have people say to me, as they have from time to time, "I like very much what you said" or other things of a complimentary nature, but to win such compliments was never my purpose. I have tried always to speak because I felt that I had something to say that was of value and in the hope that it might be so regarded by my hearers – something that might be helpful to them in the development of a larger, fuller, nobler life.

5. I have always shrunk from public gatherings, the design of which was to center attention upon me personally. Hence, I have never proposed myself, nor have I encouraged others to get up testimonials of any kind to me. During my entire ministry I have never celebrated a single anniversary of my pastorate. Some ministers are all the time having testimonials gotten up for them, or are all the time celebrating some anniversary, which carry along with them gifts of some kind, and a lot of speaking of a complimentary nature to themselves. I have no taste for, or inclination towards such demonstrations; I am glad to know that I am appreciated or what I have tried to do is appreciated, and I am perfectly content to have that appreciation shown in a private or informal way, instead of in public.

6. I have never had any desire to preach what are called great sermons – sermons which display learning or ability, and which are relished particularly by the highly educated members of the congregation; but I have desired and have sought to preach helpful sermons, sermons that meet the real needs of the human heart in the midst of life's trials, struggles, temptations, sorrows. To know that you have helped somebody, that you have cheered and comforted somebody, that you have caused somebody to turn from his evil ways, to forsake the broad way and enter the narrow way, is vastly more important than to cater to the intellectual tastes of the hearers by striving to preach so-called great sermons. The only real value of a sermon is to be found in the extent to which it ministers to the

actual, pressing needs of the soul; in the extent to which it is a quickener of life, spiritual and eternal. The function of the pulpit is not to entertain, to amuse, to satisfy an idle curiosity; it is to instruct, to inspire, to fire the heart and mind, to implant within us noble desires and ambitions, and, above all to keep ever before men the one supreme figure in history, the Lord Jesus Christ, and to beget within them a passion for him and for a Christly life.

7. I have during all my ministry never used the pulpit to chastise my enemies, to vent my spleen on those who excited my displeasure. I have never felt that the pulpit could be properly used for such an object. Besides, such conduct would be unbecoming a Christian minister. I have often been provoked with people and sorely tried with them, but I could never bring myself to strike at them from the pulpit, either directly or indirectly. I have been content to remain silent and to leave them in the hands of the Lord. That is, I believe, not only the right thing to do but is the wisest policy to pursue. Any attempt to use the pulpit to get even with your enemies will always do more harm than good. It will simply tend to make things worse and more and more to destroy the peace of the church.

8. I have always been ready to speak in behalf of the rights of the race and have never hesitated to condemn, and in the strongest terms, those who are trying to deprive us of our rights as men and as American citizens.

9. I have also always spoken strongly in favor of temperance. I have always regarded the saloon and the whole liquor business as the greatest source of corruption in the world and the greatest enemy to the human race, and, therefore, to be everywhere met with determined and uncompromising resistance. As the elder Cato felt about Carthage I have always felt about the whole horrible liquor business: it must be destroyed. "Delenda est Carthago."

10. I have always spoken strongly in favor of a single standard of morality for men and women alike. I have never been able to see that sexual impurity was any less reprehensible in men than in women. If it

is wrong in the one, it is equally wrong in the other and should be so regarded in every decent community and in every decent circle of society.

11. My experience during a ministry of nearly forty years is that if a man will put his trust in God and go straight forward and do his duty, God will take care of him. On trustee boards will often be found men who will want to pay any and everybody before the minister, not because the minister has done anything to them, but from sheer meanness. There will also, however, always be found on such boards men of high Christian character and of a proper sense of what is due the minister who will always look out for his interests. The laborer is worthy of his hire is what the Bible asserts, and if he will do his work faithfully, he need not be concerned about his support. God will see that he is cared for. [31]

In order to preach effectively, the sermon should grow not out of the head, but out of the heart. The truth presented should be first realized in the preacher's own experience. A sense of its reality and importance should first be felt with his own soul. This I always feel in reading the sermons of F. W. Robertson. They are not deficient in intellectual strength, but the appeal which they make is always to the heart, and you feel that he is speaking from the heart. I am always stirred to be or do something after laying down a volume of his sermons. [37]

Speaking with authority means speaking from conviction, from positive knowledge, with an assurance, therefore, that commands respect, that makes you feel that what is said is genuine, is worthy of all acceptation, is thoroughly reliable. [38]

I am not asking God to fill the house with listeners, but I am asking him to send to the services those who need to hear the message which I am to give and to prepare me to give it and prepare them to receive it. [40]

A lady came up to me at the close of the services and, after shaking my hands cordially, said, "I thank you for that sermon. Every time I hear you preach I feel that I want to be a better woman, a better Christian." I thanked her. There is nothing in the line of praise that she could have said to me that would have been half so acceptable as the simple assurance that what I said in the sermon had helped her, had intensified, had deepened her desire to get on higher ground. That is the only kind of preaching that counts that is of any value in the sight of God or that results in any good to man. My earnest prayer is that more and more mine may be such a ministry, that more and more I may lose sight of self and think only of the good to be done, of those who come into the sanctuary who need the helping hand, the ministry of Jove, the tender, watchful care of some loving heart. [40]

In our troubles, anxieties, perplexities, the longer I live the more am I impressed with the wisdom of speaking more to God and less to man. He can do more in the way of helping through all our difficulties than all others put together. Talk more with God, less with man. [52]

Too often, we preachers feel that we are not doing very much, that our work is not succeeding, unless someone is constantly swinging the censer under our noses. It is when we are praised, when our sermons are spoken of in complimentary terms, that we feel that we are succeeding most. And when we preach, Sabbath after Sabbath, and no words of commendation are heard, we are apt to feel a little discouraged, to think that we are not succeeding. Unfortunately, too many of us (such is poor human nature) want to be praised. We look for it; we expect it; we often think more of a word of commendation than anything else. It is certainly a weakness, a pitiable weakness, a thing to be ashamed of. We ought to be content to do our work, with no thought of self, but only of the glory of God. Too many of us are like the Pharisees in this respect. It is the glory of man that we are thinking of and that we are hankering most for. It may be natural, but it is a thing for which we should despise ourselves. [53]

It is a great privilege, a great honor, to be allowed to speak for Jesus Christ. When we speak, it is well for us to bear this in mind. We should be careful how we speak, and careful as to what we say. Everything should be in harmony with the character of the great Being that we represent. [53]

The minister should aim, in his public ministrations, to make each service a kind of mount of vision for the people. Those who come to worship should get such a glimpse of the truth, such views of life and duty, as the better to fit them to meet life's trials, difficulties, perplexities. Peter and John went down from the mount of transfiguration with impressions that remained with them ever afterwards and that helped them in the experiences that were yet before them. What an opportunity the minister has, under the guidance of the Holy Spirit, to help those who come up to the house of the Lord, Sabbath after Sabbath. Every service should be a kind of mount of vision – a means of helping the people to see God and to see things from the Divine standpoint – and so be lifted to a higher plane, so be strengthened and fortified for the immediate tasks which may be before them. [54]

We ministers ought to bring to the people Sabbath after Sabbath a message that will be helpful to them in one way or another – a message of instruction, of warning, of encouragement, of comfort, of inspiration. We ought never to be preaching in the air; we ought always to have something to say, to understand what that something is, why we ought to say it, why it is important that the people should hear it, and we should speak always in dependence upon the Holy Spirit to prepare the people to hear and to make the truth effectual. We are not to depend upon our eloquence or any trick of oratory. The only really saving power comes from the presence of the Holy Spirit in the heart of the preacher and in the hearts of the hearers. [56]

The effect of a discourse depends, in part, upon what is said, plus the character of the speaker, or the manner or spirit in which it is said, and also upon the temper or spirit of the hearers. [56]

As a minister, what especially is my duty? 1) I am to stand as the Divine representative. I am never to lose sight of the fact that I am his representative. 2) My duty is to seek in every possible way to advance his kingdom, to teach men the way of life, and to persuade them to enter it. My mission is to win men to Christ, to bring them to accept him as their Lord and Savior, and to begin in earnest to live the Christian life. [56]

Rules For Preaching:

1. Always have a message. Don't speak simply because you are asked to speak or merely for the sake of speaking or of killing time. Every time there ought to be a distinct message to be given.

2. The message to be given should be clearly and fully before the

mind. We should not only have something to say, but that something should be clearly apprehended by us.

3. We ought to be impressed with the importance of the message in itself considered, and particularly to those to whom it is about to be given. If it is not important that they should hear it, then there is no reason for giving it. If, however, it is important, the reason or reasons why it is important should be clearly before us.

4. The message ought to be a living one, i.e., given with spirit, earnestly, as if we felt the importance of it. It must be no mere perfunctory performance. It must pulsate with life. Otherwise, it cannot be made effective. [57]

~

The word CONQUER may be used in two senses: (1) in the sense of overcoming, of beating down, of subduing by superior force, and (2) in the sense of winning over, of inducing a change of views or opinions by the presentation of truth, by arguments which appeal to the reason, the conscience or moral sense, so that the enemy not only sees that he is wrong and gives up his views, but accepts yours, comes over to his own accord on your side.

And in both of these senses the Lord Jesus Christ is a great conqueror. Ultimately the wicked will, unless they repent, be destroyed by the might of his power. In the meantime, there are thousands that are being conquered by him in the other sense; they are being convinced that they are wrong in resisting his authority and are coming of their own accord over on his side, are arraying themselves with him and not against him. And this world-wide conquest that he has begun will go on to the end of time. This is the end of all preaching, that men might be reconciled to God, might cease their rebellion and fall in with his ways. [69]

~

We cannot hope to be a source of help to others in matters spiritual unless we ourselves are in touch with the sources of spiritual power. The man who preaches, if he hopes to be of any value in helping to win men to Christ and keep them won, must be a God-fearing man – a man of sincere, earnest piety. He can't be merely pretending to be a Christian, pretending to be interested in things of the Spirit, pretending to love God and to be interested in the advancement of the kingdom of the Lord Jesus Christ; he must actually be – he must himself be daily feeding upon the sincere milk of the word – must be living in fellowship with God through prayer, and must be actually at work in the vineyard of the Lord. No pretense will carry any power with it. To have power to rise ourselves or to be of help to others in rising, we have got to be really, truly alive to God and righteousness. [74]

~

The great mission of the preacher is to teach and inspire. The mission of the Christian Church is to lead men to Jesus and to build up Christian character.

The most serious problem with which any human being has to deal is the problem of right living, the problem of getting out from under the power of sin and getting into right relations with God.

The man who finds Jesus Christ, who finds him truly, has found the solution to all of his problems, both here and hereafter – in time and in eternity. It is literally true – and experience, as far as it goes, shows it to be true: "Jesus is made unto us wisdom, and righteousness, and sanctification, and redemption" (I Corinthians 1:30).

What a great thing for the world, for society, that one day out of seven people are called to leave the busy cares of merely material and worldly interests and to come up to the house of God where they are brought to think of things spiritual and eternal – where the thought of God, of right, of things that are true, just, pure, lovely, and of good report are brought to their attention and impressed upon their hearts and minds. Without it, what would become of us?

All our efforts as Christians should be to help men the better to know Christ, the better to love him, and the better to serve him. All life may be summed up in trying to get perfectly adjusted to his way of thinking, feeling, acting. To be like the Lord Jesus is the very perfection of being. And to be steadily aiming ourselves to become more and more like him and to get others to be the same is indeed the noblest aim that we can set before us. My prayer is that God would help me, through the influence of the Holy Spirit, to get a clearer and fuller knowledge of him, and to bring to others the same clearness and fullness of knowledge.

The work of the ministry is a most serious business – the business of calling men to repentance and faith, of warning them against a life of sin, and of showing them the better way through faith in Jesus Christ. It is a serious business because it has to do with the most serious thing in life, sin, with matters of the greatest importance; with issues upon which the eternal destiny of the soul depends. How important it is for all ministers to realize how really serious is the business in which they are engaged and address themselves to it under a sense of its seriousness. [77]

When I am thinking about something to preach about, as I have been today, it isn't that I might find something to fill up the time that is usually allotted to the sermon, something with which to entertain the people, not at all; what I am hunting for is something that will minister to their moral and spiritual need, something that will really be a help to them in the struggle of life, in the midst of temptations, sorrows, sufferings, in the midst of life's duties and responsibilities. It never is to entertain, but always to strengthen, to uplift, to ennoble. [80]

A man preaches effectively when the truth grips him and when it grips his hearers, in other words, when he himself fully realizes the significance of what he is saying, the value, the importance of it, and there is awakened in the hearers a like realization. A man upon whom the truth which he is seeking to present has made no deep impression cannot hope to make much of an impression upon others. [81]

We ministers must have a message, and it must be from the heart – i.e., it must be a message in which we thoroughly believe, and whose importance is mostly keenly felt by us. It must not be something spoken simply to fill an engagement, to occupy a certain amount of time scheduled in a service. It may be given at a service, but it must not be merely to fill an appointment; the truth to be presented ought to be under the conviction that it is what the people need to hear and heed. [87]

In many churches the effort on the part of the minister, as evidenced in the manner in which the services are advertised, is clearly simply for the purpose of attracting a crowd, simply for the sake of having a crowd. With this end in view, the services are so arranged as simply to entertain. I have never had any sympathy with that kind of thing. I have never had the slightest desire to have a crowd simply for the sake of a crowd. I want people to come to the services, and to come in large numbers, but the one and only reason that I want them to come is in the hope of helping them spiritually, of bringing them into contact with Christian ideals and principles with a view of getting them to order their lives according to them. I never try to entertain anybody; I never invite people to come to the services with a view of entertaining them. I want them to come because

I think I can do them good and because the services are so arranged as to be helpful to them. The church of God is not a playhouse – a house of amusement, but a school for the inculcation of right principles and for stimulating us in the direction of all that is best and noblest. This is my idea of the church, and this is what I am trying to make my church to all who come to it, not a place of amusement or entertainment, but of spiritual uplift. [88]

A service is of no value unless it draws men nearer to God, unless it sets up in the soul the purpose to do right, to live a clean, pure, upright life. Every service ought to be uplifting, ennobling – a call to higher things, to a truer, purer, nobler life. [93]

Do we live what we preach? If not, our preaching is vain; no good will come of it. [93]

The greatest source of power for good in a church is the pulpit, if it is properly filled – if it is occupied by a God-fearing man, a man who is qualified to teach the people, and who makes it his business, mainly, to feed the flock on the sincere milk of the word instead of on the husks of current happenings in newspapers and magazines. A pulpit well manned is always a source of power – is always an uplifting and ennobling influence. The more ministers themselves realize this, the more earnestly will they endeavor to qualify themselves to meet its great responsibilities and opportunities. Whenever I think of the pulpit, of the ministry, and of what it is capable of becoming and of achieving, instantly I think of the apostle Paul – of his zeal, his earnestness, his steady, unswerving devotion to Jesus Christ and the interest of his kingdom. What a record he made for himself! What a glorious record. Let us all, at least, catch his noble spirit. [95]

———

No man's ministry is a failure, however meager the results, if he has been faithfully and earnestly preaching the gospel of the grace of God, holding up to dying, sinful men God's message of redeeming love. Such a ministry is not, could not be, a failure. [97]

———

Reading a sermon is not preaching; preaching is giving a message straight from the heart; it is the proclamation of a truth which we fully believe and the importance of which we fully appreciate.

We can preach with power only when we realize the truth of what we are saying and the importance of it to those to whom we are speaking. [99]

———

George Frederick Watts, speaking of his pictures, says, "I want to make people think. My intention has not been so much to paint pictures that will charm the eye as to suggest great thoughts that will appeal to the imagination and the heart and kindle all that is best and noblest in humanity."

In reading this over, it occurred to me that we have here a noble ideal for the preacher to keep before him in preparing his sermons – not to please, to win the applause of those who may be listening to him, but to make his sermons the vehicles of such thoughts as will appeal to the imagination and the heart and call into being all that is best and noblest within them – sermons that will appeal to and call forth all that is best within them. So often the aim is only to entertain, to fill up the passing hour or allotted time for the performance, or to display one's learning or cleverness with a view of drawing attention to one's self. Such sermons are not only out of place but are absolutely no good so far as helping to advance the cause of Christ in the world. Better that they were never uttered, better that all such men were out of the ministry. The aim of the preacher ought always to be of the same lofty character as that of this artist. [100]

We search the Scriptures in order to find out what the will of the Lord is. And in preaching we endeavor to set before the people what God would have them do, but unless I myself am practicing what I preach, my preaching will be of no value. We must live what we preach if we hope to influence others, if we hope to command the respect of others. We who preach therefore should be constantly on our guard, should be careful ourselves to walk circumspectly in all our ways. [101]

The things contained in the word of God may not, in the estimation of some people, be true, but believing, as we do, that the Bible is the word of God, our duty is to preach what it declares to be true. Time will tell whether what it declares is true or not. It won't be long before the light of eternity will reveal on which side the truth is, whether with those who believe, or those who disbelieve. Jesus said, "Heaven and earth shall pass away, but not one jot or tittle of my word shall fail." Those who build on his word are building on rock foundations. When the rains descend, and the floods come, and winds blow, whatever is built on his word will stand. The old Book of God has stood and will stand for ever and ever. The only thing that we need concern ourselves about is that what we preach is really in it and that we are faithful in setting it forth. [108]

The apostle tells us, "The world by wisdom knew not God," and, therefore, any attempt to win men to Christ by appealing to their intellects, is a fool's project. Men are not won in that way. The old way, and the Bible way, of winning men is by the simple presentation of the truth of God, in dependence upon the Holy Spirit to make the truth effectual. He alone can open blind eyes, unstop deaf ears, soften hard hearts. No other kind of preaching has ever been effectual and ever will be. There is a fool notion going the rounds now that because of the great advance in education and in scientific knowledge somehow the preacher, in order to reach the young men that are in our colleges and universities and that are coming out of them, must show that he is fully abreast of the knowledge of the time and must impress the young men with his knowledge of what is going on in the intellectual world, in order to make an impression on them. It is all folly. These young men will listen, it may be, with pleasure, to the display of his learning and of his intellectual power, and go away feeling that he is a smart fellow, but no impression will be made upon their hearts; such preaching will have no power to effect in them changes for the better, no power to set their face Godward and heavenward, no power to set up in their soul the dominating and masterful influence of Jesus Christ over them. Changes like that can come only from preaching the simple truth of the gospel in reliance upon the Holy Spirit. And a man is a fool who thinks it can be done in any other way. It is well for all such preachers to read what the apostle Paul, the prince of preachers, has to say about the matter. I Corinthians 1:26-29; I Corinthians 2:1-5. [108]

A minister should enter his pulpit, not in a thoughtless, frivolous mood, but with a deep sense of the seriousness of the work in which he is engaged – the work of calling dying, sinful men to repentance and faith before it is eternally too late. The thought of the tremendous issues that depend upon the faithfulness with which he addresses himself to the work should solemnize his heart and banish every frivolous thought from his mind every time he enters the pulpit. The business in which he is engaged is a serious one, and no one should be more deeply sensible of that fact than the minister himself. [109]

I never concern myself in the least about getting invitations to speak, here or there. I always assume that if the Lord wants to use me at any time and in any place, he will open the way. If he doesn't open the way, it is clear to me that he doesn't need me there. And as I desire to speak only where he needs me, I am never troubled if I am not invited. The fact is, I never care to speak anywhere unless I feel that some good can be accomplished. Otherwise, it is simply a waste of precious time and energy. [110]

The sermon should never be made an end, but only a means to an end. This should be kept constantly in mind in the preparation of it.

It is a mistake to make it an end. That is what, it is to be feared, is done by some preachers, however. Their aim is to make it as perfect as possible as a literary production. Its construction, the choice of words, the illustrations – all have to do with its literary construction as a work of art. Not long ago, I listened to a sermon by a gifted University professor. It was remarkably well thought out, so much so that the thing about it that impressed me was not what was said in it, the truth presented, but rather how it was said – the choice language and imagery that characterized it. I was impressed with the ability of the speaker, rather than with what he said. At the close of the sermon, I found myself thinking of him instead of the truth which he essayed to present.

It is a mistake to preach such sermons. They do little or no good, except to advertise the preacher, to call attention to his ability, and so to win the applause of men. And this, unfortunately, seems to be the aim of some preachers. Their sermons are prepared and preached with a view of drawing attention to themselves which always neutralizes the effect of the sermon as a spiritual force.

The sermon, properly considered as a means to an end, should always aim to draw attention to Christ, or to enforce some truth, etc. If it doesn't make men think, of the truth, of their condition, of the claims of God upon them, it is of no value; it is simply time wasted in the preparation and in the preaching of such sermons. The value of a sermon is not to be estimated by its literary qualities but by its power to arouse the hearers and set them going in the right direction, by its power to inspire, to ennoble. If it ends with thought of the preacher, rather than of the truth presented, it has been a failure. Peter on the day of Pentecost preached a great sermon, but no one thought of Peter, it was of the mighty result which followed his words, the conversion of three thousand souls. As he preached, men forgot all about the preacher, thought only of what he was saying, of the truth which wrung from them the cry, "What shall we do to be saved?" That is the kind of preaching that counts, that makes preaching worthwhile. One such sermon is worth a thousand mere literary sermons however perfectly constructed, however finished in all of their parts. [110]

The secret of effective or successful speaking depends very largely upon our knowledge of the subject discussed and our interest in it. If we know but little about it and feel but little interest in it, we cannot hope to make much of an impression upon others. It is the man who has something to say in which he is himself interested that people care to hear, that will claim the attention of others. Interest alone, without knowledge, will not go very far. [121]

As to the congregation to which one ministers, it isn't whether it is large or small, but what are we doing for it, or with it? Are we feeding it with the bread of life? Are we properly instructing it in the ways of life? Are we setting before them proper ideals? Are we expounding to them faithfully the great principles of righteousness? Are we pointing out to them clearly the way of life, spiritual and eternal? Are we trying, earnestly, faithfully to build them up in faith and holiness? If so, whether there are few or many to listen to us need not trouble us. Our duty is to feed those who come, to point out those who come to Jesus, who is the way, the truth, the life, and leave results with God. [128]

It is a great thing in preaching to expound the word of God, to draw out of it what is in it, and not attempt to expound our own views, to set forth our own ideas. What the people need is to hear the word of God, and not the wisdom of man, not what is passing current in the newspapers and magazines. The sooner we preachers learn this lesson and stick to it the more fruitful of good will be our ministry. It is a great privilege to be permitted, week after week, to appear before the people and to unfold to them the word of God. How careful ought we to be to see that what we do present to our hearers is the word of God, the plain, simple, unvarnished truth of God, and not the speculation of men, the vagaries of the human mind – what Jesus calls the traditions of the elders, which are of no value as a means of grace. [131]

The church is the place of worship, of spiritual refreshment, where people may come and be instructed in the things of God, in things of an elevating and ennobling character – a place from which we may get glimpses of life on its highest plane – where we are forced to think of the enduring treasures – of the things that are true, just, pure, lovely and of good report.

It is not a place for entertainment or amusement, where we go to while away the time, to get away from the serious things of life. Unfortunately, that is what some ministers seem to think it is for and so arrange their services with that end in view. They succeed in attracting the people, in entertaining them, but make no serious impression upon them. They go away not only not made any better, but worse. In the atmosphere of such a service they sink to lower levels, go out to meet life's duties and responsibilities weaker, less able to resist its many temptations, less able to discern between what is right and wrong. Such services are not only of no value but a curse instead of a blessing to any community. [133]

I still hope occasionally to do a little preaching. It is what I love to do, and I realize now, more than ever before, what a privilege it is to be entrusted with the glorious gospel of the grace of God to dying, sinful men. A true minister of Jesus Christ is in a position to wield an influence for good second to no other man on earth. I sometimes ask myself the question as to how many of us who are in the ministry realize, as we ought, the nature of our calling and the sweep of great possibilities for influencing men that it opens up to us. On my way from Howard University today, after attending the morning session of the Convocation, I was talking to a brother minister (Rev. L. Z. J.), and the burden of our conversation was as to the Christian ministry and the part which it is capable of playing in the future of the race. If we can get the right kind of men in it – men who are educationally qualified and who realize that it is a high calling which will require the very best in them day in and day out, week in and week out, month in and month out, year in and year out to the end of life. It is because not a great many come to it with this overwhelming sense of obligation which it imposes and the wide outlook for usefulness which it opens up that the future is not as bright as it might be. As I look back over these seventy-five years, nothing gives me greater pleasure than the fact that nearly forty-eight of them have been spent in this highest of all callings. For this particularly, as I look back, I am thankful to God. [134]

The true mission of a church in the community where it is located is to preach the Gospel, with the double purpose, first, of winning men to an acceptance of Jesus Christ, and, second, of building them up in faith and holiness. In other words, its value to the community will be in proportion as it is helping to make its members, after they are brought in, better men and women, better Christians, getting them, in character and life, more conformed to the character and teachings of the Lord Jesus Christ. Its value to the community does not depend upon the size of its membership but upon the quality of the men and women that make up its membership. It is through the individual members, in their personal character and life, in their contact with others, that it is to do its most effective work. I have very little sympathy with the craze that is now taking hold of so many churches: merely to increase in numbers. Numbers count for nothing unless the constituent elements are of the right character. It is quality not quantity that tells in the work of the Lord.

The main business of the church, therefore, is not only to win men to Christ, but particularly to make them such in spirit, in temper, in life, as to make them powers for good, centers of life-giving and ennobling influences. The church lacks power, because so few, or comparatively few, in it are of the right stamp. It needs to bend its efforts towards making more of its members of the right stamp. The basis of all outward expansion must be first inward. [149]

It is a great privilege to be permitted to minister in spiritual things, to be called to the preaching of the word of God. And the minister who doesn't realize this and who doesn't make the most careful preparation each week to bring to the people a message, a real, true message from the word of God as will help them to be better men and women, is unworthy to fill such a position and should be heartily ashamed of himself. What the people want is the word of God; and if the preacher allows his time to be taken up with other matters so as to leave him no time for proper preparation, the sooner he gets out of the ministry the better it will be, certainly for the people to whom he ministers.

I marvel, at times, as I have listened to the kind of sermons that are preached, the subjects that are discussed, and even when the subject is all right, the manner in which it is handled, the little thought that has been given to it, the superficial manner in which it is handled, showing often no real true understanding of the thought which the passage which is being discussed is intended to convey. So, the people are starved; so, they are fed not on the finest of the wheat which they are entitled to, but upon the husk. And so, they are not nourished, are not built up, are not edified. [156]

How many, many of us who are in the ministry fail to realize the importance of the public ministrations of the sanctuary, especially of the preached word. It is the preacher's time preeminently for sowing the seed, for feeding the flock, for building the people up in faith and holiness. What an opportunity of warning sinners, of calling them to repentance, of pointing out to them the way of life. It is because so many of us do not realize the importance, do not appreciate the priceless value of these occasions in pushing forward the work to which we are especially called that our pulpit preparation is often unsatisfactory, so miserably poor, so utterly unworthy of the high and holy office which we hold. The time that ought to be given to preparation we give to other things. And so, the flock is unfed, the services are not edifying, the people are not helped spiritually, the good work languishes, everything moves at a poor dying rate. And all because of unfaithful shepherds, men who are more concerned about themselves than they are about the work to which they are called of God – the conversion of a lost world, and the building up in faith and holiness those who have started out to live the Christian life. The kind of sermons that proceed from some of our pulpits, the lack of preparation which they show, the careless manner in which they are put together, without any definite aim or object except to fill up the time allotted to the sermon, is a shame and a disgrace. When we ministers realize more fully than most of us do that the business in which we are engaged is a serious one, involving the eternal interest of immortal souls, we shall give a little more attention to our pulpit ministrations, to the work of feeding the flock of God which he hath purchased with his own blood. If we are not feeding the flock, if we are not calling sinners to repentance, if these things are not uppermost with us, we are out of place in the pulpit; we have no business in the sacred desk.

"Feed the flock of God which he hath purchased with his own blood," is an admonition which we preachers should keep ever before us. The flock, purchased at an infinite cost, is to be fed, and we are to do the feeding. And the food upon which the flock is to be fed is the sincere milk of the word. Nothing else will nourish the sheep, will build the believer up in faith and holiness. It is well for us also to remember what is said in another scripture, Mark 6:34: "And Jesus, when he came out, saw much people, and was moved with compassion towards them, because they were as sheep not having a shepherd." We must see to it that the people to whom we minister are not, through any neglect of ours, as sheep having no shepherd; in too many cases, unfortunately, such is the case. The shepherds often are so concerned about their own personal affairs as to give little thought to the flock over which they are placed. "Rightly dividing the word, showing themselves to be workmen that needeth not to be ashamed," is no part of their program. The shepherding of the flock is with many of them only a side issue and not the business in which they are engaged as a life work, subordinating everything else to it, making everything else subservient to it. And this is why the results are so meager, why the average Christian life is lived on so low a plane. [164]

In beginning my ministry, I was very fortunate:

1. In that the church to which I was called was located at Washington, the capital of the nation.

2. In that it was attended by the most intellectual and cultured group of colored people to be found anywhere in the country at that time. It was at the Fifteenth Street Presbyterian Church that this group gathered Sabbath after Sabbath. It necessitated on my part hard, hard study and the most careful preparation of my sermons. I realized what the pastorate of such a church meant and addressed myself earnestly to the task of meeting its high duties and responsibilities. It was good for me that I felt this way, and it was good for the congregation. It was a constant stimulus to me to do my best; and it brought to the people more thoughtful and helpful sermons.

No greater misfortune can come to a man beginning the ministry, unless he is an exceptional man, than to be thrown among a class of persons that will require very little study or preparation on his part in order to satisfy them. He will be sure to become careless, to do little studying, to make little or no preparation for his pulpit ministrations. It is a bad thing for a minister in beginning his career, to be so circumstanced as to make him feel that any and every kind of sermon is good enough for his people. If they are very ignorant and little given to thinking, they may be satisfied with that kind of preaching. But under such a ministry, neither they nor the minister will grow, will develop into anything of value. Whether the people are sufficiently intelligent to require it or not, it is the duty of the preacher, for his own sake as well as for theirs, to bring to them, Sabbath after Sabbath, the very best of which he is capable by hard study and preparation. This he owes to himself, and this he owes to them.

Where a man has been so unfortunate as to begin his ministry and to have continued for some time under conditions which made very little demand upon him in the shape of careful preparation in his pulpit ministrations, and when, by some chance, he happens afterwards to get into a different field where it becomes necessary for him to study, he is usually a failure; his incompetency soon comes to the surface. The habit, being formed of not properly preparing himself, has so taken possession of him, that he finds it impossible to buckle down to hard work. And the result is general dissatisfaction with his ministrations. He has disqualified himself for work among a more intelligent group that cannot be satisfied with the kind of food which he has been accustomed to feed the people on. It is better for the man, and better for the church, that the relation between the two should be severed as soon as possible. Unless this is done, dissatisfaction with him will continue to grow, and the church will steadily go down.

Men who haven't accustomed themselves to hard study and to careful pulpit preparation had better remain among a class of people who will be satisfied with little or no preparation.

And yet, I ought not to say that either. For people ought not to be satisfied with that kind of ministry. Under it they can never properly develop. They, particularly, need a ministry that will so educate them that they will not be satisfied with any kind of stuff that may be handed out to them from the pulpit. The only place for such ministers is out of the pulpit entirely. If a man doesn't intend, as far as he is able by hard study and dint of perseverance, to feed his people on the finest of the wheat, he has no business in the ministry and the people should be so educated as to make him feel it and as to shut him out of every pulpit. [180]

A great sermon is one that sets forth a great or important truth, and powerfully sets it forth, carrying conviction with it, stimulating the intellect, arousing the conscience, and moving the will. I am assuming that the main purpose of a sermon is to bring men nearer to God and to each other – is to influence character and conduct so as to bring them more and more to conform to the character and life of Jesus Christ as set forth in the Scriptures. Its greatness will depend, it seems to me, upon the extent to which it helps to bring about this result. A sermon, however well-constructed, however logical, however replete in learning and adorned with literary gems, that appeals simply to the intellect, that pleases simply the fancy, can hardly be called great. It may be great as an address or oration, but not as a sermon. The sermon ought always to minister, not incidentally, but mainly to the spiritual side of our nature.

The estimate that Jesus puts upon a sermon is the true measure of its greatness, and the estimate that he is likely to put upon it will depend upon how far it tends towards helping on the purpose which he has in view, to draw men out of the world into his kingdom, and to build them up in faith and holiness. A sermon is to be judged by its moral and spiritual effects mainly in determining whether it is to be classed as great or not. When we speak of great sermons I wonder sometimes whether we really know what we are talking about. [182]

Some preachers are entirely too mechanical in presenting the truth, i.e., they fail to vitalize it, to present it in such a way as to arrest the attention and hold it, in such a way as to excite interest, and move to action. You hear what is being said but feel no interest in it. What is being said may be true, but it is presented in such a way as to make you feel it is no concern of yours. A truth that is vitalized always grips you, makes you feel that it has a claim upon you which you must try to satisfy. How much of the preaching that you hear in many of the pulpits today leaves no impression upon you at all, or so little as to amount to the same thing. And the reason is lack of vitality in the presentation of the truth. It is well for the preacher to know definitely what he is going to preach about and have clearly before him what he wants to say about it, and to be duly impressed with the importance of the subject, and, particularly, its importance to those he is addressing. The truth thus presented will be vital and will be sure to lay hold of the hearers. The truth must first live in the preacher himself before he can hope to have it live in others. No mechanical preaching will get anywhere. The sermon is a failure before it starts.

The tendency, generally, is to forget God, to pass over lightly things which have to do with our spiritual welfare, to allow ourselves to become absorbed in the mere temporalities of life, to the neglect of things of permanent, of enduring value.

Our duty, as ministers of the gospel, is to keep the people ever in touch with spiritual things – to keep ever before them the thought of God, of their responsibility to Him, of character building, of eternity, of the endless life beyond the grave.

> 'Tis not all of life to live
> Nor all of death to die.

This we are so apt to forget but which we must not be allowed to forget. Living is a serious business, involving grave responsibilities – responsibilities that carry with them consequences that reach beyond this present life. Fortunate for us if we live in the consciousness of the true meaning of life in its relation both to time and to eternity and are steadily influenced by that consciousness. [184]

I have just finished reading a sermon by Rev. Clarence Edward Macartney, pastor of the First Presbyterian Church in Pittsburgh, entitled "Your Fellowship in the Gospel." I was deeply impressed with its spirituality and power, with its clear-cut statements of the vitally important things in our religion. And this is what I said to myself: "If we could have that kind of preaching in all of our pulpits – preaching that holds up and emphasizes the importance of a living faith in Jesus Christ as the only hope of a sin-cursed world and the duty of spreading that faith, and of living it, exemplifying it – its principles and ideals in our daily walk and conversation, instead of the stuff that goes out from so many of our pulpits, what a difference it would make, how much greater would be the influence of the church in moulding individual character and life after the pattern of Jesus Christ. How much, much depends upon the men who fill our pulpits, upon what their conception is of Christianity and of its high mission.

Only as our pulpits are filled with men of God, spiritually-minded men, men upon whom the Holy Spirit has come and upon whom he remains in quickening, life-giving power, will the preaching that emanates from them Sabbath after Sabbath count for much. The trouble is the people are not being fed with the word of God, which alone is able to save. It is amazing how much husk is given out from many of our pulpits week after week. Instead of searching the Scriptures, earnestly and prayerfully endeavoring to discover and to bring out its rich treasures of wisdom and knowledge, we find the occupants of them ransacking papers, magazines, periodicals of one kind and another, in search of something novel, something strange to talk about, forgetful of the fact that they are not in the pulpit to entertain people, to help them to while away their leisure moments, nor to keep them informed as to secular matters, but to feed their souls with the bread of life, to keep before them the things of enduring value – things which tend to build them up in holiness and comfort. To use its high and sacred privileges and opportunities for any other purpose than that for which they were designed is a betrayal of one's trust for which God will certainly hold us responsible. [187]

Sermons should be fresh, living, vital. There should be nothing hackneyed, mechanical about them; they should grow out of convictions that dominate the soul.

A man must be in touch with the source of life if he is to be a source of life to others. Life can come only from life. [190]

~

We need educated ministers, yes; we need men who know what is going on in the world about them, yes; but the great need is for men who believe firmly in the Scriptures as the word of God, and who faithfully preach the truth therein contained, in dependence upon the Holy Spirit to give efficacy to the truth, and not upon their training, their education, their ability to construct arguments in defense of the truth. The business of the preacher is to state the truth of God, clearly, fully, simply; the rest the Spirit will take care of. We need not trouble ourselves about the survival of Christianity. God will take care of that; what we need to be concerned about is that we faithfully preach it, line upon line, precept upon precept, here a little and there a little. The seed thus sown is bound to bear fruit. The promise is: "We shall reap if we faint not." [191]

~

In connection with Peter's sermon on the day of Pentecost, large results followed. Three thousand were converted and brought into the church. The truth was efficacious, not because it was uttered by an apostle, and uttered in an earnest and straightforward way, but because it was attended with the presence and power of the Holy Spirit. It was because Peter and the rest of the apostles had received the enduement from on high, which they were to tarry at Jerusalem until they had received; that alone accounts for the mighty results on that day. The simple fact is there is no other power by which such results can be brought about. "Not by might, nor by power, i.e., human might or power, but by my Spirit, saith the Lord of hosts." It has always been so, it is so now, and will always be so. No other power has ever been able to turn men from darkness to light, and from sin and Satan to God. And this explains why we fail so often in our efforts to win men to Christ, to start them on the upward way: it is because we do not depend upon the Spirit to convict and convert those we are seeking to reach. And the result is, nothing comes of our efforts, and never will until we swing in line with God's way of doing his work of soul-saving. The apostle Paul, you will recall, in setting forth the results of his great missionary journeys, never took any credit to himself; he always regarded himself only as the agent or instrument used by God. Thus, in Acts 15:12, we read: "And all the multitude kept silence; and they hearkened unto Barnabas and Paul rehearsing what signs and wonders God had wrought among the Gentiles through them." It was all the work of God; they were simply the instruments used by him. [199]

In preaching, it is well for us always to carry with us the thought that it is God who is speaking through us, that we are only his agents, and also, to preach in such a way that the people also will get the same thought that we are speaking for God. This is the ideal way to preach. If, however, we are to convey that impression to the people, what we say, as well as our manner of saying it, or in which we conduct ourselves while saying it, must be worthy of God. If what we say is of little consequence, is light and trivial, is lacking in proper preparation, we shall never be able to convince people that we are speaking for God or by his authority. The man who speaks for God must carry himself in a befitting way and must show in what he says that he is conscious of the relation which he professes to sustain to the great Being that he claims to represent. It is a great thing for a minister so to live and so to prepare himself for his pulpit ministrations that people will listen to him as to the voice of God. So men listened to Paul; so men listened to John the Baptist. The man coming to his pulpit with that kind of prestige, with that kind of authority, will always be listened to respectfully, will always speak with power. [214]

~

It is wonderful to watch the play of one mind upon another, or upon others – the effort of one mind to influence others, to get them to think, to feel, to see things as it sees them and to react accordingly. This is the aim of all public speakers; it is to influence the hearers, to bring them over to their way of thinking and feeling. Only so far as they succeed in doing so are they successful. If the address or sermon results in producing no conviction, in moving no one in the direction of the speaker's thought, it has been a failure.

That the effort of one mind to influence others may not result in failure there are certain conditions that must be fulfilled on the part of the speaker:

1. He must know definitely what he wants to speak about; his subject he must have well in hand. There must be no uncertainty on his part, no lack of information in regard to it. Ignorance on his part disqualifies him to speak.

2. He must believe that what he has to say is of value, is worth communicating. If it doesn't commend itself to him, if he attaches little or no importance to it, he cannot hope to interest others in it.

3. He must feel that what he has to say is not only of interest to himself, but especially to those to whom he speaks. However much he may be interested in it, if he has reason to believe that it holds no interest for the hearers, he is not likely to make much headway in presenting it. They may be so blind, or so stupid, as not to see the value of it, but the speaker, at least, must believe, whether the audience realizes it or not, that it is of importance that they hear it, that it is to their interest to hear what he has to say. The moment he is convinced that there is nothing in it for them, his power is gone.

4. Back of whatever he has to say, there must be conviction, and the stronger his conviction the more effective will he be in the presentation of it; i.e., what he says must be the honest expression of what he really thinks, really feels. If he is only pretending, only faking, saying what he really does not believe, it will destroy or greatly lessen the effectiveness of what he has to say. The man who hopes to move others, to carry others with him, must be honest, straightforward, sincere, must mean what he says, and say only what he means.

Knowing what we want to say, believing in the value of it, believing in the value of it to those to be addressed, backed by earnest and honest conviction, we shall be sure almost always to leave some impression upon those to whom our words are addressed. It is important for all speakers thus to fortify themselves whenever they are to appear in public, or else hold their peace, be quiet, say nothing. [227]

I listened this afternoon to an address at a funeral ceremony. It was very well done: it was flowery and abounded in many brilliant thoughts. I am sure it produced a pleasing effect upon those who were present. And yet, I said to myself afterwards, there was nothing in the address, pleasing as it was to listen to, that was calculated to leave any serious impression upon the mind in the presence of a great catastrophe such as death is. No one, I am sure, went away feeling the solemn significance of life and the challenge which death carries with it to every man. A funeral address, to be what it should be, ought to awaken in the minds of the hearers, the thought that someday, and it may be not far away, it will be their turn to go out into the boundless beyond, and to bring them face to face with the realities of that future life, conditioned upon the kind of life we have lived here.

In a funeral address there are three things that ought to be kept in mind:

1. To comfort the bereaved members of the family.

2. To extol the virtues of the deceased, to hold up and exhibit their good qualities in the hope that it may encourage others to live worthy lives.

3. To draw some lessons that might be helpful to the living – to those who are trying to live right, and to those who are careless, indifferent, unconcerned about their soul's eternal welfare. All three of these points ought somehow to find a place in every funeral discourse. If people go away without having the thought of death and eternity brought to their attention, the minister has failed to embrace one of the greatest opportunities of his life to stand between the living and the dead, to call men to repentance and lift up before them the Lord Jesus Christ as the Lamb of God whose blood alone cleanses from all sin. [236]

What are the public services in the church for? Are they to give the preacher an opportunity of showing what a clever fellow he is, how many bright things he can say with a view of enhancing his popularity? Heaven forbid! And yet that is what some preachers think of them; that is the use they make of them. The real, true purpose of such services is often lost sight of entirely, and other things are so crowded into them as to render them of no value as a spiritual agency. [242]

The aim of the sermon is not to show one's skill in the production of a literary work that will appeal to the intellect and win for the writer or speaker admiration, praise from the hearers; but rather, in fact, its aim always should be to reach the mind and heart and to influence the will in the direction of what is just, pure, lovely, and of good report, with never a thought as to the glory which it might bring to the preacher. The thought of self is sure always to destroy the effectiveness of the message. Whether men think of the preacher or not, if they hear the message and lay it to heart, the object of the sermon has been accomplished.

A man who is always thinking of himself in his pulpit ministrations is a failure before he begins. How little, how contemptible it is to be thinking about ourselves in the presence of the great and all-important issues that make up the themes of the pulpit! Not what people may think of our pulpit ability, but how far is the truth reaching them! How much are they being benefited by what they have heard. The pulpit, the sacred desk is no place for the man who wants to boom himself, to center attention upon himself instead of the Lord Jesus Christ and the truth of God. [250]

In public Sunday services, the principal thing is the sermon, the preacher standing as the living representative of God, declaring his will to the people. The preliminaries to the sermon should be brief, should not be extended too long so that the people may receive the message before they are worn out. When the sermon is over, nothing should be allowed to follow that will tend to break or lessen the effect or impression made by it. Whatever announcements are to be made should be before the sermon. This, unfortunately, is not always done. On the contrary many things are reserved until the sermon is over, which have no bearing or relation whatever on the message, but are in the nature of distractions, and so tend to destroy the effect of the sermon. Many preachers seem to lose sight entirely of what the real purpose of the service is, particularly of the message. It is a blunder, a stupid blunder, which should never occur. [252]

The only effective way of propagating Christianity is to live it. It is all right to preach it by word of mouth; but if we are not careful to live it, our words will go for nothing. It is the truth incarnate in our everyday living that gives it power. If we preach one thing and live another, our preaching is in vain. [254]

〜

This is July 7, 1928. Fifty years ago, I was ordained to the gospel ministry and installed as pastor of the Fifteenth Street Presbyterian Church, Washington, D. C. It is hard to realize that it has been a half century since I was formally set apart to this, the greatest work that can be committed to mortal man, the preaching of the glorious gospel of the grace of God in Christ Jesus. I have been trying to think myself back to the time when I began. Then I was young, not yet twenty-eight years of age, full of life and abounding energy; now I am approaching my 78th year, weak in body, and no longer capable of long and strenuous effort physically or mentally, and with the frost of many winters resting upon my head. How I have been able to meet the many obligations devolving upon me as pastor of an important city church, preaching Sabbath after Sabbath, and holding the confidence and respect of the people and satisfying their intellectual, moral, and spiritual needs, has been a marvel to me. There is only one explanation of it, and it is to be found in the fact that, realizing my own insufficiency from the very beginning, I sought, and sought earnestly, the Divine aid; I relied upon God; I sought his help in the preparation of my sermons, and in all that I had to do. I worked hard, studied hard, did everything that I could to make myself efficient and my sermons acceptable and helpful, but after all that I had done, still had I not been sustained by a living faith in God, and the abiding sense of his all-sufficiency, I never could have gone through with it. No mere human strength and wisdom, in a work like the ministry, are sufficient to insure even a measure of success. As one has said, "We must work as if everything depended upon one's self; and trust as if everything depended upon God." And I wish at the end of this half century, to bear witness to the fact that I never sought his aid in vain. I soon found out in my ministry, what Paul found out to be true in his, as expressed in the words, "I can do all things through

Christ who strengtheneth me." Only as we ministers come to realize that our sufficiency is not of ourselves, however gifted naturally we may be, but of God, will large results ever come out of our ministry, will our ministry, in any one place, be of long duration.

Another thing I may say in connection with these fifty years, and, which may account in part for the continued acceptance of my ministry, I have stuck close to the preaching of the word of God. From the beginning, and all along, I have felt that my mission was to preach the gospel, to expound the Bible as the word of God. I never attempted to make the pulpit a platform from which to discuss all sorts of subjects. The commission which Jesus gave to his disciples was "Go ye into all the world and preach the gospel unto every creature." It is the gospel which the minister is set apart to preach, and of which the people never tire. And that is what I have tried steadily to do, in dependence upon the presence and power of the Holy Spirit.

In looking back over these fifty years, two questions have suggested themselves to my mind:

1. What effect have these fifty years had upon myself, upon my personal development? What have I to show in character development – in intellectual, moral, and spiritual growth? Am I any farther on in the upward path, in the attainment of the measure of the stature of the fullness of Christ? No one knows better than I do how far I am below the noble ideal of what a Christian ought to be; and no one can more sincerely deplore it than I do. And yet, imperfect as I know myself to be at the end of these fifty years, I can truthfully say, it is not the result of indifference: it is not because I have not desired, have not tried to be a better man, a more worthy representative of the religion which I profess, and which I have sought to induce others to accept and practice. I am fully aware of the fact that I am not now, and never have been all that ought to be. All that I ought to be, however, I do most earnestly desire to be. Fortunately, it is not in our own righteousness, that we are to stand at last, but in the

perfect righteousness of the Lord Jesus Christ, imputed to us and received by faith alone.

2. The other question that presses upon me in looking back over these fifty years is: What have they meant to others through my ministration through my personal influence? It is a solemn thought, that no one liveth unto himself, that whether we want it so or not, others are constantly being affected by us for good or evil. To be functioning for fifty years as a minister of the gospel, as a public servant, cannot but raise very serious thoughts in the mind of one who stops to think.

During these fifty years thousands of people have been touched by me, have heard me preach, have listened to my words, have observed me in my daily walks and conversation. What effect have I had upon them? Have they been made better or worse, strengthened or weakened in their purpose to do right, to live clean, pure lives? Have I in any way been helpful to them in starting them on the upward way, in pointing out to them the path of life, spiritual and eternal? We cannot tell, of course. God alone knows. God alone can follow the spoken word, the act, the silent influences to their effect; he alone knows. And there we must leave the matter. All we can do is to hope that in some little way these fifty years have contributed something of good to the forces that have been and are still working for righteousness.

Whatever the effect of these fifty years of preaching and of living may be, the purpose running through them all has been to lead men to repentance and faith, and to build them up in comfort and holiness.

The close of these fifty years was marked on last Sabbath morning in the church, without any parade or demonstration of any kind, it was my request that there be none, but by the preaching of a simple gospel sermon by myself, from the text John 12:32, expressive of the character of my ministry from the beginning. I wanted to mark the close of the half century by calling attention to the fact that I began my ministry with the old, old story of Jesus and his love, and that with the same old gospel of the grace of God in Christ Jesus, it was my purpose to end it, having no faith in any other means of saving men. Looked at from whatever standpoint, the gospel which was proclaimed by Jesus Christ challenges the attention of the world as no other and vindicates its claim to be accepted by fruits far superior to any or all of its competitors. Wherever it has been proclaimed, wherever it has been accepted and acted upon, it has been a steady influence for good along all lines. Its trend has ever been upward and onward. No greater service can be done to the world, to the races of mankind, than to do all that we can to propagate it, to keep it ever to the front, ever alive in the consciousness of men.

The minister should be a man of brains, of sense, of high character, of piety. The ministry is no place for a fool, for a rogue, for a hypocrite, a wolf in sheep's clothing. He must be a man of sense, of intelligence, an upright and God-fearing man. [264]

I am distressed for the future of one of our churches. The trash that is served up to the people on Sunday mornings and Thursday evenings is deplorable. The sermons and exhortations are made up largely of the gleanings of newspapers and magazines, with precious little of the word of God in them, and, even when it comes in, is handled in the most superficial manner. No church can be built up on that kind of preaching; no church can be made strong morally and spiritually unless it is fed on the word of God, line upon line, precept upon precept, here a little and there a little. The pulpit of this particular church has been a platform from which the word of God has been faithfully and earnestly expounded, week in and week out, where people could come and be fed with the truth of God, instead of the rubbish that is now being handed out to them. It is hard to realize how rapidly the pulpit has gone down, how much lower the plane now is upon which it is moving. When I remember what the pulpit of this church used to mean to this community, and what it is today, it fills me with sadness. The pastor is manifestly a misfit in this pulpit. He is not qualified to meet its demands, or else he is not exerting himself sufficiently to do so.

How long this condition is to continue God only knows; but it cannot long continue if the church is to be saved and is to be continued as an agency for the moral and spiritual uplift of the membership and of the community. [272]

—

I was unable to go to church this morning on account of my health and a great storm that was raging. I regretted it much, and for one reason particularly, I hated to miss the sermon. I knew that I would get something worth hearing. And one of the rewards that come to a preacher who carefully prepares himself, who faithfully expounds the word of God, is that no one wants to miss hearing him. When people feel that they cannot afford to stay away, and when they do, always with regret, you may know that you are feeding their souls, that you are rightly dividing unto them the word of life. It pays a minister always to come to his pulpit fully prepared; never to be content with any slipshod preparation. To preach, in a way to make people feel that if they stay away they will lose nothing, is a sad reflection upon the preacher and should bring the blush of shame to his face. A man who is not willing always to make the proper preparation has no business in the pulpit, and the sooner he gets out of it the better. The one thing that never fails to draw is the careful, prayerful, faithful preaching of the gospel. It is mightier, more effective than all the clap-trap that some ministers are using to catch the popular attention. Paul's exhortation to Timothy was: "Preach the word; be instant in season and out of season: reprove, rebuke, exhort with all long-suffering and doctrine." It is the only sure and effective way of drawing and holding people. [275]

—

The secret of effective preaching, and by effective, I mean followed by results, depends, in part upon careful preparation, and also, and particularly, upon reliance upon the Holy Spirit to make effectual what is said. Effectiveness in the spiritual sense cannot be brought about by any amount of mere intellectual preparation or natural ability – it depends mainly on the presence and power of the Holy Spirit. Unless, as preachers, we realize this, and after we have made the most careful preparation, go to our pulpits relying upon his aid, nothing of any lasting value will result from our effort. It has always been true and is still true: "Not by might, nor by power, but by my Spirit, saith the Lord of hosts." Our duty, as ministers, is faithfully to preach the word, and the Holy Spirit will take care of what becomes of it. It is never what we do, but what the Spirit does through us or by us, as His instruments, that counts. [276]

In preaching, we drop the seed into the soil of the human heart. What becomes of it depends upon the presence and power of the Holy Spirit. Unless he attends it, nothing will come of it. Paul may plant, and Apollos water, the increase comes from God. And only as we realize this and learn to depend upon the Spirit for results will anything be accomplished by our sowing. [282]

Some sermons are too academic, they lack vitality. Nothing in them grips you; they leave no impression that counts. They may be interesting but are powerless to induce action, to influence the will; they lack force. They may show signs of careful preparation, but the atmosphere that pervades them is cold, frigid; they never reach the heart.

There is a way of presenting the truth that makes it glow, that kindles interest in the hearers. Sermons that are largely academic belong to the classroom rather than the pulpit. In listening to such sermons, they seem to be dealing with matters which in no way concerns us. The sermon to be effective must present what it has to say in a way to make the hearers feel that it is a matter that vitally concerns them, a matter that deserves their attention. Unless in some way the preacher can hold the attention of his hearers, can get them interested in what he has to say to them, can make them feel that they cannot afford to turn a deaf ear to the message, it is simply time wasted, the effort will be fruitless, of no avail. This is a point which, we, as preachers, should never lose sight of in preparing our sermons as well as in delivering them. Unless we have some vital truth to present and realize the importance of it to the heart, we had better be silent.

In preaching, it is one thing to make a point; it is a very different thing to drive that point home, i.e., to so present it that the hearers will leave feeling, I am the one that is referred to; it has to do with me; it sets forth my condition. When God sent Nathan, the prophet, to David to rebuke him for his heinous sin in his relations with Bathsheba, after he had told a most pathetic story and David's indignation was fully aroused, he was not left in doubt as to whom the culprit was. The prophet said to him directly, "Thou art the man." And this is what is meant by driving a point home, so setting it forth that the hearers will not be left in doubt as to its application to themselves. Each one will be made to think of himself or herself – of that in himself or herself to which the truth applies. "Thou art the man" is the kind of preaching that brings results, that causes people to think, to stop and consider. Be sure that we have a point to make, and see that that point is driven home, is so lodged in the minds of the hearers that the Evil One will not be able to snatch it away as soon as they are from under the sound of the preacher's voice. In other words, preaching, to be effective, must be heart-searching, must reach the conscience; must, in the language of Scripture, be "quick and powerful, and sharper than any two-edged sword, piercing even to the dividing asunder of soul and spirit, and of the joints and marrow, and a discerner of the thoughts and intents of the heart." [283]

A heart-searching sermon is not likely to call forth any flattering comments. It will be more likely to be received in silence, and the more conscious it makes us of our sins, the less disposition will there be to comment on it favorably. A sermon that flatters us, that makes us feel quite satisfied with ourselves, with our good qualities, will be sure always to be followed by favorable comments. So that when we are most praised is the time when we need to ask ourselves whether we have faithfully presented the truth or not. The sermons that make people think; that induce in them a serious attitude toward life and its great and solemn responsibilities, are not the ones that elicit popular applause. And this is the reason why sometimes in order to win applause the pulpit loses sight of its great mission and sinks to the low level of pandering to the tastes of the hearers instead of thinking of their good, their moral and spiritual uplift. More sermons that people do not feel like praising because they hit the sins of which they are guilty are what is needed in all of our churches. With such sermons people will not go to church expecting to be amused, entertained, and will not come away, as they often do, in a frivolous mood. The word preached must be made quick and powerful.

No notices should be given after the sermon, or anything said that would tend to divert attention from the thought presented in the sermon. The thought emphasized in the sermon is the one that the people should carry away with them. Some preachers, especially in Negro churches, often follow the sermon with notices and talks about all kinds of matters, so that the impression made by the sermon is partly, if not wholly, obliterated. There is great need for the exercise, in regard to this matter, of common sense. It looks as if no special importance is attached to the sermon by the preacher himself. How then can he expect the people to attach any importance to it, since, as soon as it is over, other matters are crowded upon their attention? I believe that the most important part of public worship is the preaching of the Word, and that everything should be made subservient to it, that nothing should be allowed to enter that would lessen in any way the effect of it. Every service should point definitely in some one direction, and it should never be lost sight of from the beginning to the close. The people should go away carrying with them some vital truth, some thought or suggestion that will enable them the better to meet the duties and responsibilities, the trials and temptations that await them in the actual struggles of life. The aim of every service should be to help people to be better, to live truer, nobler lives. [285]

The great mission of the church, in addition to calling men to repentance and faith, is to build up Christian character. And the only way to build up Christian character is to feed the people on the word of God. Any other kind of food, drawn from papers, magazines, current literature, will be unavailing, will have not the slightest effect. The program laid down in the Scriptures for growth, development, in things spiritual, is the careful and prayerful expounding of the word of God. There is no efficacy in man-made traditions, in what man has evolved out of his own inner consciousness. The emptiness, the shallowness of religious character and life among the Jews when Jesus Christ made his appearance was because the people were fed on the traditions of the elders, instead of upon the word of God. This was the very charge which Jesus made against the scribes and Pharisees when they said to him, "Why do thy disciples transgress the tradition of the elders? for they wash not their hands when they eat bread." His answer was, "Why do ye transgress the law of God by your traditions?" They were concerned about keeping the tradition of the elders, and not about following the inspired record. And this was why their spirituality was so attenuated, why there was so little to show of sturdy religious character of genuine religious life.

And the same is true today. The farther we get away from the word of God in our pulpit ministrations, the more of other things that we lug into our sermons, the less will there be to show of Christian character in those who sit under our ministry. [296]

It is a great privilege to be permitted to bring a message from God to the people, to be prepared by him to give the message, and to have the people prepared by him to receive it. These are the conditions that ought to obtain in every preaching service. The message ought to be from God; the preacher ought to be prepared to give the message by the enduement of power from on high through the presence of the Holy Spirit in his heart; the people ought to be prepared to receive it through the Spirit operating upon their hearts and minds. Preaching under such circumstances is always attended by results; impressions are made that are lasting and that lead to higher and better things. And yet how often services are conducted in our churches of which none of these things can be said, services therefore that are utterly valueless, that count for nothing. [300]

If God wishes to use you in giving a message on any particular Sabbath, you need not be concerned as to the state of the weather or whether there will be few or many present. Those for whom the message is intended will be there; God will see that they are there. All the preacher needs to be concerned about is to see that he has the message well in hand and that in giving it he has the unction from on high, the accompanying presence of the Holy Spirit. [300]

The prayer immediately preceding the sermon should be such as to create an atmosphere favorable to the reception of the truth that is to be presented in the sermon; it ought to be a kind of forerunner, preparing the way for what is to follow. Such a prayer will have much to do with the kind of impression the sermon will make. This is a point that is well worth thinking about in our pulpit ministrations. There are usually so many distracting thoughts that are passing through the minds of the worshippers, that, if in the prayer before the sermon, we can quiet those thoughts, can allay them, can hold them in check and center the mind upon spiritual things, it will greatly help to a favorable consideration of the contents of the sermon. The soil in this way can be prepared for the reception of the truth and very often is. The prayer before the sermon very often comes as the voice of the Master in the midst of the noise and confusion of the storm, saying, "Peace, be still." And so the calm comes on, the inner quiet, where people can listen without being distracted. [301]

A scolding ministry is not likely to be a happy one or a helpful one. It creates an atmosphere that is not favorable to profitable seed-sowing. It indisposes people to listen as they should to what is being said. The truth should be spoken, and spoken plainly, but not in a censorious, fault-finding spirit. People get tired very soon with that kind of ministry. The preacher, if he is wise, will not shut his eyes to what is wrong about him, but it is a mistake for him to be all the time harping on the dark side of things. There is a time for reproof, for rebuke, for calling people sharply to account, but that doesn't mean that it must be kept up continually. It is a mistake to do so. [307]

What we need is instruction, careful, painstaking instruction in the things of God, as set forth in the Scriptures of the Old and New Testament, line upon line, precept upon precept, here a little and there a little, if we are to develop properly, to grow strong morally and spiritually, and are to be saved from falling into error.

There isn't enough of this kind of work being done in our pulpits. So many other things are allowed to come in and take the place of the pure, unadulterated word of God. One of the things in the book of Deuteronomy that is particularly noticeable is the pains that are taken to emphasize the importance of carefully teaching the word of God (Deuteronomy 11:18-20). "Therefore shall ye lay up these my words in your heart and in your soul, and bind them for a sign upon your hand, and that they may be frontlets between your eyes. And ye shall teach them your children, speaking of them when thou sittest in thine house, and when thou walkest by the way, when thou liest down, and when thou risest up. And thou shalt write them upon the door posts of thine house, and upon thy gates." The instruction that is needed is not in the things of the world but in the things of God. A ministry that is given up to the careful and prayerful exposition of the Scriptures will be a fruitful ministry – a ministry under which the people will be able to grow in righteousness and holiness. [322]

How important it is in preaching (I am impressed with this more and more as I have listened to sermons) that we preachers should know definitely what we wish to preach about and that we carefully map out the lines along which we desire to develop the subject and under each head just what we want to say. In other words, the subject should develop and develop orderly if we are to hold the attention of the hearers and produce unity of impression. To go pell mell at a subject, beginning anywhere and ending anywhere, and dragging into it any and everything that happens to come into our mind, is to render it of no value, is to destroy its effectiveness. This is one of the things that should be particularly stressed in our theological seminaries. Much of the preaching that we hear is of no value because of a lack just here. How to present the truth in the most effective way is of prime importance in sending out men into the ministry. How much depends upon how the truth is presented, upon the intelligent presentation of it. If a man hasn't learned how to think clearly and how to present the truth clearly, the ministry is no place for him. [329]

—

I have just returned from listening to a sermon by the Rev. _____. How much we need in our pulpits men who can with simplicity, clearness and force expound the word of God so that the people may be fed spiritually. So often the message contains little of value and, apparently, has no definite, clear-cut end in view. The result is it counts for nothing, is of no value in character building. [332]

—

It is a great privilege to be permitted to preach the gospel, to expound the word of God to sinful, dying men. The minister, especially as he grows in age, as he comes nearer and nearer the end of life, realizes more and more what a priceless privilege it is. And though he may be weak of body, physically unable to do much, still the desire is there to be at work, to be breaking to others the bread of life. When the opportunity comes, after the active pastorate is over, how gladly do we respond to such calls. It is hard to get used to having no stated time and place for proclaiming the glorious gospel of the grace of God. This is the way I feel and is the way others have felt. [340]

—

In making the application in a sermon, it should be done in a way to bring the thought presented home to each one personally: each one should go away feeling called upon to do or refrain from doing certain things. If the discourse leaves us in the same state in which it finds us, if we are not quickened by it, stimulated, inspired to move forward in the direction in which it points, it is of no value to us, we are not helped by it, we are made no better by it. Every discourse should have a definite, practical end in view, and that end should be so impressed upon the hearers that they will be, at least, forced to think about it. It thus becomes a seed out of which great things may come. That is what preaching is for; it is to prepare the way for the coming of things of real value to the hearers. [340]

The subject upon which we are to speak, as ministers of the gospel, should be clearly defined in our own minds and should be so stated as also to be clearly defined in the minds of the hearers. All that is said, by way of amplification or illustration, should have reference to it. When the sermon ends, the subject should be still clearly in the minds of the hearers, and an ever-deepening sense of its importance. In no part of it should the audience be allowed to forget it or to stray off in other directions. Paul says, I press towards the mark. And every sermon, in the subject matter of it, should be a steady forward movement towards the mark, i.e., towards the subject that it is seeking to unfold. The theme should be one, and the aim should be to hold the attention to it, from beginning to end. [342]

I listened yesterday to a sermon from the text I Peter 4:12, 13. The theme of it was, "Enduring fiery trial because of the kingdom of heaven, or because of our efforts to advance it." In all probability, there was not a single person in the audience who was passing through any fiery trials because of the kingdom of God. The most of them were content to be in it but were in no way or were but little concerned about its advancement, certainly had no intention of enduring fiery trials because of it. The sermon might just as well, therefore, have not been preached. It had no reference to and was fitted to meet no special need in the state or condition of the hearers. This is one reason why many sermons fall flat, count for nothing. Two things ought to be true of every sermon:

1. The theme presented should be intelligently treated, clearly thought out, and presented in simple, understandable language:

2. It should have reference to the state, condition, or needs of the audience. To talk about matters in which those present are not interested or that in no way concern them, is simply a waste of time. Why should a man, with even ordinary common sense, preach such a sermon under such circumstances? The aim of the sermon should always be to help the people in some way to a better understanding of the truth, to warn them against evil, or to stimulate them in the direction of what is right. If it doesn't answer any of these ends, it is of no value. There is no reason, earthly or heavenly, why it should be preached. [349]

—

The pulpits in any community that have maintained their influence and held the attention of the people through a number of years have been those that have been concerned about feeding the people on the word of God, that have kept Jesus Christ steadily to the front, and spiritual things ever in the ascendancy. There is no other source of abiding influence for any pulpit in any community.

I talked not long ago to a young minister who is making quite a reputation for himself about the importance of sticking close to the word of God in his pulpit ministrations. He said in reply: I am coming more and more to see the importance of what you have said. I am realizing more and more that the only substantial food upon which to feed the people in order to make them strong, to build them up in Christian character, is on the pure, unadulterated word of God. Other things that may be lugged in may interest them for the moment but no substantial good will come from that kind of preaching. And the sooner all of our pulpits learn that great lesson the better it will be, the more commanding will be their influence, and the greater the results of their ministrations to the kingdom of God. The supreme mission of the pulpit, its only mission is to preach the gospel, is to expound the word of God. What the people need to know is not what we think, what we have to say, but what God thinks, what He has to say. And this the apostle Paul fully understood, and never deviated from it, but held fast to it to the end of his wonderful ministry. [350]

The main business of the minister each week is to be searching the Scriptures with a view of gathering food, spiritual food, for the members of his flock and all others who may be present at the public services. He is the shepherd of the flock, and it is his business, the responsibility is his, to lead his flock ever into green pastures and beside still waters. And this he will be able to do only as he is a careful and prayerful student of the Word. No outside business of a worldly or secular character, having to do with his selfish, personal interest, must be allowed to interfere with his full preparation to feed the flock over which he has been placed by the Holy Spirit. Too often this solemn obligation is not recognized as it should be, and the result is the flock suffers, the work is neglected. Other things are allowed to come in and absorb the minister's attention.

The subject of the sermon should be so presented as to arrest the attention, as to excite the interest of the hearers. How is this to be done?

1. The subject itself should be of value, of real importance – a subject worth considering.

2. It should, somehow, connect itself with some phase or matter which affects in some way the interest of the hearers. People are always ready to listen, and listen attentively, to what has to do with their interests, welfare, happiness. The subject must somehow have to do with what they are interested in, with what concerns them.

3. It must be presented in an attractive way. The minister must be wide awake, sincere, in earnest, if he hopes to get and hold the attention

of his hearers. He must show that he himself is interested.

A sermon merely as a literary production, however perfect according to literary standards, if that is its leading characteristic, its chief merit, is of little or no value as a spiritual instrument for the advancement of the kingdom of God. A minister whose aim mainly is to produce something of literary value has failed to understand what his real mission is. Paul, in speaking to the Corinthians (I Corinthians 2:2-5), said: "For I determined not to know anything among you, save Jesus Christ and him crucified. And I was with you in weakness, and in fear and in much trembling. And my speech and my preaching was not with enticing words of man's wisdom, but in demonstration of the Spirit and of power; that your faith should not stand in the wisdom of men, but in the power of God."

That is the only kind of preaching that is of any value. The aim of the minister should be to expound the word of God, to set forth clearly and forcibly the truth of God, and not to display his literary ability or attainments. It is the heart and conscience that he wants to reach, and only as he does that, however perfect his sermon may be as a literary production, it is a failure. This does not mean that a minister should not endeavor to express himself in the best literary form, but only that the great dominant thought with him in the preparation of his sermon should be the truth which it conveys, the substance rather than the form which it takes. [354]

Some sermons are made up largely of mere words, words thrown together without any center around which they gravitate – there is no central thought, no dominating idea; it is, at best, a mere conglomeration, a something loosely thrown together, an unorganized mass of anything that happens to be passing through the preacher's mind. Against such poorly prepared sermons I wish to register my emphatic protest. It is bad for the preacher, and it is bad for the hearers. We need in our pulpits clear thinking and thorough preparation.

Each sermon should be made vital, should have a definite spiritual aim, and everything that enters into it should tend to further the end sought. A sermon that is a mere formality, or that comes in simply as a part of a certain order of events merely to fill up the time allotted to that part of the service is of no value whatever. It must be something more than a mere formality. It must possess a value of its own and must convey a living message. So many sermons that we hear are mere routine performances. And so count for little or nothing. [360]

If there ever was a time in which we needed in our pulpits strong men, men of vision and of courage, it is in this degenerate age in which we are living. I see from the papers that Rev. R. W. Brooks, pastor of the Lincoln Temple Memorial Congregational Church, is being criticized because of a sermon which he preached denouncing the immodesty and indecency of the young people at an entertainment given by them which he attended. He was shocked, deeply, painfully shocked by what he saw. Instead of being blamed, he ought to be congratulated for the stand which he has taken. As a minister of the gospel it was his duty to cry aloud, to lift up his voice like a trumpet in condemnation. And the fact that he did it is greatly to his credit, and those who are now criticizing him will commend him all the more for it in their serious, sober moments. There are too many time-servers in our pulpits who, for fear of losing favor with the people, are too ready to tolerate or pass over in silence things that they know to be wrong. Such men are nothing but hirelings, a disgrace to the pulpit and traitors to the God they profess to be serving. I hope that Mr. Brooks will stand his ground and not be driven from the right and proper position which he has taken in this matter. We need, in all of our pulpits, men who fear God, but have no fear of man. Only such men are fit to stand as God's representatives in a world such as we are living in. The apostles said,

"We must obey God rather than man." And that is the spirit that must take possession of everyone who dares to call himself a minister of Jesus Christ. [361]

The mission of the minister is to teach and preach – to expound the word of God, line upon line, precept upon precept, and to proclaim the message of salvation, conditioned upon repentance toward God and faith in the Lord Jesus Christ. If he is faithful in these two particulars, he will vindicate his right to be called an ambassador of God. He is called to a specific work, and only as he concerns himself about that work and gives himself unstintingly to it is he fulfilling his high calling as a minister of Jesus Christ. He is to be instant in season and out of season; he is to show himself approved unto God, a workman that needeth not to be ashamed, rightly dividing the word of truth. [364]

In preaching it is a mistake to have too many divisions and sub-divisions, a mistake to dwell upon too many separate things. They will obscure or neutralize each other. It is a great deal better to select out of the many things that may be said three or four and concentrate attention upon them. The effect will be better and the impression more lasting. I have heard sermons interesting enough to listen to, but at the close from the multiplicity of things presented no definite impression along any one line was left on the mind. If the sermon does not focalize attention upon some one thing which it seeks to impress, it is of very little value. Have a point, and let everything move steadily toward it. [372]

I have just finished reading the life of H. B. Meyer, the noted English divine. It is the record of a most wonderful career. We are amazed at the tremendous task that he was enabled to accomplish, at his tireless efforts, his abounding energy, his never ceasing labor of love for his fellow men and for the spread of the glorious gospel of the grace of God in Christ Jesus. He seemed at all times to be intent upon the one thing, to magnify his Lord and Master and to bring men to repentance and faith. What a tonic it is to read his life, to follow him during the years that he lived and moved among men. How it shames us, many of us who are preachers, out of our lack of enthusiasm, our half-heartedness, our meagerness of effort in the great task that has been committed to us. We need his consecration, his singleness of purpose, his whole-heartedness, his abounding energy, his love for souls, which kept him ever at work, in season and out of season, which made him all things unto all men, that if by any means he might save some. I thank God that this book has fallen into my hands, and I earnestly trust that it may fall into the hands of many of our ministers. There is great need for just such an awakening, as it is fitted to give. We need more H. B. Meyers in our pulpits, men who are in actual, living touch with God, and who can therefore, speak with authority, whose words will carry weight with them. Much of the preaching that we hear is of no value because there is no evidence of the Divine touch in what is said.

The true minister must live in touch with God, in close, intimate touch with him, if he is to interpret God to men, and to bring men sensibly near to him. It is only as he has been on the mount with God, as Moses was, that he is in a condition to speak for him, and to speak in a way to make men sensible of the fact that he is speaking for him. The minister must be a man of prayer, and he must be a close student of the word of God. Without these two things, he may be able to preach interesting and eloquent sermons, but they will carry no saving weight with them. It is only as he lives in close, vital touch with God that he can hope to speak with convicting and converting power. And the sooner we understand this, as ministers, the better it will be for ourselves and for those to whom we minister. [385]

A man who preaches must be sure to keep in close touch with God if in his ministration he is to make God real to the people, if he is to make them feel his presence as a living reality in their lives. You can't talk about God and expect people to believe that you are speaking for him unless, as a matter of fact, you are living in close touch with him. You can't pretend to be, and not be, people will discern the difference. You must be what you profess to be. Unless God is really in your own life, controlling, directing it, is manifest, your preaching and ministry will avail nothing, or be of very little real value. To pretend to be what we are not will be fatal to our effectiveness. [388]

To preach so as to make people feel the value and importance of what is being said to them should be the aim of every preacher. That can be done only, however, provided he himself feels the value and importance of what he is saying. It is the truth made alive in his own heart that will come to life in the hearts of the hearers. So much of our preaching is mere empty talk with no real, deep heart-felt convictions lying back of what is said. The truth must be vital, living in ourselves if it is to be effective in moving others.

The man who has a message which he knows to be true because he has tested it in his own experience is bound to speak with power, to attract attention, to be listened to with interest and profit. It is the note of reality, that is wanting in so much of our preaching that will account for its ineffectiveness. [392]

Take a truth; lift it up clearly, forcibly; burn it into the hearts and minds of the hearers. That is the way to speak effectively, to command attention, to be sure of a hearing. [398]

A capable, efficient preacher is one who can take a truth and hold it up in such a way that people will understand it and be influenced by it. If you can't think clearly and can't present the truth in a way to attract and impress others, the pulpit is not the place for you.

Preach only on things that are real in your own experience – things that you believe in and that you are trying to exemplify in your own life.

In all preaching a note of reality should run; i.e., the thing preached about should be witnessed to in our own lives. In so much of the preaching that we hear this note is lacking; the things spoken of seem to lie outside of the preacher's own range of experience. What he says is not a part of him, but only something that he has heard or read about. You can't preach effectively under such conditions. It must be of things that we know. [408]

I listened yesterday afternoon to a talk by a young woman to the members of the Endeavor Society and was deeply impressed with it, as I am sure others were. The thing particularly that impressed me was its evident sincerity. It wasn't mere talk. Back of it was an experience; you felt that what she was saying was what she had actually experienced in her own spiritual life. What she said about prayer, what she said about the reading of the Scriptures, what she said about courage to stand up always and everywhere for what we felt to be right, you felt as you listened to her, was not mere talk, but the expression of a life; they were the channels through which her own life was flowing. And it had its effect; it went home to the hearts of the hearers. That is the only way really to speak effectively. What you say, let your life be back of it. [409]

More and more, as I listen to sermons, am I impressed with the importance of knowing just what we want to say, of having our subject well in hand, and of going directly at it, and keeping directly at it until we have said what we want to say. There is so much rambling, so much loose thinking, so much floundering about, instead of hewing to the line. This is one reason why so little impression is made by the average sermon that is preached. So many of them are gotten up simply to kill time, to fill out a program, so that any and everything flows into it, without order or arrangement, or pertinence to the subject in hand. [409]

As preachers we should exercise common sense and good judgment in the things that we take up and discuss from the pulpit. It is a mistake, a stupid blunder, to notice or call attention to what may be said about us, or about the church we are serving, which may be reported to us by some disgruntled individual or mischief-maker, reflecting or seeming to reflect upon our administration of affairs. The sermon to which I listened this morning was taken up largely with what the minister alleged to have been reported to him as said by one of the elders. It disgusted everybody and lowered him in the estimation of the well-thinking members of the church and congregation. Reference to such things do no good and is only a source of irritation. Someone has well said, "If you want to be happy, you must learn when to see, and not see: when to hear, and not hear; when to speak, and when not to speak." There is a world of wisdom in it, and the pity is that more ministers do not learn the lesson. The man that takes up and attempts to reply to every disparaging word that may come to him about himself or his work is a fool, and the sooner he wakes up to the consciousness of that fact the better it will be for him and the church which he is serving. It is one of the quickest and surest ways of destroying people's respect for us. There are some things that we cannot afford to notice and hope to retain the respect of others. [409]

The importance of the gospel message, and why it should be carried everywhere, lies in the fact that it is a call to men to escape the fate, under the moral government of God, that will be sure to come to them, unless they swing over on the side of Jesus Christ. The only way to avoid final moral disaster is to forsake our sins and put ourselves under the leadership of Jesus Christ. For the man who is a sinner, there is no hopeful outlook except in the mercy of God as revealed in Jesus Christ.

Such being the case, the preaching of the gospel becomes the most serious, solemn, and momentous task that can engage the attention of mortal man. It is a tremendous responsibility. We can understand the feeling of the apostle Paul when he said, "Woe is me, if I preach not the gospel." The gospel must be preached because in it is man's only hope. [416]

A minister may look upon the church over which he is placed as an instrument in his hand for advancing the kingdom of God on earth by drawing sinners out of the world into it, and of perfecting them in faith and holiness after they are in, by the faithful preaching of the word, line upon line, precept upon precept, here a little and there a little. Or he may look upon it only or mainly as a means for caring for himself and his family, so that if his salary is paid and his creature comforts looked after, he is satisfied. What the spiritual condition of things are, whether the gospel is being faithfully preached, whether the people are being fed with the sincere milk of the word gives him little concern. Unfortunately, that is true of too many ministers. It is of themselves that they are thinking rather than of the work of the Lord. It is what they can get out of it, rather than what they can put into it. It is not what I am worth to the Church, but what the church is worth to me, that is the dominating thought. [417]

Often when we are about to speak in public, it is not the good that might be accomplished by so doing that we are thinking about, but rather, what effect what we have to say will have in enhancing our own reputation, in setting us in a more favorable light with the public. We love the praise of men, and alas, that is what, in too many instances, we have in mind in the efforts that we put forth. Instead, what we should have in mind in all our efforts is to magnify the truth, to set it clearly and forcibly before the hearers, so that they will remember what is said, though they may forget the speaker. It is not important that the speaker should be remembered, but it is important that the truth should be. Unfortunately, in too many cases, instead of thinking about making better men and women, we are thinking about ourselves, about enhancing our reputation, of magnifying ourselves. Of such conduct we should be heartily ashamed. All such thoughts should be put far away from us. The opportunities that are afforded us of preaching the word are too sacred to be used for such unworthy purposes. The more completely we lose sight of ourselves, the more effective will our preaching be, the more good will be accomplished by it. Are we trying to help the hearers, to do them good, or to win their praise? Is it to help them to be better men and women, or to get them to think more highly of us, of our ability, of our eloquence? This should be early settled in our ministry, if we are to count for much in the kingdom of God. [427]

More and more am I impressed with the privilege, the glorious privilege which ministers of the gospel possess in the opportunities which are offered to them week after week as they face their congregations, of influencing them for good, of implanting deep in their hearts the truths of God's world, of setting clearly and forcibly before them the great ideals and principles of the Christian religion. What an opportunity, I say, they have of wielding the mightiest influence for good. And yet, I am afraid, judging from the inadequate preparation that is often made for their pulpit ministrations, that it is not appreciated. They do not come up to this great task, as they ought to, conscious of what it requires of them, and of the possibilities of good that it opens to them, as is true in too many cases. To stand as God's representative between the living and the dead is not only a great responsibility but also a glorious opportunity of doing good. And this, as ministers, we should all feel. [433]

As ministers, every time we meet the people in public gatherings, there is an opportunity of influencing them for good and for which we should always be at pains to make the most careful and thorough preparation. It is a time for sowing the precious seeds of divine truth in the hearts of those who are present. We should realize this and come to the task always with an earnest desire to make the most of such opportunities. We must not allow anything to stand in the way of the most effective use of them. We are to be always and everywhere heralds of good tidings, messengers of peace; always and everywhere lifting up a standard for the people, calling men to repentance and faith. [438]

I believe in the Bible as the word of God and that the work of the minister mainly is to expound it with a view of developing character of the type set forth in the Scriptures. If he is faithful in this, he will show himself a workman that need not be ashamed, "rightly dividing the word of life," as it is stated. In the Bible, in its great truths, in its lofty ideals and principles, are to be found material for building up character of the noblest type. To bring men to Christ and to develop in them a Christly character, is the main business of the minister. If he is not doing this, if his influence is not a positive force in that direction, he is a failure, and the sooner he gets out of it, the better. [443]

———

Much is being said about what is necessary on the part of religion or the church to meet the demands of this modern scientific age. My answer is: The great need of man in this age is the same as it has ever been, the need of salvation, of being saved from the guilt and power of sin. And there is only one way of meeting it: the way set forth in the inspired record, in the Scriptures of the Old and New Testament. It is by preaching the gospel, "not with enticing words of man's wisdom, but in demonstration of the Spirit and of power." All that the church needs is to get hold of the truth, as set forth in the word of God, and fearlessly and faithfully proclaim it, depending, as did the apostles in the early church, in the midst of conditions just as difficult as the present, upon the Holy Spirit to make it effective. There is no other way, and it is foolish and futile to think of any other. God's way of saving a lost world is "not by might, nor by power," but through the agency of the Spirit working upon the hearts of men in connection with the preached word. There are no difficulties in this modern, scientific age which cannot be met, and fully met, in this way. The plain, simple, faithful preaching of the gospel with power from on high is adequate to the needs of this age and of every age. It is foolish for us to be concerning and worrying ourselves about a matter which has already been settled by God. All we have got to do is to work his plan and leave results to him. The apostle (I Corinthians 1:22-28) says: "The Jews seek after a sign, and the Greeks seek after wisdom: but we preach Christ crucified, unto the Jews a stumbling block, and unto the Greeks foolishness: but unto them which are called, both Jews and Greeks, Christ the power of God, and the wisdom of God. Because the foolishness of God is wiser than men: and the weakness of God is stronger than men. For ye see your calling, brethren, how that not many wise men after the flesh, not many mighty, not many noble, are called: but God hath chosen the foolish things of the world to confound the wise; and God hath chosen the weak things of the world to confound the things which are mighty; and base things of the world, and things which are despised, hath God chosen, yea, and things which are not, to bring to naught things that are." [452]

⁓

In preaching, we need physical strength, mental vigor, and Spiritual power – power from the indwelling or conscious presence of the Holy Spirit. Thus equipped, we may expect results from our preaching. The minister to be effective must take care of his health, must keep his mind fed on Bible truth and his heart warm with the love of God, which will keep his heart also warm towards his fellow men. There is a physical, mental, and spiritual basis to all effective preaching. Hence, Jesus directed the apostles to remain at Jerusalem until they were endued with power from on high. And Paul directed Timothy (I Timothy 4:13): "Till I come give thyself to reading." And again (II Timothy 2:2): "And things which thou has heard of me, among many witnesses, the same commit thou to faithful men, who shall be able to teach others also." And also exhorted him as to his health, his "oft infirmities" (I Timothy 5:23). [454]

⁓

One thing every minister ought to be trained in is how to present the truth, whatever it may be, clearly, forcibly, convincingly. He must think clearly and must know how to express himself clearly, otherwise he has no business in the pulpit. [454]

⁓

In order to be most effective in speaking on a particular subject or a particular occasion, we must be sure to stick to the subject and not allow ourselves to run off into generalities. I read an address of this nature this morning. The address as an address was very good, but it failed in creating any special interest in the purpose for which the meeting was called. And it was because of taking up the special need which it was intended to forward, it dealt largely in generalities, in matters in which few present had any interest. All that was said was said well, and the illustrations used were happily chosen, but they had no bearing upon the specific purpose for which the meeting was called. If he had eliminated much that he said and had taken up the matter in hand and dealt with it, the address would have been very much more effective. I don't think it added one dollar to the collection.

Most of the preaching that we hear is of little or no value. It is lacking in sincerity and earnestness; it is not vital, it does not seem to flow from the heart, or to have back of it well-rooted convictions. It is largely on the surface, designed to catch every passing breeze of popular sentiment. If we had more of the kind of preaching as illustrated in the life and ministry of the apostle Paul, far greater results would follow than we see. Much of it counts for little or nothing, and the reason is because it counts for little or nothing with the preachers themselves. A vivid sense of the value and importance of the gospel message which is essential to good preaching comes only from the baptism of the Holy Spirit. It is where the Spirit is present that preaching is with power, that it becomes effective. Ministers must themselves keep alive spiritually if their preaching is to amount to anything. If they are dead spiritually, their preaching will be of the same character. As preachers we are so apt to neglect our own souls, to allow the well of water within us to dry up or to become clogged up by too many cares of the world. We have got to disentangle ourselves from such things and give ourselves more to the things of the Spirit if we are to increase our effectiveness as ministers of the gospel. It is when we are seeking to approve ourselves unto God, workmen that needeth not to be ashamed, rightly dividing the word of truth that we may expect the greatest returns from our ministry. [461]

One reason why much of the preaching that we hear in many of our pulpits is of no value is because it has no relation to the actual needs or experience of the people addressed. Another reason is because the subjects discussed are so bunglingly handled, with neither head nor tail, beginning nowhere and ending nowhere – a kind of vaudeville performance, or variety show, taking in a little of everything. The minister becomes simply an entertainer, with no real serious purpose in view. Sermons to be effective must be well thought out and must be directed to some worthwhile end – to instruct, to inspire, to move in the direction of what is elevating and ennobling, and not a mere makeshift for killing time, the time allotted to the sermon. [467]

Know what you want to say, and go at it. Don't be beating about the bush, running off on tangents and never getting back, saying nothing in particular and everything in general. It is better to say nothing than to be rambling about in a way that amounts to nothing. [472]

It is important to recognize the value of every opportunity that presents itself of saying a word, whether at a funeral or otherwise, and be sure to make the necessary preparation so as to present the truth in the most effective way. We are so apt to think lightly of some occasions and neglect to prepare ourselves properly. Every occasion that gives the opportunity of presenting the truth is great and should be treated as such. The best that we have is what we should always give. [472]

So few ministers seem to know how to conduct funerals. The special point or points in each particular case that should be brought out and emphasized they fail, too often, to grasp, and deal only in generalities that have no significance in the particular case in hand.

Funerals should be simple and should not be needlessly prolonged, as is too often the case. Nor should there be any special effort to increase the sadness and gloom that usually attend them, but rather to dispel the gloom, to brighten the outlook. At such times people need to be cheered, comforted, buoyed up, and this ministers should keep in mind. "To give beauty for ashes, the oil of joy for mourning, and the garment of praise for the spirit of heaviness," is their special mission under such circumstances. And this they should keep in mind. [473]

When you are going to speak, make plain to the audience what the subject is that you are to speak on, and be sure that you speak on it, excluding everything not directly bearing on it. Stick to the subject so that when you are through, the hearers will know something about it, and the importance of it. The speaker must not wander from the subject, nor should the people be allowed to. The discourse should be both interesting and informing. All the points of value should be clearly brought out and emphasized. [475]

What a privilege it is to get in touch with God and have him touch others through us so as to start them on the upward way, the way of faith and holiness.

The older I get the more do I feel what a wonderful thing it is to be a minister of the gospel, to be permitted to speak to dying sinful men in behalf of God, calling them to repentance and faith. It is because so many ministers do not feel this way that they do so little, that their ministry is so ineffectual. When we realize that we are co-workers with God, that God is beseeching men through us, and appreciate, as we ought, what a wonderful and glorious thing it is to be thus associated with him, then shall we be active, earnest, faithful in the task in which we are engaged. [475]

The great aim of the minister is to keep the people to whom he ministers in vital touch with the mind of God as revealed in the Scriptures of the Old and New Testament. The mind of God on all matters he should know himself and should keep the people constantly reminded of the same. He has got, therefore, to be a close and constant student of the word of God; he must himself be constantly feeding upon it, coming in larger measure in possession of its inexhaustible treasures of wisdom and knowledge. The truth of God's revealed will must be proclaimed, line upon line, precept upon precept, here a little and there a little. It is God's Word that the people need to hear, whether they wish to hear it or not, and it is the special mission of the minister to see that they hear it. It is not what he thinks but what God has to say that is important. And the man who doesn't realize that has no right in the ministry. [477]

Reading a sermon and preaching a sermon are two distinct things. Reading is merely to utter the words; preaching is to utter the words with power, to be so possessed by the thought which they contain as to be ourselves stirred by it. Preaching is not the mere mechanical utterance of words but words that have back of them thoughts, sentiments that flow hot and living from the heart. [478]

The effect of what we say will depend not only upon what is said, but also upon the extent to which it has taken hold of our own soul. If it comes fresh and living from the heart, it will be effective, but not otherwise. If it is given in a cold, formal, listless manner it will leave no impression. [479]

~

What a great privilege it is to speak to people on worthwhile subjects – subjects that tend to build them up in character and increase their usefulness. [480]

~

A gentleman came up to me today and said, "I heard you preach on Sunday. It was a wonderful sermon." I thanked him, told him I was glad he liked it. But said to myself, alas, such compliments are what most of us preachers like to hear. How much greater compliment it would have been if he had said: "I liked your sermon and was helped by it, and I believe that others were also helped by it." A sermon, however wonderful, as that term is usually understood, is of no special value as a sermon, unless someone is helped by it, is spurred on, stimulated in the direction of better things. And such sermons are the only kind that we should ever desire to preach. [480]

~

In preaching, it is in the hope of making an impression, a lasting impression for good upon those who are present, an impression that will work itself down into the character and life. This should be our aim. Unless some such effect is produced, the effort has been in vain. It is a mistake, in speaking, to seek to impress ourselves upon others. It is the truth, and not ourselves, that is important, and the more fully we realize this, the better it will be, the more effective will be our preaching. The work of preaching is too sacred and important a thing to allow self to intrude. We should cast self out of our thoughts and seek to be filled with the truth only that we are to present. It is when the truth takes possession of us that we may expect to preach with power, with authority. The self-seeker, the notoriety hunter has no place in the Christian pulpit. [480]

I preached this morning a sermon upon which I spent considerable time and labor, and yet, it is almost certain that in a very short time it will pass almost entirely out of the thoughts of those who heard it; little or nothing of it will be remembered. It is rather a discouraging reflection, were it not for the assurance contained in Ecclesiastes 2:1: "Cast thy bread upon the waters: for thou shalt find it after many days." It shows that our preaching is not in vain, especially when it is faithfully done. Some good is bound ultimately to result from it. Our concern is not with the result, but only with the faithful preaching of the word. "Paul may plant and Apollos water, the increase comes from God." God takes care of the results. Let us remember this, and it will keep us from ever becoming discouraged. Our labors are not in vain, as we are also told in I Corinthians 15:58. [481]

The Christian minister's great mission is to preach the Word, to be instant in season and out of season. It is the preached Word under the influence of the Holy Spirit that alone will do the work. It is profitable for doctrine, for reproof, for correction, for instruction in righteousness that the man of God may be perfect, thoroughly furnished unto every good work. The reason why we often fail, why the work lags, is because we are not always loyal to the Word in our preaching as we might be, and ought to be. Nothing can take the place of the plain, simple, earnest exposition of the Word. Where that is faithfully done, results are bound to follow. In no other way may we expect our labors to be crowned with success. [488]

I listened to a sermon this morning that had some good things in it, but which failed to grip me, which left no clear, distinct impression upon my mind. When it was over I had little or nothing to carry away with me. And the reason, as I analyzed it, was:

1. Because the subject of the sermon was not clearly stated. It evidently was not clear in the mind of the preacher himself.

2. The purpose which he wished to accomplish, if he had any in preaching it, was not discoverable from what was said. There was nothing outstanding and pointed in it. The text was: "We are saved by hope." What specifically was meant by hope? What by being saved? Saved from what? In what way saved found no specific answers in the discourse. After listening to it, it created no desire to be saved, no desire for the hope that saves. [494]

There is a great difference between preaching that merely entertains, that holds the attention for the passing moment, and preaching that satisfies, that ministers to the deeper spiritual needs of the soul – preaching that tends to fit us for life's duties and responsibilities – its trials, temptations, cares, anxieties, sorrows, and afflictions. Never mind how brilliant a man may be, how striking his oratory, if what he says does not minister to the soul-life, if the thoughts of his hearers are not turned Godward and heavenward, if they are not moved in the direction of the things that make for their highest moral and spiritual welfare, it is of no value; it is nothing but sounding brass or a tinkling cymbal. Preaching to be of any value must always have spiritual ends in view. [495]

It is a mistake to crowd too many things into a sermon and to have too many heads and sub-heads. Let it be simple in its structure and development. The thing particularly that you wish to have the hearers remember, stress.

Let everything else go. To overburden the memory is to defeat the purpose which you have in mind. Little or nothing will be remembered, and what is remembered, if anything, will be the least important. [496]

~

I listened to a sermon this morning, which, if the purpose of the preacher was to disgust people with religion, he was eminently successful. Religion, as presented, was anything but attractive. Such sermons do absolutely no good. Religion should be presented as an attractive, not as a repelling force. To tell all the bad things you know about professing Christians in a sermon is a foolish thing to do if you hope to attract people towards it. If we are to speak of religion, let us speak of the successes, not of the failures, of the men and women who reflect credit upon it, and not of those who discredit it, who are a disgrace to it. Once in a while, as in the case of Ananias and Sapphira, it may be well to sound the alarm as a warning to hypocrites; but you cannot associate too much wickedness with Christianity, as seen in its professors, and hope to draw men out of the world into the kingdom of God. We need to use a little common sense in dealing with such matters. [496]

~

In conducting a funeral our aim should be to be just to the dead and helpful to the living. Nothing should be said complimentary of the dead which is not strictly true, which his known character and life will not bear out. Nor should anything be said to the living except such as will help to make them better men and women, that will better fit them for life here and for the life beyond the grave. A funeral affords a great opportunity for most effective service if the minister only knows how to use it. A great many fool things, many unnecessary things, are sometimes said at funerals that do no good, that serve no purpose whatever, and should be omitted. There is great need for the exercise of common sense here. [498]

It is a solemn thing to stand up before an audience to break to them the bread of life, remembering that those present will soon be face to face with eternity and the judgment, and that the present may be their last opportunity to hear the word of God, and our last opportunity to give it to them. How careful we ought to be as to what we say and how we say it. The sermon I delivered this morning I prepared with great care, but I am fully conscious of the fact that the effectiveness of any sermon does not depend upon its value as a literary production, but only upon the use that the Holy Spirit makes of it. Its literary character, however perfect, counts for nothing as an agency for saving men, apart from the presence and power of the Holy Spirit. Whenever we come to break to men the bread of life, we should be sure therefore that, in addition to the careful thought we bestow upon what we are to say, that we make sure that we have the Spirit with us. [498]

In order to treat a subject intelligently, we must think it clear through so as to be able to see all of its parts separately and in relation to each other and to the whole. Some people bungle up a subject so in trying to treat it. And the reason is because it has not been clearly and fully thought out. [504]

It is amazing what little common sense some ministers seem to have. They say things which they ought not to say and things in the wrong place and at the wrong time. Sometimes they say things about themselves, from the pulpit, which a proper selfrespect would have prevented any reference to. In this way they destroy their influence, lessen people's respect for them. When to be silent, when to speak, and when not to speak, is a lesson which some of us need particularly to learn. A minister who is lacking in good judgment will be all the time blundering, making mistakes, saying and doing things that he ought not to say or do. [505]

There should be a positive note in all of our preaching. We should speak with authority; there should never be any misgivings, any uncertainty about what we have to say as ambassadors of God. Jesus said to Nicodemus, when he hesitated to accept or believe what he said, "We speak that we do know, and testify to that we have seen." And this same note of positiveness, of full assurance as to the reality, the truth of what we are saying, we must carry with us always and in all that we say. It is this lack of positiveness that is wanting in much of the preaching that we hear today and is one reason why it is not more effective than it is. In proportion as we are thoroughly convinced ourselves of the truth of what we are saying will others be impressed. It is the only effective way of preaching. [508]

Our mission, as ministers of the gospel, is to proclaim the truth of God as found in the inspired record, the Scriptures of the Old and New Testament, whether people believe it or not. We are not commissioned and sent forth to defend the truth, but to proclaim it, depending upon the Holy Spirit to make it effective. It is the Spirit that opens the blind eyes, that unstops the deaf ear, and softens the hard heart. The truth of God needs no defense from man. Back of it is the power of God, and it will always vindicate or justify itself. All that is necessary therefore is to hold up the truth, to set it clearly before men. The word of God cannot fail, will not fail, the gates of hell cannot prevail against it. Heaven and earth shall pass away but the word of God, never. [509]

Get hold of the truth, i.e., clearly apprehend it; let the truth get hold of you, i.e., be fully impressed with the value and importance of it. Only thus will you be able to present it effectively to others. The clearer you see it, and the more deeply you are impressed by it, have been brought under its power, the more effective will be your presentation of it. This is one reason why much of our speaking counts for nothing, or for so little: haziness of thought and lack of strong conviction. What we believe thoroughly and feel keenly, we will be able to make others see and feel. We should attempt to speak on no subject which to us is of little value or importance. The estimate that we put upon it is the estimate which others listening to us will be likely to put upon it. [511]

Every time a minister gets up to speak, either on the Sabbath or at the weekly prayer meeting, an opportunity is afforded him to feed the flock over which he has been placed by the Holy Spirit. It is for him to see that it is well used, that the words uttered by him shall be helpful to the people – in fortifying them against evil, in building them up in faith and holiness, in stirring them up to make the most of their opportunities for spiritual growth and service in the kingdom of God. If they go astray, if they fail to do right, if they grow cold, lukewarm, it must not be because he has failed to do his part to keep them up to the mark. It is a great opportunity, a great privilege which is thus afforded him which he must not neglect or fail to utilize to the utmost. Indolence or other things must not be allowed to lead him to fall short of making the most of all such opportunities of properly caring for the flock. [513]

One of the things, as ministers, that we should be on our guard against, is the desire for praise, the wish to be complimented for our pulpit ministrations. After we have preached what we regard as a good sermon, how we like to be complimented, to be praised for it. So much so, that if we preach a sermon and no one speaks of it, we are apt to feel that the effort was a failure. In other words, we come to measure the worth of a sermon by the compliments which it elicits. And so, we soon find ourselves preaching with a view of getting compliments, and so debasing the ministry, prostituting it to the unworthy purpose of self-laudation. If people praise our efforts, all right, but let us beware of making that the end of our preaching and looking for it as the test or evidence of our efficiency and worth as ministers. The man who puts himself in the forefront instead of Jesus Christ, thereby discredits himself, proves his unworthiness of the sacred office. [515]

A sermon to be of value should have some reference to the condition and needs of the hearers. There is no use of discussing in a sermon things that the people are not interested in, or that have no reference to matters which do not vitally concern them. There are certain things that are always appropriate, always timely, always will be sure to apply to someone in the audience. It is never amiss to tell men how to live, what to live for, things to seek after, and the things to avoid. It is never amiss to expound the word of God, to set before the people the great ideals and principles of the inspired record. Keeping this in mind it will enable us very accurately to determine the nature of the sermon to be preached at an ordinary service. Sermons that deal with subjects beyond the reach of the audience, that will not be easily comprehended by the people, should be avoided except before a select audience wishing for information on the subject.

I was forcibly reminded of this recently. I preached a sermon on a matter that, in some respects, was very important, having to do with the demands which this scientific, materialistic age is making upon the church, but it was not a subject in which the generality of ordinary church members are interested. It would have been better if I had taken another line of thought. It would have been more helpful; it would have ministered to the wants of a much larger number. I shall know better in the future and shall be more careful in adapting my sermons to the actual present needs of the hearers. [515]

~

The aim of all of our preaching should be to bring Christ to the front, to set forth his ideals and principles, and to live them ourselves and to get others to do the same. This program faithfully followed will cure all the ills of the world and will bring peace and happiness in all the walks and relations of life. It may be a slow process, but with the Holy Spirit attending our efforts, it cannot fail. To all, at least, who accept Christ and walk according to his ideals and principles, there will be peace and happiness. You can't reject Christ and his high and holy ideals and principles as the rule of life and ever hope to find inward peace or happiness. Out of the right way, the way of righteousness, there is no peace for any one. Only as we get in harmony with God, in accord with his way, can there be peace. [517]

~

How much the people lose because of inefficiency and lack of careful preparation on the part of the ministry! In listening to some sermons, I have often been painfully conscious of this fact. How we ministers often fail to appreciate what opportunities we enjoy of helping the people to whom we minister or to realize what our responsibilities are as ministers of Jesus Christ. If we did, we would be very much more earnest than we often are and very much more careful in our preparation for the great work to which we have been called of God, if we have really been. It is to be feared that many of us have been self-called, instead of Divinely called. It is a solemn thing to be entrusted with the ministry – to stand between the living and the dead as ambassadors of God. The more we feel this, the better it will be for us, and for the kingdom of God. [519]

~

The more I listen to sermons, the more am I impressed with the importance of knowing definitely what you are going to talk about and of keeping to the subject. Otherwise the sermon will be a hodge-podge, made up largely of disconnected matter thrown loosely together, with no definite purpose in view. I heard a sermon of this character this morning. What the speaker was aiming at I was not able to tell, and so I got nothing out of it, and I don't think anybody else did. A man who cannot clearly, intelligently, persuasively present the truth has no right in the ministry. All preachers should, according to the Scriptures, be "apt to teach," that is, be able to speak intelligently to others. It is not enough to know the truth, we must know how to present it. [521]

The longer I live, and, especially, now that I am nearing the end of life, the more deeply am I impressed with the great and solemn responsibilities resting upon a minister of Jesus Christ. He is charged with feeding the flock of God which he hath purchased with his own blood, and over which the Holy Ghost hath made him overseer. He is to be instant in season and out of season; he is to reprove, rebuke, exhort with all long-suffering and doctrine. He is to approve himself unto God, a workman that needeth not to be ashamed, rightly dividing the word of truth. He is to be an example to believers, in word, in conversation, in charity, in spirit, in faith, in purity.

Great and solemn indeed are the responsibilities that rest upon us as ambassadors of God! May we fully realize what is required of us and address ourselves earnestly to the task of measuring up to our great responsibilities. If we betray our trust, if through carelessness or indifference we fall short, great will be our condemnation. [522]

The subject that you are to speak on should be clearly defined in your own mind, and should be kept ever before you. The sermon or discourse should be built about it; every part of it should have some relation to it, directly or indirectly. In other words, the subject and the treatment of it should be so linked together that the hearers will not be allowed to forget the theme or the manner of its treatment by the lugging in of irrelevant matter or wide digressions. The theme should be the center towards which everything in the discourse should gravitate. This will give directness, force, and clarity to it. It is a great thing to be able to hold your own attention and the attention of the audience to the subject under discussion. It is the only effective way of speaking or of treating a subject. [526]

As a general thing, it is always best for a minister to take a text or portion of Scripture and stick to it, endeavoring faithfully to get out of it all there is in it, or so much of it as he wishes to use at that particular time. In this way, there will be variety in his preaching and growth in his knowledge of the word of God. Merely to make a text as a hook upon which to string a number of unconnected things is not a wise thing to do. It is not best for his own mental development, nor for the good of the people. Usually, it is only a lazy way of getting by, of which any preacher ought to be ashamed. In the preparation of our sermons, let us buckle down to hard work and not be seeking the easiest way of meeting a grave responsibility. [535]

It is not wise, as a general thing, for a minister to announce a series of sermons on a given subject unless it is one in which the hearers are likely to be interested, interested enough to wish to hear about it. It is best to let the serial nature of the discourses appear as you go on Sabbath after Sabbath. If it is not a specially attractive subject, people are not likely to be drawn by announcing it beforehand.

Be sure also in beginning a series that the first sermon is made particularly interesting. If it isn't interesting, the others will lag.

Another thought – each sermon in a series should be such as to whet the appetite for what is to follow. Each should be more and more interesting. [535]

Great preaching is preaching based upon the word of God and backed by the presence and power of the Holy Spirit. In other words, it is preaching that is effective, preaching that is attended with results – preaching that comes from the heart and goes to the heart. No preaching can be properly called great that is not effective, that is not followed by spiritual results. There may be preaching that shows learning, ability, eloquence, and yet be lacking in spiritual power – power to move the heart Godward and heavenward. Such preaching can never be called great, cannot even, in any proper sense of the term, be called preaching at all, if it fails to touch the heart and conscience. When we speak of great preaching, let us remember that there can be no such preaching apart from the Holy Spirit's presence and power. [537]

I am, more and more, impressed with the importance of having in our pulpits men of common sense and of capacity to apprehend truth and the ability to present it clearly and forcibly to others. For the past four Sundays I have been listening to a series of sermons based upon the text Mark 6:31, "Come ye yourselves apart into a desert place, and rest awhile." The purpose of the series, as stated by the preacher, was to give the members of the church something to think about during their vacation, based upon what he conceived to have been the lines of thought that passed through the minds of the apostles at that time while they were away in the country, thoughts about themselves, about the work to be done after their return, and about their relation to Jesus Christ and what he was expecting of them, etc.

There seemed to be no end to the things which he conceived to be passing through their minds. The probability is that not one of them ever crossed their minds. It looked as if the speaker was trying to see how many things he could conceive of as passing through their minds. The many things referred to, by no twist of the imagination, could have been drawn from the passage under consideration and the circumstances attending it.

The simple fact is, that while they went out into the country for a little rest, as a matter of fact, they got none. When they reached the place selected, the crowds were already there awaiting them, so that they had little or no time to think about themselves, or the work to be done on their return. And yet, it took this preacher four Sundays to tell the people what these apostles were thinking about during the brief period that they were away. There were a few good lessons that might have been properly drawn from this incident, that might have been helpful to think about during the vacation, but these could easily have been compressed into a single sermon and would have been very much more effective in its result. It looks as if it was simply an effort to use up the time allotted to the sermons with as little real thought as possible. Why don't such men either get out of the ministry or else buckle down to hard work in the preparation of their sermons by taking a text and getting out of it what there is in it and not try to hitch on to it, because of indolence, what has no connection with it. We need common sense; we need intelligence; we need the disposition to work, and to work hard in the ministry. [544]

Preaching is a tremendously serious business, and is fraught with the gravest responsibilities. It has to do with sin, out of which have come all the evils that afflict the human race. It has to do also with the greatest message that was ever sent to fallen humanity, the message of the grace of God in Christ Jesus. How to present such a message, and how to arouse men, dead in trespasses and sins, to a sense of their danger and the importance of accepting God's offer of mercy through Christ Jesus, is a task that calls for the highest wisdom and the most painstaking, conscientious effort on our part. We can understand how the apostle Paul felt when he said: "Knowing the terrors of the law we persuade men. Yea, woe is me, if I preach not the gospel." The nature of the message, and the condition of the world lying in sin and misery so took possession of him that it kept him ever on the go; it made him instant in season and out of season; it kept him saying, and living in the spirit of it, "As much as in me is, I am ready to preach the gospel." And in that frame of mind and under a sense of his great responsibilities he kept on to the very end of his glorious career. Realizing, while doing his utmost, his inability in and of himself to measure up to the great task, and so leaning, ever leaning upon him through whom he felt that he could do all things, he spent his days and weeks and months and years. And yet, how few of us in the ministry realize as we should the seriousness of the work and the greatness of the responsibilities resting upon us. It is because of this that so many are turning aside to other things, are allowing themselves to be diverted by other matters. The nature of the Christian ministry, its great and solemn purposes, its far-reaching consequences involving eternal weal or woe, we need to be awakened more fully to. We, as ministers, need to be constantly quickened along these lines, which is only another way of saying that we need to be more fully under the power of the Holy Spirit than we are as a general thing. No one can fully measure up to his great responsibilities as the ambassador of Christ who does not keep in close touch with him through the abiding presence of the Holy Spirit in his own heart and life. When Jesus directed his disciples to remain at Jerusalem until they were endued with power from on high, he knew that without the Spirit's presence they would soon lose sight of the work and the importance of it and, from lack of interest, give it up entirely or drift into other things. The man who is to live under the overshadowing influence of the grave and solemn responsibilities of the ministry will have to keep alive in his own soul a continual Pentecost. All believers need, but especially we who are ministers, to be constantly sending up the prayer:

> "Come Holy Spirit, heavenly dove,
> With all thy quickening power."

It is his quickening power that is needed to keep us alive and abreast of every duty and responsibility. The difference between a dead and living ministry is to be found just here – the one is Spirit-filled, the other is not; the one is absorbed about things of the kingdom, the other is not; the one is calling, ever calling sinners to repentance and faith; the other is more of the nature of an entertainment bureau; the one is seeking the approbation of God, the other of the world. [548]

I heard a sermon this morning from the text John 5:8, "Rise, take up thy bed, and walk," by the Rev. Prof. Benjamin Brawley. It was, what I would call, a helpful sermon. And by helpful, I mean a sermon that awakens us to a sense of our condition, our failings, shortcoming, imperfections, and at the same time, so sets before us the higher, purer, nobler things that are open to us as to create within us a desire for them and to start us in the direction of them. The simple fact is: every sermon should be, in some way, helpful to the hearers – helpful, if they are going in the wrong direction in restraining them, in causing them to stop and think, or, if moving in the right direction, to stimulate them, to spur them on. It should come as a retarding or impelling force to all who listen. It should be a voice of warning or of encouragement. [549]

Every minister who goes into the pulpit should go there with the distinct understanding that he is there for the one purpose of helping his hearers Godward and heavenward, of turning them from their evil ways, and perfecting them in holiness. The man who is himself in close touch with Jesus Christ, who knows from personal experience what the religion of Jesus is and its value as a soul-saving power, will show in all his ministrations the high estimate that he puts upon it. To bring others to see and feel as he does about it will appear in all that he does. And so the thought of forsaking sin and growing in righteousness will characterize all his preaching. It will have a helpful, restraining, constraining, uplifting influence.

The very atmosphere which such a man creates in and about him is very different from that of the man who has no such lofty sense of his mission as an ambassador of God. You can't sit under the sound of his voice for ten minutes without detecting the difference. What he says is different, the manner in which he says it is different, the spirit in which he says it is different. The one speaks with authority, speaks out of the fullness of his own experience – speaks because he knows the value, the importance, the transcendent importance of the message which he has to present. This thought of preaching helpful sermons is one that cannot be too strongly emphasized. If it is not to help people to be better, purer, nobler, more Christ-like of what value is it? And the more strongly, as ministers, we feel this, the more careful we will be to make our sermons helpful, adapted to the actual needs of the people to whom we minister. We must know their needs, their temptations, trials, weaknesses, failings; and, we must also know the word of God, where we learn just how to minister to them, how to meet their every want. Let us not forget that we stand in the place of the great Physician and that through him all things are possible to us in the way in helping the weary and heavy-laden, all who are carrying burdens of whatever kind. It is a glorious privilege that we have, and never should we lose sight of it or fail to do all we can to meet the pressing need of those about us. Let us aim always to preach helpful sermons, not sermons to tickle the fancy, to please the ear, to catch the applause of the passing crowd, but sermons that reach the heart and conscience, that tend to sober us, and to put an earnest, serious, worthy purpose into us.

Speaking of preaching helpful sermons, the thought occurred to me not long ago as I began reading Miss Margaret Slattery's little volume, He Took It Upon Himself. These words occur on the cover: "When Miss Slattery speaks the house is full. The audience gives her its undivided attention, and goes home with invigorated purpose and quickened faith." It was the last clause here particularly that struck me, "goes home with invigorated purpose and quickened faith." And the thought that came to me was, "That is the kind of preaching that should be going on in all our churches – preaching that invigorates the purpose and quickens the faith." [549]

Every time I stand before an audience and look down into the faces of the people, the thought comes to me, and as I grow in age, with ever-increasing emphasis – I am not here to amuse you, not here to entertain you, but to instruct and inspire you, to help you, as best I can, to realize the meaning of life and how to make it worth living.

To be worth living it must be conformed to the ideals and principles of Jesus Christ. It is by accepting him and following his lead that it becomes worth living. To set Jesus Christ before men in such a way as to draw them to him, as to lead them to surrender themselves to him, is, therefore, the great objective in all preaching. And it is with this thought before us, as ministers, that we should always ascend the sacred desk. We are there not as entertainers, but as instructors, and inspirers, and, therefore, must ourselves be Spirit-filled. [551]

Sunday is a great day for the minister, and if he is the right kind of a minister, it will also be a great day for his flock. Sunday is the day particularly on which he is to meet his flock, on which he is to feed them, to lead them into green pastures and beside still waters. It is the day particularly in which he has the opportunity of reading and expounding to them the word of God.

How anxiously he should look forward to it, and how carefully and prayerfully he should prepare himself for it, careful as to how he feeds them and what he feeds them on. It is his opportunity, preeminent, of instilling into them the ideals and principles, set forth in the Scriptures and upon which their whole future welfare will depend. It is to him or should be "the day of all the week the best." [551]

The minister to whom I listened on last Sabbath morning, at the close of the service announced his subject for the following Sunday, which, as a general thing, is not a wise thing to do, unless it is a subject of special interest, one that will make the audience curious or anxious to hear it discussed. If it isn't, instead of drawing people it will tend to keep them away. They will say, I am not interested in the subject, and so will either stay away or go elsewhere. The best way is to let them come and find out what the subject is to be, rather than attempting to draw them in this way. The best drawing card is always to see that you have something to give them when they come that is worth coming for. It is what you give them when they come that will tell most in drawing them and in holding them when they are drawn. Hard work, faithful work is the thing that tells. [552]

In Preaching:

1. The purpose of the sermon, the object which it is intended specifically to accomplish, should be clearly defined in the mind of the speaker.

2. It should be kept constantly before him in the preparation or construction of it; not for a moment should he lose sight of it.

3. Nothing should be introduced into it which does not bear directly upon the end sought, the impression which it is designed to make. These rules carefully observed will give unity to it and will tend to deepen the effect of it.

4. The end of it should not be long drawn out. In a few pointed words, it should end. Even a good sermon may be spoiled by the manner in which it is ended. [552]

So few people, comparatively, read the Bible that the work of the minister in his public ministrations, in reading and expounding the Scriptures, becomes all the more important. The only knowledge that the majority of those have who listen to him in the public services is what they will get in these services and from the pulpit.

In this fact is to be found also a strong reason why people should be urged to attend upon the public ordinances. In thus attending, whether they read the Bible themselves or not, they get to know something about it and about its great and important teachings. It is in this way, particularly, that the general lack of Bible reading is to be met or supplemented. [553]

In a sermon it is not well to use too many illustrations in elucidating any one point. One or two will be quite sufficient. [553]

The teaching of Jesus was always pitched on the highest plane. It was always a call to men to rise, to leave "their low vaulted past." And he always lived what he taught. Every truth, every virtue which he commended he exemplified in his own character and life. We need to learn a lesson here. It is one thing to lift up a lofty standard in words; it is quite a different thing to live it. And yet, if we do not live what we preach, it is of little value. Most of us need to keep this in mind. We are not always as careful as we ought to be, in seeing that we live up to or, at least, make the effort to live up to what we preach. Unless we are trying to be what we preach, we had better not preach at all. [554]

Rev. Prof. Brawley's voice is not the most musical, nor is his delivery especially attractive; but what he says is worth hearing and fully compensates for any defect in his voice or delivery. As one lady said, speaking of him, "He always has a message to give, and a message that is worth coming to hear. He gives you something to think about, and something to take away with you that pays you for coming." That was a high tribute and one that it would be well for all of us, as ministers, to think about and seek to preach in such a way as to elicit from those who hear us a like compliment. If we are not helping people by our sermons, of what value are they, and why are we in the ministry? What reason can we give for continuing longer in it? [554]

As I have listened for the past few Sabbaths, during the vacation season, to the sermons by Rev. B. B., of Howard University, sermons that help to feed the people, to build them up spiritually, and then think of what we are to go back to after the vacation season is over, I found myself saying, What is to become of the poor sheep under the husk-diet which will be given them. With such preaching and such leadership as we have been having for the past five or six years, it will be impossible to build up a strong, aggressive, efficient church organization. Unless some help comes, and comes speedily, the outlook is anything but promising. Our minister not only doesn't know anything about preaching, about rightly dividing the word of God, but he doesn't seem to have the remotest idea of what the church stands for or should stand for. The result is the church, though under his care, by some strange providence, is without any intelligent, efficient, spiritual leadership. Everything seems to be simply drifting; nobody seems to be in command. There are no great objectives, no organized movements towards the pushing forward of the kingdom of God, in making men better, in turning them from their evil ways, and setting their face in the direction of things spiritual and eternal. We are in a most unfortunate condition and from which let us hope that relief will soon come.

Any church without proper leadership, without intelligent and pious direction is in a most deplorable condition. [555]

The sermon which I heard this morning was searching, moving, illuminating: searching in the sense that it led to careful self-examination; moving, in the sense that it touched the heart and renewed the will or purpose to do better; illuminating in that it enabled one to see clearly what is required of him, whether he be saint or sinner. And that is the kind of sermons that must be preached if this sinful world is to be brought to Christ and we, as Christians, are to live the kind of life that we must live if we are to be true to our profession, if through us Christ is to be glorified.

It was virtually the same thought which was in the mind of a lady who said to me at the close of the services on last Sabbath, expressive of her approval of the sermon to which she had just listened: "That is the kind of sermons that we need, Dr. Grimke. The people need to be spiritually fed."

After I got away from her, I said to myself: What did she mean by being spiritually fed? She meant, evidently, preaching that made people think seriously of life and its great duties and responsibilities as they respect both God and man; preaching that keeps before men the fact that they are responsible beings and that one day they must answer before the bar of God; preaching that keeps before men the fact that they are sinners, and that salvation is possible through faith in Jesus Christ alone; preaching that keeps men conscious of the fact that they are both mortal and immortal beings, that their stay here on this earth is only for a little while, and yet during that little while, the issues of eternity depend; sermons that make men feel that living is a serious business, that we can't do as we please, can't spend our time and talents in frivolous amusements, in the selfish pursuit of gain, or the gratification of carnal lusts and passions and hope for any favorable outcome, any lasting peace and happiness. People are spiritually fed only when the spiritual is kept in the ascendency, when men are made to feel that life is more than meat and the body more than raiment, that the kingdom of God and his righteousness are the things to be kept ever to the front. When Christ said, "Feed my sheep; feed my lambs," that is what he meant, feed their souls, deal with them as immortal beings, made in the image of God and through whom he is to be glorified. No sermons which lose sight of these things can furnish food for the soul. [556]

We, who are ministers, when we speak to the people should be in earnest – should speak as if we realized the meaning of life, its solemn significance, its grave responsibilities, the tremendous issues which hang upon it – speak so as to make them feel, as Malthie Babcock has expressed it,

> "We are not here to play, to dream, to drift:
> We have hard work to do, and loads to lift."

Back of all of our pulpit ministrations should be the desire and the effort to awaken men to a full realization of what life holds for them. and what they may get out of it if they are in earnest and will properly apply themselves. It is a great privilege, a great opportunity which we have of properly influencing those who attend our services. See that we keep it before us, live in the consciousness of it. [558]

As a general thing, it is not well to give much attention, in preaching, to the affirmations of science which seem to conflict with religion. It is best simply to go ahead and clearly and forcibly set forth the truth as revealed in the word of God, the Scriptures of the Old and New Testament. People are not generally concerned about what science has to say when they come to the house of God to worship. Much of what is called science is mere guess work, unproved assumptions, about which, in the pulpit, we need not concern ourselves. It is with the truth of God revealed in the Scriptures that we have to do, and to which our attention should be directed. Jesus said to doubting Nicodemus, "We speak that we do know, and testify to that we have seen." It is to such things that the pulpit should address itself. [559]

The sermon which I heard this morning was not what would be called a great sermon, looked at from an intellectual standpoint, but it was what was better; it was a helpful sermon – one that had in it food for the soul, that tended to strengthen one's faith and to inspire one with courage when the way seems dark and unpromising. I never had any desire, as I have said before, to preach great sermons as viewed from an intellectual standpoint, but I have always desired, and still desire, to preach helpful sermons, sermons that are adapted to meet the actual daily spiritual needs of the hearers, that help to build them up in faith and holiness, and to bring cheer and comfort to them in the midst of life's struggles, perplexities, discouragements. One sermon like that is worth a dozen which merely seek to feed the intellect, to hold the attention for the moment. [560]

It is a great responsibility and a great privilege to be permitted to preach the gospel, to stand before the people and to break to them the bread of life, spiritual and eternal. The more fully we realize this, as ministers of the gospel, the more earnest we will be in the prosecution of the great task which has been committed to us. When we speak, we should remember that the message which we bring is a message of life and death, and that those who are listening to us may be listening for the last time, and that we who bring the message may be speaking for the last time. Before we speak again, we may be in eternity; before they hear again the message, they may be in eternity. Into every effort, therefore, we should put our best, we should enter with our whole heart, soul, mind, and strength. [560]

The seriousness of the work in which he was engaged the apostle Paul fully realized. It was the work of saving men, of turning them from darkness to light, and from sin and Satan to God.

1. He realized the awfulness of sin, its deadly character; the end to which it inevitably leads.

2. He realized that all men were sinners, hopelessly in the grip of sin, left to themselves.

3. He realized that there was but one way by which they could be saved, through repentance and faith – repentance towards God and faith in the Lord Jesus Christ.

4. He realized, fully realized, that to him had been committed the mission of telling men how they must be saved, if they are ever saved. With these great facts ever pressing in upon him, we can understand

why he was so tremendously in earnest, and why he was, as he himself tells us, "instant in season and out of season," and why, in the face of persecution and suffering, he went everywhere proclaiming the truth as it is in Jesus Christ. And no one who realizes what sin is, and what it leads to, and that the only remedy is in turning from our evil ways, and putting ourselves under the leadership of Jesus Christ, can fail to do otherwise. The reason why so little is being done, why so little zeal is shown in trying to reach men with the gospel message, is because the great facts underlying the church's mission are so little understood or believed in. There is no adequate sense of the reality of sin in all its deadly effects, no sense of the fact that through Christ alone can men be saved. Much of the preaching is only perfunctory of things in which we do not really believe, back of which there is no conviction. We do not, as a general thing, begin to realize the seriousness of the work in which, as ministers, we are engaged. [560]

A preacher may be popular, may draw people to hear him, and yet his ministry be of no real value in their lives. The test of the value of his ministry to them is not as to whether they like to hear him, but as to what effect it is having upon them. Is it elevating their standard of living? Is it making them more anxious to do right, more careful of their character and conduct? Is it helping them to be more truthful, honest, straightforward in all their dealings with others? Is it moving them to seek more earnestly and persistently the things that are true, just, pure, lovely and of good report? If so, it is a ministry that is worthwhile, that is properly functioning, that is of real value, and that under the influence of which we should seek always to come more and more. The man who draws us to hear him, but leaves no permanent, lasting effect upon our character and life, is not worth hearing, and no time should be lost on him. [564]

~

In listening to the discussion of the subject of the sermon this morning, "Holy Ghost Power," I had two criticisms:

1. Too much time was given to telling us what Holy Ghost power was not. What we wanted to know was what it was, in what did it consist. What it was not could have been disposed of in a few words, which would have left more time for telling us what it was, which, after all, was the important thing in discussing the subject.

2. My other criticism was that the illustrations used, while good, kept the attention upon the illustrations as ends, rather than as means to an end. The circuit described in the illustrations was too wide before returning to the point illustrated. This is sometimes the case. In thinking of the illustration, we lose sight of what it was intended to illustrate. [566]

~

It is a great thing to be able to speak to people in a way to awaken the good within them, to touch their better natures, to arouse them to the consciousness of the meaning of life, with its great and wonderful possibilities for growth, for development, for usefulness. The prayer which Whittier put into the mouth of Andrew Rykeman was:

> "If there be some weaker one,
> Give me strength to help him on;
> If a blinder child there be,
> Let me lead him nearer thee."

To possess that spirit ourselves, and to be able to awaken the same in others, is to make life worth living. It is power to affect people in that way that is most to be desired, most to be coveted, and that counts for most in our contact and relations with others. Unfortunately, in too many cases, the effect which we have upon others is just the reverse: it is not their better natures that we call forth, but their worse. Power to uplift, to ennoble, how glorious! [568]

Much that we hear at times in public preaching is mere talk – talk that has no real conviction back of it – talk that is meant simply to fill up a certain amount of space in a set program, with no moral or spiritual end to be subserved by it – mere padding. Sermon time is too precious to be used in this way. If we can't find enough to say, back of which are real convictions, a worthy end, then stop, even if you have to cut the discourse short. It is better to say a little to the point than to say much in a random, haphazard way. Never continue talking merely to be talking, merely to kill time.

The time preeminently that a minister has for expounding the word of God, for instructing the people out of the Scriptures, is the time set apart for preaching during the mid-week services and on the Sabbath. If he fails, therefore, to prepare himself – to have some definite portion of Scripture to expound, and to make himself thoroughly familiar with it, so that the people will be fed, properly instructed, God will hold him responsible to a strict account for his laziness, for his neglect of his most sacred duty as the ambassador of Jesus Christ.

The priceless value of such opportunities for instructing the people, there is reason to believe, is not as fully appreciated by many of the clergy as it should be. I have spoken of this before, but it cannot be too often or too strongly emphasized. [572]

In preparing a sermon, put your best effort into it; marshal all your resources; gather into it all your treasures of knowledge; beautify and embellish it to the utmost of your ability; but when you have put your best into it, made it as perfect as you are able from a literary standpoint, don't forget that its effectiveness as an agency of grace will depend mainly, may I not say wholly, upon the presence and power of the Holy Spirit. Only as the Spirit works through you, only as he uses the message will anything of value result from it. The simple fact is, both in the preparation of our sermons, as well as in the delivery of them, we need the guidance of the Spirit – need to feel his quickening, enlightening, enlarging influence. If we don't keep in touch with Him, in close, vital touch with Him, our preaching will count for little or nothing however carefully our sermons may be prepared or eloquently delivered. [578]

In preaching we should be ever holding up before the people the Divine ideal and standard of life. They must not be allowed to forget what is required of them. If they go astray, it must not be because the pulpit has failed to do its duty. The minister is particularly charged with the duty of "crying aloud and sparing not," of lifting up a standard for the people. And the proneness of the people to go astray makes it all the more necessary for him to be ever at the post of duty, ever holding up the word of God as a lamp to the feet and a light to the path. The light of truth must never be allowed by him to be put under a bushel. In this dark world it is God's lighthouse from which the light should be constantly going forth. [579]

A sermon that is searching, that causes us to look seriously into our character and conduct, to examine closely ourselves in the light of what we know to be right, will not be likely to stir a popular response in the audience. Such sermons are not popular, will not be likely to elicit many compliments. A person, here and there, may thank you, or say a complimentary word because he thinks you expect it, but, as a general thing, very little will be said about it. People don't want to be reminded of their shortcomings, don't want high standards of living held up before them. The less said along such lines the better will they be pleased. This is unfortunate: and some ministers who have itching ears, who want to be praised, knowing this will say very little in their sermons to disturb the conscience, to interfere with the self-complacency of the hearers. The truth, however unpalatable it may be, will always be courageously proclaimed by the true minister of God. He may not be praised for it by man, and it is a small matter whether he is or not, but he will have the approval of his own conscience, and the approbation of God, which is far more important than any praise of man.

Whether popular or not, it is our duty to declare the whole counsel of God. Only thus will our skirts be clean and our title to be called ambassadors of God be fully vindicated. No cowardly minister who is afraid to declare the whole word of God lest he give offense, or interfere with his popularity, has any right in any Christian pulpit. He is simply a disgrace to it and a stench in the nostrils of Jehovah. The seeking of popularity in the pulpit is a fatal defect and the surest way of not achieving true success. [580]

In preaching, the important thing is the truth of God that is presented, and we should be careful that the truth is kept to the front and not ourselves. It is the message that we should desire to have the people take away with them, rather than favorable opinions of ourselves. If the minister only is remembered and not the message, the service has been of little value. One of the most memorable sermons I ever heard was from a man whose delivery was most striking, most dramatic, but it was the truth which he presented with such power that made the deepest impression upon me. So it should always be, and so it will always be when the Spirit is back of the message, when all thought of self goes out of the preacher. That is what I call great preaching – preaching where the truth grips you even more than the personality of the preacher. [582]

—

Every sermon should have a central thought, and whatever enters into its composition should be articulated to that thought in such a way as to keep the thought before the minds of the hearers. [588]

—

After the most careful and prayerful preparation of a sermon, I am fully persuaded that unless it is used by the Holy Spirit it will accomplish nothing. The enduement from on High is absolutely necessary if results are to follow. The Spirit is needed both in the preparation and in the delivery of the message. Our hearts must be prepared under his influence, in giving the message, and the hearts of the hearers in order properly to receive it. [588]

—

I want to record here, as I have done before, my deliberate judgment that a minister who doesn't think clearly, who is not able to present the truth simply and lucidly, is not only not fit to fill the pulpit where people of intelligence, of education, worship, but unfit also to preach to the ignorant, the illiterate. The simple fact is people who are ignorant and illiterate need especially preachers who can clearly and simply present the truth. Men who cannot think clearly and express themselves simply so as to be understood by the common people are out of place in any pulpit and should seek employment in some other line of activity. The ministry is no place to display one's ignorance and incompetence. [593]

—

Curses on the minister who doesn't carefully and prayerfully prepare himself for all his public ministrations, especially the preaching of the word. The opportunity that is afforded him, on such occasions, of impressing upon the hearers some important lesson is too precious to be wasted through poor and inefficient preparation. [594]

~

Sermons, which consist of simply stringing together a number of generalities get nowhere and accomplish nothing. They simply run on, with no end in view, except to use up the time. Such sermons are a reflection upon the intelligence of the preacher as well as upon that of the congregation that tolerates such preaching. [594]

~

What a great privilege it is to be permitted to break the bread of life to dying men on their way to eternity and the judgment. How glad we ought to be of every such opportunity, and how careful we ought to be in preparing ourselves for it – careful as to what we say and how we say it. It may be our last opportunity to speak to them and their last opportunity to hear the word – God's word of warning and also his gracious words of pardon, of peace, of reconciliation. It is a solemn thought that we should not forget whenever we get up to speak. It will make us more earnest than we would otherwise be; it will fill us with a deeper sense of our responsibility and the use that we should make of every such opportunity. We cannot as ministers be too strongly impressed with the meaning of such opportunities. [595]

~

To preach, so as to induce sinful, dying men, to forsake their sins and fall in with God's way is the great problem for the pulpit. Its definite aim should always be to reach men for their good. Under its influence, under the proper kind of preaching men ought to become better, purer, nobler in character and life. [598]

~

It is a great thing, in preaching, to have a message, and to be able to give it in demonstration of the Spirit and of power. It is the only way that the gospel message should ever be given and is the only way to give it effectively. In order to do this, there must be care in preparing the message and care in seeking the enduement of the Holy Spirit in giving it. It is not a matter of chance. Preaching effectively requires careful preparation in both of these directions.

The only gospel that is exerting any real saving power in the world is the gospel of the grace of God in Christ Jesus. The only people who, in their character and lives, give evidence that they are being saved from their sins are those who have accepted Jesus Christ as their prophet, priest, and king. It alone is the power of God unto salvation to everyone that believeth. [598]

In preaching, I am not speaking for God, but God is speaking through me. That is the proper way to view it and the spirit in which, as ministers, we ought always to enter the pulpit. It is a Spirit-filled, God-controlled ministry that alone will be effective. [599]

Forget all about the preacher, think only of the message, of the truth declared by him. Let that sink into the heart, and go forth to live it, to profit by it. [599]

Every time we get up to preach, we have the opportunity of magnifying ourselves, or of magnifying Jesus Christ – of calling attention to ourselves or to him. Which is it that we are aiming to do? Which is it that we ought to be aiming to do? It is worth thinking about. Alas, too often it is only of ourselves that we are thinking. [599]

—

Preaching is a serious business – serious for the preacher, in that it lays him under solemn obligation to have something to say that will be worth hearing, something calculated to benefit the hearers, to make them stronger, to better fit them to meet the duties and responsibilities of life.

Serious also for the hearers, in that it places them also under equally solemn obligation to listen carefully, attentively to what is said, and to lay it up in their hearts and regulate their lives in accordance with it.

In going to church, go where you think you can get something of value, and go hoping to be benefited by the services. Give close attention to what is said and lay it up in your heart as a means of enriching your character and life. [599]

—

What a privilege to have the opportunity of speaking to dying, sinful men on their way to eternity and the judgment! What an opportunity of imparting truths of the highest value, of implanting high ideals and principles that may help to shape and mold character and life in the direction of what is just, pure, lovely, and of good report. And how careful we ought to be in the preparation we make for such services.

What a privilege, yes, and what a responsibility to be entrusted with the work of proclaiming the gospel of the grace of God to a world lying in sin and misery. (1) We should be sure that what we preach is the word of God, (2) and that we are in the proper condition spiritually to impart the same to others. We can't do it in our own strength. [599]

—

Every time we attempt to preach we should have a message from God, and we should have the message well in hand; and it should be given in demonstration of the spirit and of power. When we speak in the consciousness that we are speaking for God, or rather that God is speaking through us, our preaching will not be in vain, but will always be owned by God, will always be attended by beneficial results to someone. If the message is from God, is on a subject that God wishes emphasized, and it is given by one under the influence of the Holy Spirit, it is bound to result in good. Let us be sure, therefore, that our message is from God, and that we have the enduement from on high. We must be much on our knees, much in close fellowship with God if we are to speak as one having authority and not as the scribes. [600]

In preaching, be sure that you keep the subject that you are discussing clearly before you. Don't ever get so far away from it that the people will lose sight of it if you hope to produce upon them a definite effect.

In preparing and in preaching a sermon, be sure that you keep steadily in mind the impression you want to make upon the hearers, the state of mind that you want to induce in them, the purpose that you want them to take away with them. A sermon, e. g., on the Holy Spirit in relation to the Christian life, should be so presented that each one will go away feeling that he cannot get along without his aid, and the determination to seek him in earnest. If the Christian life cannot be lived apart from the Holy Spirit, in speaking of the Spirit, it should be so done as to impress that fact vividly upon the mind and so as to stir the hearers up to seek more earnestly his presence. [602]

As ministers of the gospel, we should come to the pulpit every time with a definite and live message, a message touching the actual needs of the hearers, with something that will cause them to think, to face seriously the issues of life, its grave duties and responsibilities. It ought never to be merely with something to fill up the time but always something that ought to be said, that is important to say, and the importance of which we ourselves feel, and feel keenly. It is when we go into the pulpit with a definite and vital subject before us, the value of which we ourselves fully realize, that we may expect to speak with power. Lack of something definite and vital to say and a failure to realize the importance of what we do say are reasons why much of the preaching that is heard counts for nothing. [602]

The only reason for speaking in public is in the hope of doing some good, of helping someone. It should never be to advertise one's self, to call attention to one's self. Always have something to say that is worth saying, and say it with a view of impressing others with the importance of it. If there is any advertising of self to be done, let it be by others. Be so absorbed in what you are saying that the thought of self will not be able to intrude itself. [605]

The fact that the Bible is so little read by the generality of people, and even by the great majority of professing Christians, makes it all the more necessary that it be the constant companion of every minister of the gospel, that it be carefully and prayerfully studied by him, and that he avail himself of every opportunity to expound it to the people. Unless this is done, the most of them will grow up in ignorance of its contents. It is upon the ministry that the responsibility largely rests of making known God's word and of building character upon it, upon its great and vital truths. Because the people do not read the word of God, the ministers, therefore, must make them acquainted with it. They have no time nor business to be devoting themselves in their pulpit ministration to the discussion of other matters. It is upon God's word that the people need to be fed. [606]

If men can be saved without the gospel, i.e., without a knowledge of salvation as set forth in the Scriptures, then there is no need of preaching, of calling men to repentance and faith. But if it is true, as Peter, under the influence of the Holy Spirit, said, "There is no name given under heaven whereby men must be saved, but the name of Jesus," then it is necessary to preach the gospel; otherwise none will be saved. It is this great and solemn fact that is back of all our missionary efforts and that we, as Christians, should realize more fully than most of us do. The possibility of salvation through Christ alone we do not begin to realize, do not begin to appreciate as we should. If we did, we would work harder and give more than we do in behalf of missions. [607]

There is great need in our pulpits for clear thinking, for men who know how, intelligently and effectively, to present a subject. And by this, I mean present it in such a way that the people will understand just what the preacher is driving at and in such a way as to move them to action in the direction pointed out in the sermon. Every sermon should have a definite aim, and it should be so constructed and built up as to make plain what the end or aim is. Many sermons show no clear thinking or definite aim. Know what you want, what you are driving at, and then go at it with all your might, turning neither to the right nor the left. "This one thing I do," said the apostle, and so should it be in preaching. Be always pressing toward the mark. [608]

It is absolutely a waste of time to be speaking on Sunday or at the mid-week meeting unless some results are to follow, some good is done. And, therefore, in connection with all such services there should always be careful preparation for them in two directions:

1. In what we have to say. We cannot go before the people and expect

results if we have given little or no thought to what we are going to say.

2. It should be preceded by earnest prayer for the presence of the Holy Spirit to make effective what may be said or done. The more deeply we impress ourselves with the importance of having the Spirit present, and the more earnestly we seek his presence, the greater will be the success of the meeting, the more beneficial or helpful will it be to those present. It should be preceded by much prayer. [608]

RULES FOR SPEAKING OR SERMONIZING:

1. Know what you want to speak about.

2. Know why you want to speak about it.

3. Keep the end ever before you, from start to finish. Keep from wandering, from straying, from lugging in other things.

4. When you have said what you wanted to say, stop. To go on after that is simply to weaken the effect of the discourse or address. It is a good thing to know when to stop. So many of us don't seem to know. [612]

Every sermon should have a definite subject for presentation. and everything that enters into it should tend to fix attention upon it, to illuminate it, and to increase interest in it, so that as the discussion proceeds, the clearer will the subject become, the more will its importance be perceived and the purpose which it is intended to subserve be apprehended. [614]

I have said several times before, and say again, I am more and more impressed with the importance of having in our pulpits trained men – men who can take a subject, think it through, analyze it, and clearly and forcibly present it.

I heard a sermon this morning which illustrates the importance of what I am saying. It was on the subject of lukewarmness in the spiritual life. There was no definition of the subject, no attempt made to analyze it, to show what it was, how it was brought about, and how it was to be remedied. It was not long before all trace of the subject was lost and several others taken up, with running comments on each. The preacher evidently did not think his subject out clearly and so was easily drawn away from it in other lines, ending in leaving no definite impression of the subject or the importance of it. How important it is that we know how to deal with subjects when we attempt to discuss them! [616]

The truth to be presented should be clearly apprehended by the speaker and its importance fully realized by him. The more fully he realizes its importance, and the more fully it takes possession of him, the more effective will be his presentation of it. If the speaker is not impressed with the importance of what he is saying, he will not be able to impress others with it. All we can do, therefore, to impress ourselves with the value and importance of what we are saying the greater will be the prospect of leaving a like impression upon others. If we are not really interested in a subject, if it doesn't take hold of us, we had better let it alone or leave the discussion of it to someone who is interested in it. There is no use wasting time. [617]

There is great need for the exercise of common sense on the part of preachers in adapting their discourses to the actual present need of the hearers and not to be discussing subjects which they are not likely to be interested in or that have little or no bearing upon matters that concern them. Such discourses are simply a waste of time and never accomplish anything. The exercise of a little common sense in the pulpit would save from such blunders. Talk of things that are of present concern to the hearers; let things that are of remote interest go by. There is always a sufficient number of things of present interest to engage the attention, and such things only ought, as a general thing, to be taken up for discussion. [617]

In inviting men to preach to the students in our colleges and universities, those in authority are too apt to select what they regard as brainy and scholarly men rather than men of spiritual insight and power. This has always seemed to me to be a mistake. The men who are likely to do the most good are spiritually minded men, men who can clearly and forcibly present the truth of God, and who depend upon the Holy Spirit to make effectual the message which they bring. It is the gospel preached not in the wisdom of man, but in demonstration of the Spirit and of power that is needed. These officials in our colleges would do well to keep in mind what the apostle Paul said to the Corinthians (I Corinthians 2:3-5). "And I was with you in weakness and in fear, and in much trembling. And my speech and my preaching were not in persuasive words of wisdom, but in demonstration of the Spirit and of power: that your faith should not stand in the wisdom of men, but in the power of God." The more we come to understand that the effectiveness of preaching does not depend so much upon the intellectual ability and scholarly attainments of the preacher, as upon the extent to which he realizes his dependence upon the Holy Spirit – the extent to which he realizes that it is only as the Spirit uses him, works through him, that anything of any value will be accomplished. The men best adapted to speak to our college students, and to speak to men anywhere, are Spiritfilled men, men clothed with power from on high. Paul was a man of brains, a man of culture, but most of all he was endued with the unction from on high, and there was the secret of his power to move men and set their faces in the right direction.

And not only those in our colleges who invite the preachers, but the preachers themselves are apt also to think of their mission from the intellectual rather than the spiritual standpoint and aim to preach what might be called great sermons instead of helpful ones. The fact that a college is a seat of learning, and often is nothing more, is all the greater reason for injecting into the life of its student body sermons that will tend to brace them up spiritually, to impress upon them the importance of religion as a stabilizing force in life. Unsanctified knowledge, knowledge divorced from the thought of God and our responsibility to him is a curse and not a blessing. It is to keep that thought before the student body that is most important.

As ministers, our duty is to preach what the Bible teaches, its ideals, principles, great truths concerning God and man, sin and righteousness, never mind what others may think or say, whether they believe or disbelieve in what is declared to be true in the Scriptures of the Old and New Testament. The minister stands as the Divine representative and is bound to declare what God reveals to him in his inspired Word and to declare it fearlessly whoever may assert the opposite or however high his standard in the estimation of the world may be. Jesus said, "We speak that we do know." And the preacher, as long as he sticks to the clear declarations of the word of God, may say the same. He is not guessing, speculating, surmising, theorizing. What he asserts is true and may be relied upon with absolute assurance. It is not sand but rock that he is building upon. [617]

Plan your sermon. Make the plan simple. Follow the plan. Don't stray from it; don't mix things up, and so muddle the minds of the hearers, confuse their thoughts, leave them with no clear definite idea to take away with them. If the sermon is not planned, there will be no order in it, and if there is no order there will be confusion. And if there is confusion, no clear impression will be taken away. It shows a lack of proper training on the part of the preacher and his unfitness therefore for the pulpit. [619]

Every sermon should have a definite end in view, and that end should be kept steadily in mind in the preparation of the sermon. All that enters into its make up should not only have some bearing upon the end but should tend to make clear what the end is and help to enforce it. I have written this before in this journal, or something like it, but it will bear repeating, because, in so many sermons it is overlooked or disregarded. The result is the value of the sermon or its effectiveness is entirely destroyed or greatly diminished. It is a point that is well worth remembering for the sake of the preacher as well as for his hearers. [630]

WHAT

IS

JUDAISM?

An Interpretation
for the Present
Age

Emil L. Fackenheim

SYRACUSE UNIVERSITY PRESS

First Syracuse University Press Edition 1999

99 00 01 02 03 04   6 5 4 3 2 1

Originally published in 1987 by Summit Books,
a division of Simon and Schuster, Inc.

The paper used in this publication meets the minimum requirements
of American National Standard for Informational Sciences—Permanence
of Paper for Printed Library Materials, ANSI Z39.48-1984. ∞™

Library of Congress Cataloging-in-Publication Data

Fackenheim, Emil L.
What is Judaism? : an interpretation for the present age / Emil L.
Fackenheim. — 1st Syracuse University Press ed.
p. cm. — (Library of Jewish philosophy)
Originally published : New York : Summit Books, c1987.
Includes bibliographical references and index.
ISBN 0-8156-0623-0 (pbk. : alk. paper)
1. Judaism. I. Title. II. Series.
BM561.F24 1999
296—dc21   99-37825

Manufactured in the United States of America

To Henry Fischel
and the memory of
Heinz Warschauer
and
my brother Alan
Companions of a Lifetime

CONTENTS

Part II. PRESENT
The Life of Judaism Through the Ages   105

Part III. FUTURE
Judaism in an Age of Renewed Jewish
Statehood   221

PREFACE

I have written this book for two interrelated reasons. First, contemporary Jewish history is marked by events so momentous that Judaism, the Jewish religion, cannot remain unaffected. These events, of course, are the Holocaust and the birth of the State of Israel. Second, those bearing the brunt of these events, and of their impact upon Judaism, are not just rabbis, professors, intellectuals, and the like. They are the Jewish people as a whole. The wicked ones did not single out pious or learned or committed Jews for defamation, persecution, and eventual murder: To be born a Jew was enough. And the defense, development, and support of the state that has risen from the ashes is not in the hands of an elite: If anything unites the Jewish people today—produces a *k'lal yisrael* ("united Jewish people")—it is the determination that Israel shall not go under. How is this commitment to a Jewish state related to the Jewish religion? And can there still *be* that religion after the scandal of the Holocaust? Ordinary Jews are asking these questions. They have every right to ask them. And they have a

9

right to an answer, however tentative and fragmentary. Or if not
to an answer at least to an attempt at one.

I have found that a book with this purpose had to be written
in a very special way. This was dictated by the moral necessity of
not keeping out anyone—anyone, that is, who would be sufficiently
concerned to open this book. I could therefore not begin with God
or even the Torah, as a book silently assumed to be divinely revealed. I had to begin with a simple Jewish commitment to Jewish
survival. Only thereafter could I turn to the Jewish Bible, and
even then to it as the Jewish book, not yet as *the* Book, seeing that
many good Jews find their identity through this book but in all
honesty cannot accept it as a religious one. Only thereafter was it
possible to raise the climactic question of part I of this book:
whether a Jew of today can have access to this book as "Torah,"
and if so what Torah means. I call this part "Past," not in the ordinary sense of the word, but in the sense that a reader who proceeds
to the second part has taken the steps of the first part or at least
holds himself open to the possibility of taking them.

Part II of the book is called "Present," in the sense that it gives
an account of what Judaism has been in the past, is in the present,
and will continue to be in the future. (It will continue to be so,
that is, so long as there is at least a remnant faithful to Judaism.)
This part deals, as it were, with the present of Judaism as it always
is, although, as references to contemporary events are meant to
indicate, Judaism has never been indifferent to events of the times.

Only the title of part III, "Future," is to be taken in the ordinary
sense of the term. It opens with a chapter on the State of Israel. I
have heard arguments to the effect that Judaism will continue to
be after the Holocaust what it was before, wholly unchanged and
unaffected. I do not share that view. I am not even sure that I understand it. And I most emphatically think that those defending
it should keep it, instead, in suspense for a few centuries, so as to
be sure that they do not simply abuse the tradition in order not
to have to face the great anguish. Still, it is possible that in the
end this view will be defensible. Quite indefensible to me is the
view that Judaism would be unaffected if the State of Israel were
destroyed. Except among fringe fanatics (ignored in this book),

this view is not often openly expressed. On the few occasions that I have heard or seen it expressed, it has always been accompanied by a "God forbid." But whether expressed or merely implied, this view strikes me as a religious obscenity. It is one thing to survive with one's faith intact after a past catastrophe. It is quite another to hedge one's bets against a future disaster while dwelling at ease in some safe place, so as not to have one's ease disturbed. A Jew today dare not hedge his bets against future disaster but must instead attempt to prevent it with all his heart, with all his soul, with all his might.

If I tried to mention all to whom this book is indebted I would not know where to begin. I therefore confine myself to two without whom it could not have been completed; Arthur Samuelson, my editor, who not only gave invaluable advice but also bore the passing of one deadline after another with angelic patience; and Nehemia Polen, who introduced me to the subtleties in the thought of Rabbi Kalonymos Shapiro, the last representative of Polish Hasidism. Without this I would not have known how to complete the last, crucial chapter of this book.

Jerusalem
Elul 5746 (September 1986)

INTRODUCTION

There was a depressed silence in that jail cell in my hometown of Halle, Germany, meant for at most six people but now crowded with twenty-odd Jewish men. Then an older man spoke up. "You, Fackenheim! You are a student of Judaism. You know more about it than the rest of us here. You tell us what Judaism has to say to us now!" But I, then a rabbinical student aged twenty-two, said nothing.

This book is my attempt to answer that man's question, nearly half a century later, after momentous events, and to a new generation.

The question was asked on November 11, 1938, two days after the so-called *Kristallnacht*. Synagogues had been burned all over Germany. Jewish stores had been smashed and looted. Jewish men aged sixteen and over had vanished one knew not where, preferred not to guess, and most certainly did not dare to inquire. In that one night the one-thousand-year history of German Jewry had been brought to a brutal, bloody end. Much worse was to come, of course, for the Jews not only of Germany but most of Europe.

However, the soul of German Jewry was destroyed in that single night, when houses of worship from which prayers had soared heavenward, in many cases for centuries, were burned down. And now the twenty-odd of us, rounded up a day later, were in that cell, our fate uncertain.

I might have said quite a lot to that man from my hometown whom I knew slightly. (Most of us knew each other at least slightly, for our community, though old, consisted of just little over a thousand souls.) Hitler had come to power when I was sixteen years old, and by the time I finished high school in 1935 what mattered to me most was how to be a Jew. Certain that what was needed was to be found in Judaism, I went to Berlin to study at the famed *Hochschule fuer die Wissenschaft des Judentums* (Academy For The Scholarly Study of Judaism). To prepare for a profession was only vaguely in my mind. I simply wished to become knowledgeable. By the time I landed in that cell, three and a half years later, I had learned a great deal.

The Berlin of 1935-38 was a place of nearly unbearable distress, for it was Nazi. But insofar as it was Jewish it was also a place of inspiration and strength. In those brief years German Judaism, the center for which was Berlin, experienced a profound if short-lived renaissance. Jews flocked to the synagogues on Shabbat and listened to stirring sermons. Study groups sprang up. And we at the *Hochschule* studied the Jewish sources with deep intensity, and had much to say to each other.

But what was I to say to that man on that November day? I had no idea whether he believed in God, and in the circumstances did not have the nerve to ask. Was I to drag in conventional wisdom and suggest that once more we were being punished for our sins? But that particular wisdom, time-honored though it is, was preposterously inapplicable. My community was not particularly pious and contained no saints I was aware of. However, those in that cell were decent men, struggling hard to be good citizens and upright Jews: They in no way deserved what had befallen them since 1933. Was I to suggest, then, that the meaning of this was mysterious, a secret known only to God? But I was already deep into my lifelong love affair with Midrash. (Of this the reader will find a lot in this book.) In Midrash a humble agnosticism, expressed in story and parable, often ranks higher than theological certainties, and even in those days I already preferred Midrashic parables to certainties of that kind—and was not going to associate storm troopers with a divine purpose, however mysterious. So it has taken me all these years to answer that man's question, in anything like a comprehensive way. And what years they have been! In Jewish history there has been nothing like them, certainly not since the Bar Kochba revolt in the second century, and possibly not since the Exodus from Egypt and the event at Mount Sinai.

My questioner in 1938 was no intellectual, let alone a scholar or philosopher. As to whether he subscribed to Orthodox, Conservative, or Reform Judaism (or rather, their German-Jewish equivalents) I had no idea and did not much care. I did not even know whether he attended synagogue services regularly or only occasionally. The man, in short, belonged to *amcha*, the ordinary Jewish folk who may not be learned or saintly but are far from frivolous, unintelligent, unwilling to learn and—most important of all—thoughtless. It is for *amcha* that this book was written.

This is not to say that I wish to exclude intellectuals, scholars, professors, and the like. Jewish tradition warns such as these against separating themselves from the community. I like to think that this is not only because they owe the community solidarity, but also because with regard to the simple but great questions— life and death, good and evil, love, God and man—human beings are not groups apart. Among these simple but great questions is what Judaism can mean to a Jew today. It was a great question half a century ago. If anything, today it is greater still.

In that cell back in 1938 we were filled with foreboding. But not even our worst nightmares contained the possibility of the Holocaust. The murder of every available Jew, pursued as an aim more important than the thousand-year Reich's very survival? Such a thing was impossible "in this modern day and age!" Why, it was impossible in *any* age, for not even the "dark" (medieval) age had seen anything like it. The impossible, however, has become actual, and the result is not only a threat and a challenge that even in

1938 was unimaginable, but also the need for a radical reassessment of modernity. Once the question was what a modern Jew could believe, with "modernity" supplying the criteria, and it stood for Spinoza and Kant, Newton and Einstein, Voltaire, Locke, and Jefferson. (Even then the Marquis de Sade was conveniently forgotten, and the antisemitism of Voltaire was ignored.) The problems of modernity are still with us, as are its great representatives. But our modern (or if we prefer, postmodern) world now includes also Auschwitz and Buchenwald. What can a Jew believe in *that* world? Possibly this question has at best only inadequate answers. The greatness of the question is undeniable. And is it for Jews only? Can anyone be indifferent to what a Jewish Holocaust survivor can believe? Anyone at all? The world of today is never far from the thought and fear of collective death. Who can disregard a people that has already suffered collective death, the survivors of which yet rehear words first heard at Sinai, "Thou shalt choose life"?

They ever rehear these words: I am bold enough to assert this because, without such a rehearing, at least one Jewish reality would be unintelligible, the State of Israel—the fact that it was born and has managed to survive to this day. Let me go back once more to that day in November 1938. We were in jail and subsequently transported to a concentration camp. This was of course because of Nazi policies. But it was also because of the refusal of the civilized countries of the world to take more than a few of us. We appreciated that the immigration policies of some of these countries were generous by the standards of the time; that the standards themselves were low we experienced every day. Would any one of us then have believed that within a decade a Jewish state would be born that would actually obligate itself to take each and every one of us? And that in the wake of that step there would be a worldwide ingathering of homeless and persecuted Jews that would dwarf the boldest of Zionist dreams? Such a thing has never happened in history. Its results are taken for granted today but ought not to be. Unbelievable then, they ought to be astonishing still. Astonishment, I have learned over decades of reflection on the matter, is the deepest source of religious faith.

"For believers there are no questions, and for unbelievers there are no answers." Those who subscribe to that epigram will find little of interest in this book. In response to the events of our time, the cited epigram is often invoked by religious apologists who wish to evade the questions of others, and who have (or claim to have) no questions of their own. But Judaism has been a questioning faith ever since Abraham called God to account in the matter of Sodom and Gomorrah. What would a Judaism be that had no questions at all, after what has occurred in the last half-century? Or had no answers whatever to those who, no longer able to believe everything, or in danger of being left with nothing? It is a Judaism that both does have answers, yet is left with unanswered questions, that I have found over the decades. It is to such a Judaism that this book seeks to guide the reader.

1. THE RELIGIOUS SITUATION OF A JEW TODAY

SUMMARIES OF JUDAISM

The story is told of how a donkey driver once came to Rabbi Akiba (ca. 50–135 C.E.) and asked him, "Rabbi, teach me the Torah all at once!" Akiba replied: "Our teacher Moses stayed on Mount Sinai forty days and forty nights, and you want me to teach it to you all at once? Still, this is the basic principle of the Torah: What is hateful to you do not do to your fellowman."

A similar, more famous story is told about a pagan who wished to learn the Torah in the time he could stand on one foot, and who went first to the stern Shammai (who chased him away angrily) and then to the latter's contemporary and opponent, the gentle Hillel (ca. 30 B.C.E.–10 C.E.) who, like Akiba, cited the golden rule. A good deal more will be read in these pages about these and other great representatives of rabbinic Judaism.

There are many other summaries of Judaism in the rabbinic writings. Perhaps the most comprehensive is the following, by the third-century Rabbi Simlai.

Six-hundred-and-thirteen commandments were imparted to Moses, three-hundred-and-sixty-five negative (corresponding to the number of days in the year), and two-hundred-and-forty-eight positive (corresponding to the number of bones in the human body). Then came David and reduced them to eleven in Psalm 15.

Thus the rabbi begins. He quotes the psalm in full, proceeds to cite other texts that reduce the number of commandments further and further. He reaches Micah, who reduces them to three:

It hath been told thee, O man, what is good, and what the Lord doth require of thee: Only to do justly, and to love mercy, and to walk humbly with thy God. (Mic. 6:8)

The climactic conclusion of the Midrash is as follows:

Then came Amos and reduced them to one, as it is written (Amos 5:4): "Seek ye Me, and live." Rabbi Nahman, the son of Isaac, suggests an alternative conclusion: Then came Habakuk and reduced them to one (Hab. 2:4): "The righteous shall live by his faith."

From texts such as these we learn that while no summary exhausts the teachings of Judaism—Hillel, having given his pagan the golden rule, admonishes him to "go and learn"—to give such summaries is not only an obvious pedagogic necessity but also a genuine possibility. For this reason the Jewish tradition has not only the activity of the commentator (through which the Torah becomes ever more complex, subtle, esoteric) but also the opposite activity of the teacher who, though ever fearful of distortions, yet takes his courage into his hands and simplifies. After all, are not in general all great things, even if complex or even inexhaustible, at the same time simple?

Of Judaism in particular, we here learn a great lesson at the very outset. The rabbis of the Talmud and their predecessors, the Pharisees, are often pictured as lost in hair-splitting distinctions of legal minutiae; and since Judaism does in fact contain 613 commandments there may seem to be justice in this picture. Yet the same Rabbi Simlai who quite explicitly accepts all the 613 also sees Amos as reducing them all to one. There are many trees in Judaism. But only in times of decay has there been a loss of sight of the forest.

This is one lesson we learn from our texts. Another is that the answer to be given to a questioner for the Torah "all at once" depends on that questioner's situation. Thus the progressive reduction of all the 613 commandments to Amos's climactic "seek ye Me, and live!" (or, alternatively, Habakuk's "the righteous shall live by his faith") may be infinitely meaningful to one who has studied the Torah all his life and lives by it. But to Hillel's pagan (who comes to Judaism from without) or Akiba's donkey driver (who is born into Judaism but has remained ignorant) these two climactic reductions would be quite meaningless. "Righteousness"; "faith"; "live"; and, above all, He in whom there is life: Of all these the ignorant know as yet nothing.

JUDAISM AND MODERNITY

That the situation of the questioner may concern his age rather than his individual circumstances may be learned from the most famous of all summaries of Judaism, the thirteen principles of Maimonides (1135–1204). (Of him, too, much will be read in this book. He is popularly referred to as the Rambam, RMBM being the Hebrew abbreviation of Rabbi Moses Ben Maimon.) So authoritative did his principles become as to be made into a hymn, the *Yigdal*, one of two with which Jewish religious services are customarily concluded. The other, the *Adon Olam*, will concern us toward the end of this book. (See chapter 14; section 2.) The *Yigdal* concerns us at the very start. The Maimonidean text itself, put into the form of a creed several centuries after his death, reads as follows:

1. I firmly believe that the Creator, blessed be His name, is the Creator and Ruler of all created beings, and that He alone has made, does make, and ever will make all things.
2. I firmly believe that the Creator, blessed be His name, is One;

that there is no oneness in any form like His; and that He alone was, is, and ever will be our God.

3. I firmly believe that the Creator, blessed be His name, is not corporeal; that no bodily accidents apply to Him; and that there exists nothing whatever that resembles Him.

4. I firmly believe that the Creator, blessed be His name, was the first and will be the last.

5. I firmly believe that the Creator, blessed be His name, is the only one to whom it is proper to address our prayers, and that we must not pray to anyone else.

6. I firmly believe that all the words of the prophets are true.

7. I firmly believe that the prophecy of Moses our teacher, may he rest in peace, was true; and that he was the chief of the prophets, both of those who preceded and those who followed him.

8. I firmly believe that the whole Torah which we now possess is the same which was given to Moses our teacher, may he rest in peace.

9. I firmly believe that the Torah will not be changed, and that there will be no other Torah given by the Creator, blessed be His name.

10. I firmly believe that the Creator, blessed be His name, knows all the actions and thoughts of human beings, as it is said, "It is I who fashions the hearts of them all, He who notes all their deeds" (Ps. 33:15).

11. I firmly believe that the Creator, blessed be His name, rewards those who keep His commands, and punishes those who transgress His commands.

12. I firmly believe in the coming of the Messiah; and although he may tarry, I daily wait for his coming.

13. I firmly believe that there will be a revival of the dead at a time which will please the Creator, blessed and exalted be His name forever and ever.

In what follows I shall refer to quite a few of these principles, which is the reason why at this point I quote the text in full.

To quote them will of course not necessarily mean assenting to them. Maimonides expected every Jew to be able to subscribe to each of these principles. The reader of today who has problems with quite a few should know that he is not the first. A Hasidic student once studied the very first words, *Ani ma'amin be'emuna sh'lema,* "I believe with perfect faith." He was stuck already. He could not go on: There was *nothing* he believed with perfect faith! Then how could the Rambam expect him to say such words? He went to his rabbi. "This is not a statement," the rabbi explained. "It is a prayer: May I believe!" (Of Hasidism, too, much more will be found in this book.)

Assent to creeds, then, is not automatically demanded in Judaism; indeed, according to the story just related, doubt has a legitimate place. In addition, not a few of the Maimonidean articles have given rise to specific doubt over the centuries, some only at some times, others, notably the thirteenth, at virtually all times. But the characteristically modern difficulty is surely caused by articles six through nine. Possibly trouble can still be avoided with the sixth article, provided one distinguishes the "prophecy" of ancient times not too sharply from the "insights" of "sages" or "seers" of modern times. Any such possibility, however, comes to an abrupt halt when in the seventh article Moses is exalted above all prophets before and after, and when, in consequence of this, the Torah of Moses, affirmed in the eighth principle, is declared in the ninth to be unchangeable forever. The modern reader may appreciate these articles of faith in their historical setting, that is, as part of a medieval Jewish reaction to Christianity and Islam, both of which claimed to possess Scriptures that rendered the Torah of Moses anachronistic. But can he accept in any sense whatsoever the traditional principle of *Torah min ha-shamayim—* that "the Torah is from heaven"?

Three reasons may be cited, in ascending order of importance, of why any such acceptance seems in conflict with what may be called an enlightened modernity. First, there is the broad modern conviction (doubtless inspired by the success of modern science and its offspring, technology) that the more recent is always the truer and more advanced. To be sure, this broad modern view has met with protests ever since nineteenth-century romanticism: Why should the later always be better, say, in matters moral, aesthetic, religious? Still, protesters of this kind, now as then, are always suspect of resembling the nineteenth-century English Luddites, who tried to solve the social problems created by the machine age by smashing the machines.

Still, this first objection rests only on a suspicion: Surely not all harking back to the past is romantic escapism, to say nothing of being "reactionary"! More serious is the objection implicit in the modern world view that reality is a continuum and that the same is true of our knowledge of it: that there are no breaks in either the knowledge or the reality. Thus, if an event in nature seems to fall straight into the miracle class, we moderns do not accept it as such, but merely conclude that we have yet failed to explain what in principle can be explained and we hope some day will be explained. And if in history a new truth appears we do not consider it as having, as it were, dropped from heaven, but at most as the work of something we call "genius," to be absorbed by future history and superseded by the work of future genius. Thus the very possibility of a unique revelation to a unique Moses at a unique Sinai seems to have vanished with the advent of modernity.

What then, third, of the actuality of that revelation? Here the conflict between traditional Judaism and modernity seems to reach its climax. It is a standard premodern argument that an unbroken chain of reliable witnesses connects the present Jewish generation with that at Sinai, and that the revelatory event at Sinai was witnessed by no fewer than 600,000 Israelites—too many to be mistaken. (Premodern Christian and Muslim thinkers make parallel appeals to authorities of their own, and while their great trump card generally has been that their revelations not only came later but were more universally accepted, the great Jewish trump card always was that neither Christianity nor Islam could boast of anything like a comparable number of witnesses present at the original event.) To the modern minded, this sort of argument conjures up theological debates as futile as they are wrongheaded—futile because each debater appeals to authorities rejected by the other, and wrongheaded because there are appeals to authority at all. The medieval Gaon Saadia (892–942) was able to list "reliable tradition" as a source of knowledge equal in certainty to reason and the five senses. (Saadia was a philosopher, exegete, grammarian, and liturgical poet. The title "Gaon" ["Majesty"] has been given to heads of Talmudic schools since the sixth century. Saadia is the most celebrated Gaon.) To the modern historian, "tradition" is not an authority on what actually occurred but only a "source," generally one among several, enabling him to *reconstruct* what actually occurred. Moreover, his reconstructions are subject to revision in the light of possible new future evidence.

We must go a crucial step further still. Suppose the relevant facts were as described in the Book of Exodus. Suppose 600,000 Israelites had actually stood at the foot of Mount Sinai and heard not only the thunder but also the divine voice. Suppose further that the historian could construct a time machine that projected him back into their company and made him share their experience. Since this could conceivably be a case of mass delusion, his "facts" would still include only a human hearing of a divine voice, not a divine voice itself. To the modern minded, then, "tradition" is at most only a source of historical probabilities. A source of knowledge it is not.

The religious implications of this difference between the premodern and the modern mind were stated with unsurpassed power and simplicity by the eighteenth-century poet and critic Gotthold Ephraim Lessing (1729–81), who might fairly be called the first truly modern theologian. Unlike "truths of reason" (which are "necessary"), Lessing states, "truths of history" are at best only "probable." Then how, he asks, can he as a Christian stake his "eternal beatitude" on truths having no more than probable certainty? That, he laments, is the "nasty, broad ditch" that he cannot "get across, however often and however earnestly . . . [he has] tried to make the leap." For premoderns with their appeal to authorities, this problem did not arise. For moderns such as Lessing it is inescapable—and it is as inescapable for modern Jews as it is for Christians. What difference does it make if no fewer than 600,000 are said to have been present at Mount Sinai, whereas only

a handful are said to have stood at the foot of the Cross? Both
assertions are to moderns, not facts, but only what certain of the
sources claim to have been facts.

Such, in outline, are the chief challenges of modernity. How is
one to respond to them? Some twenty years ago or so I came upon
a striking passage in an autobiographical sketch, then just published, by the late Leo Strauss, a well-known political philosopher
whose Jewish writings impressed me greatly in my Berlin student
days. (They impress me still.) Of German Judaism in the 1920s
Strauss writes as follows:

> . . . it was granted by all except the most backward that the
> Jewish faith had not been refuted by science and history. The
> storms stirred up by Darwin and, to a lesser extent, by Well-
> hausen had been weathered; one could grant to science and his-
> tory everything they seem to teach regarding the age of the world,
> the origin of man, the impossibility of miracles, the impossibility
> of the immortality of the soul and the resurrection of the body,
> the Jahvist, the Elohist, the third Isaisah [and other theories of
> modern Biblical criticism claiming to refute the traditional view
> of the literary origin of the Bible] without abandoning one iota
> of the substance of the Jewish faith.

We shall have to come back to this statement several times and,
in so doing, shall find that much depends on what is meant by the
phrase "substance of the Jewish faith."

When I first came upon this passage it arrested me at once. I
found it striking because my experience in the 1930s was the same
as Strauss's experience a dozen or so years earlier. So, presumably,
was the source of inspiration. Martin Buber (1878–1965) and
Franz Rosenzweig (1886–1929) were the pioneers of a way of
Jewish religious thinking which, to use a convenient label, might
be called existentialist, a way of thinking of which, within a Christian context, the lone nineteenth-century pioneer had been Søren
Kierkegaard (1813–55). Kierkegaard's Christian thought can be
understood as a response to Lessing's challenge, and may be sum-
marized in three fundamental points. What is revelation? If there
is such a thing, it is not the product of man—conscious or uncon-

scious, "neurotic" or "creative," individual or collective—within the world of man, but rather an incursion of a divine reality *other* than man *into* the world of man. Being a true modern, Kierkegaard conceded that there was no authority of a person or a text that could prove the reality of such an incursion. Nor was there anything in philosophy or theology that could demonstrate it. Yet he also found that there was nothing in science, history, or philosophy that refuted the possibility of such an incursion. Whether or not the world of man is open or closed to incursions of the Divine into it, then, remains objectively undecided.

This is Kierkegaard's first fundamental point. His second is to endorse what had already been stressed by Lessing (for whom he had great admiration): There was indeed a "nasty, broad ditch" between himself, the would-be Christian, on the one hand, and the basic fact sacred for him, on the other; and no authority existed to bridge it for him. Indeed, were he himself projected into the company of the disciples of the Christ, the only facts he would perceive—if facts they were—would be a crucified man and an empty tomb.

Kierkegaard's third point was the decisive one: If a "leap" were needed to bridge Lessing's "ditch," it could only consist of a subjective act of commitment: The leap was a leap of faith. Revelation, then, was what it claimed to be only if it was an objective reality; yet what a Christian was to stake his very life on was at the same time a radical risk, for it was "objectively uncertain."

Such was Kierkegaard's Christian existentialism. In the above-cited statement Strauss could say what he did because of Buber's and Rosenzweig's Jewish existentialism. This latter arose far less because of any Kierkegaardian (or other Christian) influence than because of parallels between the Christian and the Jewish religious situation within the context of modernity. Strauss asserts that not an iota of the "substance" of the Jewish faith needs to be surrendered. This is possible, however, only because of a radically altered foundation. For the premodern Gaon Saadia "tradition" had been a source of knowledge on a par in certainty with other forms of knowledge; hence the past Sinaitic event and its product, the Torah, had come to the present on the authority of the 600,000 present at Sinai and the unbroken chain of trustworthy witnesses. His modern heirs (who are bereft of authorities) must reach out from the present for the past, in an attempt to *recover* it; but they *can* recover revelation in that past only if it is not only a past fact but also, potentially, a present experience. Much will have to be said in elaboration of this point (see chapter 4). The basic one, however, has had to be made here, at our very start.

That revelation cannot be just a past fact but must also be a present experience is not an altogether new idea in Judaism. In the Midrash we read:

> Never let the Torah be an antiquated decree for you, but rather like a decree freshly given, no more than two or three days old . . . Ben Azzai said: "Not even as old . . . but as a decree given this very day!"

Another Midrash could serve as a motto of this whole book: "When was the Torah given? It is given whenever a person receives it."

To sum up, then, what is this, to "grant to science and history whatever they teach . . . and yet not to be compelled "to give up one iota" of the "substance" of Judaism? It is to give that "substance" a new foundation, namely, personal commitment instead of authority. In a post–World War II joke two U.S. Army chaplains, one Protestant and the other Catholic, have served faithfully in a common cause and are close friends after their long shared experience. The war has ended and the time has come to part. The Catholic sighs and says to his friend, "So now we go back each to his task, you to serve God in your way and I in His." The recent rise of fanaticism in many quarters shows that this joke is not as out of date as it ought to be. Yet for those who have not surrendered their modern critical mind the situation is clear. If the Catholic's way is "His way," it is so not on grounds of some objective, let alone infallible, authority but only on those of his own faith and commitment; as for the Protestant's way, it is, to be sure, "his" way only, but quite possibly it is "His" way also. To apply this to Judaism, Orthodox Judaism remains a modern-minded possibility— if it is open-minded regarding the possible validity of other, non-

Orthodox forms of Judaism as well. This line of thought, to be sure, produces the specter of an all-encompassing relativism. But however one may cope with that specter, the fear of it does not justify resort to a medieval-style authoritarianism that can no longer be honestly maintained. As the late Abraham J. Heschel once put it in my hearing, before a group of Roman Catholics who at that time were quite startled by the boldness of his expression: "Pluralism is the will of God."

OF JEWISH PEOPLEHOOD, JEWISH SECULARISM, AND ZIONISM

Thus far in this account the religious situation of a Jew today is parallel to that of a Christian, although that the two faiths differ goes without saying. Now comes a crucial difference. In order to face up to that difference one need not consult learned theologians. It may even be better to do without them. All that is necessary is to consider one basic Jewish institution, namely, bar mitzvah. A Christian child is born pagan, becomes Christian through baptism, and baptism itself is provisional until at confirmation the confirmand makes a conscious commitment to the Christian faith. A Jewish child, in contrast, is born Jewish, is Jewish even before, if male, he is circumcised. He is and remains a Jew even if he is not circumcised. And that there is nothing provisional about either Jewish birth or circumcision is fully disclosed at the time of bar mitzvah. If a Christian boy or girl cannot in good conscience make the Christian commitment, confirmation can be postponed, if necessary indefinitely. If a Jewish boy has corresponding scruples, he and his family may decide, to be sure, to postpone or cancel a bar mitzvah *ceremony*. The *event* of bar mitzvah cannot be postponed or cancelled: In Judaism a Jewish boy becomes a "son of duty"— obliged to keep the commandments—quite regardless of his wishes, beliefs, or twinges of conscience. There is in Judaism an altogether crucial togetherness of what may be called faith and fate. Of this the rabbis are fully aware. Why, asks one Midrash, was the Torah given in the desert? The desert has no borders and belongs to no

one, is the reply. All nations might have come and were invited
to come; yet only Israel came. Why, asks another Midrash, was
the Torah given on a mountain? The mountain provided God with
a threat: "Either you take the Torah, or the mountain will bury
you!"

But how can one be obligated to a faith when integrity may require one to suspend or even reject it? And how can one be obligated to practice that faith when doing so may run counter to
one's conscience? These questions may not have bothered Jews
overly in premodern times that staked so much on authority. They
have been bothering them greatly in modern times that, in free
societies, have been staking so much on self-determination, autonomy, the freedom of the individual conscience. Consequently, in
such societies Jews of modernity have been making attempts to
redefine their own religious identity. With the advent of political
emancipation such a redefinition seemed in any case mandatory:
In premodern times Jews had been a nation in exile; but one could
not very well demand and accept equal rights in a modern state
and still consider oneself in exile. "Exile," therefore, became "Diaspora," and the former "Jewish nation" became "Germans (or
Frenchmen, Englishmen, Americans) of the Jewish faith." The
political aspects of this attempted self-transformation have often
been discussed and are in any case outside our present concern.
Often overlooked, but well within our present concern, is the question: Just what, in terms of the new definition, was the Jewish
"faith?" The fatherhood of God; the brotherhood of the one mankind; the prophetic ethics that were to help realize these ideals,
and the Messianic hope that they would one day be approximated
or even fully realized, and possibly that the approximation was
under way even now: This broad message was clear enough.
Equally clear was that these ideals were far from being present
realities. Jews were therefore to be "missionaries" of the "ideals of
Judaism" to "mankind." This could be by precept. Since Jews do
not believe in seeking converts it was, more aptly, by example. To
be sure, all this is not easy to believe today: In our grim century
many are more likely to fear that we approach disaster rather than
Messianic peace. One must stress therefore all the more that once

many Jews sincerely believed in this "mission of Israel" and also practiced it. Thus they have often been in the forefront of fighters for freedom and justice for all, and indeed continue to be so today. However, there was one great difficulty with the whole idea from the start: Except for converts to Judaism, Jews continued to be born Jews—and no one is born a missionary.

The modern redefinition just sketched in effect makes Judaism into a faith wholly parallel to the Christian. For the reason just given, it has a nemesis that reveals its inadequacy. Eastern Europe was where the European Jewish masses lived till they were murdered in the Holocaust. It was also the part of Europe never sufficiently penetrated by modern ideas of freedom and equality to result in Jewish emancipation. Yet the penetration was sufficient to produce in a large number of Jews a revolt, if not necessarily against religion, at any rate against religious authoritarianism. Here, then, Jews in effect remained a premodern nation in exile, denied as they were civic freedom and confined as they remained in ghettos, while at the same time widely expressing the modern freedom of religion—as freedom *from* religion. The nemesis of modern Jewish fideism in the West—the Jewish self-definition as members of a faith, and a people no more—thus became a secularism in the East that created a Yiddish culture but ignored the Jewish religion when it did not actively reject it. If at its best Western Jewish fideism showed fidelity to the God of Israel but abandoned the Jewish people, Eastern Jewish secularism at its best showed fidelity to the Jewish people but abandoned the God of Israel.

It is possible (though, I believe, not fair to the realities) to view this latter, vital though once it was, as a product of mere nostalgia, as a phenomenon that could not long have survived in the modern world, even if the two great twentieth-century catastrophes—Hitler's Nazism and Stalin's communism—had not destroyed it. No such cavalier attitude is possible toward the other great product of modern Jewish secularism, Zionism. This has often been deprecated as a mere imitation nineteenth-century European nationalism, espoused only by maladjusted members of what long has been only a "chimerical" nation. (This latter notion, accepted among

others by Karl Marx, has its ultimate origin in the Christian view
that Jews have ceased to be a living people since the advent of
Christianity.) Yet not much more than half a century after Theodor Herzl (1860–1904) the movement founded by him has produced results that no other modern nationalism can boast of,
among them a state founded, maintained, developed, and defended
by a people that—so it was once thought—had lost the arts of state-
craft and self-defense forever; the replanting and reforestation of a
land that—so it once seemed—was unredeemable swamp and desert; the ingathering of a people from all corners of the earth on a
territory—so the experts once asserted—with not enough room left
to swing a cat; the reviving of a language that—so even Herzl once
feared—was dead beyond revival; and, last but not least, the physical rebuilding of the one city on earth, Jerusalem—so the consensus
of mankind once held, Jews only excepted—that was meant to remain forever of the spirit only, i.e., holy ruins. Today only outright
lies can dispose of the Jewish people as a chimerical nation. Every
honest person, and certainly every Jew seeking to come to grips
with his religious situation, must come to confront the fact of the
State of Israel. He must do so for better or for worse.

For some among the religious, this is for worse. If modern nationalism is a form of modern secularism, then the Zionist version
of it could be considered as one of its purest manifestations, and
hence to religious Jews as the most threatening. By its own best
and most challenging definition, modern secularism consists of the
taking of human destiny into human hands alone, and this definition does fit the Zionist movement. Through the centuries pious
Jews waited for God to restore them to the land, with a patience without parallel. Then the modern Zionists came, stopped
waiting, and did the job themselves. Other forms of secularism,
Jewish or general, could exist side by side with the traditional Jewish piety, ignored by the faithful. This form of secularism seemed
to come on the scene as a rival and a direct challenge.

But *is* Zionism but another modern nationalism? Is it secularism
and nothing but it? A modern secular impulse made Zionists stop
waiting for emancipation by either God or men and instead seek
"auto-emancipation." (This is the title of a pamphlet by an early

Zionist, J. L. Pinsker [1821–91].) What but a (possibly unconscious) religious impulse led them to seek it, not in some new land such as Uganda, Brazil, or Argentina but rather, of all difficult places, in the old, religiously hallowed Palestine? And if through the ages religious Jews went to die amid the ruins of Jerusalem, what but a modern secular impulse led them to join secular Zionists not only in living in Jerusalem but also helping rebuild it? As these lines are being written clashes occur between extremists in the religious and secular camps in the rebuilt Jerusalem, clashes which, if unchecked and spreading, could endanger the state as nothing else could short of annihilation by its enemies. This very fact, and awareness of the danger in all responsible quarters, is proof that neither Zionism nor its chief product, the State of Israel, can be understood in either purely religious or in purely secular terms: that with the advent of the state a new page has been opened in the history not only of Jews but also of Judaism.

Even so a religiously motivated Jewish anti-Zionism—Orthodox, Conservative, or Reform—has accompanied the Zionist movement all along. It survives to this day, and hardly does an Israel Independence Day pass without some ultra-Orthodox fanatic scribbling on some wall in Jerusalem words to the effect that the Zionists are the new Nazis. However, all anti-Zionism, Jewish and Gentile, should have come to a total end with the gas chambers and smokestacks of Auschwitz.

JUDAISM IN THE AGE OF AUSCHWITZ AND A REBUILT JEWISH STATE

The Jewish policy of the Third Reich fell into two main phases. The first, lasting from 1933 to the outbreak of the Second World War, may be described as the phase of the *St. Louis*. This was a German passenger ship that sailed for Cuba in March 1939, with some nine hundred German and Austrian Jewish refugees on board, fleeing for their lives. Denied entry on arrival when their visas were declared invalid, the refugees sought a haven elsewhere—*anywhere*—and organizations acting in their behalf telephoned and

cabled up and down the Atlantic Coast, in vain. Finally the ship
was forced to turn back, and the captain, the sole hero in a story
otherwise uniformly dark, issued orders to sail as slowly as the engines would permit, in the hope that someone, somewhere, might
take his hapless cargo, and determined, it is said, to wreck his ship
on a rock rather than return these refugees to Germany, concentration camps, death. In the end several European countries did
take them, one a few, another a few, and so on. And when some
months later the Germans invaded Holland, Belgium, and France,
those unlucky enough to be on the Continent rather than the
British Isles were, for the most part, caught and murdered.

This was the first phase in Nazi Jewish policy. The second, of
course, was Auschwitz. This symbol of unsurpassable horror, long
become universal, has its literal, nonsymbolic counterpart in a carefully devised, vast network of factories of degradation, torture, and
death in which the degraded, tortured, murdered human beings
were not means to an end or by-products in the manufacture of
some product needed more urgently, such as uniforms produced
by slave labor or gold from Jewish teeth. The human victims *themselves* were the product, and those most single-mindedly intended
were Jews. (As Elie Wiesel has said, not all victims were Jews, but
all Jews were victims.) Degradation of Jews was an end in itself.
So was torture. So, finally, was "extermination." And while the
trains rolled and the murder factories operated no one tried to slow
down if not stop the process by bombing the railways or the gas
chambers themselves. Not the British. Not the Americans. Not the
Canadians. Not the Russians.

At first one thought it was not known. But enough was known.
Then one believed those who argued that the bombing was techni-
cally unfeasible. But a factory a few miles from Auschwitz was
bombed. Never in all human history was a people as radically
homeless as Jews under Nazism in the first phase of Nazi policy;
as for the second phase, never in all human history was a people
as radically abandoned.

The Third Reich lasted from January 30, 1933, to April 15, 1945.
The State of Israel was proclaimed on May 14, 1948. A decade is
not much in Jewish history; in world history it hardly counts at all.

Let us conduct an experiment in the historical imagination. Let there be a change of dates by less than a decade; let May 14, 1948, be shifted to March 1939. The news is flashed around the globe that a Jewish state has been proclaimed in Palestine. It reaches the *St. Louis* in mid-Atlantic waters. Having restrained his ship's progress as much as the engines permit, the captain now shouts orders "full steam ahead," and, needless to add, to change course. Their anguish turned into sudden gladness, his passengers break out into dance and song, and do not cease dancing and singing until they reach the beaches of Netanya and Naharia, where joyful, tearful Jews await them by the thousands. So much for the Jews. As for the world, or rather the part of it that is human, its burden of guilt, though not removed, is greatly lightened. A sudden light has appeared in the midst of the universal darkness, shedding its rays everywhere.

Our experiment in the historical imagination has yielded no less remarkable a result than the most characteristic of all Jewish experiences, the experience of salvation. This side of eternity, salvation in Judaism is not of individual souls. This side of the end of history, it is not the Messianic event that, so is the hope, will remove from humanity as a whole the evils of poverty and injustice, hatred, and war. Characteristically, paradigmatically, it is the sudden removal of a radical threat—a removal so astonishing that the more it is explained the deeper the astonishment becomes. So it was first at the Red Sea, when Jewish history almost came to a catastrophic end when it had hardly begun. (See Exod. 14; 15:1–20.) So it was, or at any rate seemed—to make a huge leap from the most ancient to the most recent example—in May and early June 1967, when for three long weeks annihilation threatened the State of Israel less than two decades after its birth; when the threat was removed in six days; and when the remnant of the Jerusalem Temple came under Jewish control, for the first time since it was lost in the Bar Kochba catastrophe, way back in 135 C.E.

So much for the first phase of Nazi policy toward Jews. Had there been a Jewish state at the time, it is arguable that the second phase would never have occurred. But even if it had occurred, salvation, albeit in a sense tragic without precedent, would not have been altogether absent. No one attempted to bomb the railways to Auschwitz or the gas chambers themselves: Had there been a Jewish state at the time, armed with ten rickety planes, the planes would have done so or perished in the attempt.

Imagine the victims inside those cattle cars, with young children, aged parents, other loved ones, half-crazed already with hunger, thirst, exhaustion, the filth all around, destined they do not know to what fearful fate. (I confess I have imagined myself in one of those cars many times, and consider any Jew less than Jewish—any human being less than human—who knows what happened then and has not imagined himself in that position at least once.) Suddenly there is a roar of planes overhead, anti-aircraft fire, bombs exploding all around. Those inside the cars are not saved. Indeed, their fear has increased, for before the bombs they could still cling to the slimmest of hopes, while now there is fear of imminent death, for the bombs might kill them. Even so a redemptive moment—the fragment of a miracle—has occurred: Someone has cared; abandonment is no longer complete.

We have completed our experiment in the historical imagination. Forced to return to reality, we conclude the following: *Salvation came once again to the Jewish people in our time, just as it did in previous times; this time, however, it came too late, and all that is new and unprecedented in the contemporary Jewish religious situation is due to this circumstance.* Nothing remotely comparable happened in premodern times. Nothing remotely comparable happened in modern times. This is what makes the religious situation of a Jew today unique, and whoever believes, prays, celebrates, mourns as though it were otherwise has not yet noticed—or does not wish to notice—what is the case.

A Jew today rightly celebrates the birth of the State of Israel, an event that a prayer composed by the Israeli chief rabbinate describes as "the beginning of the growth of the redemption" of the Jewish people. He cannot, however, celebrate that event on Yom Ha-Atzmaut (Independence Day) as he celebrates Pesach (Passover), Hanukkah, and Purim (see below, chapter 10, section 5). In each of the three last-named cases, catastrophe was averted, if but at the last moment. The Jewish people were saved. Coming as it did when it did, the State of Israel could save only the survivors. For us to celebrate Yom Ha-Atzmaut as we celebrate the festivals of redemption would be to give meaning to Auschwitz through the rebuilt Jerusalem, and this is impossible.

We cannot give meaning to Auschwitz with Jerusalem. Still less is it possible, however, to give meaning to the catastrophe without Jerusalem: Indeed, we cannot give meaning to Auschwitz at all. Just as for a Jew today Yom Ha-Atzmaut cannot be but another day of celebration, so Yom Ha-Shoah, the day of remembrance for the Holocaust, cannot be but another day of mourning. If this were possible we should abolish Yom Ha-Shoah altogether, and mourn the Holocaust on the ninth of Av, the day already set aside in the Jewish liturgical calendar for the remembrance of the destruction of the first Temple, of the second Temple, of the expulsion of the Jews from Spain in the fifteenth century, the Chmjelnizki massacres in Poland in the seventeenth century, and of all the other Jewish tragedies. (See below, chapter 10, section 5.) The rabbis wisely put the mourning for all these into one day: How much mourning can be borne by a people composed of men, women, and children, and bidden, moreover, to rejoice at the appointed festivals? Yet for us to lump the Holocaust with all the others would be to act as if nothing new had happened in the history of horror when the attempt was made to "exterminate" the Jewish people, that is, to murder saints as well as sinners, newborn babies as well as adults, and no exception was to be made even for those already near the grave; and the attempt was successful beyond the wildest nightmares of anyone. Even the expellees from Spain remembered their particular catastrophe in its own right, and in due course found a response to it, in the form of kabbalistic Judaism founded by Isaac Luria (1534–72). However, the expellees from Spain lived; the victims of the incomparably greater catastrophe of the Holocaust, for the most part, are dead: If there is to be a response, it cannot be left to their children's children.

Could the "Final Solution" conceivably be final? The Third Reich aimed at the end of the Jewish people. It also aimed at the end of Judaism. It failed in the first aim, for it succeeded in murdering "only" one-third of the Jewish people. Is it conceivable that it succeeded in the second, the end of Judaism for the survivors? This apprehension becomes a vivid fear if, for the second time in these pages, we conduct an experiment in the historical imagination. Imagine the Holocaust happening exactly as it did, but no Jewish state coming into being thereafter. Surely the Jewish religious condition today would be one of total demoralization, of a complete failure of nerve. To be sure, there would still be some Orthodox pockets here and there that behaved as though nothing had occurred; but precisely for that reason they would be inconsequential. Doubtless there would also be well-to-do congregations in well-to-do countries whose way of Jewish life were based on the assumption that their accidentally privileged condition is somehow deservedly privileged: These too, however large and wealthy, would be inconsequential. But in a world with a Holocaust but without a Jewish state, all Jews truly sensitive to what has occurred would surely be in a flight from their Jewish condition that would dwarf anything known as "assimilation" now. And who could blame them? Not long ago the world was divided into one part bent on the murder of every available Jew, and another that did less than was possible to prevent it, to stop it, or at least to slow the process down. If after that there had been no *radical* change, who would want to be a Jew? Who could be expected to remain one? And by what monumental affront could anyone—Jew or Christian, man or God—actually lecture to Jews on the duty to remain with their Judaism? Or to bring up Jewish children?

Once again, however, ours was only an experiment in the historical imagination, and events did not happen as we have imagined them. Once again, therefore, we must return from imagination to reality. This time, however, the return generates, not an astonished horror but an astonished rejoicing, the joy over a restored Jewish state and a rebuilt Jewish Jerusalem. To be sure, in the day-to-day course of day-to-day troubles there occurs a loss of the astonishment and hence also of the joy. Jews in the Diaspora read about these troubles, while Jews in Israel endure them. However, in great moments the astonishment and the joy come to life again and again. And with the help of the religious imagination this coming to life is an ever-present possibility. In my lectures I often promise Diaspora friends, Christian as well as Jewish, a mystical experience in Jerusalem. All they need is imagination and a sense of Jewish history. Perhaps they are not religious, and do not go to the Wall. Let them go to Yafa Road, the busiest of Jerusalem streets, try to get off a bus, on a bus, and just barely manage either on account of the crowds. Then let them close their eyes for a moment, remember the past and the opening verse of the biblical book that confronts it at its darkest: "How doth the city sit solitary, that was full of people!" (Lam. 1:1) Let them ponder this and all it means, and then open their eyes again, and they are gripped by the mystical experience: How is the city full of people that only yesterday, it seems, did sit solitary! A sublime joy and a unique astonishment comes over a Jew of today: the wonder at the fact that, after the greatest catastrophe in Jewish history, a new page is being opened, in the history not only of Jews but also of Judaism. Who would not wish to have a share in the writing of it?

EPILOGUE

The Torah is said to be unchangeable: For this we have no better authority than the Rambam. How the great sage would react to modernity remains a matter of dispute. For the necessity of a change in our time we can cite him against himself.

In his ninth principle Maimonides affirms that the Torah is unchangeable, and in his twelfth that the Messiah will come "even though he tarries." (The words, as we have mentioned above, are not his own, but the thought is.) Elsewhere he explains that the "sole difference between the present and the Messianic days will be deliverance from servitude to foreign powers," and elsewhere still he advises a community that would risk death were it to practice the Torah to refrain from doing so, that the Torah bids Jews not to die but live by it. However, he proceeds as follows:

If a person is forced to transgress the commandments, he is forbidden to remain in that place but must emigrate, leave everything behind, wander day and night, until he has found a place where a person can observe the commandments. The world is wide and large.

This was solid counsel through the ages: not so during the reign of the Third Reich. In the first phase of its Jewish policy the world was not "wide and large," and in the second phase not even outright apostasy could save a Jew's life. The Rambam would therefore have been compelled to alter two interrelated teachings of his today: Jewish "servitude to foreign powers" must come to an end, not in some unspecified future, but here and now; and what is needed to end it is not patience and waiting, and prayer only if it is accompanied by resolute action.

In the Midrash we are told that when at the Red Sea the Egyptian army came closer and closer and the sea itself had parted, the Israelites did not dare walk between the two columns of water. Even Moses hesitated. Then a certain Nachshon from the tribe of Judah jumped in, and the whole people followed. (In another version the waters did not part until Nachshon jumped into them.) The Jewish people today is a collective Nachshon, with two differences, however. Then catastrophe only threatened and was averted by a miracle: In our time it has already occurred. And then the miracle came first, and the human action needed was only a response to it. In our time there was no time to wait for miracles. The Nachshon of our time had to jump into the raging sea, hoping that a miracle might come to his aid but determined, if necessary, to swim alone.

PART I

PAST

PRESUPPOSED COMPONENTS OF JUDAISM

2. A JEW
AND
HIS FIDELITY

HOW TO BEGIN

"God, Torah and Israel are one": This is a much-quoted saying in the Zohar, a major work of Jewish mysticism, probably composed by the Spanish Kabbalist Moses de Leon in the thirteenth century. Though quite mysterious, its minimum meaning is obvious enough: There can be no Judaism without all three—God, Torah, and Israel. Without "Israel" there may be an abstract "monotheism," and also a "Torah" in heaven; but there could be no presence of either God or Torah on earth. Without "Torah" there would be no bond between "God" and "Israel." And without "God" there would either be no Jews at all, or else they would be (as so often they have wished to be) a nation like others.

But in a book on Judaism for a Jew today, how shall we begin? With "God"? But many a good modern Jew can at best only find Him, not have Him from the start; and after what has happened in this century, even many Jews of veritable saintliness cannot find Him at all.

43

Begin with "Torah," then? Many Israeli Jews are steeped so deeply in the Jewish book as to have found their very identity in it, not only as Israelis but also as Jews. Yet in all honesty it can be for them only the Jewish book, not *the* Book. A lesser case against beginning with "Torah" is that of Diaspora Jews who lack knowledge of Torah through little fault of theirs. Most compelling of all is the case of refuseniks, Jews in the Soviet Union dedicated enough to have applied for emigration to Israel, and this with the knowledge that as a result they might lose their jobs, face discrimination, as well as indefinitely be denied the permission applied for. If such as these have no knowledge of Torah, it is due to no fault of theirs at all. It has long been deliberate Soviet policy to drive a wedge between the Jewish people and the Torah. At this time of writing Josef Begun is in prison for the "crime" of "parasitism." To be sure, prior to being jailed this dedicated Jew had worked hard as a private teacher of Hebrew. He had also been careful to list both his work and his earnings in the tax return that he had duly submitted. If nevertheless he is guilty of the crime of parasitism, it is because one cannot, after all, teach a nonexistent language. Such is the notion underlying current Soviet policy.

We must, then, begin with the third term in the above-cited saying, with "Israel"—with Jews as they actually are. In beginning in this manner we try to give due weight to the realities of our time. Yet we shall not lose sight of the fact that, whatever the shifting realities of Judaism in a history spanning nearly four millennia, "God, Torah and Israel," in however changing constellations, are the lasting components. They are, as it were, the ever-presupposed past.

I must confess that at one time my approach would have been quite otherwise. When in 1935 I came to the Berlin *Hochschule*, I was in search of sublime expressions of Jewish faith—that and little else. Consequently I was quite deflated when the director of the school and our history professor, Ismar Elbogen, spent what seemed far too much time on how in times of darkness and persecution the ordinary Jew managed to survive. How could he manage to make a living and look after his wife and children? Who cared about things so lowly! What about the great martyrs and saints? And where was the deeper meaning of Jewish history?

That was way back. When I recall that time now, I think fondly of my late history professor, a great scholar but a greater Jew. Large changes have occurred in my attitude over the decades, some gradually but others quite abruptly. I began this book with an incident in that jail cell on November 11, 1938. Here is another incident that occurred only two days later. We had been taken on trucks to the concentration camp of Sachsenhausen, and forced to stand all night. Next morning a procedure took place that was obviously standard. An SS officer walked up and down our front row in leisurely fashion, now looking at this one, now at that one. Then began the "interrogation." He stopped in front of someone: "What's your job? You are a doctor? You Jewish swine, you have defiled Aryan women!" To the next: "A lawyer? You have perverted German law!" To the next: "A rabbinical student? The Talmud says that all Gentiles are pigs!" And so on, with blows inevitably following the insults. At length he came to a man who said he was a bricklayer. "You Jewish liar, you are a banker, and you have swindled your Aryan customers!" But throughout the "interrogation" and the blows that followed the man kept insisting that he was indeed a bricklayer, even though "conceding" that he was a banker would have stopped the process; and I shall never know whether it was because he was too proud to tell a lie or too simple to understand what was going on. I think of that Jew also when I begin this book not with "God" or "Torah" but with "Israel."

This does not mean that I exclude Jews who are not simple people. Henri Bergson (1859–1941) was the greatest French philosopher of his time. Attracted to Catholicism and considering conversion, he changed his mind with the advent of Nazism. After the German conquest of France, he rejected the Vichy French offer to be exempted from its anti-Jewish measures, and, though ill and weak, he queued for many hours with his fellow Jewish victims. Also, he returned all his French decorations and awards to a government that he held in contempt as a Frenchman and as a Jew. I think of Bergson also in beginning with "Israel" and wonder whether, had he lived longer, he might have found his way back to Judaism.

All this, of course, happened long ago, and I anticipate the objection that this is all over and done with, and that this man Fackenheim lives in the past, whether or not on account of some trauma or other. But very much of the present are Soviet Jews who, though denied all Jewish knowledge, persist in their Jewish identity; Israeli Jews who, though wearied of a siege by hostile neighbors that shows few signs of ending, resist the temptation to leave for safer, easier lands; and of the present are also students in Western universities who have every opportunity simply to merge in a benign environment but repudiate that opportunity since they view it as a betrayal. In the 1960s, when the student rebellions were in full swing, two Jewish students, one male and the other female, enrolled in my own University of Toronto. They had no particular Jewish commitments that I ever discovered, let alone religious ones. Yet they were shocked and insulted to discover that in so renowned a university Jewish studies had so small a place. And they did not rest until they had achieved what at that time no professor could have achieved, something at least approximating the place for Jewish studies that they deserve. (When it was over, the university president remarked that this had been the most constructive of all the student rebellions that had occurred during his tenure.) I think of these two students also when I begin with "Israel."

The great event in Israel in this year of my writing has been the arrival of Anatoly Shcharanski at the Western Wall in Jerusalem. The greatest moment of the great event occurred when a black Jew from Ethiopia, himself a recent arrival, walked up to Shcharanski, shook his hand and said: "Welcome from one Oleh to another!" These two men, all the others mentioned previously, and many others I might have mentioned, as well as countless others unknown to me, possess what of all Jewish virtues is the most indispensable, namely, a very special fidelity. Without other virtues Jews cannot be pious, learned, saintly, heroic. Without fidelity they would long have vanished from the earth.

THE TRADITIONAL DEFINITION OF A JEW

Who is a Jew? The child of a Jewish mother or a convert to Judaism. This is the definition given in the Halacha, the traditional law of Judaism. It seems straightforward enough, yet is far from unproblematic. For it states, on the one hand, that one is not a Jew by virtue of one's faith since no one is born with a faith; and on the other, that one is not a Jew by virtue of belonging to a national, tribal, or ethnic group, since converts become Jews in every sense of the term, so explicitly as to be given the name of son/daughter of Abraham, as though they were physical descendants of the ancient patriarch. And that a convert may assume a pivotal role in the history of Judaism could be shown no more dramatically than by the tradition according to which the Messiah himself will be a descendant of Ruth. No greater words were ever spoken by a convert than these of the Moabite Ruth to Naomi, her Jewish mother-in-law:

> Entreat me not to leave thee, and to return from following after thee; For whither thou goest I will go; and where thou lodgest I will lodge; thy people shall be my people, and thy God my God; where thou diest I will die, and there will I be buried; the Lord do so to me, and more also, if aught but death part thee and me. (Ruth 1:16–17)

The difficulties in "Who is a Jew?" are largely removed by the Halachic answer to the question "What is a Jew?" (Others, however, will be seen to take their place.) A Jew is one obligated to the covenant that God made with Israel, a process that began with Abraham, was resumed with the Exodus from Egypt, and reached its climax thus far—the ultimate, Messianic climax is yet to come—with the revelation of the Torah at Mount Sinai. It is this obligation that converts to Judaism take upon themselves voluntarily. For one born of a Jewish mother, however, it is not voluntary. Originally, to be sure, choice played a role. We have already cited one Midrash to the effect that the generation at Sinai made a voluntary commitment. The same point is made more powerfully still

in another Midrash, this one known to every well-educated Jewish
youth. *Na'asse v'nishma* ("We shall do it and hear it," Exod.
24:7), the people reply to Moses when confronted with the momentous challenge. Is this not a corrupt text, an imaginary biblical
critic might ask, for how can the doing come prior to the hearing?
But no, the Midrash says as if in reply. So deep, so unconditional
was the faith, the love of God of that great generation as to make
them accept His task and only thereafter ask what the task was.

The first generation, then, made a choice. But what of future
ones? The book of Joshua ends with a dramatic encounter. Moses
had been denied entry into the promised land. Joshua had led a
new generation to take possession of it. Now, just prior to his
death, he calls an assembly and makes a speech. "Your fathers,"
he begins, "dwelt of old time beyond the River, even Terah, the
father of Abraham, and the father of Nahor, and they served other
gods" (Josh. 24:2). He goes on to rehearse how He, the God of
Israel, led Abraham from beyond the River, into Canaan; how He
multiplied his seed and did all His great deeds, until finally they,
the generation addressed by Joshua, came into possession of the
long-promised land. Then comes the climax of Joshua's speech and
the purpose of the whole assembly: They, the second generation
following the Exodus, are to be given a second choice. They may
either renew the commitment made by the first generation at
Sinai, or else they may reject that commitment, whether in order
to go back to the gods from beyond the River, or to go on to the
gods of the Amorites, who inhabit the land in which they now live.
"But as for me and my house," Joshua concludes his speech, "we
will serve the Lord" (Josh. 24:15). It is when the people respond
that they too will serve the God of Abraham and Moses that
Joshua utters the words that were to reverberate through the generations: "Ye are witnesses against yourselves. . . ," he says, and
the people confirm that witnesses, indeed, they are.

No more fateful words were ever spoken in Jewish history: The
choice given to the first and second generation was withheld ever
after. The generation of Joshua was witness not only against itself
but also against its children and children's children, from then on

and forever after, until the Messianic end of days. This is a fact of the Jewish religious life that has often puzzled, annoyed, and infuriated others. It has often puzzled, annoyed, and infuriated Jews themselves as well. But whether we accept it, reject it, or simply remain puzzled, we cannot hope to come to grips with the Jewish religious condition unless we confront that unique fact.

ASSIMILATION AND JEWISH FIDELITY

But how can one human being, by witnessing against him/herself, bind another? Or, to put it less abstractly and philosophically, but more relevantly and poignantly, how can one Jewish generation witness against Jewish generations yet unborn? This question assumed a new dimension of anguish when the 1935 Nazi Nuremberg laws defined a Jew as "a person with two Jewish grandparents, if they belonged to the Jewish religion." But it has been a special burden upon the Jewish self-understanding at all times, and the wish to be "like the other nations," as old as biblical times, can be viewed without sympathy only by those whose piety is doctrinaire and insensitive. As for modern times, we have already seen that their belief in "autonomy" and "individual conscience" has led to attempts at changes in Jewish self-definition (see chapter 1, section 3). Thus a modern Jew committed to Judaism may act as though his commitment were purely a matter of personal choice— and then is hard put to explain why he did not choose Unitarianism or Bahai. Or he may view his "Jewishness" as a matter of "ethnicity" wholly parallel, in North America at least, to, say, the Irish or Hungarian. But then he is hard put to explain why the Jewish ethnicity should have survived so long and under circumstances often so adverse, and also why to preserve this particular ethnicity seems to be some sort of moral imperative. The most recent, most radical attempt at change not only of the Jewish self-understanding but also the Jewish condition is of course that streak in the Zionist movement that would make Jews wholly into a nation like others, the most radical form of which is the attempt to make Jews into "Canaanites" on arrival on Israel. However, Israeli "Canaanism" has been overrun by the course of events.

Minimally, then, the modern Jewish quest for a change in the Jewish self-understanding is for some sort of "normalization" of the Jewish condition that would get Jews away from that fateful tradition of the parents witnessing against their children's children. Maximally, it is the reduction of Jewish birth to an "accident," and, "now that the walls of the ghetto have fallen," the quest, in various forms and to various degrees, for assimilation.

Assimilation is not a uniquely Jewish fact of modern times. In our time, urbanization, social and geographical mobility, and other well-known factors have made it a universal Western phenomenon; and, despite the recent "rise of the ethnics," the process continues apace. Jewish assimilation, however, differs from others in at least two respects. The children, say, of an Irish Catholic or Hungarian Protestant in America may cease to be Irish or Hungarian yet continue to be Catholic or Protestant; in the case of their Jewish counterpart, both the Jewishness and the Judaism will have disappeared. And whereas the Irish or Hungarian parents may lament the loss of ethnic identity in their children, the loss of *their* identity in their children is likely to be viewed by their *Jewish* parents as something close to a betrayal. As for the children, they may try to assuage a vague sense of guilt by such acts as joining the local Unitarian church. (In this, the wish to escape antisemitism too may play a role.) So well known is this phenomenon as to have generated a joke. Someone remarks that Smith has died, and that he will be buried in the Unitarian cemetery. "The Unitarian cemetery?" a listener exclaims. "I didn't know Smith was Jewish!"

Along with assimilation there exists resistance to it, among the Irish, the Hungarians, the Jews. Does the Jewish resistance differ from the other two in any respect other than its greater tenacity, a difference that can be ascribed to a religious tradition armed with once-powerful sanctions? If so, they could all be viewed as so many rearguard battles, waged in behalf of anachronisms. Even among those who look kindly upon Irish and Hungarian group survival, this has been a widespread view about Jewish group survival in the

Western world, ever since the age of Jewish emancipation. The conservative Right (which opposed Jewish emancipation) was obvious in its view that both Jews and Judaism had been an anachronism since the advent of Christianity. Because of the obviousness of this fact it was often overlooked that the liberal Left (which supported Jewish emancipation) too was apt to view Jews and Judaism as an anachronism, for in return for being emancipated "as men" Jews were generally expected, silently or not so silently, to disappear "as Jews." In his time the liberal-minded philosopher Immanuel Kant (1724–1804) looked forward to the "euthanasia" of Judaism. In our time Arnold Toynbee, no less liberal minded, viewed Jewish group survival as that of a "fossil." The most up-to-date version of this kind of liberal mentality is illustrated in an Israeli joke in which an Englishman asks an Israeli: "Why are you people so parochial? Why do you insist on a state of your own, a language of your own, a culture of your own? Why don't you dissolve in mankind?" The Israeli replies: "After you, sir!"

But this joke, though nicely militant, is not nearly militant enough. Kant, Toynbee, and the mythical Englishman of the joke all adopt, as beyond criticism, a modern universalist stance, and view in its light a Judaism seemingly parochial and anachronistic. The joke fails to bring to light a doctrinaire parochialism implicit in that very stance, despite its self-styled universalism. Self-limited to modernity, those adopting that stance all fail to notice, let alone take seriously, the fact that Jewish assimilation, unlike the Irish or Hungarian, is not a purely modern phenomenon: It is as old as Jewish history itself.

This is a fact that deserves close attention. The Bible has much to say of those Israelites who left Egypt; of those who stayed behind it is silent. It dwells at length on those who, carried off to Babylon in 586 B.C.E., returned some fifty years later, unable as they were to forget Jerusalem; not a word is said of the ten northern tribes that had been carried off to Assyria some 125 years earlier. To be sure, fundamentalists of many kinds and many times have looked for these "lost" tribes among the British, the Japanese, and the American Indians. The obvious fact is that these tribes are the classic case of Jewish assimilation. They were carried off in order that they should assimilate—a well-tried strategy of ancient empires with obstinate subject peoples—and assimilate they did.

These reflections could give rise to speculations as to how many Jews there might be today had no Jew ever assimilated. More importantly, they revolutionize one's entire perspective on the subject of Jewish assimilation. If the Bible pays heed not to those who stayed behind in Egypt or Assyria but to those who left Egypt and returned from Babylon, it is because whereas the behavior of the first was "natural," only that of the second was of historic significance. To go further, its significance was *world* historical. What would have been the history of the Middle East, of Europe, of the West, of the world, had *all* stayed and assimilated, whether in Egypt or Babylon? Even just to raise this question is to abandon the view of Jewish group survival as that of a fossil or anachronism. (That view is in fact nothing more than an age-old Christian prejudice, even if given a modern secular form.) Conceivably and maximally, Jews might once more have a new role in a new age. Even minimally, however, it emerges that something quite other than parochial bigotry is involved in Jewish group survival. We in any case nowadays view Irish- and Hungarian-Americans who wish to remain hyphenated as heir to a certain fidelity rather than as enemies of progress. Yet a unique fidelity is shown by Jews who reject the lure of assimilation. Without *their* special fidelity the history of the Irish and the Hungarians would come to an end, in countries other than Ireland and Hungary. Without the special *Jewish* fidelity, Jewish history would never have begun.

This insight was given classic expression by the medieval poet-philosopher Yehuda Halevi (1080–1145). In his *Kuzari* a pagan king, dissatisfied with his paganism, consults in turn a philosopher, a Christian, a Muslim, and a rabbi and, having considered the teachings of them all, ends up by converting to Judaism. (The book is based vaguely on historical fact: The Khazars, a Tartar tribe, did in fact embrace Judaism sometime in the eighth century.) Already on the verge of conversion, the king expresses some remaining doubt with the observation that he has noticed greater saintliness and humility among Christians and Muslims than among

Jews. Why, Jews do not even have monasteries! The rabbi agrees but adds that the characteristic Jewish virtue is another, namely, fidelity. "Consider," he says to the king, "how thoughtful men among us could escape the degradation [of persecution in exile], by a word spoken lightly," [a lip-service conversion to Christianity or Islam]. Only in two respects need Halevi's point be brought up-to-date in our time. First, at least in free, democratic societies it is no longer necessary to "speak a word"—convert—in order to assimilate. (Also, if being a Jew involves some discomfort here and there, it hardly involves "degradation.") Second, disappearance through assimilation is no longer a possibility confined to the "thoughtful"; it is open to all. Without fidelity, Jewish history in ancient times would never have begun; without fidelity, Jewish history, in our time, would come abruptly to an end.

ANTISEMITISM AND JEWISH IDENTITY

But an account quite other than the above could be given of Jewish survival through the ages; indeed, in some respects it is diametrically opposite. Jewish survival, according to that account, is the product of antisemitism. The case is made most brilliantly in the French philosopher Jean-Paul Sartre's *Antisemite and Jew.* Many years later Sartre admitted that when he wrote the book in wartime France he had no knowledge of Jews or Judaism but wrote merely on the basis of personal experience. In the book itself he says that he confines himself to Jews in France only. Of these he says that they are without a religion of their own, without a culture of their own, without a historical consciousness of their own. Then why do they survive? Because their enemies give them no choice! It is true that the Jew has a "friend" in the "democrat," but this is a weak friend. First, because his friendship lacks passion; second, because he has many victims of injustice to defend of whom the Jew is but one; and, third and most seriously, because whereas the enemy attacks the Jew as Jew, the democratic friend defends him only as man. The antisemitic enemy, in contrast, is relentless and passionate in his hatred of Jews, and is not deflected from his goal—

ultimately it is to kill the Jew—by other goals or endeavors. The Jew, then, is made a Jew by enemies that permit him "no exit." (This is also the name of one of Sartre's plays.)

It goes without saying that the "no religion, no culture, no historical consciousness" part of Sartre's theory applies only to assimilated Jews; such, indeed, are the only Jews he seems to have known when he wrote the book. The "no exit" part of it was true of his own wartime France, both the Nazi-occupied part and the part governed by the Vichy regime, a nasty collaborator with Nazi policies. Since in all Nazi-occupied Europe even a single missing Jew was hunted down coldly, systematically, and until the second and third generation, Sartre's "no exit" theory was absolutely true of that time and that place. That it has some truth also for other times and places may be illustrated by two examples. In fourteenth- and fifteenth-century Christian Spain Jews were severely persecuted. In reaction, they for the first time in history converted to Christianity en masse. This produced two Gentile reactions. One, the Inquisition, implied that Jewish conversion to Christianity mattered a great deal, for Jewish converts to Christianity were tortured in order that the genuineness of their conversion might be established. The other Gentile reaction implied that Jewish conversion to Christianity did not matter at all: a new, unprecedented distinction was made between these "new" Christians and the old Christians—those of "pure blood." The old Christian Jew-hatred, expressed in the Inquisition, allowed Jews one "exit," namely, baptism. This is done away with by the new "racist" Jew-hatred, which made its first appearance in Spain at that time.

The second example is more striking still. The enemy makes Jews a nation whether they like it or not: This was said by Theodor Herzl, the father of the Zionist movement and the grandfather of the State of Israel. Herzl was a correspondent for a Viennese newspaper. In 1894 he was sent to Paris to cover the Dreyfus trial. A Jewish officer in the French Army, Alfred Dreyfus had been falsely accused of espionage for Germany, was found guilty and sent to prison, and "the affair" was not fully settled until 1906, with the discovery of the guilty party and the rehabilitation of Dreyfus. Meanwhile, it occasioned an explosion of antisemitism in the press, the streets, the political life of the Republic—and converted Herzl to Zionism. Quite possibly without that experience Herzl would have remained just another of the many assimilated Jewish journalists who were at the time in so many capitals of Europe. Is Jewish survival, then, in modern times at least, the product of anti-semitism?

The ultimate expression of any such theory is the view that the grandfather of the State of Israel was not Theodor Herzl but Adolf Hitler. Were he alive, assuredly the *Fuehrer* would seek the death of the Jewish state as passionately as do all living Nazis, old and new. (So passionate are some in their hatred that they make themselves over into "leftists" so as to be more respectable "anti-Zionists.") Nevertheless, so the theory holds, just as the Jew-hatred of the antisemite creates the Jew's very identity, so the genocidal Jew-hatred of the ultimate antisemite caused Jews to embrace Jewish statehood.

"Hitler as grandfather of Israel": this is the ultimate consequence of the view that Jewish survival is the product of persecution. It is also its *reductio ad absurdum*. The most dramatic example of this is B'richa ("flight"), the "illegal" postwar immigration movement of Holocaust survivors to Palestine, in the waning days of the British manadatory regime. Hitler had not only practiced antisemitism, and this in its ultimate form of mass murder. He had also done his best to export it; and that his efforts had been successful was proved, among many other facts, by the fate of the survivors who, virtual prisoners in "D.P." camps still, had to wait endlessly for someone, somewhere, to offer them a place of refuge, of peace, and, above all, of anonymity and a chance to forget. Hitler had robbed the Zionist movement of those Jews it counted on most, the Eastern European masses; he had also done his best to rob Jewish survivors of any wish for any future Jewish identification. Then why did even a small minority of Jewish survivors choose to defy the legal niceties of the world, "illegally" cross borders, board unseaworthy ships—all this in order to reach the only country where there would be no prospect of early peace, no flight from the Jewish condition, and no chance to forget? The B'richa movement cannot be understood as a passive, mechanical "effect" of the Holocaust as its "cause." One can understand it only as an *active response* to a challenge without precedent; and expressed in it was a Jewish fidelity long dormant, perhaps, but awakened by catastrophe to new life.

Had Herzl's Zionism been an "effect" "caused" by French antisemitism? Many journalists covered the Dreyfus trial. Some were assimilated cosmopolitan Jews like Herzl himself. Of these at least one, Bernard Lazare, reacted similarly to Herzl. Others we know of reacted quite differently, and the reaction of yet others we can only guess. One of these latter may have been as outraged as Herzl by the judicial murder he had to report, but went out of his way to ignore the antisemitism at the heart of it. Another may have sought refuge in "objectivity," for who knows, maybe Dreyfus was guilty. Yet a third may have felt that to a degree Dreyfus's misfortunes were his own fault, that he should not have "pushed himself" into the reactionary French officer corps or that, if push he must, he should have had the "tact" to convert to Christianity first. I do not know whether any of the reactions were actual. I do know that all would have been possible. And against them all Herzl's Zionist reaction stands out, minimally, as an act of Jewish self-respect.

It was this and more. Jewish self-respect was shown also by Jewish students in pre–World War I Germany who, denied admission by antisemitic fraternities, formed their own. Self-respect was shown by an acquaintance of my father's who, insulted by an antisemitic fellow-student, challenged the latter to a duel and was killed. Like the fallen in Israel's defense forces, my father's acquaintance died; but unlike them he died in vain.

Beyond self-respect, Herzl's Zionist response to the Dreyfus trial was a new expression of the age-old Jewish virtue of fidelity; and beyond that it was an intimation of what through the ages had been its source. This is expressed in the very title of his novel that depicts a future Jewish return to the ancient land: *Alt-neuland* ("Old-newland"). Herzl knew no Hebrew. Yet such was his genius that he hit on as close to a German equivalent of a Hebrew word that is not quite translatable but signifies the innermost secret of Jewish survival. The word is *teshuvah*.

TESHUVAH AS THE SOURCE OF JEWISH FIDELITY

> I remember thee for the affection of thy youth,
> The love of thine espousals;
> How thou wentest after Me in the wilderness,
> In a land that was not sown. (Jer. 2:2)

What a moving image of fidelity, that of a lover following after a beloved! This Jeremiah passage must surely move even the most doctrinaire atheist, despite the fact that the beloved referred to in it is God.

The passage is thought-provoking as well as moving. The prophet utters his words in anguish, for it seems that Israel's youth and the affection of her youth are both over and done with. Yet generations upon Jewish generations were moved by this and similar passages, to an affection rivaling if not surpassing that of the wilderness generation: the Maccabees with their heroism; such as Rabbi Akiba with his martyrdom; and *amcha* as a whole when it endured degradation and exile rather than abandon the Torah and the God who at Sinai had given it. Youth normally gives way to old age. Throughout Jewish history youth was ever-renewed. Israel's affection for her Beloved was ever old-new.

Nor is this all. According to a Midrash whenever Israel went into exile God Himself went with them. The Midrash obviously was written in exile, in circumstances that might well have produced the belief that, abandoned by men, Israel was abandoned by God as well. Yet when Jews in exile read the Torah in some miserable hovel, they had with them not only a scroll of parchment but also the presence of God. To the ever-renewed affection of one of the lovers corresponded an ever-renewed affection in the Other.

This renewal as the source of Jewish fidelity has remained misunderstood by the non-Jewish mind through the ages; it very largely remains so to this day. The Christ tells his followers that whereas in the world they will have trouble he has "overcome the world" (John 16:33); hence to the Christian mind Jewish fidelity *in* the world is an anachronism. To the pagan mind, old and new, it is a fossil, for the central pagan idea, expressed most profoundly by the ancient Greeks, is that time is the river Lethe, forgetfulness; that existence is tragic since time devours all: Youth is lost in old age, life yields to death, and Hades is inhabited by shades whose yearning for a retrieved life is frustrated in all eternity. Both these forms of the non-Jewish mind, then, find it difficult to grasp and do justice to the basic Jewish idea, *teshuvah*, a turning and returning in which the old is renewed. According to tradition Jeremiah, who wrote of the affection of Israel's youth, also composed *Lamentations*, which mourns the destruction of Jerusalem, a catastrophe that he himself had prophesied. The book ends as follows: "Thou canst not have utterly rejected us, / And be exceeding wroth against us" (Lam. 5:22). The threat that confronts Israel is the end of affection, of youth, of life itself. Yet tradition forbids a reading of the book that ends with its last verse. The second-to-last verse is to be repeated, and this is done when the book is read on the ninth of Av, the day of mourning for the destruction of Jerusalem. That verse reads as follows: "Turn us unto Thee, O Lord, and we shall be turned: / Renew our days as of old" (Lam. 5:21). To this day this verse is recited whenever the Torah, having been read in a synagogue service, is returned to its ark. Throughout the ages *teshuvah* has been the source of Jewish fidelity and Jewish renewal. It has been the innermost source of Jewish survival.

Will *teshuvah* be operative in the future? In our time there *is* occurring a great *teshuvah*, if not to the God of Israel so to the land of Israel, and signs of a renewal of the old-new people in the old-new land are not difficult to find. Even so it would be foolish to make predictions about this great but perilous *teshuvah*. (On this subject, see chapter 11.) We do not know the distant future. We do know, however, the distant past. The first mention of the name of Israel known to archaeologists is in the following passage: "Israel is laid waste, his seed is not." The words are on the so-called Israel stele of the Egyptian Pharaoh Mernephta (reigned ca. 1224–1214 B.C.E.) Mernephta and his boasts have long vanished into the river Lethe. The people whose seed he claimed to have destroyed still lives. After what has occurred in this century, this is a fact fraught with astonishment.

EPILOGUE

In 1977 my wife, Rose, and I undertook a pilgrimage to the Soviet Union. Our purpose was to impart some Jewish knowledge to refuseniks. Denied access to such knowledge by a dictatorial regime, these men and women nevertheless apply for exit visas to Israel, knowing full well that they are subject to penalties for so risky a step, yet without any assurance that their request will ever be granted.

We visited four cities. Our first was Riga. The leader of the local study group of some twenty people requested us over the phone to arrive an hour or so early, in order that we could discuss the topic for the evening. "What do you suggest?" I asked Arkady Tzinober on arrival at his tiny apartment. "Jewish philosophy," he replied. "And what do you mean by Jewish philosophy?" I went on to ask. I had been asking myself that very question over the decades, and the more I had thought about it, the more problematic the accepted answers—for our age!—had become. Tzinober gave me what I consider the best answer yet. It certainly was the best answer for him and his like. "We already know that it is our duty to survive as Jews," he said. "Jewish philosophy will tell us why."

3. THE JEW OF TODAY
AND THE JEWISH
BIBLE

PORTABLE FATHERLAND

I remember a picture from my childhood. It was the sort of picture that used to adorn the salons of Eastern European, Orthodox, petty-bourgeois families. It was not our kind of picture, not only because it was rather poor art but also, more importantly, because what it portrayed was not a German-Jewish experience: Jews fleeing from a pogrom. Even so it moved me deeply, and I remember it well. The fleeing Jews in the picture are bearded old men, terrified, but not so much as to leave behind what is most precious to them. In the view of antisemites these Jews would doubtless be clutching bags of gold. In fact each of them carries a Torah scroll.

Perhaps the picture moved me because the pogrom experience was not altogether alien even to German Jews, much though we felt at home with our German identity, our Jewish identity, and a harmony between the two. (That this was in our own minds only, not in the minds of our neighbors, was soon to become grimly evident.) If identification with the experience of these old men was not what moved me, it is what should have moved me. In my view, the greatest of German Jews was Heinrich Heine (1797–1856). That he was a great German poet no one except antisemites has ever denied. If I consider him a great Jew also, it is despite the fact that, like so many of his generation, he underwent baptism. These many did so, to use Heine's own expression, in order to obtain their "entrance ticket" to European culture, and Karl Marx's father had his son baptized in childhood for just that reason. Unlike most of these many others, however, Heine never got over the cravenness of his act, and expressed in his work is not only his own torn condition but also an admirable fortitude that atones for his craven act. A German romantic himself, he flayed mercilessly the bombastic, antisemitic, narrow German patriotism of many of his fellow romantics. Having abandoned Judaism, he yet in a beautiful poem celebrated the "Sabbath Jew" for whom his contemporary Marx had nothing but words of slander. No honest and knowledgeable person can consider Marx a great Jew. If Heine is to me the greatest of German Jews, it is because he experienced so deeply, and at so early a time, the torn condition of German Jewry, which was ultimately to end in disaster. It is this Jew that wrote words that could never have come from the pen of Marx. "The Torah," he wrote, "is the portable fatherland of a Jew." The expression is hauntingly beautiful. But the idea is the same as in that picture of *amcha* in Eastern Europe, the picture from my childhood, unforgotten to this day.

JEWISH FIDELITY AND THE TORAH

"A Jew and his fidelity": This has been our subject hitherto. The critical reader may have wondered about a fidelity so unfocused, with an inspiration so obscure, and—so it may have seemed—without any particular goal or object. We have been at pains to show, however, not only that such a fidelity does exist but also that it is not to be dismissed lightly or without respect. No better proof of this could be given in our time than persons such as Arkady Tzinober, who defy the most powerful dictatorship of our time—

in behalf of a cause which they yet have to learn about from "Jewish philosophy"! The critical reader who still objects does have a point, however. Throughout the ages Jewish fidelity was not a commitment in search of a cause. As is articulated both by that picture from my childhood and Heine's dictum, Jewish fidelity was to the Torah.

Consider the following passage. Every well-educated Jewish child knows it by heart. Observant Jews recite it twice daily in their prayers. And its first sentence is the dying words even of many Jews who have observed or believed little or nothing Jewish during their lifetime:

> Hear, O Israel, the Lord our God, the Lord is one. And thou shalt love the Lord thy God with all thy heart, with all thy soul, and with all thy might. And these words which I command thee this day shall be upon thy heart; and thou shalt teach them diligently to thy children, and shalt speak of them when thou sittest in thy house, and when thou walkest by the way, when thou liest down and when thou risest up. And thou shalt bind them for a sign upon thy hand, and they shall be for frontlets between thine eyes. And thou shall write them upon the door-posts of thy house and upon thy gates. (Deut. 6:4–9)

In a way, the key sentence in this passage is the one about teaching the children. It has many implications, some profound but all important. An important (if depressing and sobering) implication: If to this day the *melammed*, the Hebrew teacher of the children, enjoys little respect, it is because he does only what anybody can do. Of course, the father is supposed to do it, but he is generally too busy doing "more important" things. I myself was once told just that, and in those very words, when, a penniless refugee but after all at the age of twenty-three an ordained rabbi, I arrived in Aberdeen, Scotland, and earned part of my living as a *melammed*. I would bicycle from home to home and teach the dozen or so kids of the small community for two shillings and sixpence per hour. It was there that a father told me that he would teach his child himself if he had the time. I was not particularly pleased by this experience, my first as a *melammed* and refugee but by no means the last.

The passage about teaching the children, then, does have depressing implications. Under no circumstances, however, must these obscure the profound ones. A profound implication: Not the least Jewish answer to the question, "How do you know that there is a God?" is this: "My father told me—would he tell me a lie?"

THE IDEA AND REALITY OF A CANON

But how does the father himself know? The answer "he was told by his father" is, of course, inconclusive. The real answer is that he learned it from a book—*the* Book. The book in question is known in Judaism as the *TeNaCh*, an abbreviation of its three parts, Torah, Nevi'im ("Prophets") and Ketubim ("Writings"). There are, of course, numerous Jewish books. The Tenach is *the* Jewish book because it was revealed through prophecy and because, with the last of its twenty-eight books, the second Book of Chronicles, prophecy came to an end, to be given thereafter to "fools and children." Such, at any rate, is the traditional Jewish view.

This distinction between divinely revealed books and books merely humanly composed has given rise to the idea of a canon. This idea came into the world with Judaism but spread to Christianity and Islam, and what spread to these religions from Judaism was more than just that idea. The Tenach, the Jewish canon, was to become the "Old Testament" within the Christian canon, its other part being the New Testament. As for the Koran, this is deeply influenced by Jewish ideas, postbiblical as well as biblical. It is this kinship between the Jewish canon and the Christian and Muslim that has given rise to the image of these religions as "daughters" of Judaism, and without doubt this image discloses a truth.

But it also conceals another. I remember first hearing of this image at bar mitzvah lessons from our local rabbi, a man of wide learning and broad sympathies, and while the image inspired me—

my best friend was not only a Christian but also, at least partly, my best friend *because* he was a Christian—but also puzzled me. If Judaism was a "mother" with "daughters," why were these latter so often so nasty to the mother? Of Muslim nastiness I knew nothing at the time, for while we learned of the "golden age" of Judaism in medieval Muslim Spain, barely touched on was the fact that Maimonides had to flee twice from Muslim fanaticism. But no Jew in Germany could be ignorant of the nasty behavior of the Christian daughter. "His blood be on us and our children" (Matt. 27:25), Jesus' Jewish contemporaries are made to say in the Christian canon, calling a curse not only upon themselves but also upon their children's children. Hardly less devastating in nastiness are passages in the Muslim canon, such as: "Then were they smitten with abasement and poverty and met with the wrath of God . . . because they had disbelieved in God's signs . . ." (Sura 2:58). At a conference held in Cairo in 1970 a Syrian Muslim leader went out of his way to emphasize that this passage applied to Jews not only of Muhammed's time but of all time.

Such hostility springs at least in part from the very idea of a canon and the possibility, if indeed not inevitability, of conflict between different religions based on Scriptures claiming canonical status. Of "sibling rivalry" between the two "daughters" of Judaism the most telling historical example are the Crusades. That the Jewish "mother" considers prophecy to have come to an end with the end of the Tenach we have already mentioned, and what this means for Jewish relations to non-Jewish religions in general and to Christianity and Islam in particular will have to be considered subsequently. (See chapter 12, section 5.) On the part of the "daughters," much of the hostility stems from the facts that in their respective canons the "mother" is understood in terms other than those of its self-understanding in its own canon. For those who wish to overcome the traditional hostility, then, much of the task depends on whether the conflict between the different canons that has been a historical fact is inevitable.

In this modern day and age, it would of course be an easy step to dismiss the very idea of a canon, and this in behalf of a critical, enlightened modernity. Perhaps, however, the step is too easy. For us in this book, it would in any case be premature. We cannot do other than consider Judaism as it is on the basis of the Jewish book as *the* Book, as Scripture accepted as divinely revealed and canonical, in order first to understand what Judaism traditionally is, and only thereafter to ask what of it remains acceptable. We must, that is, consider the role of the Tenach as canonical within Judaism itself.

Why are the first book of Maccabees and the Wisdom of Solomon outside the Jewish canon, in the so-called Apocrypha? (They are part of the Roman Catholic and Greek Orthodox canon. They are excluded from the Tenach, possibly because they are extant only in Greek. But then, why and how were the Hebrew originals lost?) And why are the Song of Songs, Ecclesiastes, and Esther inside the Jewish canon when, on the face of it, the first is a secular love poem, the second is full of skepticism, and in the third the Deity is not so much as mentioned? However, these questions concerning the relation between canonical and noncanonical books, important though they are within the life of Judaism, pale in importance compared to at least one question concerning the relation between parts within the canon itself. All the twenty-eight books of the Tenach are divinely revealed. "Prophets" (Nevi'im) such as Amos and Isaiah spoke truly when they prefaced their messages with the words "thus saith the Lord." "Writings" (Ketubim) such as Psalms, Proverbs, and Lamentations were composed—so the tradition has it—respectively, by David, Solomon, and Jeremiah, the last-named a prophet and the two kings retroactively elevated to the stature of prophets. However, of the three parts of the Tenach only the Torah was given directly to the whole people at Sinai, and Moses is unique among the prophets. And it is he who committed to writing the whole of these five "books of Moses," except only for its last eight verses. These, beginning with "So Moses, the servant of the Lord died. . . ," were written by Joshua. The scrolls carried by those bearded old men in that picture from my childhood do not contain the Tenach in its entirety. They contain the Torah alone.

This distinction between the Torah and the remainder of the Tenach was to be of enormous consequence for the liturgical life of the synagogue and, beyond that, for Jewish life as a whole. In a church service the pastor may generally select texts from the Christian Bible according to the exigencies of the moment and the prompting of his own heart. In the synagogue Shabbat service it is obligatory to read the Torah in its entirety once each and every year—a practice that includes not only ever-meaningful portions such as those about Creation, the Exodus, or the Ten Commandments, but also portions concerning animal sacrifices, leprosy and its cure, and dire threats of the evils that will befall Israel if she fails to heed the divine commandments. There are two weekly portions in the Torah containing these threats (Lev. 26:14–45; Deut. 28:15–68). It is true that when the time for the reading of these comes, they are read with a low voice. The point is, however, that they are being read—even after the Holocaust. And, despite or perhaps even because of such portions, the festival in the liturgical year on which the cycle of the reading of the Torah ends—and is immediately begun again—is termed Simhat Torah, "The Joy of the Torah." It is this stern yet joyous discipline that has been the deepest source of Jewish fidelity through the ages—a fidelity extending beyond liturgy to the whole or Jewish life. And when during the Holocaust Nazi *Einsatzgruppen* burned synagogue after synagogue in Eastern Europe, in more than one reliably reported case Jews rushed into the flames to save the Torah scrolls, only to be burned with them or else shot when they emerged. The picture from my childhood is out of date. It ought to be replaced by one depicting "a certain Schlesinger, his son and his son-in-law, emerging from a burning synagogue in Bendin, Poland, carrying each one Torah scroll in each arm," just before they were "shot by the wicked ones." I quote the report of the chronicler Shim'on Huberband, who wrote his chronicle before he was murdered himself.

WRITTEN AND ORAL TORAH

The image of a people clinging faithfully to the Book may move us. But to the modern minded it is also likely to suggest all the stereotypes they ever heard about Jews blindly obeying outdated authorities, about a "slavish" Jewish "legalism" and "literalism," and, consequently, about Jews themselves as a "fossil" in history. (It also brings to mind stories heard from time to time about odd Christian sectarians who refuse blood transfusions for their children on the grounds that the Bible forbids the eating of blood.) However, while such a literalistic stance toward the Tenach is found here and there among Jewish sectarians—the Karaites come to mind, a sect originating in the eighth century and surviving in very small numbers to this day—the Jewish people as a whole, simply because they are a people, could never have embraced such a sterile literalism and survived. (What is more important, the slavish clinging to a misread text, or the life of your child?) Indeed, this particular conflict was settled within Judaism once and for all when, roughly at the time of Jesus, the Pharisees, the precursors of rabbinic Judaism, won out against the literally minded Sadducees. The Pharisees in turn were preceded by the Maccabees; indeed, the issue of biblical literalism was settled in principle as early as in the Maccabean war, although to explicate it in its details and the consequences was the work of centuries.

In 169 B.C.E. the Syrians under Antiochus Epiphanes invaded the land and tried to suppress the Jewish faith through measures such as forcing Jews to eat pork in public and killing those who refused. The Maccabees took to arms. Two nova occurred with the Maccabees in world history. They, as it were, invented martyrdom, the witnessing to God unto death. Also, theirs was the first war in history fought in defense of a faith.

The war itself, however, produced a dilemma. Fighting in defense of the Torah against the Syrian attempt to destroy it, the Maccabees were naturally scrupulous in observing it themselves. Observing the Torah, they would not fight on Shabbat—and were slaughtered wholesale by the enemy. Quite possibly they might have died a martyr's death with serenity had they been a sect of monks or other isolated adults. They were, however, the leaders of a flesh-and-blood people; what is more, the Torah they were defending was given to that flesh-and-blood people, and therein consisted the dilemma. The Maccabees could either go on observing Shabbat as ordained in the Torah, but this would be one way of destroying Judaism since there could be no Judaism without living Jews—men, women, and children. Or else they could fight on Shabbat so as to defend that people; but in fighting on Shabbat they would violate the Torah themselves. It was the first but by no means the last time that an enemy confronted Jews with an impossible dilemma, whether the purpose was to annihilate Jews, Judaism, or both.

But was the dilemma impossible? Could the God of Israel be in league with the enemy, endowed, as it were, with a sadistic sense of humor, permitting situations to arise in which a Jew could serve him neither by observing Shabbat nor by *not* observing it? In answering this question with a resounding no the Maccabees produced a revolutionary thesis: Violation of the Torah in defense of it is not a violation; it is an interpretation. Long before Jesus of Nazareth the Maccabees discovered—and this by dint of the direct existential necessity—that man was not made for Shabbat only, that Shabbat was also made for man.

But how could the mere word of man—the interpretation—be pitted against the Word of God—the Torah itself? Only if the word of man was not, after all, merely human but itself divinely inspired. There was not only a "written" Torah; there was an "oral" Torah as well. The implications of this monumental response to an unprecedented challenge became explicit only in centuries to come, in a tradition that includes Pharisaic Judaism, rabbinic Judaism, and extends to the present day whenever learned rabbis foregather to relate the Torah to problems of the age. (The greatest document of that tradition is the Talmud.) The response was present in principle, however—it is necessary to repeat this point for emphasis—ever since the first Maccabee decided that he *must* violate the Torah in order to save it, and that he *may* do so because the "violation" is no violation but an interpretation.

ORAL TORAH AND AUTHORITY

The Talmud is a vast work consisting of numerous heavy tomes. Its style is so terse and dense as to require, even of the learned, days of concentrated study for the mastery of even a single page. Is that "oral"? And is it "Torah"? Even the casual reader of a Talmudic anthology comes easily upon material with little or no obvious connection with the "written" Torah. Rabbinic Judaism itself makes this point in a tongue-in-cheek Midrash in which Moses, residing with God in heaven, looks down and sees and hears some rabbis engaged in a discussion of which he, Moses, understands not a single word. (Akiba is one of the rabbis.) So he turns to God and asks what it is these Jews are talking about, and the Almighty replies: "They are studying the Torah given to Moses on Mount Sinai."

The modern, historically and critically minded reader may wish to go without ado much further than this tongue-in-cheek Midrash. He is tempted to dismiss the whole concept of "oral Torah" as nothing but a pious fiction invented by later generations that wished to pay lip-service to the sacredness of the biblical texts while deriving from them (or rather, *reading into* them) what was wanted or needed by their own time and circumstances. But it is by no means obvious that so radical a step is required by a critical modernity. In any case, before taking it we must dwell on the incredible fact that the Talmud was in fact orally transmitted for the longest of times, and committed to writing only when the upheavals of the time plus the limitations of human memory made the taking of this step necessary. Of the work as now in our possession the Mishnah, its first part (consisting in turn of six parts devoted, respectively, to laws of agriculture, festivals, marriage and divorce, civil affairs, sacrifices, and ritual purity), was redacted by Yehuda Ha-nassi around the year 200 C.E. The second, vastly larger and more complex part, is the Gemara, formally a commentary on the Mishnah but breaking the bound of commentary and having a style, logic, and life of its own. It exists in two versions. The so-called Jerusalem Talmud was completed around 500 C.E. The much larger and more authoritative Babylonian Talmud was not completed until some decades later.

Whatever a modern reader's own eventual views about the concept of "oral Torah," he cannot but ask some questions of the tradition that subscribed to and lived by it. What makes the "oral"

Torah an authoritative interpretation of the "written" one? What makes it even legitimate? And what is the limit beyond which exegesis—finding in the text—becomes "eisegesis," a reading into the text of what is not in it?

That the tradition takes these questions with the utmost seriousness is perhaps best illustrated by the fact that to this day in America the two great movements that break with the "oral Torah" of rabbinic Judaism, Reform and Conservative Judaism, are themselves forced to struggle with the "problem of authority." (See below, chapter 6, section 6.) The traditional stance toward the above questions may be summed up in four principles.

First, an unbroken tradition links the "written" Torah with the "oral" one. The most popular treatise of the Mishnah, *Pirke Abot* ("Sayings of the Fathers"), begins as follows:

> Moses received the Torah and handed it down to Joshua; Joshua to the Elders; the Elders to the prophets; and the prophets handed it down to the men of the Great Assembly.

Second, the "oral Torah" must be in the hands, not of individuals, however outstanding in spirit and learning, but of a scholarly community. As portrayed in the New Testament, Jesus differs from the "scribes and Pharisees," not in interpreting the Torah, nor even in offering new interpretations, but rather in doing so on his own, personal authority. No corresponding claim was ever made on behalf of such as Hillel or Shammai, learned and pious though they were. As for the schools founded by these two rabbis, it is indeed the case that they often clashed. Yet the rabbinic view was—*had* to be—that "both are the words of the living God."

Third, there could be no "oral" Torah that was not steeped in the study of the "written" one. The claim that our human interpretation of the Word of God is itself part of that Word is an enormous one, and the rabbis rarely lost sight of its enormity. This awareness expressed itself in a tradition productive not only of "oral" commentaries on the Torah but also of commentaries on them, subcommentaries, and so on. It also produced a piety at once grandiose and unique to Judaism, but also not lacking a certain harshness. None other than the gentle Hillel said the following:

"An ignorant person cannot be pious." (*Abot* 2:6; more on this subject in chapter 7, section 5.)

But there is yet a fourth principle governing the rabbinic attitude toward the possibility, necessity, legitimacy, and vitality of the "oral" Torah in its relation to the "written" one, and this is most important of all. The modern reader may have his difficulties with it, yet without noticing it, meditating on it, and treating it with empathy and understanding even if he cannot subscribe to it, he cannot hope to understand why and how Jews in past ages studied the Torah, lived by it, died by it, or why any Jew who ever fled in terror from a pogrom staged by drunk Cossacks should have carried the Torah with him. Briefly put: The Torah is inexhaustible. In the words of Rabbi Ben Bag Bag: "Turn it and turn it [the Torah scroll], for everything is in it" (*Abot* 5:25).

AGGADA AND HALACHA

But how can "both are words of the living God" go with authority, to say nothing of any "orthodoxy"? One ponders the relation between that dictum and authority, and conjures up visions of theological schools denouncing or even excommunicating each other. Yet, unlike in Christian history, conflicts of this sort have happened in Jewish history with surprising rarity. To be sure, the institution of excommunication does exist in Judaism, and the most famous (or notorious) case is the excommunication of Spinoza by the Amsterdam rabbinate in 1656. But even here the action was probably taken for political rather than theological reasons, the rabbinate's fear of offending the Protestant establishment by harboring a notorious free-thinker. And then, consider the far more characteristic case of Elisha Ben Abuya. This learned and once-pious second-century rabbi became an apostate, one suspects losing his faith as a result of the persecutions following the Bar Kochba Uprising (135 C.E.). So shocked were his former colleagues that they referred to him no longer by name but as *acher* ("the other one"). No one, however, excommunicated him, and one rabbi, his former pupil Rabbi Meir, continued to associate with him. Moreover, rabbinic legend, so to speak, posthumously exonerates him: He is said to have become a *ba'al teshuvah* just prior to his death. (The role of *teshuvah* in Judaism has already been touched on. That of the *ba'al teshuvah* ["one who returns"] has yet to come.)

A Hasidic tale sums up well the general Jewish attitude toward theological dissent. A disciple comes to his rabbi, inquiring whether it is not the case that everything in the world has a purpose. The rabbi agrees. "Then what," the disciple demands, "is the purpose of atheism?" The rabbi answers: "When a poor person comes to you asking for help, then be an atheist! Don't tell that person that God will help! Act as though no one existed to help except you!"

The spirit reflected in this tale is sometimes taken to mean that one can believe anything one likes and call it Judaism. This is of course completely false. The rabbi in the tale might find all sorts of uses of atheism. The possibility of its being true he would reject out of hand. And what holds true of this tale also holds true of Midrashic literature, of which Hasidic tales may be considered as rightful heir. (I have mentioned my lifelong love affair with Midrash at the beginning of this book, and Midrashim have appeared and will continue to appear throughout its remainder.) Midrash is the profoundest and most indigenously Jewish and hence most authoritative theology ever to emerge within Judaism. What makes it both profound and indigenously Jewish is that it takes the form not of propositions and systems put forward (or perhaps even "demonstrated") as true, but rather of stories and parables: These never pretend to have all the answers; moreover, the beliefs expressed in them are not binding. If, nevertheless, the world of Midrash is authoritative, it is because there are limits to the liberty of the Midrashic story teller. To illustrate with the issue uppermost in the theological mind of the second half of the twentieth century, there are Midrashim relating that God weeps, is in exile, accuses Himself, or in other ways suggest that God has not, or could not have, prevented catastrophe. The divine powerlessness suggested here, however, is always only temporary, and the faith in God's redemptive power, to be sure, is tested but not destroyed. Nietzsche's tale of the death of God (taken over by the recent

God-is-dead theologians) may doubtless be considered a Midrash. It is, however, a Christian or "post-Christian" Midrash. Within Judaism it is impossible.

Midrash is the term for an individual story or parable. It is also used for the numerous Midrash collections that generally take the form of commentaries on books of the Tenach. (Thus there is a Midrash Genesis, Midrash Exodus, and so on.) Within the Talmud, the Midrashic element is known as Aggada. The far larger, more difficult, and also more authoritative element of the Talmud, however, is legal discussions, or Halacha. If the Halachic parts of the Talmud surpass the Aggadic in authority (though not, I believe, in importance), it is because of one altogether crucial difference between Aggada and Halacha: Unlike the beliefs expressed in the former, the laws expressed in the latter are binding. There is therefore strictly speaking no such phenomenon as "Orthodox Judaism," and we employ that term in these pages only because it is universally accepted. The correct term would be not "orthodoxy ("correct belief") but "orthopraxy" ("repository of correct practice").

Then how can the teachings of the schools of Hillel and Shammai both be "the words of the living God" when the controversies between them are mostly of a Halachic nature? In theory both are true, is the reply, and consequently both are to be studied. In practice, however, only one can be followed, and the school to follow was generally ruled to be that of Hillel. This, however, is only an immediate answer; left undecided is what authority will decide which school, in each given case, one is to follow, a question the import of which is still further accentuated by the fact that in many a Halachic debate in the Talmud no conclusion is reached. As we shall see in the section immediately following, many a modern wishes that the question of authority had been left undecided. In point of historical fact, however, it was decided. Orthodox Judaism has a third great book, next in importance only to the Tenach and the Talmud—the Shulchan Aruch, composed by Joseph Karo (1488–1575).

The Talmud is not a code of law. Legal decisions are preceded by lengthy, complicated discussions and sometimes not reached at all. The legal decisions, moreover, are not systematically arranged.

The first attempt at a code, composed of legal decisions alone and arranged in systematic order, is the Mishne Torah of Maimonides. But it was the Shulchan Aruch that became authoritative. And so complete was its acceptance that an abbreviated, simplified version of it, the Kitzur Shulchan Aruch, intended for the use of *amcha*, became the most widely read book among Eastern European Jewry. It is said to have remained most widely read until both that Jewry and its Judaism were murdered in the Holocaust.

PROTEST MOVEMENTS

Our present theme "The Jew of Today and the Jewish Bible" has thus far led us to rabbinic-Halachic Judaism alone; and that this latter was in fact normative from the Pharisees to modern times is undeniable. Even so it is erroneous to believe that the advent of pluralism in Judaism coincides with the advent of modernity. This is shown by the fact of protest movements against the dominant rabbinic-Halachic Judaism, in premodern as well as modern times. Perhaps the most powerful of these is kabbalistic Judaism. This form of Judaism was in due course to return to Halachic orthodoxy. But it began as a protest movement against this orthodoxy, and in its bolder spirits continues to seek to go beyond it, or even circumvent or reject it outright, in order to seek a direct, Halachically unmediated, mystical access to the Deity. Rabbinic Judaism warns against the study of Genesis, chapter 1, and Ezekiel, chapter 1, by those too young or too unlearned: Speculations on the origins of the world or the nature of the Deity, the subject of these two chapters, can lead to dangerous error. It is precisely on such speculations, however, that the Kabbala concentrates. (For more on this subject, see chapter 14.) Hasidism, too, is a premodern movement that ends up returning to orthodoxy but begins as a protest movement. A Hasidic story tells of a unlearned, nearly illiterate youth who attends Yom Kippur services all day long, from the early hours of the morning until the shadows of evening fall, until the "gates of *teshuvah*," having been open, are about to be closed. His heart is full, but all he knows is the Hebrew alphabet. So he spends the entire day reciting the alphabet again and again, saying each time he comes to the end, "O God, I cannot put the letters together! You do it for me, please! You know what is in my heart!" The prayer, we are told, was accepted. Once Hillel had uttered the profound but harsh dictum that an ignorant person cannot be pious, and a vast tradition of pious learning had been built on that belief. Now Israel Ben Eliezer, the so-called Ba'al Shem Tov ("Master of the Good Name," 1699–1760) and founder of Hasidism, initiated a protest movement against the exaltation of the learned mind in behalf of the purity of the heart—a protest epitomized perfectly in that Yom Kippur prayer that, though all but illiterate, is yet accepted. There is, then, a Jewish pluralism in premodern times, and more examples than just these two could be given. Jewish legitimacy, therefore, cannot be denied to modern protest movements simply because they are modern.

The Italian Jewish scholar Samuel David Luzzatto (1800–1865) was a fervent traditionalist. He also was a fervent Jew. Yet it was because of and not despite these commitments that he made one of the keenest attacks ever made on that cornerstone of orthodoxy, the Shulchan Aruch. It was an "Atticist" streak, he argues, that caused Maimonides to compose his Halachic code, its order systematic, its paragraphs fixed and frozen, i.e., Halachic conclusions divorced from the living debates that precede them in the Talmud. Had this unfortunate Greek import into Judaism not prevailed through the Shulchan Aruch, Luzzatto argues, the Halacha might well have retained the living flexibility that it possessed in former times. Luzzatto was an early pioneer of Conservative Judaism.

Of liberal or Reform Judaism the profoundest exponent thus far has been the German-Jewish philosopher Hermann Cohen (1842–1918). Superficially this movement within Judaism may seem to be nothing more than an attempt to keep up with modern times. At its most profound, however, it springs from the conflict between the claim of past authority, that of a revealed canon included, and the modern claim of the free, "autonomous" moral and religious conscience. No modern thinker sides more emphatically than Cohen with the claim of conscience against authority, that of a divinely revealed Tenach included. Yet he finds that very claim

not merely endorsed in the Tenach but proclaimed with a radicalism that dwarfs the radicals of modernity. "Make you a new heart
and a new spirit," the prophet Ezekiel makes God say unto Israel
(Ez. 18:31). To Cohen this passage is fundamental, and he sees
it as dwarfing in radicalism nearly all modern claims in behalf of
human freedom and moral responsibility. Hence it is from the
ancient "sources of Judaism" that the modern Jew—nay, modern
man as a whole—must learn "the religion of reason." Moreover,
from the knowledge of an unheard-of human freedom springs an
unheard-of hope. That hope is needed by modernity, but on its
own is inaccessible to modernity. Modernity must "borrow" it from
the Jewish prophets. It is the hope for the Messianic unity of
mankind.

There is yet a third modern protest movement of which mention
must be made. In our time it has moved into the center of most
things Jewish. It is the Zionist movement and its chief product,
the State of Israel. The relation between these and Judaism in our
time it would be premature to consider at this point. (See below,
chapter 11.) The mention of Zionism as a protest movement is
not. Modern Zionism protests, minimally, against the pious acceptance of exile and, maximally, against Judaism altogether. That
even in its maximal form its protest falls within our present theme
is shown in contrast with Christianity. Like all the others mentioned, Christianity is a protest movement against rabbinic Judaism. Unlike the others, however, it takes the Jewish book outside
the sphere of the Jewish people and its history. Zionism, in contrast, is of the Jewish people and its history; and that without the
Jewish book it is unthinkable its very name suffices to prove. Zionism is yet another protest movement within the theme "The Jew
of Today and the Jewish Bible."

BIBLICAL CRITICISM

On learning of modern protest movements within Judaism a Jew
today is tempted to side without further ado with one of these, if
only because he shares their modernity. He cannot in honesty do

so, however, without first contemplating the amazing vitality of Orthodox Judaism through the ages and in our own time. Kabbalistic Judaism may have begun as an anti-Halachic protest; it soon returned to the Halacha. And what has been true of the Kabbala has also been true of Hasidism, one of the most vital forms of Jewish orthodoxy in our time. Let us give three further examples of such vitality.

First, in the view of Spinoza, Judaism "emasculates" its followers since it makes them pray to God for help against their persecutors rather than inspiring them to help themselves: On beholding Orthodox Jewish soldiers in Israel today, he would be forced to concede that Judaism no longer emasculates. Second, Luzzatto once accused the Shulchan Aruch of reducing Jewish tradition to sterile fixity: He would have to withdraw this judgment, at least in part, on beholding a feminist movement within Orthodox Judaism, small but vigorous, that keeps insisting that "where there is a rabbinic will there is a Halachic way." Third, there are today *ba'al teshuvah* who would invoke Ezekiel's "make you a new heart and a new spirit" in order to justify, not the freedom of the newest, but a free submission to the authority of the oldest: These would require a Hermann Cohen today at least partly to revise his philosophy.

In short, justice in modern protests against traditional orthodoxy lies automatically as little with the protests as it does with the reality protested against. We have above cited Abraham J. Heschel to the effect that pluralism is the will of God. His Jewish statement to a Roman Catholic audience, a critique, to be sure, of Catholic claims to a monopoly on truth, had its heart and soul in a spirit of mediation. It is well to bring this spirit to bear on differing—nay, conflicting—forms of Judaism as well, to approach these conflicts with the belief that here too pluralism is the will of God.

But there is surely one subject on which mediation is impossible, and possible is at most an agreement, more or less amicable, to disagree. That subject is biblical criticism. We have seen from the start that whereas those of premodern mind receive the past on the authority of a "tradition" at least equal to other forms of knowledge, those of modern mind can only reach out for the past in an attempt to reconstruct it. It is this modern stance, manifest not only in science but also in the writing of critical history, that once gave rise to Lessing's modern theological dilemma that in turn necessitated a new way of theological thought. (See above, chapter 1, section 2.) And it was only a question of time for this new way of thought to give rise to a new discipline, known as biblical criticism.

Modern historiography understands itself as critically reconstructing the past rather than passively receiving it from past authorities. Once this step is taken no distinction is possible either between secular and sacred facts, or between the sources through which the facts are to be reconstructed. Hence as early as in the seventeenth century various writers used literary and historical criteria for the study of the Torah and came to postulate a plurality of sources from which an unknown redactor had composed the whole. The Torah uses two words for God: YHVH and *Elohim*. The critics postulated two different authors, the so-called Jahvist ("J") and the so-called Elohist ("E"). On the grounds (among others) of the relative self-containedness of the book, "D" was postulated as author of Deuteronomy. Then came "P" as author of most or all of the legal and priestly material. And then of course there had to be "R," the redactor who put it all together. Much of this preceded the works of Julius Wellhausen (1844–1918). If it is his works that are correctly described by Leo Strauss as "stirring up the greatest storms" (chapter 1, section 2), it was not only because Wellhausen, a gifted writer, found his readers far beyond the circles of professional scholarship. More importantly, it was because the so-called Graf-Wellhausen hypothesis made "P" into a very late source—as late as the period following the Babylonian exile. Thus the book once believed to have been written by Moses came to be viewed as written over a period of many centuries; and its legal materials, so important to Orthodox Judaism, fell into so "late" a period in the history of Judaism as to lose, by dint of that fact alone, much of their former authority. No wonder the first reaction to biblical criticism by Jewish spokesmen was negative, and by no means only from the ranks of orthodoxy. Isaac Mayer

Wise (1819–1900), the founder of American Reform Judaism, rejected biblical criticism.

But can biblical criticism in principle be rejected by those of modern mind? One may charge rightly that such as Wellhausen dealt rashly and in a debunking spirit with a text that, after all, had been preserved with minute care by many generations of devoted scholars: More recent biblical critics have had to become much more conservative. One may also charge fairly that bias invariably crept into the supposedly "scientific" theories of the earlier critics: Biblical Judaism was almost invariably seen as somehow "evolving" in the direction of Christianity; postexilic Judaism, though biblical still, became "late" Judaism, as if destined to die with the advent of Christianity; and more of the same. All this led Solomon Schechter (1848–1915), a great figure in American Conservative Judaism, to quip that the higher criticism was the higher antisemitism. His quip is not wholly out of date yet: The critics, mostly Protestant, to this day are markedly more enthusiastic in operating on the "Old Testament" than on the New.

All this, however, while justifying suspicion of this or that theory of this or that critic, does not justify the rejection of biblical criticism. Consider the following, purely speculative, possibility. A young Jewish scholar has been brought up as an Orthodox Jew. But he is also a modern critical historian, committed to the methods of modern scholarship. Much to his joy and astonishment he comes upon new evidence indicating not only that that man Moses actually existed but that he composed the entire Torah (save only the last seven verses), exactly as the tradition has maintained all along. Would this reinstate the premodern, authoritarian basis of Jewish belief? Unless the principles of scholarship were abandoned, it would not. The new theory replacing Wellhausen and all the rest would still be only just that—a theory. It would be one theory among all the others, that is, subject to future revision or replacement in the light of possible future new evidence. The dilemma of Lessing would still be with us, and with us it will remain.

Then what did Leo Strauss mean when he wrote that in his time "it was granted by all except the most backward that the Jewish faith had not been refuted by . . . history," that "the storms stirred up by . . . Wellhausen had been weathered," and that one "could grant to . . . history everything . . . [it] seem[s] to teach regarding . . . the Jahvist, the Elohist . . . and so on, without abandoning one iota of the substance of the Jewish faith?" Perhaps he had in mind a letter written in 1927 by Franz Rosenzweig (1886–1929) to Jacob Rosenheim, a leader of German-Jewish orthodoxy. (Strauss had dedicated his first book, published in 1930, to the memory of Rosenzweig, who had died the year before.) Together with his friend Buber, Rosenzweig was then engaged in translating the Tenach into German, a great project which, following Rosenzweig's death, Buber completed alone. In his letter Rosenzweig confesses that Buber and Rosenzweig felt as close to no previous translation as to that of Samson Raphael Hirsch, the nineteenth-century founder of modern orthodoxy. (Hirsch's influence is felt to this day.) He went on to state one difference, however, between Hirsch on the one hand, and his colleague and himself on the other: Unlike Hirsch, they "could derive no conclusions concerning the literary origin and philological value of the Biblical text handed down to us" from their "belief in the holiness . . . and revealed status of the Torah." If all of Wellhausen's theories were correct, he went on pursuing the point, Buber's and his own faith would "not be touched in the slightest," whereas for Hirsch it was obviously otherwise. He concluded by saying that here there was obviously a gulf that could be bridged by mutual respect but not by mutual understanding. At any rate, he, Rosenzweig, "did not understand the faith-foundation of Hirsch's commentary."

Then why was the Buber-Rosenzweig translation, nevertheless, closer in spirit to that of Hirsch than to any of the others? Rosenzweig does not say, but the answer is obvious. If "no conclusions" can be derived from the "belief . . . in the revealed status of the Torah" concerning the "literary origin and philological value" of the present biblical text, then the reverse is true as well: The belief in the revealed status of the Torah does not depend on the Wellhausens of this world and their theories. They may refute what theologians call "verbal inspiration," the doctrine of a divinely handed-down text. But we have already indicated and shall show more fully later on (see chapters 1, section 2; 4, sections 1 and 5) that Jewish thought rarely embraced so primitive a view of revelation, implying as it does that, had there been tape recorders at the time, Moses could have spared himself the trouble of ascending the mountain and sent a machine instead. Revelation is primordially a divine presence, an incursion into the world of man, necessitating a distinction between the event of revelation itself and a text that it "stimulates." (Buber's expression; see further chapter 4, section 5.) This is the doctrine that Rosenzweig embraces, and it implies both that biblical criticism cannot refute revelation, and that no objections in principle can be made to biblical criticism in the name of faith.

Objections may be made, however, to *irreverent* criticism. I remember an incident from my student days at the *Hochschule* when I was already influenced by Buber and Rosenzweig without, however, a sufficient grasp of their thought. Our Tenach professor was Moshe Sister, an outstanding teacher and a temperamental person whom we loved dearly for his sense of humor, his complete lack of professorial pomposity, and above all, for the high philological and critical demands he made on us. (No one made us work as hard as Moshe Sister, and now that I struggle again with Hebrew in Israel, one thing supports me greatly—grammar as drilled into us by Sister nearly fifty years ago.) Sister was a radical critic, his negative attitude toward the text reinforced by his Marxism. This is why, though I loved him, I always fought with him. Once when his tearing the text apart seemed too much I kept on arguing for the text's integrity. At length he hollered: "Use your reason, man! Then you'll admit that the text is corrupt!" I shot back: "Maybe my reason is corrupt!" Such obscurantism left Sister speechless.

My argument, of course, was clumsy and incompetent. Only much later did I come upon the way Rosenzweig makes the point beautifully, at the end of his letter to Rosenheim. The critics who so rashly dissect the text, ever-ready to declare this or that text corrupt, presuppose a low view, not only of all those generations of scribes who so devoutly preserved every word of the text, but also of "R," the anonymous redactor. But why would anyone except a "higher antisemite" assume that "R," presumably himself devoutly concerned with the text, was careless, foolish, or both? Rosenzweig writes: "We do not know who was the concluding redactor of the Torah. . . . That it was Moses we cannot believe. . . . However, for us "R" stands not for 'Redactor' but for 'Rabbenu'—our teacher."

THE TENACH—SACRED OR NATIONAL HISTORY?

There is a Christian theological term that is applied especially to the "Old Testament." Like so many others, the term is German and used untranslated by English-speaking theologians. *Heil* ("salvation") has a *Geschichte* ("history") in which the Jewish people have a well-defined role. From Adam through Abraham, through the Exodus, through Sinai unto the last of the prophets there is manifest a *Heilsgechichte* until finally, at the proper *kairos* (Greek, "ripeness of time") salvation reaches its climax in the Christ of Christianity. Consequently the "Old Testament" is both contained in, and superseded by, the New Testament, and the *Geschichte* of the "old" Israel is over and done with, or very nearly so, with the advent of a "new"—the Christian church.

In these days of pluralism, the case for Christian supersession over Jews and Judaism is not often stated as baldly as once it was. Among Christians seeking "dialogue" with Jews, supersession may even be abandoned altogether, for one does not, after all, seek dialogue with an anachronism. (On this subject, see chapter 12, section 5.) However, even when Christians view Judaism as alive and Jews as living dialogue partners, they are very nearly bound to continue to read their "Old Testament" differently from the way in which Jews read their Tenach. We have already mentioned that in a church service the Bible, both "Old" and "New Testament," is quoted selectively, whereas in the traditional synagogue service at least one-third of the Tenach is read in its entirety each and every year. Let us look somewhat closer at the Christian selectivity. Rare must be the pastor who would select the book of Esther for his Scriptural reading with a view to preaching his sermon on it. One theologian I know has gone so far as to suggest that the book be dropped from the Christian Bible. For a Jew, the dropping of this book from the Tenach would be unthinkable.

Never was this as evident as it is today. Several schools are located near our Jerusalem apartment. We walk the streets at Purim time and see children by the hundreds, dressed up not only as Mordecai, Esther, Ahasverus, and the "bad guy" Haman, but also as Superman, Wonder Woman, and the like. Purim is supposed to last for a day, and to be celebrated in the synagogue and the home. The children have decreed that it is to be celebrated in the streets as well, and that it is to last for the better part of a week. The Christian reader of his "Old Testament" skips from prophet to prophet, from saint to saint, on the grounds that "not all Israel is Israel" (the apostle Paul in Romans 9:6). For him, in short, the "Old Testament" is *Heilsgeschichte* only, and would remain so even if Christian supersession over Judaism were totally abandoned. For the Jewish reader, in contrast, the Tenach contains not only sacred but also plain history, the history of one people—his own. And that for him all Israel *is* Israel is never more evident than during that week in Jerusalem when the children decide to celebrate in the streets, and for more than just the one day. (Last year our Yossi, aged six, wavered between being a gobot and Superman, but decided on Superman.) Never does the view of Jews as a fossil, a ghost people, an anachronism, seem as plainly absurd as during that week in Jerusalem; and never does our Aliyah seem so meaningful to Rose and myself as when we contemplate the fact that in coming we brought with us not only Suzy and David, both now grown up, but Yossi as well. ("Aliyah" ["ascent"] is the term for immigration to the land of Israel, just as "Yeridah" ["descent"] is the term for emigration from it. Both terms are hallowed by tradition and charged with emotion to this day. That the emotion has religious overtones, even in the case of Aliyah by secularists, is best indicated by the fact that "Aliyah" is also the term for being called to the reading of the Torah during a synagogue service.)

A Jew must recover his Tenach from Christian spiritualizing at all times. In our time, however, he is faced with the new task of recovering it from Jewish spiritualizing as well. Consider the following examples. In the traditional Purim and Hanukkah liturgies it is God whose miracles have saved the Jewish people, respectively, from the plot of Haman and the assault of the "wicked Hellenistic regime." In the biblical book of Esther, what saves are the courage and fidelity of Mordecai and Esther, assisted by luck; and in Maccabees I—the book is not in the canon but in my view ought to be—the crucial role in salvation belongs to the valor of the Maccabees. That a Jew today identifies as much with the account in Esther as with the Purim prayer is evident from the example already given—the children in the streets of Jerusalem. And since there would *be* no Jewish children in Jerusalem without the Israeli army, even a Jew continuing to thank God for his miracles feels closer to Maccabees I than he ever did before. Vis-à-vis Jewish as well as Christian piety, then, a Jew today must emphasize that the Tenach is the book of his people as well as *the* Book, the "secular" bound up with the "sacred," a history that affirms a deeper meaning and a divine purpose together with the plain relating of historical facts that claim to be only what they are and nothing more.

Of this togetherness a striking example is found in a text relating to the very beginning of Jewish history. The four long centuries of Egyptian slavery are about to end. The covenantal relation between God and Israel, begun with Abraham, is about to be resumed. At this juncture we find the following passage:

> And it came to pass in the course of those many days that the king of Egypt died; and the children of Israel sighed by reason of the bondage, and they cried, and their cry came up unto God by reason of the bondage. And God heard their groaning, and God remembered His covenant with Abraham, with Isaac, and with Jacob. (Exod. 2:23–24)

Had God forgotten? Heaven forfend, a pious tradition replies whenever the question is raised, and proceeds to ascribe meaning to those grim four hundred years. Perhaps they were deserved punishment, perhaps discipline needed for their future mission, and more of the same. Significantly, however, neither Rashi (1040–1105) nor Nachmanides (ca. 1195–1270)—the first the most popular Tenach commentator, the second perhaps the most profound—comment on the passage "God remembered," and perhaps this omission by both must be taken together with a Midrash cited by both: In this Pharaoh bathes in the blood of Jewish children, in an attempt to be cured of his leprosy. How could a God remembering *that* fail to redeem His people at once? Yet the years of slavery continued to wear on. (Incidentally, Nachmanides is referred to as Ramban, an abbreviation of Rabbi Moses ben Nachman.)

Who is "a Jew today?" He feels at one with Israel if he is not himself Israeli. He also feels at one with Holocaust survivors if he is not himself a survivor. As such he cannot but follow in the footsteps of Rashi and Nachmanides. He too thinks of the blood of the children—and all talk about meaning in those grim four centuries is wiped from his lips. Instead, as he reads the Tenach itself, he has nothing but that bold, powerful, magnificently anthropomorphic phrase: "And God remembered." That and nothing else.

For a Jew today, then, the Tenach is a book of national as well as one of sacred history. For many a good Jew, especially in Israel, it is national history and nothing else. More precisely, since much of the history harks back to the mythical past, it contains the national mythology of the Jewish people, much as the Homeric epics contain the national mythology of the Greeks.

There is much to be said in favor of this comparison. "Athens and Jerusalem" is an abiding theme in Western civilization. The Tenach and the Homeric works are classics by any literary standard, and classics are inexhaustible. A Jew in our time, however, cannot dwell on such similarities without also being struck by at least one difference, the implications of which are of great moment: There is a Greek as well as a Jewish Diaspora; but no Greek ever returned to Greece because of the *Iliad* or the *Odyssey*.

EPILOGUE

Rose and I met Arkady Tsinober at the beginning of our 1977 pilgrimage to refuseniks in the Soviet Union, in Riga. Our meeting with Col. Lev Ofsischer of Minsk occurred close to the end of our journey. Tsinober has long been permitted to leave for Israel. Ofsischer is in Minsk still, and one fears that permission to leave will be denied him again and again.

Who is Lev Ofsischer? As a flier in World War II he downed a large number of German planes in the battle for Stalingrad, that great turning point in the war. He was recognized as Hero of the Soviet Union, with his name and photograph appearing in a book that he showed to us. But he also showed us the latest edition from which his name and picture have been excised. He is a hero no more. Nor is he still a colonel, for he was reduced to the rank of private and deprived of his pension. All this happened because some time after the Six-Day War Ofsischer applied for permission to leave for Israel. Why is it denied him? With the KGB one never knows, and this uncertainty is surely part of deliberate policy. In Ofsischer's case, however, the reason seems plain: The Soviet authorities do not wish the world to know how their state rewards its heroes.

Why did Ofsischer take his fateful step? We know only what he told us himself. Some time in the early sixties a Baptist of his acquaintance told him that he knew why he himself remained in the Soviet Union but that he, Ofsischer, ought to be in Israel. Having said this, he presented Ofsischer with a Bible. During the two hours or so of our visit our host excused himself several times, opened his Bible, and read a page or two in it.

Has Ofsischer become a religious Jew? We did not ask him in 1977, any more than I asked such questions of that Jew way back in that jail cell in 1938. All we know is what he himself told us. On the VE Day observances that had occurred just before our visit, he had addressed a group of Jews, had told them to be proud of their Jewish history, and had warned them against being affected by the semiofficial antisemitic slander. (He made a tape of his speech for us.) When urged by friends to withdraw his application and have his pension restored, he replied that he must choose between his pension and his honor. And when urged by the KGB to give up, seeing that he had already waited for nearly a decade, he crystallized the theme "The Jew of Today and the Jewish Bible" as few other testimonies do. "You are wrong," he replied, "I have waited for nearly two thousand years. And I can wait a few more."

4. RECEIVING THE JEWISH
BOOK AS TORAH,
OR, REVELATION BETWEEN
CREATION AND REDEMPTION

HOLDING ONESELF OPEN TO FAITH

Not too long after I entered the *Hochschule* I had an experience
of the kind that occurs but rarely in one's lifetime: I read an essay
that changed my life. To put it less grandiosely, it gave me the
first glimpse of what I was looking for. But has it stood the test of
time? The test even of *our* time? Over the years I have reread it
with this question in mind, most recently in connection with this
book. And I concluded: Yes, on the whole, this essay, written by
Martin Buber in 1926, has stood the test of time. The test even of
our time.

Not that it has done so in every respect. The most important
exception is indicated in Buber's title: "The Man of Today and
the Jewish Bible." Way back in 1926, who was Buber's "Man of
Today"? Since Europe was still considered the heart of civilization,
he was the central European intellectual, a child of modernity and
enlightenment but disillusioned with both, who wondered whether
intellectual honesty might not permit him to find his way back to

his ancestral faith; and of this European man in general a Jew in particular was but one case. More than half a century later, we find ourselves in a very different situation. Even after World War I Europe was no longer the heart of civilization. Following World War II it has become more marginal than could have been imagined even in 1926. "Worlds" have emerged—"first," "second," "third," the last subdivided into who knows how many—most of which were beneath serious notice then. Indeed, the very meaning of "modern" and "today" has changed when savage fanatics, religious and other, can no longer be dismissed as relics from the Dark Ages.

Is there, then, any one single "Man of Today"? Even if, despite all, there is such a person, the Jew of today could no longer be viewed as but one of his several manifestations. Throughout the ages a Jew has had a unique relation to the Jewish Bible, his Torah. This was so until modern times. A unique relation has reemerged in our time between "The Jew of Today and the Jewish Bible," and one need but think of Col. Lev Ofsischer of Minsk in order to recognize the fact. Not accidentally does the chapter just completed bear the title just mentioned—or end with Ofsischer, a man still waiting for his share in the writing of a new page in Jewish history: a man armed in his heroic patience, so far as my wife and I know, with nothing but the Jewish book.

What, then, in Buber's essay has stood the test of time?

> Biblia, "books" [in the plural] . . . is in truth one Book . . . , united by the basic theme of the encounter between a group of people and the Nameless One, whom they dare to name as they are being addressed and in turn address Him—the encounter between the two in history . . .

What an opening sentence! Pushed to the margins are all scholarly disputes, important though they doubtless are, about the origin of this or that source of this or that biblical book. Moved into the center is the crucial issue—"the encounter between a group of people and the Nameless One." That the biblical authors believed in such encounters is doubted only by Marxist and similar ideologues who view them as swindling priests scheming to manipulate "the masses." And no one at all can doubt that such as Abraham, Moses, the prophets, the psalmist believed themselves not to be alone in the world but rather "addressed" by God as well as "in turn address[ing] Him."

One may of course doubt the truth of what they believed. It is possible even to deny that Abraham and Moses ever existed. But both they and their belief most certainly did exist in the minds and hearts of countless Jewish generations. They did believe in the "encounters with the Nameless One" of ages past—and not infrequently had such encounters of their own. Buber employs the expression "Nameless One" in order to indicate that these were not encounters with the long-familiar gods of whom Thales, the first Greek philosopher (ca. 636–546 B.C.E.) had reported that "the world" was "full." These encounters were with the one God beyond the world (hence nameless) who yet entered into the world. That the world is open to His incursion is the core of what may be called biblical faith. And that core was stubbornly held fast to—both by the biblical writers and by Jewish readers of their writings—even in times when no such incursion took place, when the "Nameless One" was said to "hide His Face," to "have abandoned," to "hear not" (e.g., Ps. 22:2, 44:24, 88:28).

Such was the faith of "the group of people" whose history the Tenach records; its faith and that of the authors of their history; the faith of both these and of the countless generations of Jewish readers. We cannot but grant that *they* believed it. Informed as we are, however, by Copernicus and Galileo, by Newton and Einstein, by Darwin and Freud, can we believe it ourselves? Must we not rather reduce all such supposed encounters to so many illusions? Does not intellectual integrity require us to view the world as closed to incursions of divinity into it?

For my part, if Buber's opening sentence defines the core of biblical faith, his answer to the question just posed has occupied me for a lifetime. Probing it, testing it, refining it, over the decades I have sought out not only the Jewish sources but also the great modern philosophers, Spinoza and Kant, Schelling and Hegel, Nietzsche and Heidegger, to name only the most important. (In the process I discovered—not that it matters—that Buber is not all that original.) And I come back to that Buber passage that has accompanied me for a lifetime and say: Yes, it has stood the test of time. The test even of our time. The passage reads as follows:

> Certainty of faith is not accessible to the Man of Today, nor can it be made accessible to him. . . . But he is not denied the possibility of holding himself open to faith. . . . He too may open himself to this book and let its rays strike him where they will . . .

Buber proceeds to explain that a person who follows this counsel "does not believe anything a priori; he does not disbelieve anything a priori. . . . Nothing is prejudged. The current of time flows on, and the contemporary character of this man becomes itself a receiving vessel."

As over the decades I have examined and reexamined that passage and its implications (and, of course, many other passages by Buber as well as many other thinkers), I have come to conclude that nothing in science, history, psychology, philosophy, or any other relevant discipline demonstrates that the world of man is closed to the incursion of the Divine; as well as that nothing in theology, philosophy, or any other relevant discipline demonstrates that it is open. To "hold himself open" to faith was the appropriate religious stance for Buber's "Man of Today" several generations ago. It remains the appropriate religious stance for our "Jew of Today." He is a Jew who wonders whether what already is the Jewish book for him can be received by him as Torah.

CREATION

My thoughts go back to *amcha* in general and that man in that jail cell in particular. How are such as he to hold themselves open to faith? It cannot be necessary for them to study this or that philosophy or theology. Yet if without doing so they open the first page of the Tenach and read of how in the beginning God created heaven and earth and on the sixth day created Man in His own image, they can hardly avoid becoming involved in debates about science and religion. They have learned in school about dinosaurs and cavemen. So, at any rate, one hopes—that their school was not so bigoted as to ban the teaching of Darwin's theory of evolution. Then how without philosophy can they avoid becoming involved in debates that according to Leo Strauss were already "backward" more than half a century ago?

Whether or not the biblical creation story was ever meant to provide information about the origins of the universe is a question best left unanswered in these pages. (We have no need of an answer.) What matters for us is that within Judaism Creation has always been a *present* experience also—and that for one who "holds himself open to faith" a possible present experience it remains. On waking each morning a Jew at prayer acknowledges the Creation renewed, for not only he but the world might have passed out of existence overnight. And the Creation thus acknowledged each day is experienced each week on Shabbat, for Shabbat is the feast of Creation.

The shadows of Shabbat eve fall, and a solemn serenity descends upon a Jew as he makes himself ready to participate in *kabbalat Shabbat*, the "reception of the Sabbath." (According to tradition a "higher soul" enters into him for that day, to depart when the day is done.) Part of that reception is the chanting of six psalms. Anyone who truly receives the Shabbat experiences Creation. Anyone who understands these psalms understands what Creation means. The last, climactic psalm of the group of six reads as follows:

Ascribe unto the Lord, O ye sons of might,
Ascribe unto the Lord glory and strength.
Ascribe unto the Lord the glory due to His name;
Worship the Lord in the beauty of holiness.
The voice of the Lord is upon the waters;
The God of glory thundereth, even the Lord upon many waters.
The voice of the Lord is powerful;
The voice of the Lord is full of majesty.
The voice of the Lord breaketh the cedars;
Yea, the Lord breaketh in pieces the cedars of Lebanon.
He maketh them also skip like a calf;
Lebanon and Sirion like a young wild-ox.

The voice of the Lord heweth out flames of fire.
The voice of the Lord shaketh the wilderness;
The Lord shaketh the wilderness of Kadesh.
The voice of the Lord maketh the hinds to calve.
And strippeth the forests bare;
And in His temple all say: "Glory."
The Lord sat enthroned at the flood;
Yea, the Lord sitteth as King for ever.
The Lord will give strength unto His people;
The Lord will bless His people with peace. (Ps. 29)

We have cited this psalm in full. We have had to cite it in full, because of its testimony. It testifies neither to a divine omnipotence that is absent, nor to a divine presence that is lacking in omnipotence. What the psalm does testify to is the presence of divine omnipotence. This presence is therefore overwhelming and all-shattering. The cedars of Lebanon are broken, or—a different image—they skip like a calf. The wilderness is shaken. The forest is stripped bare. And then it comes, the wonder of wonders: One opens one's eyes, as it were, and behold, the cedars, the forest, the desert are not, as they ought to be, annihilated. The cedars, skipping and broken, stand before us unimpaired. The wilderness is steadfast. The trees of the forest are rich with foliage.

Why is nature not annihilated by the presence of omnipotence? And why is the psalmist who experiences that presence not *himself* annihilated—annihilated at least in experience, dissolved into stark terror? These questions do not arise for one to whom his world is closed to the incursion of the Divine: For him the presence of omnipotence is merely a "subjective experience," and the psalm that testifies to it, only "poetry." The questions are fully real, however, for one who "holds himself open to faith."

The answer to the question is Creation. There is an initial terror in the psalmist's experience; but it transmutes itself into awe, into reverence, and at length into praise. And as the experience occurs and is transmuted, nature, annihilated by the presence of omnipotence, is restored and handed over as a gift; and the one that receives the gift is restored to himself as a gift also. Hence the psalm ends with praise unto Him who gives unto His people strength and peace. Such is the experience of Creation. For him who holds himself open to faith, such, also, is the reality of Creation.

The liturgy of *kabbalat Shabbat* has led us to a remarkable conclusion. Over the centuries deep thinkers—Jewish, Christian, Muslim, philosophical in general—have pondered the enigma of Creation. If God is everything, must the world not be nothing? And if the world is something, must not God be less than everything? At length these deep thinkers found no way of "saving" Creation except the mystery and miracle of a divinity that in its power needs no world yet in its love wishes or chooses to need it. Our remarkable conclusion is this: The miracle and mystery discovered by deep thinkers only after much labor of sophisticated thought has been experienced by *amcha* whenever and wherever Shabbat has been truly "received." And the Shabbat eve service that begins with *kabbalat Shabbat* ends with the Kiddush ("sanctification") "in memory of the works of the beginning."

A WORLD IN NEED OF REDEMPTION

This is how Shabbat begins. Its end could be in no sharper contrast. Psalms recited express apprehension. (A sample: "Thou shalt not be afraid of terror by night, nor of the arrow that flies by day" [Ps. 91:5].) And as one reaches the *havdala*—the liturgical "separation" of the "holy" Shabbat from the "profane" week—there occurs one of the most haunting passages in the entire liturgy of Judaism:

> O Guardian of Israel,
> Guard Thy people Israel,
> Lest those perish
> Who proclaim "Hear, O Israel [the Lord thy God,
> the Lord is One].

The people that have just spent Shabbat celebrating the goodness of the Creation fear—have reason to fear—that it might not survive until the next Shabbat. The world is not—no longer is—what it is said to be in the opening chapters of the Tenach and in such texts as the Twenty-ninth Psalm.

Then why did these texts not become in the course of time for Jews what Homer and Hesiod became for Greeks? The *Theogony* of Hesiod bears a striking resemblance to the opening pages of the Tenach. Both works begin with a golden age. In both texts, too, that age is past, in the one case because of the expulsion from the Garden of Eden, in the other because the golden age has yielded, successively, to one of silver, bronze, ending up with the present age of iron. There is, however, no Greek counterpart to Shabbat on which the world is ever again received, renewed, and celebrated as Creation. Hesiod's myth of the golden age therefore serves but to disclose the tragic discrepancy between the condition a Greek longs for and the condition in which he exists. If it is otherwise for a Jew, it is because of Shabbat. Shabbat survives to this day and, as a passage in the Reform Jewish *Union Prayer Book* puts it, "Just as Israel has kept Shabbat so Shabbat has kept Israel." Hence whatever the condition in which a Jew may exist, "tragic" is not the correct word to describe it.

Because of their love for—nay, infatuation with—all things Greek, Western intellectuals have therefore often charged Judaism with a superficial, crass, and vulgar optimism. The Creation is good? Is there no Jewish sensitivity to the evils of pain, disease, hatred, war—indeed, to the fundamental contradiction between the eternity that is man's aspiration and death that is his lot? Socrates dies giving thanks to Asclepius, the Greek god of medicine, on the grounds that death will relieve him of that great disease, life itself. Abraham dies of good old age, full of years (Gen. 25:8), satisfied for no more profound reason than his knowledge that Isaac will live.

That a certain optimism is a basic trait of Judaism is undeniable. But is it a crass, vulgar, "materialistic" clinging to the goods of this world, insensitive to its evils? "The inclination [*yetzer*] of man's hearts is evil from his youth" (Gen. 8:21), God exclaims when, after having destroyed a wicked world through the flood, he vows not to do such a thing again. In the Midrash a *yetzer* is called poor indeed if it is called evil by its own Creator (*Yotzer*), and else-

where that Creator is pictured as accusing Himself for the damage
He has caused by creating the evil inclination.

In Midrashim such as these, then, the Creation is viewed as
flawed. Elsewhere the rabbis go a huge step further. Consider the
following Talmudic report:

> For two-and-a-half years the schools of Shammai and Hillel car-
> ried on a dispute. One said it would have been better for Man
> not to have been created; the other, that it is better for Man to
> be created. Then they voted and agreed that it would have been
> better for him not to have been created. However, since he is cre-
> ated, let him examine his past deeds. Another interpretation: let
> him reflect on his future actions.

In a debate basic enough to last for two and a half years, and between two schools than which none are more authoritative in
Judaism, the vote finally cast was in favor of a view fully as stark
about earthly existence as that expressed by Socrates on the thresh-
old of death. Yet the theme with which that vote ends is quite
other than the tragic theme of the Greeks. What emerges here for
us, for the first but by no means last time in this book, is a trait
essential to Judaism, namely, a very specific stubbornness. A Jew
may find himself assailed by the worst of miseries of this world,
yet he refuses to let go of the goodness of the Creation; and this
stubbornness gives birth to a twofold conviction: that the world
is in need of redemption, and that the redemption needed is sure
to come.

REDEMPTION

> The Lord's mercies are not consumed. . . . They are new every
> morning; great is Thy faithfulness. (Lam. 3:23)

This passage is found, of all incongruous places, in the Book of
Lamentations. In the context of that most grief-stricken of all bib-

lical books, however, the passage is all but lost, all the more because the book ends on a note of near-despair. Such is the Jewish stubbornness, however, as to cause two rabbis not only to take the passage out of its context but also to comment on it as follows:

> It is written, "They are new every day; great is Thy faithfulness." Rabbi Shim'on bar Abba interpreted this: Because Thou renewest us every morning, we know that great is Thy faithfulness to redeem us. Rabbi Alexandri interpreted it: From the fact that Thou renewest us every morning, we know that great is Thy faithfulness to resurrect the dead.

What a giant leap, beyond the world and all its ills, from Creation, an absolute beginning, to a Redemption that is said to be an absolute end! Fully as conscious as a Greek of the fact that history is full of unjust suffering and meaningless strife, a Jew yet looks to its Messianic end that is to redeem it. Fully as aware that "the hope of man is but the worm" (*Abot* 4:4), a Jew yet persists in an ultimate hope in a life beyond the grave.

Not that the hope of a Jew is confined to the sphere of the ultimate. The biblical Hannah, the future mother of Samuel, prays "in the bitterness of soul," for "the Lord has shut her womb"; but she "rejoices" in her "salvation" when her prayer is answered (I Sam. 1:10; 2:1–10). The exiles weep by the rivers of Babylon when they remember Zion (Ps. 137); but when they are "brought back by the Lord" have their "mouths full with laughter," and their "tongues . . . [with] praise" (Ps. 126). Such, for a Jew, is "salvation" within life—that of both man writ small and writ large—when his prayers are answered. When his prayers remain unanswered he yet remains with hope, for his hope has an ultimate dimension, and is universal in scope. There is a world to come, and the righteous of all nations have a share in it. This is for man writ small, the individual. As for man writ large—history—so profound and powerful is the Jewish hope that when, for the first time in history in our own time, the nations of the world united—or attempted to unite—they could find no better motto for their collective enterprise than these words from the Jewish Bible:

And they shall beat their swords into plowshares
And their spears into pruning-hooks;
Nation shall not lift up sword against nation,
Neither shall they learn war any more. (Isa. 2:4)

REVELATION

"When is the Torah given? Whenever a person receives it!" We
have already considered this Midrashic dictum. Now we proceed
to ask just when this "whenever" occurs, and just how the reception of Torah takes place. To turn to the "when" of it first, a Jew
receives the Torah when in his morning prayers he acknowledges
the Creation, and when on Shabbat he celebrates it. He receives it
whenever, tarry though the Messiah may, he renews his stubborn
hope for his eventual coming and when, though at the brink of
the grave, he trusts in God beyond it. Revelation, in short, is the
"midpoint" between Creation at the beginning and Redemption
at the end, and "only on the premise that revelation is a present
experience [that the Torah is given whenever a person receives
it] . . . Creation and Redemption are true." Thus writes Buber
in the essay that, way back in Berlin, gave me a first glimpse of
what I was looking for.

That Revelation is between Creation and Redemption no Jewish believer has ever denied. (With a Christian it is otherwise,
since his climactic revelatory event, the Christ's coming, has itself
redemptive significance.) But just where in this "between"? At
some precisely circumscribed point in history well over three millennia ago, and in a lesser way for some further centuries until
prophecy and revelation ceased altogether? But that even for premodern Judaism this is not the whole story is already obvious from
the Midrashic dictum just recited. On behalf of a modern account
of Revelation Buber writes:

> Revelation is not a fixed, dated point between . . . [Creation
> and Redemption]. The revelation at Sinai is not this midpoint it-
> self, but the perceiving of it, and such perception is possible at
> any time.

It is on this assumption, and on it alone, that "R" can be "Rabbenu" even if he was someone other than Moses. (See above, chapter 3, section 8.) It is on this assumption alone, too, that the modern dilemma concerning a revelation in past history can find a
modern resolution. At the very outset we cited G. E. Lessing as
asking how he could stake his eternal blessedness on a past fact—
his Christ—when this was at best only probable, and we found a
modern Jew confronted with the same dilemma concerning the
event of Sinai. And we could find a resolution only by revolutioniz-
ing the relation between past and present: The past does not come
to the present, through the authority of a "reliable authority":
rather, the present must reach out for the past, and just this is
done by a Jew who, on reading the age-old Book, "lets its rays
strike where they will."

So much for the "when" of receiving the Torah. What of the
"how" of it? One way of answering this question is through the titles
of the chapters to follow in this book. A Jew receives the Torah
whenever he accepts anew his covenantal relation with the God of
his fathers. (See chapter 5.) He receives it whenever he studies the
Torah (see chapter 7), and whenever he walks in its ways (chapters 6, 8, and 9). And all this occurs throughout the cycle of the
Jewish year, a perpetual reenactment of Jewish existence between
Creation and Redemption as it has been, is, and will continue to
be (see chapter 10). It will continue to be so at least among the
faithful, even if these should be reduced—to allude to an image
used by more than one prophet—to a mere remnant. This is one
way of answering the question of the "how" of the reception of the
Torah, and it would be complete were it not for the fact that in
our own time epoch-making events have occurred, in the history
not only of Jews but also of Judaism (see chapters 11–14).

But the "how" question of receiving the Torah requires also another, deeper answer that goes to the bottom for one who, though
thoroughly modern, yet "holds himself open" to the possibility of
revelation. Just how is it possible to "receive" the Torah when its
Giver is said to be divine while its recipients are merely human?

One may hear the question and wonder what the problem is. I
remember once reading somewhere in Muslim literature a story of

how Muhammed received the Koran. One day he was walking
about in the desert. He was alone. He looked at the sky. Something
was falling on to earth. He picked it up: the Koran! There is nothing uniquely Muslim about this story. It could exist in Jewish literature also, and many a Jew acts as though it were the truth. In
the view symbolized by any such story the text has canonical authority since, dropped from heaven by God, He Himself is its
backer; second, while dropping the book on to earth, God Himself
remains in heaven, and a divine presence does not occur even in
the supreme revelatory moment. A Jewish view such as this would
treat texts such as Psalm 29 as "poetry" and nothing more. It
would not even be very good poetry since the experience it conveys means little or nothing.

As if meant to contradict in every respect the image of an authoritative book dropped onto earth by an absent God, one Midrash, in a bold metaphor, has God bend the upper and the lower
heaven upon the top of Mount Sinai, going on to say that only
thus was it possible for the "glory to descend and spread over
Mount Sinai." Another Midrash is more explicit still:

> When God created the world, He decreed: "The heavens are the
> heavens of the Lord, but the earth He has handed over to the
> children of man." (Ps. 115:16) Yet when He was about to give
> the Torah, He rescinded the first decree and said: "Those who
> are below shall ascend to those on high, and those who are on
> high shall descend to those that are below, and I will create a
> new beginning," as it is said, "And the Lord came down upon
> Mount Sinai" (Exod. 19:20), and later, "And unto Moses He
> said, "Come up unto the Lord." (Exod. 24:1)

So radically other than all things human is the God of Israel that
at Creation their dwelling places are set wholly apart, with God
dwelling in heaven even while handing over earth to the children
of man. Yet so radically present is He in the moment of revelation
that a "new beginning" alone can make it possible.

But if God Himself is present in the relevatory moment how
can the divine Word be humanly understood? No such question

arises in the case of a God dropping the Book from heaven: What needs comprehension, in that case, is not God but the book and nothing but the book, and this latter—after all, dropped on to earth!—is fit for the human mind. But what if the divine Speaker Himself is present even as His Word is to be heard?

Once I visited the late Abraham J. Heschel, with whom I was on friendly terms, and found him greatly excited. His excitement was caused by a Midrash he had just read (or, more likely, reread), and which he wished to share with me. The verse immediately following the Ten Commandments reads as follows: "And the whole people saw the voices . . ." (Exod. 20:18). They *saw* the voices? Why, a corrupt text, a biblical critic may say, and quite possibly he is right. What does the Midrash say? "They saw the audible and heard the visible." What may well be a corrupt text has been turned into a religious profundity.

Consider the limitations of human perception. We see the visible, hear the audible, and so it is with the rest of our five senses. Could a divine presence that communicates be subject to limitations such as these? Yet if it is not, then its very presence must wholly upset our senses; and a translating effort is required if what is divinely given is to be humanly received, with the visible to be seen, the audible to be heard, the written to be read; even so, however, no translating effort can ever either exhaust the original revelatory presence or remove its fundamental upset to a mind that is merely human. In a Midrash the Torah is compared to fire that warms a person but burns him if he comes too close.

I reponder the Midrash that excited Heschel so greatly. It deserves the attention of deep and sophisticated thinkers. But then my mind turns to *amcha*; this time, however, not those of its representatives considered hitherto—that man in that jail cell, Arkady Tzinober of Riga, or Lev Ofsischer of Minsk. All these have yet to study Torah. *Amcha* is represented also by those who have studied Torah all along, and in former times these were *amcha*'s chief representatives. It is such as these that would carry the Torah with them as they fled in terror from a progrom, and that during the Holocaust would rush into burning synagogues, in vain attempts to save the holy scrolls. These, if anyone ever, were close to the Torah. None could have been closer. That they were burned by it one cannot believe. Their study of Torah was a way of receiving it, a way of knowing how to receive it that, for the most part, a Jew today has forgotten. He is well advised to relearn at least some of it: This advice from the past is part of the liturgy, and continues to be so even in the most modern minded of synagogues. The scroll is taken from its ark and read. Then it is returned. As it is being returned the congregation chants these verses from the Tenach:

> Behold, a good gift I have given unto you,
> My Torah, forsake it not!
> It is a tree of life for those who hold fast to it,
> And those who support it are happy.
> Its ways are ways of pleasantness,
> And all its paths are peace.
> Turn us back unto Thee, O Lord, and we shall turn.
> Renew our days as of old. (Prov. 4:2, 3:18, 17; Lam. 5.21)

EPILOGUE

In 1921 Rosenzweig had published his *Star of Redemption*, a deep philosophical work that he had written during the war and completed immediately after its end. Having done so, however, he concentrated his attention on *amcha*. Spurning a prestigious academic appointment, he in 1920 founded the soon-to-be-famous Frankfurt *Lehrhaus*, the aim of which was not to be another school of academic research and instruction but rather to bring the ordinary modern Jew to the ancient Torah, and the ancient Torah to the ordinary modern Jew.

In a draft of an opening address Rosenzweig stresses that the Torah is the only book of antiquity that is still in living use, and that the Jewish people owes its survival to it. He goes on to say that, situated as he is, the modern Jew needs a new kind of learning, "a learning that no longer starts from the Torah and leads into life, but . . . from life, from a world that knows nothing of the Torah . . . back to the Torah." He proceeds:

There is no one today who is not alienated, or who does not contain within himself some small fraction of alienation . . . [However, far from turning our backs on the world we live in, as being "secularist," "Gentile," "pagan" or the like] we must not give up anything, but lead everything back to Judaism. From the periphery to the center; from the outside, in.

PRESENT

THE LIFE
OF JUDAISM
THROUGH
THE AGES

5. THE IDEA
AND REALITY
OF A DIVINE-JEWISH
COVENANT

A STRIKING CONTRADICTION

A good teacher provokes thought. I have mentioned two teachers of my Berlin *Hochschule* years, Ismar Elbogen, the great scholar and greater Jew, and Moshe Sister, the hard taskmaster and Marxist biblical critic. Max Wiener was a philosopher. Of considerable originality, he never received the recognition he deserved, for he did not write much. Moreover, what he did write was on the obscure side, and he was a rather dry lecturer to boot. But he knew how to provoke thought. Once he asked us to ponder, for next week's class, a certain question. I pondered that question not just for next week's class but have been pondering it ever since.

Wiener's question was this. Like Christians and Muslims, Jews lay claim to a universal religious truth. Unlike Christians and Muslims, however, they seem to keep that truth to themselves, for though accepting converts they do not attempt to missionize the world. Except during brief periods generally considered aberrations, they never have. Isn't that incongruous? Shouldn't it be one way or the other? Shouldn't Jews opt either for a universalism that aims, successfully or not, at converting all humanity to the one true faith, or else for a particularism that is satisfied with being a tribe or nation or ethnic group and makes no claims to a universal truth? Addressed to second-year students, it was quite a question.

In a way, the answer is in the opening chapters of the Tenach. But it could also be said that these chapters give rise to that same question—and for one "open to faith," ready to let the "rays" of the Book "strike him where they will," in a more nagging form still. One imagines such a person as reading the first two chapters of the Tenach, and being baffled by the story of Creation. Then one imagines him as reading a mere ten further chapters and prey to a new bafflement. Hitherto the God of the Tenach has shown Himself as the Creator of heaven and earth, as the Lord of the universe and all humanity. Yet henceforth he seems to focus His attention on just one man and his family, for the Lord of the world becomes the God of Abraham, Isaac, and Jacob! Max Wiener had asked, "How can a Jew lay claim to a universal truth yet keep it to himself"? Some, Christians as well as Jews, may read the opening chapters of the Jewish Bible (which is also the Christian Old Testament) and be satisfied with the answer they find in them. But others will restate Wiener's question as follows: "How can He who is Lord of all humanity have a 'special relation' with one particular people"?

The contradiction does seem striking. Let us consider it in some detail. The Tenach opens with a sweep of such broad majesty as to make it a book for all humanity. Perhaps it is the only such book. Like most Europeans of my generation I have a bias toward things Greek. In high school I read Homer in the original without a dictionary, and when I graduated in 1935 I still listed in my plans for future study Greek philology in addition to Jewish theology. To this day, whenever I seek to locate things Jewish in a wider context, what comes first to my mind are matters Greek. What comes to my mind now is the *Theogony* of Hesiod. This begins with a primordial chaos. The gods come forth from that chaos and hence are derivative to it. This is in the origins of Greek civilization. At its apex, the God of Aristotle is no longer derivative to chaos but rather its radical opposite. He is the prime mover of the universe and the ultimate cause of what order there is in it. Even so, however, he is not beyond the universe but only the highest part of it. All this is in sharp contrast to the God of the Tenach, who makes His first appearance as Creator of heaven and earth. He does not create earth alone while dwelling Himself in heaven. He rather *creates* heaven—heaven fully as much as earth. And yet, though infinitely above the world and the humanity that is part of it, He creates man—him alone—in His very own image! The God of Aristotle does no such thing. Yes, its opening chapters do make the Tenach a book for all humanity—perhaps the only such book.

Nor has Judaism failed to hold fast to the teaching of these chapters. A Midrash asks why God created only one pair of humans. The answer is worthy of the Tenach itself: "So that no person can say, 'my ancestor was better than yours!' " Never was a more exalted view of man conceived than that of the divine image, and never one more radically antiracist, for if indeed the divine image exists in man, it exists in *every* man, woman, and child. *Everyone?* To weaken the idea, or even abandon it altogether, must often have been tempting, but Jewish tradition held fast to it. It was therefore grimly logical—if to be sure uniquely horrifying—that the most radical racists of all time decreed a unique fate for the Jewish people. "Inferior races" were decimated, persecuted, enslaved, viewed and treated as "human animals." The Jewish "race" was to be "exterminated"; and had Hitler won the war not a single Jew would be likely alive today. No Jew would be left to bear witness to the divine image in man—an image not in some chosen master race but in every man, woman, and child ever born into this world.

So broad, so majestic, is the sweep of the opening chapters of the Tenach. The sweep remains broad as mankind's present condition comes quickly into view. Though created in the divine image, man lapses into sin, so thoroughly as to cause God to destroy the entire human race save only for Noah and his wife, the second parents of subsequent humanity. Again there is one pair only, again only one human race. And then it comes, the good news in the midst of all the grimness. Man has sinned prior to Noah.

Doubtless he will continue to sin after him. Yet God promises
never again to destroy humanity as He did in Noah's time. He
makes a covenant with Noah that contains seven laws henceforth
to be obeyed. However, the survival of mankind does not depend
on their being obeyed: The divine promise not to destroy mankind again is unilateral and unconditional. (On this see further
chapter 12, sections 3 and 4.) Numerous must have been those
who in times of war or pestilence staked their hope on this biblical
teaching. More numerous still may be those who would love to do
so today. These latter must bear in mind, however, that God's
promise to Noah is not to destroy the world; it is not to prevent
men from destroying it themselves.

Thus begins the Tenach, the Jewish book but a book also for all
peoples. Yet barely a few pages later the God of all peoples turns
to just one people and seems to confine His effective attention to
that people, from then on to the end of the Tenach.

> Now the Lord said unto Abram: "Get thee out of thy country,
> and from thy kindred, and from thy father's house, into the land
> that I will show thee. And I will make thee a great nation, and I
> will bless thee, and make thy name great; and be thou a bless-
> ing. And I will bless them that bless thee, and him that curseth
> thee will I curse; and in thee all the families of the earth shall
> be blessed." (Gen. 12:1–3)

Thus the Creator of the world introduces Himself as the God of
Abraham, and that God He henceforth remains. Only the end of
the passage just cited gives an indication that He remains the God
of mankind still. And to this day all Jewish religious life is marked
by the fact that the One God invoked as the Lord of the world is
also the God of Abraham, and that the God of Abraham is also
the Lord of the world.

AN "EVOLUTION" FROM
"PARTICULARISM" TO "UNIVERSALISM"?

To a Jewish reader of the Book "holding himself open to faith"
this "universalist-particularist tension" may well seem puzzling. To

a Gentile reader—unless he is a Christian—it may seem downright offensive: From Creation to Noah he was included, and now, so it seems, he is shut out. Were he to read Homer he would find Athene bound up with Athens and her alone; if, however, dissatisfied with such "particularistic narrowness," he were to turn to Plato or Aristotle he would find their God no longer concerned merely with Athenians or even Greeks but, if with humans at all, only with humanity in general. In short, there seems to be in the history of the Greek mind an evolution from "tribalism" or "particularism" to "universalism."

Whether or not under the impact of the Greek examples, in modern times it once was widely popular to dispose of the biblical "universalistic-particularistic conflict" in terms of an evolutionary process also, the beginning of which was the "tribal" particularism of such as Abraham, and the end, the "pure" universalism of the Hebrew prophets. The theory was especially popular in the nineteenth century, the "century of progress." But what added not a little to its popularity was the dominance of a liberal Christianity that fancied itself to have risen above all parochial, tribal, particularistic "narrowness." In typical accounts of that period even prophetic Judaism falls short of "pure universalism"; this comes on the scene only with Christianity.

But this whole theory, now more or less in disrepute, is little but a modernistic prejudice projected on the ancient sources. We have seen that the "early," "tribal" God of Abraham already blesses all the families of the earth. We must add that the "late," "universal" God of Jeremiah—a God so "universalistic" as to destroy the "particularistic" Jewish state for the sins of its people—continues to be concerned with a weeping Rachel: He bids her refrain from weeping, promising her that her children will return from the land of the enemy (Jer. 31:16). If there is a universalistic-particularistic "tension" or "conflict" or even "contradiction" in the Jewish Bible, then, it is not to be disposed of by an "evolutionary process." It is rather endemic to the Book, and the need arises to understand it.

A corresponding "tension" or "conflict" or even "contradiction" exists in another book, the Christian Bible. Liberal Christians try in vain to blame all particularism in their Bible on their Old Tes-

tament. To be sure, the apostle Paul breaks down all barriers between Jews and Gentiles, men and women, free men and slaves.
He does so, however, through his Christ, and through him alone;
hence Paul's universalism, far from overcoming particularism, re-
tains and in a way even radicalizes it. It is Christians rather than
Jews who are apt to speak of a "scandal of particularity": With
this they refer to the Christian belief that the universal God of
heaven and earth has assumed flesh in one particular human being
in one place at one time, and that through him alone all are saved.
Sometimes the word *scandal* applies in a sense other than that intended by the theologians. Judaism teaches that the righteous of
all nations have a share in the world to come. Christians have
often found it hard to avoid the doctrine that only those within
the church are among the saved. Never was that doctrine applied
more scandalously than when in 1961 a Baptist missionary traveled
all the way from Canada to Jerusalem. He had come to convert
Adolf Eichmann, then on trial for his life. When asked by re-
porters whether a last-minute conversion would get the Nazi arch-
criminal into heaven, the missionary replied in the affirmative.
When asked whether his unconverted Jewish victims, among them
the children, were in heaven, he replied in the negative.

A universalistic-particularistic tension or conflict or even contradiction, then, does exist for Christians as well as Jews. The need
to understand it is as urgent within Christianity as it is within
Judaism. But our concern in this book is, of course, with Judaism.

THE BIBLICAL IDEA OF THE
CHOSEN PEOPLE

To try to understand that tension or conflict or contradiction
within Judaism is to be faced with that most uncomfortable of all
Jewish teachings—the chosen people. That this is biblical is undeniable. Equally undeniable is that in it the elements "universal"
and "particular" are both contained. A purely universal God would
not choose this or that people, for He would not choose at all: His
concern with mankind, if such there be, would be with humanity

in general. Neither would a purely tribal or particular god choose: Such a god would be bound up with his tribe or people, as if saying "right or wrong, my people." In contrast, the God of Israel proclaims:

> You only have I known of all the families of the earth;
> Therefore I will visit upon you all your iniquities. (Amos 3:2)

Jews often do behave as though theirs were indeed a tribal god, who had been theirs alone ever since He led them out of Egypt. But then they are promptly reminded that their God also led the Philistines out of Caphtor, and Aram out of Kir (Amos 9:7). Moreover, reminders such as these are not confined to the "later, more universalistic prophets." Nor are they tangential to the biblical understanding of the chosenness of the chosen people. Immediately preceding the climactic event of choice—the revelation at Sinai—we find the so-called eagle speech:

> You have seen what I did to the Egyptians, and how I bore you on eagles wings and brought you unto Myself. Now therefore, if ye will hearken to My voice indeed, and keep My covenant, then ye shall be Mine own treasure from among all peoples, for all the earth is mine; and ye shall be unto Me a kingdom of priests and a holy nation. (Exod. 19:4–6)

Martin Buber comments sensitively on this crucially important speech. The image is of an eagle carrying its young until they can "dare the flight" themselves and "follow the father." It contains "all in one" three activities, "election, deliverance and education." Like all images, however, this one falls short of perfection, suggesting as it does a "particularistic restriction"; and the danger of such restriction is implicit also in the expression "peculiar treasure." However, the danger is immediately countered with the verse "for all the earth is mine." Writes Buber:

> It is impossible to express more clearly and unequivocally that the liberation from Egypt does not secure the people of Israel any monopoly over their God.

What is true of the climactic moment just prior to the gift of the Torah has remained true in Judaism ever since. The liberation from Egypt, the revelation of the Torah, the entry into the promised land, the preservation through one long exile and another seemingly interminable, and this latter ending thus far with an unprecedented catastrophe and an unprecedented return to the land: Through all this, so a Jew of traditional piety would wish to claim, Jews have remained the chosen people; yet none of this has secured the people of Israel a monopoly over their God.

Not that the wish for a monopoly is not human. It is all too human. This would make the God of Israel into its tribal deity, and Israel herself into a tribe or nation like all the other tribes and nations on earth. The universal God over whom Israel has no monopoly, in contrast, is the God of all nations that sets Israel apart from all nations: He singles this nation out—and who wants to be singled out? The pagan prophet Bileam, called by Balak, the king of Moab, in order to curse Israel, blesses her instead, saying, "Lo, it is a people that shall dwell alone, and shall not be reckoned among the nations" (Num. 23:9). But cursed or blessed, what people wishes to dwell alone? Or not to be reckoned among the nations? It is thus not surprising that, when confronted with that eternally uncomfortable teaching, the chosen people, Jews have often pleaded (or acted as if they were pleading), "Please God, if choose a people you must, choose someone else!"

THE COVENANT: HOW WITH ANYONE? WHY WITH ISRAEL?

The eagle speech refers to a divine-human covenant. This is the central idea of Judaism. Through Judaism it becomes the central idea of Christianity as well. In both the idea is mind-staggering, and the reality, of revolutionary impact on world history. That the gods of pagan antiquity mingle freely with finite humans is natural, for they are themselves finite; equally natural is an infinite God who is humanly inaccessible. But what of an infinite, universal God who not only chooses one finite, particular people but enters with that people into a covenant, a relation that is meant to be mutual? How can there be such a relation between partners of whom one is Infinite and Divine while the other is finite and human? The grappling with this question permeates the length and breadth of the Jewish (as well as the Christian) religious mind. Yet the question, though seemingly unanswerable, again and again finds a positive answer as the Divine-human covenant is reconfirmed, renewed, extended. The eagle image itself is an answer, implying as it does not only "election" and "deliverance" but "education" as well: The one carried is not a nobody, and the God that does the carrying wants and teaches him to be somebody; moreover, once grown up and taught, he is to "dare the flight" on his own.

The idea is of a covenant of God with man. The reality is not with man in general—an abstraction—but with a people in its flesh-and-blood particularity. But why of all peoples with this people, with Abraham and his seed, with Israel? In a way, this question is unaswerable. How can any individual or people be worthy of being chosen by God when all individual or collective humans, simply because they are humans, are unworthy in His sight? So unworthy as to cause the difference between one human and another to approach the vanishing point? The Tenach constantly castigates the Jewish people for their unworthiness: This is one feature that makes the Jewish book Jewish. They were chosen not because of their size or power but because God loved them and wished to keep His covenant with Abraham (Deut. 7:7). But if a covenant at all, and if all are equally unworthy, why single out Abraham to begin with? "Get thee out of thy country . . ." (Gen. 12:1) are God's first words to Abraham. This revolutionary incursion of the Divine into the world of man is not preceded by any indication of any special merit in either Abraham or his ancestors. The election of him and his seed, then, is radically unmerited; humanly speaking, it is arbitrary; religiously speaking, it is an act of pure, divine grace.

But if an answer to the question "why Israel?" is impossible, it is also necessary. In idea any human partner in the covenant may be equally unworthy. In the attempt to live the reality of it, it has always been necessary to invoke, however hesitantly, human worth.

For if the human partner is and remains radically unworthy how can he either hope or be expected to be a partner? How can the "education" by the parent eagle bear any fruit, to say nothing of its young one ever "daring the flight" on its own? A Jew shrinking from invoking his own merit in God's sight, and yet needing to invoke merit, falls back on his ancestors: It is because of Abraham and Moses, a Midrash declares, that grace came plenteously into the world. The idea that human merit does, after all, enter into the election of Israel is expressed with great boldness in a Midrash known to every boy or girl attending a Jewish religious school. One day Terach, Abraham's father, left his son, then a young boy, in charge of his store. The store sold graven images. On his return he found all except the largest image smashed and destroyed. When asked about the cause of this commercial disaster, the lad reported that the largest of the idols had got angry, grabbed a stick and smashed all the others. And when the father objected that no mere piece of clay could do such a thing, the son rejoined, "Then how can you worship it"? In the case of idolatry, a matter desperately serious in Judaism, the reverence normally due to a parent takes second place.

Thus, whereas in the Torah God's election of Abraham is preceded by no act on Abraham's part making him worthy, in the Midrash young Abraham does show a merit than which none could be greater: He is first in the history of humanity to smash the idols. This is not, however, to pit postbiblical against biblical Judaism. The same Midrash that teaches that grace came plenteously into the world on account of Abraham and Moses adds that they too needed grace, since there is no man that lives and sins not. And on Yom Kippur the whole house of Israel stands nakedly before its God, confessing, "We have no merit."

THE COVENANT: CAN A FLESH-AND-BLOOD PEOPLE ABIDE BY IT?

"A kingdom of priests and a holy nation": This and similar passages have on occasion inspired Jewish sectarians to go into the desert, let their beards grow, abstain from wine, and in similar ways to withdraw from the world and its worldliness. Christian sectarians have been similarly inspired much more frequently. I remember studying at a university Christian tales about saints in a course on Syriac literature and reading the story of a holy man who did nothing but sit on a pillar in the desert. Awed by his holiness, people would come and bring him food; and when they came they could smell him from afar, for such was his spiritual unconcern with things material that he never washed. I confess this particular kind of holiness did not inspire me.

Neither, of course, would it inspire all but very few Christians. Christianity has monasteries, inhabited by monks withdrawn from the world and its worldliness. But the monks wash. They do not rely for their sustenance on the alms of others but earn their own livelihood. They even produce wine and other strong drink, although many may not partake of it themselves. If meditating on God in the purity of the heart is part of holiness, then doubtless the existence of the monk is one form of it.

It cannot, however, be the Jewish form, if only because this is to be the holiness of a "nation," not of isolated spiritual adults, but of flesh-and-blood men, women, children, the old, the senile, the sick—the holiness, in short, not of outstanding saints alone but also, indeed in a sense above all, that of *amcha* or ordinary folk. Once on being told that two unauthorized persons were prophesying, Moses expresses the wish that all the people were prophets. This is not so, however, and Moses is well aware of the fact. And not only for Moses but also for an ordinary Jew reading his Tenach—unlike for the apostle Paul reading his Old Testament—*all* Israel is Israel.

Then what sort of "holiness" is this to be? What sort of "priestly" existence? Exploiting a remote philological possibility, Rashi's commentary on the text renders "priests" as "princes," while the Ramban renders it "servants": Between them, the two suggest some sort of normalcy. The same idea is suggested, more profoundly, in a Midrash in which the angels come to God and, on the grounds that the Israelites do not observe the Torah, volunteer to take over the task. In response, God cites the very first commandment: "Be fruitful and multiply!" He cites a further commandment, to eat, to be satisfied, and to bless the Lord. "You are not fruitful! You do not multiply! You do not eat," says the Almighty to the angels, declining their offer. "The Torah was not given to angels; it was given to human beings." To beings that eat, are fruitful, multiply— and for whom these and other "worldly" functions are part of holiness.

Just how such a flesh-and-blood, worldly holiness is to be achieved is a never-ending quest that is part and parcel of the Jewish religious life. That it can be achieved is the promise of the Torah itself:

> For this commandment which I command thee this day is not too hard for thee, neither is it far off. It is not in heaven, that thou shouldst say: "Who shall go up for us to heaven, and bring it unto us, and make us hear it, that we may do it?" Neither is it beyond the sea, that thou shouldst say "Who shall go over the sea for us, and bring it unto us, and make us hear it, that we may do it?" But the word is very nigh unto thee, in thy mouth, and in thy heart, that thou mayest do it . . . I call heaven and earth to witness against you this day, that I have set before thee life and death, the blessing and the curse; therefore choose life, that thou mayest live, thou and thy seed. . . . (Deut. 30:11–14, 19)

THE COVENANT: ITS PURPOSE

How a Jew lives rather than dies by the Torah, and with the covenant constituted by it, is the theme of the remainder of this book. But why a covenant at all? Why with Israel? Why with anyone? This question must have a definite answer if the persistent Jewish wish to be "like the other nations"—a wish not only persistent but also all too understandable—is not to have the last word.

But the question is more easily asked than answered. The nations are to be blessed in Abraham and his seed. Are they, then, to be led by Israel to the God of Israel? But unlike Christians and Muslims, Jews do not engage in active missionizing. Is the universal blessing, then, to flow from the keeping of the covenant by Jews themselves? This is suggested in many ways, such as in the Midrash according to which, were all Jews to observe but a single Shabbat perfectly and with a pure heart, all mankind would be redeemed at once. But this same Midrash that stresses this Jewish role also serves to put it into question. A few saintly but isolated individuals might succeed in observing one Shabbat perfectly; for a flesh-and-blood people the Redemption would have to arrive first to make such an observance possible.

What, then, is the purpose of the covenant? Many fragmentary answers have been given in the trimillennial and variegated history of Judaism, and perhaps only this much of a generalization is possible, that, located between Creation and Redemption, a Jew testifies to the reality of the first and the hope for the second. This testimony has a positive and a negative aspect. The positive is the possibility, unheard of prior to the advent of Judaism, of a mutual relation between a God beyond the heavens of heavens and man on earth. The negative is against all the false gods—against idolatry.

Of the two the second testimony is the more urgent. The Tenach belittles atheism, for only "the fool hath said in his heart, there is no God" (Ps. 14:1, 53:1). The fear of idolatry, however, is so pervasive that the Book cannot be understood without it. The most fearful case of idolatry mentioned is that of Mesha, the king of Moab, who "took his oldest son that should have reigned in his stead and offered him for a burnt-offering upon the wall" (II Kings 3:27). Idolatrous child sacrifice is condemned with horror throughout the Tenach, most eloquently so by the prophet Micah, who goes on to declare that the true service of the true God consists of doing justly, loving mercy, and walking humbly with God (Micah 6:6–8). A seemingly strange Midrash asserts that Micah's reference to child sacrifice is only apparently a condemnation of what such as Mesha did, and in reality a praise of what Abraham was prepared to do, but at the last moment was stopped from doing— sacrifice Isaac as God had commanded. But how can the intention be praiseworthy when the execution must be shrunk from with horror? Another Midrash supplies the answer. When Abraham ascended Mount Moriah, intending to follow God's command, all the nations of the world watched. And when they saw what Abraham was prepared to do they abandoned all their idols. But alas, they soon forgot their great resolve and returned to their former ways.

The first part of the last-cited Midrash indicates the rock-bottom purpose of the divine-Jewish covenant; its last part, that this purpose is not accomplished and over and done with, but rather remains indispensable until the end of days. What is that rock-bottom purpose? "Who is a Jew?" a Midrash asks. "One who testifies against the idols."

THE CHOSEN PEOPLE AND MODERNITY

But who "in this day and age" would accuse his neighbor of idolatry? Who is himself afraid of it? What to the Tenach was a most fearful fact has trivialized itself for moderns into a mere species of superstition, surviving only in insufficiently enlightened corners of the earth; and considerable contemporary relevance attaches to the hoary joke about a man who listens to a sermon about the Ten Commandments, gets more and more depressed because he has violated them all, but cheers himself up with the thought that at least he has never worshiped graven images. Is not a Jew who in modern times testifies against the idols engaged in a "trivial pursuit" that, to put it mildly, is not worth the cost? Moses Mendelssohn, the first modern Jewish thinker (1729–86), made a weak case for the world's continued need of Jews and Judaism when he cited the need to testify against idolatry, but made idolatry into a mere superstition already beginning to vanish under the impact of enlightenment. So at least three of his five children must have thought when they converted to Christianity, as their "entrance ticket" into enlightened modern Europe. A grandson of his was Felix Mendelssohn-Bartholy, the rediscoverer of Bach's St. Matthew Passion, which had been all but forgotten.

Idolatry trivialized itself into a mere species of superstition when Europe became modern and enlightened. This was a process taking several centuries. A further change has occurred in the present century. Two European wars have destroyed the world hegemony of

Europe. They have also produced a certain European humility. This in turn has produced Western-Christian doubts about missions to Muslims, Hindus, Buddhists, with their place now widely being taken by an activity called "dialogue." (On this, see further chapter 12, section 5.) In dialogue Jews, Christians, Muslims, Hindus, and Buddhists are all to listen to each other, prepared not merely to tolerate, but also to see truth in, each other's faith. In a climate such as this, does not one person's idolatry emerge as another's religion? Modernity has already trivialized idolatry by coupling it with superstition and the lack of the proper enlightenment. Now the climate of dialogue seems to wipe out the very concept of it, by marking those holding on to it as narrow, medieval-style fanatics.

The implications of these developments for the notion of the chosen people may well seem obvious. "Who is a Jew? One who testifies against the idols." This once grandiose definition lost most of its former grandeur ever since the Age of Enlightenment discovered that there was little idolatry left in the civilized world, and that little if any help was needed for its elimination elsewhere from a people chosen for the purpose. Since the end of World War II there has been another discovery—that the pluralism that is the will of God has no limitations that anyone dare so much as hint at. Today it is widely believed that in order for Judaism to be included in the "family of world religions" it is necessary that the whole doctrine of a chosen people be completely abandoned.

RECONSTRUCTIONISM

Within Judaism, the doctrine of the chosen people has been uncomfortable at nearly all times. In modern times, at least among the non-Orthodox, most Jews have felt apologetic and awkward about continuing to affirm it. It was reworded, redefined, suspended. And of course Jews abandoning Judaism abandoned that doctrine also. However, a forthright repudiation of it, for the sake not of repudiating but "reconstructing" Judaism, had to await the advent of Reconstructionism—not accidentally the first indige-

nously American movement within Judaism. (Reform, Conservative, and even modern Orthodox Judaism all originated in nineteenth-century Germany, but the United States has always had a
potential for religious pluralism until recently unknown in Europe.) The philosophy of its founder, Mordecai M. Kaplan (1881–
1982) may briefly be summed up as follows. There is an upward
development in the religious history of mankind, culminating in
"higher" religions. In all these latter God is both One and the
source of a higher morality, hence inspiring its adherents to ever-
greater human heights and thus being the "source" of their "salvation." But while thus the conceptual content of all "higher" religions is the same it is so only in abstract thought. No religion is
alive unless it expresses itself in *sancta*, i.e., symbols manifest in
prayers, songs, rituals and the like, and these are as numerous and
different as are "civilizations." Judaism is one of these. It is a "religious civilization." As such it is different and indeed unique, but
only in the sense in which *any* religious civilization is different and
unique. Thus the distinctiveness of Judaism and its people is preserved while yet the doctrine of the chosenness of Israel—always
uncomfortable but now untenable—is, at long last, forthrightly
abandoned. Among the Jews attracted to Reconstructionism, one
almost hears the sigh of relief.

A SINGLED-OUT PEOPLE TODAY?

Kaplan's foundational work, *Judaism as a Civilization*, appeared
in 1934, and a year later he founded his *Society for the Advancement of Judaism* that was meant to put his teaching into practice.
In the same year a process began to take shape on the other side of
the Atlantic that was to single out Jews for curse and death more
inescapably than they had ever been singled out for blessing and
life. It was the year of the Nuremberg laws. From then on, except
for the lucky ones, first in Germany and subsequently in all of
German-occupied Europe, Jews had no choice but to *be* singled
out. Across the ocean, Jews had no *decent* choice but to be singled

out in solidarity with their European brethren. Solidarity with them was a moral—if often uncomfortable—necessity. Both the moral necessity and the discomfort were discovered, for example, by Chaim Weizmann on a visit to the United States in 1940 when (to quote his words) that country was still "violently neutral" and any mention of the European Jewish catastrophe was decried as "war-mongering." The moral necessity, and the discomfort caused by it, continued to be rediscovered when the country was no longer neutral. It was rediscovered by any American Jew who urged his government to mount rescue operations, only to be told that Europe's Jews would have to wait for victory—when few of them would be left alive by the Nazi murderers. (The experience of British and Canadian Jews was much the same.)

The experience just alluded to is political but not confined to politics. For the first time in our time, some Jews have found themselves compelled to reject outright, and this for religious reasons, the doctrine of being singled out by God. In that precise moment many Jews, whether of their number or not, were compelled by events to *accept themselves* as singled out by the most elementary moral necessity—solidarity with their brethren who were being murdered on the other side of the Atlantic Ocean. The shock of this experience is as yet far from fully absorbed or comprehended. A response to it will be the work of centuries. And among the tasks that arises for religious Jews is a reconsideration of the age-old doctrine of the divine covenant with Israel.

For twelve long years the world was divided into those bent on persecuting and at length murdering Jews, and those who did less than they could about it: Is this abandonment by man an abandonment by God also, an additional reason over and above that articulated by such as Kaplan for rejecting the doctrine of a covenant between God and Israel? Or is it, on the contrary, a new reason for reaffirming the age-old doctrine, and for Jews who had long abandoned it to become *ba'al teshuvah* and reaffirm it?

Among those confronted with this question are survivors. Some of them have answered it in one way, others in the other way. Others still are haunted by the question but have left it suspended.

As for those among us who seek to chart a path for a future Judaism, we cannot answer this question lightly. Indeed, it is only in fragmentary ways that we can answer it at all.

AN UNPRECEDENTED IDOLATRY

In the records of the Nuremberg trials we find the following testimony:

WITNESS (a Polish guard at Auschwitz): Women carrying children were always sent with them to the crematorium. The children were then torn from their parents outside the crematorium and sent to the gas chambers separately. When the extermination of the Jews in the gas chambers was at its height, orders were issued to the effect that the children were to be thrown into the crematorium furnaces, or into the pit near the crematorium, without being gassed first.

SMIRNOV (Russian prosecutor): How am I to understand this? Did they throw them into the fire alive, or did they kill them first?

WITNESS: They threw them in alive. Their screams could be heard at the camp.

SMIRNOV: Why did they do this?

WITNESS: It is very difficult to say. We do not know whether they wanted to economize on gas, or if it was because there was not enough room in the gas chambers.

The Russian prosecutor surely was tough. He surely had been made tougher still by what he had already heard during the previous trial proceedings. But this he could not believe until the witness had explained it. For my part, I have pondered and repondered this testimony to a horror without precedent, ever since I first found it cited in one of Irving Greenberg's writings; and the more I ponder it, the less am I satisfied by the explanation given by the Polish witness. Perhaps the gas chambers were full, but gas was cheap and plentiful. And if the screams of the children could be heard at the camp, they could be heard also by those giving those orders and, more loudly still, by those executing them. How could those orders be given? And how could they be obeyed? We are stunned by the "how" of it. But it is the "why" that shatters mind and soul. The biblical mind and soul were once shattered by ancient idolatry. The prophets could not understand it but only shrink from it with horror and fear, and, of course, oppose it with all their might. We must shrink with horror and fear from what they did to the children of Auschwitz, oppose anything even slightly resembling it; but, however much we try, we cannot hope adequately to understand it. We have no choice but to describe it, as well as Nazism as a whole of which Auschwitz was the most characteristic expression, as a modern idolatry. It was idolatry without precedent. It differed from its ancient predecessor in its scale and the systematic, cold-blooded manner of its execution. But it also differed in its quality. The ancient worshippers of Moloch threw their own children into the flames. The Nazi idolaters too threw children into the flames. But their victims were Jewish children, not their own.

"Who is a Jew? One who testifies against the idols." This once was a grandiose definition of a Jew. Subsequently it was trivialized. It ought to be trivial no more. Many will wish—nay, be religiously compelled—to reaffirm it. Those doing so, however, must face a new fact in the history of Judaism. Abraham testified against the ancient idols when he was prepared to sacrifice Isaac. Of the new idolatry of Auschwitz, Jews were the chief and singled-out victims.

EPILOGUE

The Midrash tells how once Nebuchadnezzar erected an idol and ordered three men from each of the nations conquered by him to come and bow down to it. Hananyah, Mishael, and Azaryah, the three Jews selected, consulted the prophet Ezekiel as to their duty, and the prophet cited Isaiah and advised them to flee and hide. But who, the three rejoined, would then testify against the idols? Whereupon Ezekiel went to God and said: "Sovereign of the universe, Hananyah, Mishael and Azaryyah, are prepared to risk their lives for the sanctification of Thy name. Wilt Thou stand by them or no?" Whereupon God replied, "I will not stand by them, as it is written, 'As I live . . . , I will not be inquired of by you!' " (Ez. 20:3) Ezekiel broke into tears, for did not Scripture say that these three alone were left in Judah, and would not this small remnant now perish? Yet Hananyah, Mishael, and Azaryah, informed of the divine reply, responded, "Whether He does or does not stand by us, we shall risk our lives for the sanctification of the divine name."

Nebuchadnezzar was eclipsed in our time. Having subdued the Jewish nation along with so many others, the ancient tyrant was satisfied. Nothing less would satisfy his twentieth-century successor than the murder of every Jewish man, woman, and child. The ancient oppressor bade representatives of every conquered nation bow down to his idol: thus he set the Jewish representatives free to testify against it, as it were *creating* Jewish martyrdom. Nothing less would satisfy the modern Nebuchadnezzar than the murder of Jewish martyrdom. As for the Jewish representatives, the *Judenraete*, they were sometimes chosen by Jews themselves; for the most part they were chosen by the tyrant's own henchmen. But whether one or the other, and whether saints or sinners, they but rarely—as it were, accidentally—had any choice but either to kill themselves or help kill other Jews. The *Judenraete* are the most unjustly maligned victims of the ultimate idolater. They also include the most unsung heroes and saints.

One day in 1942 the head of the *Judenraete* in the small Polish town of Kosoff received a phone call from his counterpart in nearby Kolomeya: SS troops had been seen to move in the direction of Kosoff, obviously in order to "relocate" its Jews. (In the end it turned out to have been a false alarm: The Jews of the town were not dealt with until half a year later.) The twenty-four members of the *Judenraete* assembled: what to do? Obviously the Jews must all be warned. Some had prepared hiding places, others might flee into the nearby forest. But would this be enough? In order to finish preparing the hiding places, in order to find places in the forest safe from discovery, more time would be necessary. So some Jews would have to stay behind to delay the SS, to lead the pursuers on a false trail. Who? Who else but the members of the *Judenraete*, or at least some of them! They looked at each other in silence. One stole away, then another, then a third. Twenty left, to join the rest of the Jews who attempted to hide. Of the four who stayed, one failed to leave because he had fainted, and when he recovered he too joined in the flight. Three stayed behind.

Why does the world still stand, when after Abraham's testimony at Mount Moriah idolatry did not come to an end? The Midrash replies that the world still stands, even after Nebuchadnezzar's scheme, and that while some say that the pillars on which it stands are Abraham, Isaac and Jacob, others say that they are Hananyah, Mishael and Azaryah. Why does the world still stand today, after an idolatry worse than the ancients ever imagined? Surely it is because it stands on three pillars, those three members of the *Judenraete* of a small town in Poland.

6. HALACHA, OR, LIVING
BY THE TORAH

SIX HUNDRED AND THIRTEEN MITZVOT

As early as in the Mishnaic period of rabbinic Judaism (first to third century C.E.) it was already an accepted fact that the number of commandments contained in the Torah is 613. ("Commandments" is the best translation of *mitzvot* but, as will emerge in context, it does not quite convey the flavor.) As already mentioned (chapter 1, section 1), of this number 365 are negative and 248 positive, the former number corresponding to that of days in the year, the latter, as folklore has it, to that of bones in the human body. Obviously few people can remember so large a number, and no one can observe them all. Hardly less obviously, there are bound to be differences among the authorities as to what is or is not to be counted among the *mitzvot*. (One difference catapulted into prominence in our time is between the Rambam who does not, and the Ramban who does, count Aliyah ["going up" to the land, immigration to Palestine] among them.) And yet, the tradition insists, 613 is the correct and precise number—no more and no less.

None are to be added in the course of time and, more importantly still, none abrogated. It is true—to cite the most traumatic event in the history of Halacha, the "way" of the *mitzvot*—with the destruction of the Temple in 70 C.E. a large number of the 613 became unobservable, namely, the sacrifices bound up with the Temple cult. Despite this trauma the tradition insists that these unobservable *mitzvot* are only temporarily in disuse, not permanently abrogated. (Who except the Messiah, as yet only hoped for, would have the authority?) No more striking confirmation than this could be found of our above assertion that while strictly speaking there is no such thing as a Jewish "orthodoxy," there very definitely is a Jewish "orthopraxy."

THE CENTRALITY OF *MITZVOT* IN JUDAISM

So central are *mitzvot* in Judaism that Rashi, already referred to as the most famous and most popular of medieval Jewish commentators, finds it necessary to defend the fact that the Torah begins as it does and not with Exodus 12:2, the first commandment addressed to the Israelites after the Exodus from Egypt. And the fact that centrality belongs not to some privileged group of *mitzvot* but to Halacha as a whole is put well by the Ramban, already referred to as probably the most profound of medieval commentators, when he takes Exodus 24:12 to mean that Moses received both the tables of the Ten Commandments and all the rest of the 613 during the forty days he spent on Mount Sinai. The passage reads: "And the Lord said unto Moses: 'Come up to Me into the mount, and be there; and I will give thee the tables of stone, *and the law and the commandments which I have written,* that thou mayest teach them.' " (We italicize the words on which the Ramban's interpretation is based.)

The centrality of the commandments does not of course mean that the role of belief in Judaism is reduced to insignificance. Thus the Rambam counts the basic beliefs of Judaism as themselves among the commandments, and in a similar vein a Midrash asserts that on the Day of Judgment a Jew will be asked, on a par with such questions as "Have you been honest in business," "Have you believed in and hoped for the Redemption"? This is on the one hand. On the other, the Ramban goes so far as to assert that the Torah begins as it does because God and Creation are the "roots of the faith" without which a Jew "has no Torah at all." Still, a Jew who practices the Torah and yet has doubts even about basic beliefs—there have always been such Jews—can take heart from the fact that the view of both the Rambam and the Ramban were probably provoked by medieval controversies, with Christianity, Islam or both. And, whether or not this is so, he can in any case take heart from the fact that a God from whom no *mitzvot* issue can never be the God of Israel. Christian theology has often taught that a Christian is saved by faith and faith alone. Among the teachings that the Jew Jesus himself derived from Judaism, however, is that by his or her fruits shall a person be known.

THE *MITZVOT*—A BURDEN OR A JOY?

To outsiders it must seem that "the Law" is a burden for those subject to it, even if they observe but a fraction of all those commandments. In times or under conditions of religious decay, it is so also for insiders, who then follow the "letter" without any "spirit," without feeling or knowledge of any wherefore and why. And then, there have been some great ones among the insiders, who may have had the feeling and the knowledge—or some of it—yet did shake off "the burden of the Law." Of these some, in shaking it off, shook a whole world. One, the apostle Paul, founded a new religion. Another, the philosopher Spinoza, rejected all religions or, more precisely, replaced all past religions in particular with a new religion in general, the essence of which was but one law in general, a universal morality. Yet a third among the great ones had no need to shake off "the Law," for his father had already done it on his behalf. (He had him baptized as a child.) Still, Karl Marx found it necessary to slander the "Sabbath Jew" and his *mitzvot*.

For Spinoza (and, needless to say, Marx) "the Law" was an unnecessary burden. For Paul the burden was impossible. According

to his own testimony (Acts 22:3), the apostle was once a pupil of
the first-century Rabban Gamliel. When subsequently he set out
to bring his good news to the Gentiles, could he seriously expect
them to submit to circumcision or to practice the dietary laws? Yet
this was not the core of his difficulty with "the Law." Its core was
this: How can a law or commandment that is divine be observed
by such as himself, who are merely human? That the Torah was
given to humans and not to angels we have already seen. Still to be
answered—or answered in depth—is how commandments divinely
given can be humanly obeyed.

In no way at all was the answer that emerged from Paul's agonized struggles. And since this "no" went together with a continued
belief in the God of Israel and His commandments he arrived at
the view that "the Law" had been revealed, not in order to overcome sin but rather in order to disclose it. Gentiles without the
law are sinners. Jews with the law *know* themselves to be sinners,
or at any rate acquire this knowledge when, overcoming a false
pride at having punctiliously performed this or that *mitzvah*, they
reach the supreme stage possible for man on his own—the humility, at once desperate and hopeful, that man's only salvation lies in
divine grace. And then comes for Paul the miracle of miracles, a
grace that has in fact come for Jew and Gentile alike in the incarnate God who, crucified, has suffered death and vicariously atoned
for all sin and, resurrected, has overcome both. This, and not some
liberalized or simplified version of "the Law," was the good news
that Paul carried, most successfully, to the Gentiles, and sought to
carry to the Jews as well. In this, however, he failed.

To Christians this failure on the part of Paul and all subsequent
missionaries to the Jews has always been a source of theological
perplexity. At worst they blamed it on Jewish blindness, stiff-
neckedness or willful perversity. Even at best they considered it a
mystery. The "mystery of Israel" is quite secondary, to be sure, to
the great mystery, that of the incarnate, crucified, and resurrected
God. Even so, however, it is of considerable moment for Pauline
theology: It is that whereas Paul's good news was accepted by millions of Gentiles who never groaned under the burden of the Law
(see e.g. Rom. 4:15, Gal. 3:10-14, II Cor. 3:6-11), it remained un-

accepted by Jews who did groan under it, and who therefore had (and continue to have) most reason to understand that news's goodness.

Does a Jew groan under the burden of the *mitzvot*? That these are indeed a "yoke" is stressed consistently by the rabbis, and is evident from the fact that the majority of the 613 consists of prohibitions: that Judaism is "fun" is a modernistic distortion, deriving from a confusion of joy with pleasure. Yet the distortion derives from a truth: The stern yoke of discipline is part and parcel of a more ultimate joy. It is with joy that, on each Shabbat, a Jew reads the Torah portion assigned for that particular week. It is with joy that on Simhat Torah ("The Joy of the Torah") the annual cycle of reading the Torah is ended—and immediately begun again. Hasidic Jews go so far on that day as to dance with the Torah scrolls. But even more sober-minded Jews rejoice on it. This is once a year. But the liturgy for every evening of the year includes the following prayer:

> Thou hast loved Thy people Israel with everlasting love. Thou hast taught us Torah and precepts, laws and judgments. Therefore, Lord our God, when we lie down and when we rise up, we will speak of Thy laws and rejoice in the words of the Torah and Thy precepts for evermore. For they are our life and the length of our days . . .

A Jew groaning under the burden of the Law would not carry the Torah with him as he fled from a pogrom: He would rather use the need to flee for his life as an excuse, whether sent by God or drunken Cossacks, to leave the burden behind. In effect, this was in fact the practice of many a Jew who fled from the czar's Eastern Europe to the freedom of America; but it was not the practice of religious Jews bent on remaining religious, and on continuing to live by the ancient covenant even on the new continent. Such Jews carried the Torah with them to America.

Does this Jewish joy in the *mitzvot* reflect a mere lack of religious profundity? As for positive *mitzvot*, does a Jew rejoice in no more than this, to be fruitful and multiply, or to eat and be satisfied? As for negative ones, does he thank God for no more than this, to be kept by the prohibitions from straying into false paths and to his own hurt? In observing either the positive or the negative ones, are his joy and satisfaction nothing better than self-satisfaction, the pride in having done what is required? In all this, is he too shallow to so much as notice the question that so deeply, so movingly tortured the apostle of the Christian good news: How can commandments given divinely be obeyed by mere humans?

LAW, GRACE, AND GOD-GIVEN *MITZVOT*

The picture just drawn of a Jew is much like the picture of the Pharisee in the New Testament. As in the earlier cited story about Muhammed and the Koran, the Tenach of that Jew is a rule book dropped from above by a God remaining above, and all that he does or needs to do is follow the rules. He observes these rules punctiliously, and is self-righteous in consequence. When his observance is mainly or merely show, he is hypocritical. And when he sees a sick person lie in the street he walks by on the other side. (About compassion prompted by ordinary human decency, the rule book has nothing to say.) This is the picture in the New Testament, and so influential has it been that to this day "Pharisaical" remains a synonym for "hypocritical" and "self-righteous" in most languages of Christendom.

What the New Testament rarely hints at, and certainly does not go out of its way to emphasize, is that its criticism of the Pharisees is nothing but part of the Pharisees' own self-cirticism, and that indeed this latter surpasses that of the New Testament in thoroughness and comprehensiveness. The Anglo-Jewish scholar Herbert Loewe lists as follows the types of "Pharisee," false and true, that he has collated from the rabbinic sources:

(1) The shoulder Pharisee (who carries his good deeds on his shoulder ostentatiously; or, according to another interpretation, tries to rid himself of the commandments); (2) the sit-a-while Pharisee (who says, "wait until I have done this good deed"); (3) the bruised Pharisee (who breaks his head against the wall to avoid looking at a woman); (4) the pestle Pharisee (whose

head is bent in mock humility, like a pestle in a mortar); (5) the book-keeping Pharisee (who calculates virtue against vice, or who sins deliberately, and then attempts to compensate for his sin by some good deed); (6) the God-fearing Pharisee, who is like Job; (7) the God-loving Pharisee who is like Abraham.

With this information we can dispense with all the false Pharisees. What of the true ones? Job feared God (Job 1:1), so much so as in extremity to affirm, "Even though He slay me, yet will I trust in Him" (Job 13:15). (In the same verse he adds, though, "But I will argue my ways before Him.") What of Pharisees like the God-loving Abraham? The second-century Rabban Gamliel—not the teacher of Paul—used to say:

> Do His will as if it were thy will, that He may do thy will as if it were His will. Nullify thy will before His will, that He may nullify the will of others before thy will. (Abot 2:4)

But how is such a thing possible for people of flesh and blood, to make their will like unto that of the God of heaven and earth? To nullify their will before His? Did the enormity of this not strike the later Rabban Gamliel—or his earlier predecessor of the same name who had been the teacher of Paul? Or the rabbinic tradition as a whole?

We have cited earlier a Midrash according to which for the divine-human meeting on Mount Sinai to be possible the primordial decree at Creation must be "revoked" that had set heaven and earth light years apart. We have also cited another, according to which for "the Glory" to "descend" on the mountain no less a divine action was necessary than the "bending" of the heavens, "upper" and "lower" alike, to make them touch the mountain. And when at length the divine communication occurred, the Israelites, a mere flesh-and-blood people, "saw the audible and heard the visible." Focusing now on the fact that the divine presence *commands*, and that for divine commandments to be humanly performed they must be *humanly heard*, we read the following Midrash:

Rabbi Aha in the name of Rabbi Yohanan said: "When at Mount Sinai the Israelites heard the word 'I' [the first word of the Ten Commandments], their souls left them, as it says, 'If we hear the Voice . . . anymore, we shall die,' (Deut. 5:22) and as also it is written, 'My soul failed me when He spoke' (Song of Songs 5:6). Then the Word returned to the Holy One, blessed be He, and said, 'Lord of the world, Thou art life and Thy Torah is life, yet Thou hast sent me to the dead, for they are all dead.' Thereupon the Holy One, blessed be He, sweetened [softened] the Word for them . . .

Rabbi Shim'on bar Yochai taught, 'The Torah which God gave to Israel restored their souls to them,' as it says, 'The Torah of the Lord is perfect, restoring the soul.' " (Ps. 19:8)

I ponder this Midrash afresh as I put it into my word processor, as I have pondered it ever since, so many years ago, I first came upon it, and I discover once again that it epitomizes, as perhaps no other text, my lifelong love affair with Midrash. It plumbs the depths of a Jew's love of the Torah, of his life with it and through it, of his joy in the *mitzvot*. Permitting myself to be carried away, I say: One understands this Midrash, and one understands what Judaism is.

What does the Midrash say? The Word descends and touches the flesh-and-blood Israelites, and they all die. They die, like such as Job, in the absolute fear of the absolute Presence: paralysis. Or they die, like such as Abraham, in the absolute love of it: becoming one with the One, mystics of all times and all places swoon away into the All, like individual drops of water into the ocean, their individuality surrendered and lost. But whether dying away in fear or love—or in something more ultimate than both—their death makes "the Word" come to naught, for it commands, and to naught it comes if there is none to respond by accepting or rejecting it. How can divine commandments be humanly obeyed? Such a thing is impossible, the Midrash is saying, just like Paul—and for reasons more ultimate still than those that emerged in the apostle's agonies.

Then how is the gift of Torah nevertheless possible? And how does it "restore the soul"? This emerges from how "the Word," having failed of its purpose in its first descent, is sent a second time: the Word is "sweetened" or "softened." Those formerly dead now remain alive or, more precisely, are brought back to life as their souls are "restored." This means nothing less than that a grace has entered into the commandments that makes them, though divine, capable of human observance. And as this grace permeates the whole length and breadth of the 613 *mitzvot* it enters even into those the observance of which is so "natural" that grace, and indeed the *mitzvah* itself, seems unnecessary or even altogether out of place. Like all flesh and blood, all human flesh and blood is fruitful and multiplies, eats, and (one hopes) is satisfied. It is one thing, however, to do these things, quite another to do them as *mitzvot*. In blessing the Lord for the gift of food a Jew does something quite other than, say, a beggar who thanks a charitable donor. Eating itself is a necessity. In thanking God for having eaten and been satisfied, a Jew accepts eating *itself* as a *mitzvah*, the observance of which is a response to a grace that has accepted the one observing it in his flesh-and-blood reality.

For a Jew, then, grace did come into the world through Abraham, through Moses, and in particular through the gift of Torah in which commandments divinely given have become capable of being humanly observed. This is why the *mitzvot*, though a "yoke," are not a burden, whether (as for such as Spinoza and Marx) unnecessary or (as for such as Paul) impossible. They are a joy, causing even the least theological of *amcha* to recite whenever the Torah has been read in synagogue, "It is a tree of life to those who take hold of it, and happy are those who support it. Its ways are ways of pleasantness, and all its paths are peace."

Its ways may be ways of pleasantness, yet its "yoke" is not easy to bear, for all men sin, Abraham and Moses not excluded. At times the yoke seems too heavy. In a Midrash the Israelites ask God to extirpate the evil inclination since they themselves cannot cope with it. God responds: "You remove it a little now, and I shall wipe it out in the end." Placed between Creation and Redemption, a Jew is given the burden of the *mitzvot* in order that he may testify to Creation at the beginning and help prepare for

Redemption at the end. The grace in the *mitzvot* gives him strength as he takes on his task, at times so much so as to make him feel that he can do nearly everything. Yet at other times he feels that he can do nearly nothing. Between these extremes lies "a little." But how much a little is the Midrash does not say, nor can it be said.

According to his own testimony Paul went to school with Rabban Gamliel. A Jew pondering his agonized struggle with "the Law" cannot but admire him for his religious honesty and profundity that compare so well with all the smug pieties of the world. Even so he must conclude that Paul's study with the rabbi was either not long enough or not deep enough.

"MORAL" VERSUS "MERELY CEREMONIAL" *MITZVOT?*

A Midrash draws a distinction between "laws that, had they not been revealed would have had to be invented," and such "against which Satan and the Gentiles argue." The distinction is plain and obvious. No society or state can exist without laws, or without a power that, if necessary, enforces them. The first-century Rabbi Hanina, the vice-high priest, goes so far in recognizing that necessity as to urge his disciples to pray for the (Roman!) government, on the grounds that, but for the fear of government good or bad, people would swallow each other alive (*Abot* 3:2). Certain necessary laws, then, can be humanly invented and have in fact been invented. This means that valid laws do exist quite apart from the Torah given to Israel. (For the seven laws given to Noah, see chapter 12, sections 3–4.) Philosophers, Jewish as well as gentile, have argued through the ages whether their validity was merely pragmatic—whether they were human inventions, arbitrary but dictated by necessity—or rather that of moral laws rooted in "nature," recognizable as such by a human "reason" that, too, is "natural." But whatever the grounds and scope of their validity, the Torah did not contradict but rather recognize and support such laws, if indeed its 613 commandments did not actually include them.

Such, at any rate, is the view implied by the above-cited Midrash, and the bulk of Jewish tradition shares it.

What then of the remainder of the *mitzvot*? The Gentiles argue against them since they either do not know or do not accept the Torah. Satan does likewise in order to lead Israel into temptation. We have cited the Ramban as asserting that on Mount Sinai Moses received all the commandments, not the tables of the ten commandments alone. If this be so, must the "orthoprax" view not ascribe equal weight and validity to all, deriving as they do for that view from the same divine authority? The first-century Ben Azzai and the second-century Rabbi Yehuda both urged their disciples to be as serious in observing a seemingly slight *mitzvah* as a seemingly grave one, the first of these teachers on the grounds that one *mitzvah* leads to another, the second on the grounds that the reward of any *mitzvah*—be it slight in our eyes or grave—is humanly unknown (*Abot* 4:2, 2:1). The profounder teacher, Ben Azzai, does seem to weigh the *mitzvot* and indeed has a concept of the dynamic of *mitzvot* as a whole when he adds that just as a lighter *mitzvah* leads upward to one graver, the same logic is operative with transgressions: a slight transgression, having been committed, paves the way for one greater. Yet Rabbi Yehuda's view is not to be ignored. To be sure, the *mitzvot* are to be performed not for the sake of a reward but for their own sake alone (*Abot* 1:3). Yet a reward there is, and the reward of each *mitzvah*—what a *mitzvah* counts in the sight of God—is humanly unknown. Are then all *mitzvot* to be viewed as of equal weight? But not even the most rigid of "orthoprax" rabbis ever embraced any such view. To cite the most radical case at once, nearly all *mitzvot* may be broken *al pikuach nefesh*, for the sake of saving a human life. No Orthodox Jewish parents have ever denied their child the blood transfusion that would save its life, on the ground of the (misunderstood) Biblical injunction against eating blood. Nor has any Orthodox Jewish physician ever hesitated to perform on Shabbat a life-saving operation that could not safely be postponed. Whatever the purpose of Jesus was in healing on Shabbat, it was not to save lives.

When and when not *pikuach nefesh* warrants the breaking of a commandment has always been the subject of serious, meticulous discussion among rabbinic authorities, never more so than during the Holocaust. Is it permitted to steal food or medicine and smuggle it into the starving, disease-ridden ghettos, when theft is forbidden? Is it permitted to violate Shabbat for that purpose? Never in history did Jews show so heart-rending a fidelity to the Halacha than when they considered such questions seriously in these circumstances—a fidelity never to be forgotten even by Jews who have no use for the Halacha themselves.

The *mitzvah* to save lives includes the *mitzvah* to save one's own. Some *mitzvot*, however, may never be broken: There are things for which a Jew must be prepared to give his life.

> All commandments of the Torah have been given that one may live by them, and where it is a question of *pikuach nefesh* none remains valid except the prohibitions of idolatry, incest and the shedding of blood.

Thus we read in a rabbinic text. Why idolatry? All that has preceded in this book gives the answer, though it should be added that such as the Rambam stress that a Jew should never seek a martyr's death, that so holy is life that even the temporary pretense of apostasy is permitted in order to preserve life. However, if *in extremis* there is no honest choice but martyrdom, then—and only then—a Jew "has been found worthy by God of reaching the highest stage" of religious virtue.

Why incest? The authorities seem unanimous about the fact but not the reason; but it may be surmised that incest destroys the family, that Israel begins as a family and in a sense always remains a family, and that its witness to the nations includes the sanctity of family life.

Why, finally, murder? Once a Jew came to the second-century Rabbi Yehuda, who has already been cited. He reported that the prefect of his town had ordered him to kill a certain person and threatened that in the case he refused he would himself be killed. "You must let yourself be killed," the rabbi ruled, "and refuse to commit murder. What makes you think your blood is redder than his?"

Rabbi Yehuda's reply is an application of the belief in the divine image in every human. It is also a testimony to the ethical element in the Halacha as a whole, a subject so important as to require treatment apart from the Halachic whole and in its own right. (See chapter 8.) Furthermore, it gives rise to a question implicit in this book ever since our first mention of the 613 commandments, and one much discussed throughout history by Jewish thinkers. Our first mention occurred with Rabbi Simlai's reduction of the commandments, successively to eleven, six, three, two, and one, in each case with the support of biblical authority (chapter 1, section 1). It would not of course occur to this "orthoprax" rabbi to do away with, say, the 602 not mentioned among the 11 in Psalm 15. Still, a question arises. One can see why, as in that psalm, righteousness, truthfulness, and the like are divinely commanded, and why bribe-taking, slander, and the lending of money on interest are forbidden. One can see the reason also for a good many others, with moral commandments being, perhaps, in first place. But what is the reason of the laws "against which Satan and the Gentiles argue"—the reason, say, of the dietary laws, or the prohibition against making a fire on Shabbat, when to start a fire no longer requires the labor of rubbing dry sticks but only a match?

In response to this, there have always been what may be called "rationalists" among Jewish thinkers who sought to find reasons for what moderns are fond of calling "merely ceremonial" laws. Kashrut is a means to strengthen Israel for her vocation, the Shabbat laws are a means to securing physical and spiritual rest, and so on. (In much the same vein medieval Muslim rationalists argue that the five times ordained for daily prayer in Islam are a means to elevating soul and mind.) This way of thinking has a built-in antiorthoprax potential: If the "ceremonial" laws are a mere means to "rational" or "moral" or "spiritual" ends, why not change the means according to the exigencies of the times, or indeed abolish them altogether in case spiritual progress has been such as to make them dispensable? The fateful step of abolishing or even altering the "ceremonial" laws is of course not taken by premodern "orthoprax" thinkers since, after all, the whole of the commandments remain divinely revealed; and in their view whatever our reason might do to fathom their purpose, it does not and cannot exhaust it. The step is not taken even by the Rambam, perhaps the arch-rationalist of them all, in his account of the laws concerning animal sacrifices. These were given by God to Israel, he states, since they were universal custom at the time, and since the Israelites could not be torn from universal custom too abruptly but only be gradually weaned. For moderns the implication clearly is that "evolution" has done away with animal sacrifices, that they are gone never to return.

Moderns may wish to do with a good many "ceremonial" laws of Judaism what they perceive the Rambam as doing with sacrifices. (This latter may imply the once-and-for-all abolition of sacrifices, but he never quite states it.) The Torah prohibits eating pork for reasons of health, but modern sanitation and medicine have disposed of both the reason and the prohibition. The Torah commands rest on Shabbat for one's animals and hence prohibits riding one's horse; but driving a car is not riding a horse. And more of the same. Modern non-Orthodox Jews quite naturally embrace such views. But before they invoke the tradition in their behalf they are duty bound to consider that the "rationalist" attempt to find reasons for laws "merely ceremonial" has no monopoly in that tradition. Its rival is its complete opposite, and its greatest representative is Yehuda Halevi.

We have already referred to this medieval thinker as the most eloquent exponent of that most indispensable of Jewish virtues, namely, fidelity (chapter 2, section 3). Now he appears as the most eloquent exponent of the *mitzvot* as a whole, and of the unique joy that lies in them. What of the *mitzvot* that "would have had to be invented had they not been revealed"? Why, even a band of robbers could not exist without at least some of them, is Halevi's reply. And while a decent state may have something much better than a band of robbers, its laws, being humanly invented, would still fail to produce that for which Israel was brought into the world, namely, a bridge between the God beyond the heaven of heavens and humanity on earth. Halevi asks:

> Can it be imagined that the Israelites observe the doing of jus-
> tice and the love of mercy but neglect circumcision, Shabbat and
> the other [ceremonial] laws, and are happy withal?

The happiness Halevi refers to is the happiness alluded to in the
Midrash when the commandment, sent down "sweetened" a second time, "restores the soul" of the Israelites since divine grace has
accepted them in their flesh-and-blood humanity. It is the joy experienced by *amcha* on Simhat Torah, whether or not a Jew goes
so far as to dance with the Torah. It is the hope expressed on behalf
of all humanity when a Midrashic author expresses the view that,
if only all Jews observed even one Shabbat perfectly—that is, in
letter as well as in spirit—the Redemption for all mankind would
come at once.

MODERNITY AND THE PROBLEM
OF AUTHORITY

Our account of Halacha thus far has been almost exclusively in
terms of "normative" or "orthoprax" Judaism. This has been necessary, in no case more so than in that of Halacha; and, as will be
seen, modern forms of Judaism that reject Orthodox authority find
themselves sooner or later forced to grapple with "the problem of
authority" themselves. Still we must now return to the fact stated
previously that not only have there always been protests against the
normativeness of rabbinic Judaism but that modern protests have
a new quality that at least a modern Orthodox Judaism is itself
bound to recognize. For the premodern mind, the past comes to
the present through the medium of "reliable tradition," as a form
of certainty equal if not superior to other forms of knowledge. For
the modern critical mind, the present can do no more than reach
out for the past, in an attempt to recover it. In consequence, even
the most Orthodox but modern-minded Jew can never say, "This
is the truth and the will of God" but at most only, "This is the
truth according to my belief and my testimony, and I am committed to it with my whole life." Such is a "neo-orthodoxy" that

may testify against other forms of Jewish commitment but can neither refute them nor wish to ostracize or excommunicate them; and, if tempted to do any of these things through the happenstance of power coming within its reach—as is the case in Israel today, but not in Israel alone—it will firmly, devoutly repudiate the temptation. But the reader familiar with contemporary Jewish affairs knows, putting it mildly, that what ought to be the case is not always the case.

In our opening chapter we have described the modern Jewish religious situation in general. With respect to Halacha in particular, the crucial problem arises from the fact that the modern Jew, coming as he does from the present to the past, does not come empty-handed. He comes with vital commitments already made, some of which he not only will not but also cannot surrender; and foremost among these latter are moral principles. What if a conflict arises between modern moral principles already accepted and past *mitzvot* making a claim to being accepted? In such cases a modern neo-orthodoxy may invoke its conviction already cited—that where there is a rabbinic will there is a Halachic way. But is there *always* a Halachic way, even with the best of rabbinic wills?

To have confronted conflict between present and past most forthrightly has been the great merit of Reform (or "liberal" or "progressive") Judaism. It has also been its chief contribution to Judaism as a whole, for not only have modern Reform Jews been in the forefront of virtually every modern moral cause, but Conservative and even Orthodox Jews have often followed where Reform Jews have led. The *Siddur*—the traditional orthodox prayer book—asks a male Jew to thank God daily for having him made a man, and a Jewish woman, to thank Him for having made her "according to His will." Can there be any modern Jew, regardless of belief or affiliation—of either sex—who can recite this prayer with a good conscience? Surely it is best to alter this prayer, or not say it at all.

But corresponding to the great strength of Reform Judaism there has been a weakness, evidenced by the fact that this prayer, as well as nearly all others in the *Siddur*, have been altered or expunged with great ease, and often without any twinges of conscience. We have referred to a conflict, potential or actual, between present and past. In Reform Judaism there has often been no conflict, for the superiority of present over past in all things has been presupposed. "Progress" was the great god of "liberal" or "reform" or "progressive" Judaism in the nineteenth century, the century of progress, and in consequence there exists to this day a self-styled "progressive" tendency within Judaism to confuse the most serious contemporary religious or moral challenge with the latest fad. All this disposes lightly of past, of tradition, of history, yet what is a person without a past? If a Jew, a *Luftmensch*. The sociological definition of this "human being living on air" is a poverty-stricken ghetto Jew who has a few old pairs of pants to sell that no one wants to buy, and tries to live on that "business." This definition is hardly relevant to Jews of today. But the religious definition of a *Luftmensch* remains relevant. This is that of a progress-worshiping Jew who through that worship has destroyed for himself the possibility of *teshuvah*, of a turning and returning through which a Jew's "days" are "renewed" as "of yore." Today there is rightly some considerable respect for "the search for roots." This has some of the connotations of *teshuvah* but does not exhaust its profundity.

To protest against this progress-worshiping, past-abandoning tendency within Reform Judaism (and worse forms among Jews abandoning Judaism altogether) has been the chief merit of Conservative Judaism. We have above cited S. D. Luzzatto as a pioneer when he attacked the Shulchan Aruch not in order to get rid of the Halacha but rather in order to restore the vitality which, so he held, it possessed until the Shulchan Aruch mentality destroyed it. Solomon Schechter (1847–1915), the founder of Conservative Judaism in America, carried Luzzatto's thought forward in asking—and seeking to answer—the question most urgent for the Halachic life once the norms of orthodoxy are abandoned. If change there must be in Halacha, and yet not every change is legitimate, what authority decides? Or rather, what is the standard of authoritativeness? Not the Tenach itself, Schechter replied, but rather the Tenach "as it repeats itself in history," in interpretations given "not by any section of the nation, or any corporate priesthood or rabbihood, but by the collective conscience of Catholic Israel, as embodied in the Universal Synagogue."

But what is "Catholic Israel," what is its "conscience," what is the "Universal Synagogue"? At Schechter's time these may still have been viable terms. In our time the synagogue is not universal but plural, and if there still is such a reality as Catholic Israel, its "conscience" is embodied, fully as much as in the synagogue, in some Jews representing new Jewish realities outside the synagogue, among them Holocaust survivors, Soviet refuseniks, and, perhaps most strikingly, a good many Jews in Israel who never set foot into a synagogue. Conservative Judaism, then, has a weakness of its own as well, corresponding to its virtue, namely, a tendency to seek refuge in "history" from difficult dilemmas, thus making timidity and lack of principle into a virtue.

No Jew ever tackled the modern problem of Halacha with greater depth and courage than Franz Rosenzweig. Rosenzweig was a *ba'al teshuvah*, returning to Judaism after having been on the verge of conversion to Christianity. He was a modern *ba'al teshuvah*, fully aware of the fact that his turning and returning were based not on past authorities but rather on his own present, personal commitment. Finally, his return was not either to some abstract Jewish ethical monotheism or to some concrete but non-religious Jewish nationalism, enriched though this latter may have been by Jewish "customs and ceremonies." It was to the life of the covenant as embodied in the Halacha, through which Israel is bound up with the God of Israel, a witness between Creation and Redemption to all humanity. Not accidentally did he produce a translation of the poems of Yehuda Halevi.

How was the return to Halacha possible for this modern *ba'al teshuvah?* He was on his way from "outside-in," but was unable to jump in with the help of medieval authorities. He could only move in, and in the process ask what of tradition that to begin with was mere custom and ceremony could become *mitzvah* for him, that is, no longer a ceremony practiced according to taste but a commandment given by the Commander; and if and when a *mitzvah* was "doable" the doing of it brooked no compromise.

Since Rosenzweig's time one event has occurred that has an epoch-making potential for Halacha: the establishment of a Jewish state. One aspect of this potential is negative, the other positive. On the negative side, the existence of a Jewish state encourages a premodern Orthodox fanaticism more extreme than that of the Catholic chaplain in the joke. This latter, while identifying his way of serving God with "His way," at least concedes a Protestant way of serving Him, even if it be nothing more ultimate than the Protestant's own way. Tempted by the possibility of the use of political power for religious purposes, there exists in the Jewish state an orthodoxy for which there is no way other than its own, and that is "His" way; and it shows little hesitation to put this belief into practice through the use of political power. However, this negative potential, upsetting and even alarming though it is, must not overshadow the positive potential that the state is creating for the future of Halacha. Yehuda Halevi once taught the joy of the *mitzvot*, a possibility only through a perpetual *teshuvah* through which the old is perpetually recovered by the new and thus is itself renewed. In this century Franz Rosenzweig, a modern Yehuda Halevi, carried out a personal *teshuvah* "from outside-in," as what had not been "doable" for him gradually became doable, thereby ceasing to be mere "custom and ceremony," and becoming instead commandment of the Commander. However, Rosenzweig's "way" had one crucial limitation: It was purely personal. The great positive potential created by a Jewish state is that what for Rosenzweig was only personal might become communal. Here and there, especially in kibbutzim, that potential is already actual. And whenever a group finds a new meaning and a new life in a long-forgotten *mitzvah* it rediscovers a little of what Yehuda Halevi meant when he said that the *mitzvot*, far from a burden, are a source of joy, for they are a bridge between God and the world.

EPILOGUE

It is a biblical injunction to "count the Omer" for forty-nine days, from the second day of Pesach to Shavuot, the feast of weeks.

(Lev. 23:9 ff. In the Christian calendar there is the corresponding "Pentecost," the fiftieth day after Easter.) The injunction is bound up with harvesting in the land and harvest-connected sacrifices ("Omer") to be offered in the Jerusalem Temple. However, the Temple has long been destroyed, and even those praying for its rebuilding pray at best only awkwardly for the restoration of the sacrificial cult. Less meaning still than to sacrifices in general could long be attached to the Omer sacrifice in particular: The harvest with which the "Omer" is connected is harvest in the ancient land, not in lands into which Jews have been scattered for nearly two millennia. Consequently the counting of the Omer has long been the most lifeless of rituals, even in Orthodox synagogues in which, being biblical in authority, it is punctiliously observed. "This is the first day of the Omer, this is the second day . . .", and so on. Conservative synagogues seem to hold on to the ritual only because of timidity, and from Reform or liberal prayer books it has long been dropped.

Yahel was the first Reform kibbutz in Israel. (Now there exists a second.) Located in the Arava Desert at its most arid, it is inhabited by Jews, mostly Western, of complete modernity. They have labored and created fields and vineyards. Enough grass has been grown for their cows. Few places in Israel can show as forcefully that the desert has indeed been made to bloom. Few places can show as forcefully that the bond between the land and even the most modern of Jews, never broken, has been renewed, is being renewed.

In 1982 our daughter Suzy worked for eight months in Kibbutz Yahel. The kibbutz invited the rest of our family to join them for Pesach. I looked forward with great expectancy to the Seder. This has always been my favorite celebration. Jews sit down during the first night of Pesach. They reread the story of the Exodus from Egypt while admonishing themselves—my favorite passage in the Haggada, the book that is read that night—that in each generation each Jew should regard himself as though he had personally gone forth from slavery unto freedom. What would Seder be like in a kibbutz, some of whose members might have literally come from slavery to freedom?

But in Israel you never know. The Seder turned out to be nothing special, what with the noise of small children and more than the usual disorder not uncommon during public celebrations that include a meal. To be frank, it left me feeling flat. Then someone announced that the kibbutzniks would go next evening into the fields, to count the Omer. And count the Omer we did, with prayers, song, dance, to the accompaniment of sweet strains of guitars.

I gazed at the arid surroundings: Can anything ever have been made to grow in this place, even way back in biblical times? I then gazed at the fields and the vineyards, and at the people that had made them grow, and was filled with awe and wonder, at the land, at the people, but most of all at a *mitzvah* that, once moribund if not dead, has been brought in our time to new life.

7. ON LEARNING
TORAH

THE TORAH SCHOLAR AND THE PEOPLE

According to a time-honored rule a Torah scholar is to spend eight hours of the day on making a living, eight hours on sleeping, and eight hours on studying Torah. (In this context, this is of course "oral" as well as "written" Torah [see chapter 3, sections 4–6], and the heaviest emphasis has always been on the Talmud, the most complex and difficult part of oral Torah.) This rule is startling: what about meals, playing with the children, spending time with one's wife, to say nothing of relaxation, hobbies, friends? One asks these questions because the Torah scholar is not a monk. He has a wife. He has children—a great many since to "be fruitful and multiply" is the first and most basic of all the *mitzvot*. Moreover, he does not live in a monastery but in the midst of his people.

The last-named fact arrests our immediate attention. In medieval Europe the great majority of Jews was poor, and all were subject to legal discrimination and frequent persecution, expropriation and expulsion. Yet they were Europe's most literate people.

Among Christians generally only priests and monks could read and write. Yet though their *melammed* may have been a poor teacher, every Jewish child had the Hebrew letters drilled into him, sufficiently so as at least to read the *Siddur*, even though he may have been unable to translate and understand much of what he was supposed to recite at prayer. The Torah scholar, then, not only lived in the midst of his people but in some way was also of it. Just what kind of study—to use the Yiddish expression for Torah study—was his *lernen?* To correct myself, what *is* his *lernen*, for whereas Torah study does not have the role in Jewish life today that once it had, it not only survives: In circles that seem to become larger and stronger, it actually thrives.

It is easier to say what *lernen* is not, and this will take up much of our present reflections. The above rule itself, however, suffices to show that, whatever *lernen* may be, it is not making a living. The early rabbis all had a profession, one as a shoemaker, another as a blacksmith, and so on. The second-century Rabban Gamliel praises the combination of Torah study with a worldly occupation (*Abot* 2:2), and the first-century Rabbi Zadok warns against making the Torah a "crown" wherewith to "aggrandize" oneself, or a "spade wherewith to dig" (*Abot* 4:7). The latter warning is against taking payment for teaching Torah, making the rabbis resemble in this respect Socrates, who dissociated himself sharply from the sophists, who charged a fee for teaching what they considered philosophy. Socrates refused payment because he sought and taught truth. The rabbis too sought and taught truth; their truth, however, was holy as well—so holy, in fact, that it ought to take up all a scholar's time were it not for the two great necessities of survival, one being sleep, and the other, the provision of food and shelter. Food and shelter not only for himself but also, and indeed above all, for his wife and his children. What would be the fate of the Torah, and that of the study of it, if there were no Jewish children? Children who—so one could hope and pray—would become Torah scholars themselves?

Eight hours each, then, for sleep, making a living, and studying Torah, for scholars not only in the midst of the people but also in some sense part of it. Not of the people, however, in the sense that all could be scholars, or even begin to attempt to abide by the rule governing a scholar's day. The first and most obvious exception were women. In an age in which even a movie celebrates a young woman's war on the traditional male monopoly on Torah study, one is tempted to dispose of that exception as a mere case of male chauvinism, the existence of which in Jewish tradition we have already mentioned. That this does injustice to the tradition is shown by the case of two women, Rachel, the wife of Rabbi Akiba, and Beruria, the wife of Rabbi Meir. Akiba was to become a great Torah scholar—in the view of many the greatest of them all. Yet he spent his early years in total ignorance, as a poor shepherd in a rich man's employ—one who, not surprisingly, objected to Akiba's marriage to his daughter Rachel. More importantly, however, Rachel herself would marry Akiba only on condition that he became a Torah scholar. On his part, Akiba consented, even though it meant beginning from scratch, on a par and together with his young son. And on her part, Rachel persisted in her commitment even though it meant years of separation from the husband she loved. Akiba must have loved his wife as much as the study of Torah, and Rachel must have loved Torah study as much as she did her husband. Akiba was to become the great rabbi who lived for the Torah, and eventually died a martyr's death for its sake. But the heroine of the story is clearly Rachel.

Still it may be objected that hers was but a supporting role—looking after the children, encouraging her husband, making sacrifices so that he could study—whereas his role only was the essential one. It was otherwise with Beruria, the wife of Rabbi Meir, who exceeded her husband in piety and matched him in learning. It would be false to cite her case (as apologists sometimes do) in order to deny the existence of male chauvinism within rabbinic Judaism: To deny it is impossible. Yet the rabbis do praise not only her piety but also her learning. The togetherness of the two is contained in an anecdote. Once the second-century Rabbi Yose the Galilean met her along the road and asked her, "By which road should I travel in order to reach Lydda?" Beruria replied: "Galilean fool! Did not the rabbis say, 'Do not talk overmuch with women?' You should have asked, 'How to Lydda?'" The learned Beruria

presumably refers to a warning by the second-century Rabbi Yose
ben Yohanan against much talk with women, one's own wife
included. (*Abot* 1:5. Two Orthodox translations I have checked
have "gossip" instead of "talk," but this is sheer apologetics.) Did
Beruria say what she did with tongue in cheek? We do not know.

Women are the first and most obvious exception to the rule
that is to govern the life of the Torah scholar. The next are the
poor—those so poor as to need more than eight hours a day in
order to eke out a living. If the very poor are those who cannot
study, the very rich—or rich by the standards of the time—are those
who will not study: They are too busy adding to their wealth or
managing what wealth they have, and are thus a third exception
to the rule that is to govern a Torah scholar's life. Yet despite these
(and other) exceptions, Torah scholars were not really a group
apart from them. The poor revered them, even if they had little
idea of the nature of their scholarship. As for the rich, unwilling
or unable as they were to be Torah scholars themselves, they felt
duty bound to support others in their scholarship. Such support
went far beyond mere charity. In the Eastern European ghetto,
where poverty was the rule and even a modestly prosperous Jew
was considered a Rothschild, the traditional *shadchan* (professional matchmaker) would naturally try to find a "rich" husband,
even for a girl who had "rich" parents herself. One husband, however, was more desirable still, even if he was abysmally poor: a
brilliant student who promised to become a famous Torah scholar.

In Eastern Europe, Torah study was destroyed by the combined
assault of Nazism and Communism. In the rest of the world—
except for the circles in which it thrives, circles referred to above—
it has been diluted if not dissolved altogether by the forces of
secularism and assimilation. If a hope for reviving the old study
remains, possibly in quite new ways, it is because the old respect
for learning remains, this itself in altered ways. A rabbi may no
longer be a very eligible son-in-law. But a doctor or lawyer is, for
he is learned as well as well-to-do. Indeed, in present-day North
America even a college professor, hardly among the well-to-do, is
in the process of becoming eligible.

TORAH STUDY AND ACADEMIC SCHOLARSHIP

In Western and especially North American universities, there are now professors of Jewish studies, a subject that has come to enjoy a prominence and respect undreamed of even a few decades ago. The phenomenon is of obvious importance not only for Jews but also for Judaism. Its role for Judaism remains yet to be seen. For us here the question arises whether the academic study of Judaism is the heir of, substitute for, or in any way otherwise related to, the traditional Torah study.

For me the question arose soon after I entered the Berlin *Hochschule* in 1935. The full title of the school, as stated above, was *Hochschule fuer die Wissenschaft des Judentums.* Translated accurately if not literally, *Wissenschaft des Judentums* means "academic study of Judaism." The founders of the discipline in nineteenth-century Germany were towering scholars such as Leopold Zunz (1794–1886) and Moritz Steinschneider (1816–1907); and founded it was at a time when German academic scholarship enjoyed a worldwide, well-earned fame. The *Hochschule* itself had been founded in 1872 by Abraham Geiger (1810–74), himself a towering scholar, the stated aim of the institution being to establish with the greatest possible objectivity and accuracy the facts of the Jewish past, not as believers or ideologues might imagine that past to have been, but "as it really was." (This is the much-quoted dictum of Leopold Ranke, a great historian of the time.) At least in theory, therefore, the institute could be attended by Gentiles as well as Jews, and, among the latter, equally by Orthodox, liberal, secularist, and even atheist Jews. After all, the facts, as well as the objective method required for their study, were the same for them all. And, up to a point, all this was true.

But it was never true in its entirety, if only because the *Hochschule* ordained liberal rabbis. After 1933 it was less true than ever. The majority of the students that then flocked to the *Hochschule* were less concerned with the Jewish past than with a Jewish future, and with the past less in search of facts than of a truth. For my part, I wished to discover—with a naivety for which even now I do not apologize—not only what such as Maimonides taught but also whether it was true. Such questions, however, were not objective enough to be part of the *Wissenschaft des Judentums.* Yet my friends and I kept asking them.

Among the subjects studied academically at the *Hochschule* was, of course, Talmud. No one studying the subject at the *Hochschule* alone could hope to penetrate deeply into that tremendous, many-volume work, for it was only one of ten subjects studied, and the whole course of study was only six years. For my part, I had less chance than others, for my studies were abruptly ended after only three and a half years, with the *Krystallnacht,* arrest by the Gestapo, and imprisonment in Sachsenhausen. Even so a friend of mine and I decided that what we were getting was not all there could be to Talmud study, and that we wanted more. So the two of us took our courage into our hands, went to an ultra-Orthodox rabbi in the Berlin of 1937 and asked him to teach us a little Talmud. Aware though he was of our "heretical" liberalism, he received us with the greatest warmth, agreed to teach us twice weekly, and refused payment with a gentle smile. I cannot say that I learned a great deal in the few months that we studied with him. But I did learn two things, never forgotten. The traditional *lernen* of the Talmud is as disciplined, methodical, and intellectual as is its study at a modern Western academic institution. This is the first lesson I learned. The second was that *lernen* is a discipline quite other than that practiced in the modern university. It more closely resembles prayer.

The rabbi had many sons. Once I asked him about his plans for their future. He was surprised. "Why, they of course will study Talmud," he replied. "And what about their livelihood?" I went on. His answer: "Torah study is our task. Our livelihood is in the hands of God." Actually, the livelihood of his whole large family, if coming from God, came through the instrumentality of one single businessman, wealthy and devout.

I have often wondered what happened to the rabbi and his family—whether God continued to provide their livelihood or even saved their lives. I shall never know. I cannot even remember the rabbi's name.

CONCERNING THE VIA CONTEMPLATIVA

By virtue of divine munificence (and that of the wealthy business-man who was its instrument), the Berlin rabbi was able to spend not one- but two-thirds of the day on the Torah, the study and the teaching of it, the latter of course without payment. This brings to a modern mind, seeking to understand Torah study, one great ideal of the Western spirit, the *via contemplativa*, the "way" of contemplation as the way to ultimate meaning in human life.

The ideal of the contemplative life has emerged at many times and in many places. In the West, its origin is in Greek philosophy, and from there it penetrated, for example, into the monasteries of medieval Christendom, whose purpose was a contemplative piety. Judaism, of course, has no monasteries: As we have been at pains to stress, the Torah scholar is in and of the community, a husband and father of children. Yet no one can say that in its history Judaism has been indifferent to matters Greek. According to Jewish legend—false, of course, but not without poetic truth— Plato studied with Moses.

Let us consider the *via contemplativa* as deriving from the Greeks. What distinguishes man from the lower animals? Reason, or the capacity for thought. What is the highest thought? To borrow a phrase from the twentieth-century Platonist A. N. White-head, not the thought that Ulysses shares with the foxes but that which Plato shares with the gods. (Ulysses and the foxes think up clever means, each to his own ends; Plato and the gods contem-plate ends, or rather one end only, namely, truth.) What is the highest truth? To this ultimate question Socrates, Plato, Aristotle, and all their heirs have—*can* have—only one answer: The highest truth is the Divine, and the highest thought at which man can aim is the contemplation of it. The *via contemplativa*, then, does not find its highest expression in the study of books, or in the pursuit of knowledge or even the possession of it. It is the *exercise* of the highest knowledge—the contemplation, however rarely and fragmentarily this may be possible, of God. According to Aristotle, God is the pure life of mind, the eternal contemplation by God of the highest reality, namely, Himself. If this is so, then a person who achieves the contemplation of the Divine—perhaps on rare occasions but occasions infinitely precious—lives, "so far as is possible," in the "imitation" of God.

That the *via contemplativa* has always had a strong appeal to the Jewish mind is shown, for example, by the abundance of Jewish mathematicians. Albert Einstein (1879–55) was once asked what of irreplaceable value would be lost if mankind were to vanish from the universe. He replied that no one would be left to hear the music of Mozart. (So precious is this anecdote that we shall return to it and discuss its significance in our last chapter.) On another occasion, giving a quasi-Midrashic account of the astounding fact that mathematical thought can uncover the mysteries of the universe—or what of its mysteries can be humanly discovered—he remarked that God is subtle but not malicious. The vanishing of mankind from the universe, then, though marking the end of anyone hearing Mozart, would not be the end of mathematical thought in the universe. For Einstein God Himself is, as it were, a mathematician.

But can human thought contemplate the God of Israel, when even Moses was denied his wish to see His face, on the grounds that no man can see His face and live? (Exod. 33:20) Christian theologians who love their Aristotle, yet wish to follow the God of Israel, have often postponed the contemplation of God to the hereafter: The blessedness of heaven consists of the "beatific vision" of God. Jews too have been among the lovers of Aristotle. However, they have generally been much more reticent than Christians about the hereafter. (See below, chapters 13 and 14.)

Among the great Jewish lovers of Aristotle is Maimonides: He is the greatest. What makes him greatest is his *Guide for the Perplexed*, the most clearly authentic and authoritative book in Jewish philosophy ever written. It deserves the title "Jewish philosophy" because it combines two commitments, to Judaism and to philosophical thought; because it confronts the "perplexities" resulting from this dual commitment; and because it resolves these perplexities by means not of evasive apologetics but of profound and honest thought.

The pursuit of his goal required Maimonides to probe not only Aristotle's claim to a contemplative knowledge of God but also to assess the *via contemplativa* as a whole. Was this the ultimate "way" that a person could seek? Or was it, as proclaimed by the prophet Micah and cited in his list of summaries of Judaism by Rabbi Simlai (see above chapter 1, section 1), to do justly, to love mercy, and to walk humbly with the God of Israel? Maimonides—thus, rather than "the Rambam," one should call him whenever he leans toward matters Greek—was torn, and at the end of the book he squarely confronts the question. Listing the degrees of perfection that can be achieved in a human life, what could be higher than to rise above things earthly and human, so as to contemplate things eternal and divine? Maimonides goes so far as to invoke a passage from the Tenach in support of the Greek ideal. (". . . Let the wise man glory in this, that he understandeth and knoweth Me" [Jer. 9:23].) Yet Maimonides ends his book as the Rambam. Like Aristotle's philosopher, his Jew is to "imitate" God. He is to do so, however, not by contemplating a God who, on His part, is lost in self-contemplation. The God of the Rambam "delights" in lovingkindness, judgment, and righteousness; and one can imitate Him only if one so lives as to cause lovingkindness, judgment, and righteousness to increase on earth. In Judaism not contemplation but action has the last word.

CONCERNING THE VIA ACTIVA

What is Torah study? Its place is not taken by the modern academic study of Judaism. Neither is it reducible to a form of the age-old, venerable *via contemplativa*. Both these facts—the first as if by inspired anticipation—are clearly stated by the first-century Rabbi Hanina ben Dossa:

> He whose fear of sin precedes his wisdom, his wisdom shall en-
> dure; he whose wisdom precedes his fear of sin, his wisdom shall
> not endure. He whose deeds exceed his wisdom, his wisdom shall
> endure; he whose wisdom exceeds his deeds, his wisdom shall not
> endure. (*Abot* 3:11, 12)

The academic study of Judaism is neither true nor false Torah
study, for it neither precedes, nor is preceded by, the fear of sin:
To its objective stance sin and the fear of it are irrelevant. As for
the *via contemplativa*, the study of Torah could conceivably reduce
itself to it; if so, however, it would have become a wisdom that
exceeded deeds, destined not to endure. Was such the wisdom
of the Berlin rabbi whose very name I no longer recall? But then,
he was a teacher as well as a student, and teaching is among the
greatest of deeds. Moreover, if his portion was to study and teach,
that of others was a great variety of deeds, and who was to say
what was greatest in the sight of God? Not genuine Torah students
themselves. In the Talmud we read:

> It was a favorite saying of the rabbis of Yavneh: I am a creature
> of God and my neighbor is also His creature. My work is in the
> city and his in the field. I rise early to my work, and he rises early
> to his. As he cannot excel in my work, so I cannot excel in his
> work. But perhaps you will say, I do great things and he does
> small things. We have learned, however, that it matters not
> whether a person does much or little, if only he directs his heart
> to heaven.

It would be difficult to find a greater expression of intellectual
humility, or of the fact that the Torah study of the scholar and
the life of the people are intertwined.

Still, the argument as to which is greater, the "study" of Torah
or the "doing" of it, is carried on in numerous rabbinic texts, and
is resolved only in characteristic rabbinic fashion: It is the study
of Torah that is greater—but only because it leads to the doing of
it! However, this, of course, is not necessarily so. (See section 5
of the present chapter.)

It is deeds, then, that do rank highest in Judaism. Is this to say that Torah study, in the last resort, is a mere means to action, and that Judaism as a whole may be understood as a form of that other great ideal of Western civilization—the *via activa?* All ought to do *mitzvot,* and we have already seen that for all to have a deep knowledge of the why and wherefore of them is impossible. However, if Torah study is in the end a mere means to practice, one might have to go a considerable step further: For all to study Torah might then not only be impossible but also unnecessary. Indeed, since only few can have true expertise, it might even be undesirable. An Israel covenanted to the God of Israel, and given His Torah on Mount Sinai, would thus be divided into the many who would be told what to do (and perhaps given here and there a morsel of the why of it), and the few who would do the telling, possessing as they did a monopoly of Torah expertise. Judaism, in short, would be a form of intellectual elitism.

Intellectual elitism was involved when the medieval church common folk, widely unable to read the Bible, were discouraged from even hearing it read. Jews, in contrast, were required to hear the Torah read once every year even if they were unable to read it themselves. To be sure, medieval Christian elitism was smashed— smashed doubly!—when Martin Luther translated the Bible into German, in order to teach common Christian folk both to read the Word of God and to read at all. Even so, in Jewish eyes at least, modern Protestant Christianity did away with premodern Catholic intellectual elitism only to replace it with a spiritual elitism of its own. In the Protestant church the Christian Bible is read selectively, and the one who both selects the texts and preaches sermons based on them is a "pastor" inspiring his "flock." The imagery, of course, derives from the Twenty-third Psalm, the most famous and widely recited of them all. In the psalm, however, it is God who is the shepherd, and the flock is all the people, rabbis and other learned folk included. Moreover, there is no one to do the selecting from the Torah: It is read entire. Modern liberal Judaism did not err in reducing the weekly Shabbat readings: these readings are lengthy, a fact that often causes Orthodox readers to hurry through them and thus destroy them. The liberals did err, however, in introducing the principle of selective reading from the Torah where none had ever existed: The desired end could be achieved by replacing the dominant one-year cycle of readings with a three-year cycle that once had its adherents. That the whole people is to hear all of the Torah regularly is a principle too precious to abandon for those serious about both the Torah and the people. That principle is not incompatible, of course, with an elite of the learned. But it is in total oppositism to a Torah elitism, whether practiced by an intellectual clergy, by a pastor prompted by the spirit, or by a committee of rabbis claiming a monopoly over what of the Book ought and ought not to be brought to the people.

By an ironical logic, intellectual elitism is absolutized when the claims of the *via activa* are themselves absolutized. Never in modern times was this done more radically and uncompromisingly than by Karl Marx and his followers. "The philosophers have only in various ways interpreted the world," is one of Marx's most famous and most characteristic assertions. "The point, however, is to change it." Thus with one blow all knowledge of God, man or world, for their own or for truth's sake, is destroyed, to be replaced by a knowledge that gets rid of God and changes man and the world. The task of changing man and world rests on the many; the strategy and tactics required for the task, however, is an expertise of the few, and this gives them a claim to a monopoly over power. Rivals to expertise are "reeducated" or otherwise destroyed. As for the inexpert many, they are "the masses." To be sure, the expert few act (or claim to act) on their behalf. Yet the masses have no right to a share in the power, or even to be consulted; and a more condescending, contemptuous phrase to describe human beings than the masses it is not easy to imagine.

For Marx himself, to be sure, the view that praxis is more ultimate than theory remained itself a theory, and the same has been true of sundry Marxist theorists after him, maverick or not so maverick. It would be difficult, however, to point to "orthodox" Marxism-in-power anywhere of which the above-sketched condition has no element of truth.

The word *hamon* means "the masses" in modern Hebrew for, being in the modern world, that language cannot help being also part of it. In the Tenach, however, *hamon* means "raging mob," and only here and there refers to a multitude. There is no Biblical word for "the masses." For the Book that begins with describing man as created in the divine image, the concept does not exist.

What then of Torah study, the people, and the relation between the two? All are to practice the *mitzvot*. But all are also to acquire some knowledge of the why and wherefore of them. If Torah study without deeds does "not endure," neither do deeds without any Torah study whatever—deeds that would make those performing them less than human. Above we considered the harshness in the dictum that an ignorant person cannot be pious. We also considered protests within Judaism against it. Now we have come upon its positive significance. Study of Torah is not confined to an elite among the people of the covenant. In however varying degrees, it belongs to them all.

CORRUPTIONS

Eight hours a day on making a living, eight hours on sleeping, and eight hours on the study of Torah? Is so stern a program, impossible for all, possible for *anyone*? We have seen that the rabbis list five types of corrupt Pharisees, as contrasting with two true types, the Pharisee who, like Job, fears God, and the one who, like Abraham, loves Him. As through subsequent centuries Torah study was preserved and intensified—this often against obstacles nearly past belief—new corruptions made their appearance. The Torah student is to be humble, yet scholarly arrogance is a widespread phenomenon. The paths of the Torah are said to be peace, yet there is much quarrelsomeness among its scholars. A scholar's heart is to be directed toward heaven, yet much Torah study has degenerated into an arid cleverness bent on scoring points against others and devoid of all thought of heaven. Indeed, since Torah study is of ever-increasing complexity, the last-named has been of all corruptions the most persistent and widespread, inevitably so whenever what was stated in this book at the outset is ignored, belittled or forgotten: that in Judaism the activity of the commentator and subcommentator is balanced by that of the summarizer and simplifier.

He is needed not only as a teacher of such as Hillel's pagan or Akiba's donkey driver, but also as one to remind even the most learned that, however complex, Judaism, like all great things, is also simple.

We have listed corruptions—or a few of them—that have existed through the ages. A new corruption of Torah study has appeared with the advent of a Jewish state. The state has enemies whose wish to destroy it shows few signs of weakening. To this day it has survived only because its soldiers are prepared to risk their lives for it, and many soldiers have given theirs. Numerous Torah students can live and study in the state because the state exists. Facing up to this fact, some of their number do their share in defending the state's existence and even insist on doing so. Yet many let others risk and even give their lives in order that they, the scholars, can study in peace. One cannot say for sure what Rabbi Zadok would say about such as these, for the situation is unprecedented. I suspect he would consider it a case of making the Torah a spade to dig with.

TORAH STUDY

Once a friend took Rose and myself into a large Yeshiva in Tel Aviv. He told us its story. An Eastern European rabbi's whole family had perished in the Holocaust. He alone had managed to escape to Shanghai. There he vowed that if God would let him reach the Holy Land he would build a Yeshiva in His honor. And here it was.

The story raises grave questions we cannot ask till the very last chapter of the present book. While we were in the Yeshiva they were suspended. There they were in the large hall, hundreds of Torah students, at each table two studying together; and whenever they came upon a problem they could not solve, one of the two would go for help to the rabbi sitting in front. A gentle, reverent humming sound permeated the hall, confirming the view I first formed when I studied with that Berlin rabbi—that of all activities Torah study is most akin to prayer.

That this is so is the explicit and unanimous teaching of the rabbis. The second-century Rabbi Hananya ben Tradiyon states that if two sit together, and words of Torah are between them, then the *shechina* dwells between them (*Abot* 3:3). His contemporary Shim'on bar Yohai is on record to the effect that if three have spoken words of Torah while eating at a table, it is as though they had eaten at the table of Him who is omnipresent (*Abot* 3:4). The near-contemporary of both, Rabbi Halafta ben Dossa, is most explicit. Giving Scriptural proofs for each case, he asserts that the *shechina* dwells between ten who occupy themselves with the Torah, and that the same applies to five, to three, to two, and even to one (*Abot* 3:7). His saying is of special interest for two reasons. It emphasizes that what matters with the *shechina* is not the number of the Torah scholars but their devoutness. And it has some difficulty when there is only one. The *shechina* dwells *between* those studying Torah; and in the Tel Aviv Yeshiva (and others like it) students are divided into groups of two, studying together. Just as it is not good for man to be alone, so it is not good for a student to study Torah alone. Then how can the *shechina* dwell even with one? Perhaps he is the only one left. Perhaps there are other good reasons for his solitariness. The God who gave the Torah, I take Halafta as teaching, does not abandon such as him to his solitariness. In support of his view, Halafta cites Exod. 20:21: "In every place where I cause My name to be mentioned I will come unto thee and bless thee."

What is the *shechina*, and what *ha-makom*, i.e., God referred to as the Omnipresent One? What is referred to with these terms is the presence of God. We have already come upon this fundamental commitment of a Jew. We shall come upon it again. It raises many questions, perhaps best articulated succinctly in the fact that a Jew at prayer addresses God both as *ribbono shel olam*, "Master of the universe," and as *avinu she-bashamayim*, "our Father in heaven." How can He who is beyond the heaven of heavens also be the father of puny ones such as we? This question will be with us to the end. For the present the following must suffice. *Ha-makom* is He who can be present, and who is present when scholars study Torah in earnest. The *shechina* is the "indwelling" of what, for want of a better rendering, we must refer to as the spirit of God between those studying Torah, provided they direct their hearts to heaven. Here lies the innermost secret of Torah study, and the source of its life.

A few illustrations should be provided. Should I, an amateur in complicated Halachic disputes, provide samples of these? I think not, and in deciding otherwise I have in mind not only my own limitations but also those of *amcha* who, I fondly hope, will be among the book's readers. In thinking of *amcha* what comes to mind is the Haggada, the slim volume read not only by scholars but by every family during the Seder, celebrated on the first night of the Pesach festival. (This is in Israel. In the Diaspora the Seder is celebrated for two nights.) In the volume we are told of five second-century rabbis, Eliezer, Joshua, Eleazar ben Azaryah, Akiba, and Tarfon, who once spent a whole Seder night discussing the great wonder celebrated that day, the Exodus from Egypt. One takes it that even few of the ultralearned and ultrapious ever repeated the marathon feat of these five. Even *amcha*, however, spend several hours that night on the Torah study that the Haggada contains. Inserted in the textual commentaries are several monumental assertions. One is that in each generation a Jew is to regard himself as though he had personally come forth from Egypt: This *amcha* have done through the ages. Another is that whereas in each generation those arise that plot to exterminate the Jewish people, the Holy One, blessed be He, saves it from their hands. This to *amcha* have lived by at all times. Whether a Jew can do so still in our time has become questionable.

But those who would quickly despair of the possibility should consider the Ginsberg family. They are refuseniks in Leningrad whom Rose and I visited in 1977. Already then they were waiting for permission to leave for Israel, and so far as we know they are waiting still. We spent a Shabbat evening in their small apartment, crowded for the occasion of our visit by similarly minded Jews. I no longer remember the subject of our discussion. But unforgettable is a sign that hung on the wall and, I am sure, hangs there still. It was yet another of the monumental assertions contained in the Haggada: "Praised be He who keeps His promise to Israel."

The popular imagination has all sorts of stories about the end of days. In a song loved by *amcha* the question is asked what will happen when the Messiah, having hesitated for so long, will arrive at last. There will of course be a feast, but there must be more than just eating and drinking. The great figures of the ancient past will reappear to help in the celebration. Who will make music for us? David will play the harp, and Miriam, the drum! And who, is the climactic question, will teach us Torah? Why, it will be Moses himself, our teacher! Presently not all can study Torah equally, and many, not at all. With Moses himself as teacher, Torah study will belong equally to the whole people, in the end of days.

EPILOGUE

On top of Mount Scopus in Jerusalem stands a building. It houses the Institute for Contemporary Jewry, an institute that is part of the Hebrew University. With a well-deserved reputation for academic excellence, it houses scholars whose scholarship is above reproach. Their subject—not ancient but contemporary history—poses many temptations for lapsing into ideology, politics, and even propaganda. The institute possesses the reputation it has because its members resist such temptations. They adhere to Ranke's thesis that a scholar must study the past "as it really was."

At the entrance of the building sits a guard. The threat of terrorism necessitates his presence. His task is to guard the professors, them and their research. The guard is, as he must be, a man of action. He must be willing to act, able to act, and to act swiftly, decisively, and without intellectual ifs and buts. But in his job he has a great deal of leisure time. He spends his time studying books of Torah. I have entered the building on many occasions. Rarely have I seen him do anything else.

Doubtless this man holds the professors he guards in high

esteem. Most folk in Israel do. As once I walked past him an idea crossed my mind. What if for a change the roles were reversed? In Israel most professors know how to guard. What if guard duty were assumed by one of their number while Torah was taught by the guard to the rest? The rabbis advise us to be prepared to learn from any man. In our time, this ancient advice could have a new significance.

8. THE ETHICS
OF JUDAISM—
GOD'S LOVE OF
WIDOWS, ORPHANS,
THE STRANGER, THE POOR

ON BEING A *MENSCH*

A great many Jews have but a nodding acquaintance with Torah study, and hence little if any concern with the 613 *mitzvot;* and as is only to be expected, fewer still wrestle seriously with that most uncomfortable of traditional teachings, the covenant and the chosen people. Quite remarkable, in contrast, is the fact that many of even otherwise quite assimilated Jews still know the meaning of "a *mitzve.*" (I am using the Yiddish pronunciation of the Hebrew word.) Someone will say, "For so-and-so to do this was a real *mitzve,*" or, "I simply must do this, it is a *mitzve,*" and the otherwise quite assimilated Jew understands and in all likelihood approves. I ponder this fact and conclude: Perhaps for many an assimilated Jew who wonders whether it is possible for him to become a *ba'al teshuvah,* the best way to start is by himself pondering the meaning and implications of "doing a *mitzve.*"

The word is hard to translate. "Good deed" sounds too pious and solemn, "duty" too much like something one ought to do but doesn't really want to do. Perhaps the best translation is this, that to do a *mitzve* is to behave like a *mensch*. But then, "human being" is not quite the right translation for the Yiddish *mensch* either. Perhaps the only way is to give an example, and the best possible example is this: God Himself behaves like a *mensch* when He loves widows and orphans.

But who except Jews (and following them, Christians) has ever heard of a God loving widows and orphans? A God (or gods) loving heroes, sages, and martyrs one has heard of. All these, however—the martyrs included—are winners. Widows and orphans, in contrast, are losers. Perhaps Divinity can love even these, provided they are its own, much like a person who loves his widowed mother or his orphaned nephew or niece. That this is so with the "Old Testament" God has long been stock-in-trade propaganda of the kind of Christian who knows no other way of exalting his New Testament than by denigrating the Old. However, this particular canard—that the Jewish God loves Jews only—is disposed of by the fact that He loves the stranger as well:

> The Lord your God . . . executes justice for the fatherless and the widow, and loves the stranger. (Deut. 10:17–18)

Does God merely execute justice for widows and orphans, whereas the stranger He loves? Be that as it may, the stranger is the third in the trinity of losers, beloved of the God of Israel.

Our use of the paradoxical expression "God behaves like a *mensch*" is of course quite deliberate. It brings to light the question of why God, being God, does not make losers into winners. The question is all the more puzzling because on many occasions He does just that. We have already referred to the hymn of thanksgiving offered by the childless Hannah after her prayer is heard and she has given birth to Samuel. Her hymn includes the following passage: "He lifts up the needy from the dunghill and makes them into princes" (I Sam. 2:8). More striking still in the present context is the following passage:

> He raises up the lowly out of the dust, and lifts up the needy from the dunghill, that He may set him with princes, even with

the princes of His people. He makes the barren woman dwell in her house, as a joyful mother of children. (Ps. 113:7–9)

Hannah's prayer is the spontaneous outburst of a happy woman. The psalm is part of the liturgy of a whole people—part of the so-called Hallel (composed of psalms 113–18) that is recited when communal thanksgiving is in order, i.e., on the festival of the new moon, Pesach, Shavuot, Succot, and Hanukkah. (See more on these festivals in chapter 10.) If the divine making of losers into winners is part of the faith of Judaism, so much so as to be institutionalized in its liturgy, why are there losers that *remain* losers? The question becomes all the more striking because of the rule that in houses of mourning the Hallel is not to be recited on the new moon and Hanukkah festivals. God may make some losers into winners, but losers there still are. So are there houses of mourning.

THE MAINSPRING OF JEWISH ETHICS

This question permeates the faith of Judaism, after the Holocaust shaking it to its foundations. For the present the relevant fact is that since losers there are, and since God does love them, it is a *mitzve* for us to love them as well, and to do what we can to relieve their condition. One might call this the mainspring of Jewish ethics. It is, at any rate, what gives it its special flavor.

The mainspring or foundations of Jewish ethics are subject of a debate between Akiba and Ben Azzai, two second-century rabbis of whom mention has already been made. Both look for a verse in the Tenach containing a "great principle" of the Torah. Akiba cites Lev. 19:1, "Thou shalt love thy neighbor as thyself." Ben Azzai cites Gen. 5:1 as being greater still: "This is the book of the generations of Man." In another version of the text the order is reversed: Ben Azzai comes first with his verse, and Akiba after him, maintaining that Lev. 19:1 is greater than Gen. 5:1. A case can be made for both.

The case for Akiba is obvious: A neighbor is neither an abstraction nor an ideal but rather a mixture of good and bad, and, more importantly still, a flesh-and-blood person living next door; there is no word for the abstraction "mankind" in the Tenach. What then is the case for Ben Azzai? It is possible to make friends even with a total stranger if he lives next door. One cannot make friends even with a cousin one has never met and with whom one has never been even in correspondence: The "brotherhood of man," unless it is part of a messianic hope, is a romantic illusion. Hence people distant and unknown threaten to reduce themselves for us to "the masses," quantifiable, replaceable, or even expendable. Ben Azzai's point is that, simply by virtue of being human—created in the image of God—even the least of humans is unique and irreplaceable, and that no one at all is expendable.

One takes Akiba and Ben Azzai together and arrives at a much-quoted rabbinic statement: "He who saves but a single human life is regarded as though he had saved the whole world." The statement has a simple and obvious moral significance. But behind its obvious meaning lies one so deep as to encompass the ultimate moral condition of all humanity as perceived in Judaism. Its condition is wedged between the extremes of despair and hope. On one side, there is helpless despair at the prospect of thousands or millions who, by dint of hunger, war, or pestilence, will soon be as though they never had been—a "whole world." On the other side, there is the bright hope that, except for the utterly wicked, in the end of days no one at all will be as though he never had been. Wedged between these extremes lies the *mitzve* of taking the saving of even a single human life—any life, or almost any— with the most radical seriousness. Why only "almost any"? And why the exception of the wicked? To put the two questions to-gether, is there a wickedness so extreme as to be beyond redemp-tion? Such has always been the sober view of the tradition. Imbued with the modernistic belief that idolatry is a mere species of super-stition, and wickedness a mere sickness, modern Jewish thinkers have often belittled that view if they have not openly rejected it. After the Holocaust, however, the existence of a wickedness beyond redemption is undeniable. It is necessary to reconsider the tradi-tional view and indeed, to deepen and extend it.

HOW TO LOVE THE POOR

The mention of starvation brings to mind the poor, making the trinity of losers beloved of God into a quaternity. Are these, however, in the same class as the other three? This is the view of those for whom the poor are all innocent victims, though in this case not of nature but of robber barons and similar exploiters. But there exists also the exact opposite view, that the poor, far from innocent victims, are responsible for their own condition. The first is the view of doctrinaire socialists and certain Christians—those for whom not only are the holy poor but also, *ipso facto*, the poor are holy. The second is the view of doctrinaire capitalists, as well as certain other Christians, for whom wealth is the reward of hard work and thrift, and poverty the punishment for wastefulness, shiftlessness, and sloth. Doubtless Jews have often been blown by the winds of fashion, just as Christians have. But that neither of the extremes just mentioned is the teaching of Judaism is expressed with great clarity in *Eight Degrees of Charity*, a text of the Rambam that deserves to be quoted very nearly in full:

> There are eight degrees of charity. . . . The highest degree is that of a person who assists a poor Jew by providing him with a gift or loan or by accepting him into a business partnership or by helping him find employment—in a word, by putting him where he can dispense with other people's aid. . . . A step below this stands the one who gives alms to the needy in such a manner that the giver knows not to whom he gives and the recipient knows not from whom he takes. This exemplifies performing the meritorious act for its own sake. . . . The rank next to this is of him who drops money into a charity box. One should not do so . . . unless one is sure that the person in charge is trustworthy, wise and competent to handle the funds properly. One step lower is that in which the giver knows to whom he gives but the poor person knows not from whom he receives. . . . A step lower is that in which the poor person knows from whom he is taking but the giver knows not to whom he is giving. . . . The next degree lower is that of him who, with his own hand, bestows a gift before the poor person asks. The next degree lower

is that of him who gives less than is fitting but gives with a gracious mien. The next degree is that of him who gives morosely . . .

This classical and authoritative text suffices to show that the social ethics of Judaism cannot be reduced to the capitalist, socialist, or indeed any socioeconomic scheme of things. The attempt has of course often been made, the most recent case being the attempt to understand the Hebrew prophets as forerunners of socialism. And it is indeed the case that, in the Messianic age as perceived by the prophets, economic competition (to say nothing of exploitation) will have ceased. Private property, however, will continue to exist. This is why, on the one hand, each will sit under his own vine and fig tree and, on the other, none will make them afraid (Micah 4:4).

THE ETHICS OF PERSONAL CONDUCT

That God behaves like a *mensch* is not an idea brought to the sources by us, from without and arbitrarily; it is found in the sources themselves. It is an answer to a seemingly impossible question. It is hard enough for Aristotle to ask man at his highest to "imitate" God, yet his God is only the highest part of the world. How can the Torah ask a Jew to do likewise, when its God is the Creator of heaven and earth, and infinitely above both? The Midrash replies: because God Himself, as it were, behaves like a human at his most humane.

> Rabbi Simlai expounded: the Torah begins with an act of lovingkindness, and ends with an act of lovingkindness. It begins with an act of lovingkindness, as it is written, "the Lord God made for Adam and his wife garments of skin and clothed them." (Gen. 3:21) It ends with an act of lovingkindness, as it is written, "He buried him [Moses] in the valley of Moab . . . (Deut. 34:6)

Neither Adam nor Eve nor Moses were exactly losers. Thus we learn that God's behaving like a *mensch* is not confined to losers;

neither is it so confined for a Jew who acts in imitation of God. Jewish ethics covers the whole range of personal conduct, between parents and children, husbands and wives, brothers and sisters, friends and enemies; and it does not forget *mitzvot* owed by a person toward himself. This is obviously a vast subject in its own right. Here only a few samples will be given, and we advisedly confine these to the already much-quoted *Pirke Avot*. Not only is this the most popular treatise of the Mishnah; the rabbis *meant* it to be popular, and it is included to this day in the *Siddur*, for reading in the synagogue on Shabbat afternoons between Pesach and Rosh Hashanah. This treatise was meant to be studied by *amcha*, and studied by *amcha* it once was. Here are some samples:

HILLEL: Be of the disciples of Aaron, loving peace and pursuing peace, loving your fellow-creatures and drawing them near to the Torah. (1:12)

HILLEL AGAIN: Judge not your neighbor until you are in his place. (2:5)

SHAMMAI: Say little and do much, and receive all men with a cheerful countenance. (1:15)

BEN ZOMA: Who is wise? He who learns from all men. . . . Who is mighty? He who subdues his passions. . . . Who is rich? He who is satisfied with his portion. . . . Who is honored? He who honors others . . . (4:1)

BEN AZZAI: Despise not any man, and carp not at anything; for there is not a man who has not his hour, and there is not a thing that does not have its place. (4:3)

ELEAZAR BEN SHAMMAI: Let the honor of your disciple be as dear to you as your own. (4:15)

The male chauvinism in *Pirke Abot* and other rabbinic texts has already been dealt with. So has the fact that by most standards the rabbis' emphasis on Torah study is excessive. But that otherwise this ethics reflects a humane, utterly decent outlook on the world can hardly be denied. If by modern standards it seems somewhat straitlaced, it should be mentioned that the same ethics that has produced the statement that "God loves one who never gets angry or drunk," has also produced the statement that "he who refrains from wine is called a sinner." Indeed, Rav, the third-century founder of the great Babylonian Talmud academy of Sura, went so far as to say: "On Judgment Day every person will have to give account of every good that he might have enjoyed and did not."

JUSTICE

We turn to the subject of justice last. Most readers would expect it to be the first if not sole subject in an ethics of Judaism. This is due to a Christian polemic beginning with the New Testament. Just as Old Testament "law" has over the centuries been contrasted with New Testament "grace," so through these centuries the ethics of the Jewish Bible has been said to consist of justice only, with an ethics of love having to wait for the advent of Christianity. Not infrequently the polemic has been extreme. In the Gospel of Matthew Jesus is quoted as saying, "You have learned how it was said, 'You must love your neighbor and hate your enemy'" (5:43). But there is no commandment to hate the enemy in any Jewish source I have ever read or heard of. Again, Christian polemics frequently make Jewish "justice" into "vengeance," a polemic that has had its effects to this day. When in 1961 the most horrendous criminal ever to be tried by a Jewish court was brought for trial to Jerusalem, the Canadian Broadcasting Corporation featured a nationwide television program. It was entitled: "The Eichmann Trial—Justice or Vengeance?"

The most powerful and influential Christian critique of the ethics of Judaism is doubtless the Sermon on the Mount (Matthew 5–7:27). That it is a great text in the religious ethic of mankind I have never doubted, but always with certain reservations. "Happy are those who are persecuted in the cause of right, for theirs is the kingdom of heaven." So it is with those who offer the wicked man no resistance, who, with respect to food, neither sow nor reap but imitate the birds, and with regard to clothing, neither work nor spin but imitate the flowers. (That the flowers are "more splendid than was Solomon in all his regalia" one is glad to concede.) I can think only of two ways in which the Sermon on the Mount is to be understood. It is either an ethics for saintly individuals, with no children to feed, to clothe, or to protect from attacks of the wicked. Or else it is a message to the losers among the losers, such as those so poor that the *mitzve* to love the losers, practiced here and there by the charitable, is of small help to them, or else the incurably ill that are altogether beyond human help. The kingdom of heaven that, with Jesus, is theirs is a kingdom either within or beyond. But it is not a kingdom of this earth.

But what of an ethics for this earth? Doubtless the advice to turn the other cheek when the wicked man smites is meant to shame this latter out of his wickedness. But what if instead the wicked man smites the other cheek harder, to the accompaniment of Nazi-style laughter? I withdraw the expression "Nazi-style." For behavior such as this, a Nazi is not required. Ordinary thugs or sadists are quite enough. No Christian state or society has ever been based on the Sermon on the Mount, nor could it have been. This side of the Messianic age, no state or society can be based on love alone. Not a good but only an utterly wicked state or society can dispense with justice.

"Justice, justice, shalt thou follow . . . !" (Deut. 16:20) According to one Midrash the Torah begins and ends with an act of lovingkindness. According to another the whole Torah rests on justice; and whereas history does not begin with justice but rather the fall of the first pair of humans, with justice it will end: Not until just judgment has come, on the one hand, for the poor and the meek, and on the other, for the wicked, will it be possible for the wolf to dwell with the lamb (Isa. 11: 4–6).

What is justice? It is not to respect persons in judgment (Deut. 1:17). Justice is obviously perverted if "the person of the mighty" is "favored" (Lev. 20:15), or a bribe is taken from the rich (Deut. 16:19), or on account of their impotence the justice "due to the stranger or the fatherless" is denied them (Deut. 24:17). Less obvious, but no less essential, is that in judgment the poor are to be respected no more than the rich. Love regards persons. Justice does not regard persons but the nature of the case. On justice, a

Midrash asserts, the world depends, and when the second-century
Rabbi Simon ben Gamliel lists three pillars on which the world
rests, justice is among them. (The other two are truth and peace.)

Love is not among these pillars. Can it be dispensed with? Can
it be dispensed with even in judgment? The "written" Torah repeatedly demands "an eye for an eye, a tooth for a tooth" (Exod.
21:24, Lev. 24:20, Deut. 19:21). These repeated demands notwithstanding, the "oral" Torah takes them to mean that appropriate
compensation is to be paid. The Torah permits the death penalty.
Yet the rabbis considered a court that decreed one death penalty
in seventy years to be a murderous court. As for a court pronounc-
ing such a sentence, Rabbi Akiba taught that its members should
fast on that day, on the grounds that "ye shall not eat anything
with the blood" (Lev. 19:26).

The ultimate ground for the indispensability of love in justice
is implied in a custom of Rabbi Akiba's. When people came before him in a trifling case, he would tell them the following:
"Know before whom you stand—not before me, Rabbi Akiba, but
before the Creator of the world." But who can stand in judgment
before God? All need love even in justice, since justice alone would
destroy them. And we all stand in judgment before God.

But who is this God before Whom we stand? This question has
a clear-cut answer in Judaism in all of its forms. The biblical critics
postulate an "Elohist" and a "Yahvist" among the sources of the
Tenach, according to the two words used for the Deity, Elohim
and YHVE. (See chapter 3, section 8.) For the rabbis one signifies
the divine attribute of judgment; the other, that of mercy. On the
highest of holy days Jews recite the *avinu, malkenu,* a plea addressed to a God who is both loving "father" and judging "king."
The two attributes are both necessary and mutually irreducible.
The grounds for both are given in a Midrash in which God is compared to an owner of precious glasses. If the owner pours hot water
into them they will break, and so also if he pours cold water; so
the owner mixes hot and cold, and his glasses are saved. Even so
the Master of the universe said unto Himself: If I judge the world
in all-forgiving love, sins will abound; if in strict justice, no one
will live. So He decided to mix the two, and the world is preserved.

The God of Israel loves the losers of the world; but because losers they still are we are bidden to love them. He also loves justice; but because injustice is rife still we are bidden to seek justice. But when we mete out justice we must take care lest the glasses handed over to us for stewardship break.

AMALEK

May no enemy be hated? Is it always commanded to punish the sin but hope for the repentance of the sinner?

> Remember what Amalek did unto thee by the way as ye came forth out of Egypt; how he met thee by the way and smote the hindmost of thee, all that were enfeebled in thy rear, when thou wast faint and weary; and he feared not God. Therefore it shall be, when the Lord hath given thee rest from all thine enemies round about, in the land which the Lord thy God giveth thee for an inheritance to possess it, that thou shalt blot out the remembrance of Amalek from under heaven; thou shalt not forget. (Deut. 25:17–19)

This is of course a frightening passage: It commands genocide. Moreover, there is one case in which, for once, the commandment was at least partially obeyed. Samuel orders the newly anointed Saul, the first king of Israel, at long last to obey the ancient commandment to wipe out Amalek, to spare neither "man or woman, infant or suckling, ox or sheep, camel or ass" (I Sam. 15:3). Saul wins a great victory but obeys Samuel's orders only partly: He spares not only the best of the sheep and the oxen but also Agag, the king of the Amalekites. Whereupon the Word of God comes to Samuel bidding him take away the kingship from Saul for his disobedience. Samuel does as he is bidden. Also, he has Agag, a prisoner in chains, brought before him. He says to the king, "As thy sword has made women childless, so shall thy mother be childless among women" (15:32). Then he hacks the helpless man to pieces.

Deeply troubled, an Orthodox Jew once came to Martin Buber

and asked him: "How is such a thing possible? Saul shows mercy yet is punished, and the one who is cruel and without mercy is a prophet of God!" Buber was silent for a moment. Then he replied, "I believe that Samuel misunderstood God." Buber's answer provokes thought, but fails to satisfy on two points. The first might not overly concern a Jew today: There are false prophets, but if even true prophets can err—err in a matter so crucial!—have there ever been prophets at all? The second point, in contrast, ought to concern a Jew today greatly: Buber disposes of radical evil, for if even Amalek is not a case of it, then radical evil does not exist. Here we are served better by the tradition: Amalek continues to be recognized but is symbolized; and the result is that both radical evil is deprived of its hereditary character, and that the specter of genocide disappears. One may wonder, for example, whether after so many centuries even the biblical "Haman the Agagite" (Esther 3:1) is meant to be literally a descendant of Agag. When in the end Haman's ten sons as well as Haman are put to death (Esther 9:7–9), the rabbis are careful to stress that this was because they had participated in Haman's crime. Adolf Eichmann was captured, abducted, and sentenced to death by an Israeli court; but it occurred to no one to go after his children. Dr. Josef Mengele, the murderous Auschwitz doctor, kept in hiding for decades, the fruitless object of a worldwide hunt; but his children lived in Germany openly, without having to fear being abducted by Israeli agents. And in 1950 the Israeli Parliament passed two relevant laws; one abolishing the death penalty, the other, establishing the death penalty for "crimes against the Jewish people," i.e., Nazi murderers. Eichmann was sentenced under this law. But, whether prudently or not, to this day no Arab terrorist, however bloody his crime, has been sentenced to death by an Israeli court.

The crime of the biblical Amalek consists of attacking "the hindmost," the weakest. What is the criminality of the rabbinic Amalek? He attacks the weakest because they are weakest, in the imagery of one rabbi, like a fly looking for sores on which to feed. He singles out Israel for attack *because* Israel is singled out by God for a covenant, his aim being to destroy the covenant as he destroys Israel. In an anachronism one Midrash goes so far as to assert that

Amalek destroys Torah scrolls. The anachronism is surely deliberate, for the biblical attack by Amalek occurred just prior to the Sinaitic revelation (Exod. 17:8–16). But just this deliberate anachronism serves to both symbolize the biblical Amalek and universalize what Amalek stands for. Destroying Torah scrolls was a favorite sport of Amalek's heirs, from the Middle Ages to the Holocaust. Most significant, perhaps, of all of the rabbinic Amalek's characteristics is this, that he does not repent even at the very gates of hell.

To distinguish between Amalek and evil in general is always a difficult task for the ethics of Judaism. At one extreme lies the danger of making every enemy into Amalek, when in fact the rabbis bid a Jew to try to make an enemy into a friend. (The rabbis try to lessen this danger by suggesting that even Amalek, or at any rate his continued existence, is often caused by Jewish sins.) Our own age has shown, however, that no less great is the opposite danger, the belief or dream that Amalek does not exist. The rabbis teach that the righteous of all nations have a share in the world to come. (See chapter 12, section 6.) If Eichmann is not in hell, hell does not exist. If he is in heaven, the righteous of all nations have left it in protest.

EPILOGUE

> Beloved is man in that he was created in the image of God. Greater love still was shown to him in that he was informed that he was thus created, as it is said, "For God made man in His own image." (Gen. 9:6; *Abot* 3:18)

This saying of Rabbi Akiba's raises a great question: All are created in the image of God; but how can all have the knowledge of the fact when only some have the Book in which it is disclosed? This question will require scrutiny. (See chapter 12, sections 3–6.) Obvious is the fact that some lack the knowledge, that others possess and accept it, and that others still hear the message but do all they can by word and deed to reject it: This is Amalek. The behavior of Amalek has always existed. But not until this century was a world created in which the divine image was systematically destroyed. In manufacturing *Muselmaenner*—walking corpses—the Auschwitz criminals destroyed the divine image in their victims; and in doing what they did they destroyed it in themselves as well.

In consequence a new necessity has arisen for the ethics of Judaism in our time. What has been broken must be mended. Even for a Jew who cannot believe in God it is necessary to act as though man were made in His image.

9. STANDING BEFORE GOD
IN PRAYER

PRAYER, ANIMAL SACRIFICES, AND "MODERN MAN"

No account of Jewish prayer that is both honest and thorough can ignore the subject of animal sacrifices. For "modern man," this is embarrassing. But, as we have already mentioned, it was already so for the premodern Maimonides. At least in his capacity as the philosopher Maimonides, he viewed the ancient practice in terms approximating those of modern evolutionary thought, as surpassed by subsequent developments, and never to return. However, as the Orthodox Jewish Rambam he kept on reciting the prayers that call for their eventual restoration, at the time of the Messianic rebuilding of the Jerusalem Temple. And these same prayers are part of the Orthodox prayer books to this day. It is true, however, that all liberal as well as a good many Conservative Jews have dropped them, as the case may be, shamefacedly, forthrightly, or even with enthusiasm.

But might not the same reasons that cause modern man to

dispose of animal sacrifices apply also to prayer? Is prayer petitionary? But if this is for things trivial, are we not like children
asking gifts from their parents? And if it is for things serious (such
as health in grave illness), are we not well advised to rely on the
medical arts rather than prayer? And if, finally, petitionary prayer
comes into its own only when matters are beyond human help—
what are we to say of humanity, of its courage, its maturity? It is
said that there are no atheists in foxholes: This does not say much
either for man or his religion. Moreover, this particular proverb
is far from universally true. In World War I German soldiers were
given a choice as to which of two books they wished to carry with
them in battle. One was the Bible, the other, the atheist Nietzsche's
Also Sprach Zarathustra. The German military authorities were interested not in religion but in making their men fight for the fatherland; and, in their view at least, some would risk death as bravely
without God as others would with Him.

Is all prayer, then, ultimately thanksgiving? Even an agnostic
or atheist can be filled with a deep—if unspecified—gratitude for
good fortune, freedom, the gift of life itself. But how can anyone
thank God for the evils that have befallen him? It may be possible
to *accept* these, resignedly and with fortitude. But to *thank* God
for them seems positively demeaning.

Does all prayer, then, in the last analysis reduce itself to praise?
This many thoughtful religious people have often seriously considered: We shall find a degree of truth in this ourselves. Yet this
view too has its difficulties for modern man. There may be something akin to prayer in the ultimate wonder that at times grips us—
at the order of the universe, at its beauty, at the sheer fact that
anything at all exists rather than nothing. Yet there still remains
one fundamental difference between this kind of wonder and
prayer: Prayer is addressed to someone, and it presupposes that,
if not necessarily answered, it is at any rate "heard."

Yet what would happen if prayer were to go the way of animal
sacrifices, to vanish? When the Temple was destroyed its place
was taken—in the view of some temporarily, in that of others,
permanently—by the synagogue in which prayer was offered instead of sacrifices, and prayer is "the sacrifice of the lips." But

would Judaism survive the abolition of prayer, with the "syna-gogue" becoming what the Greek word literally means—a "house of assembly"—and nothing more? But through the ages it has been a "house of prayer" also.

The question is of crucial importance to one who "holds him-self open to faith." Reviewing the "Life of Judaism" as thus far considered (chapters 5–8), a Jew may consider himself "chosen" yet remain uncommitted to the One who may—or may not—do the choosing. (Some modern Jews have asserted that God did not choose the Jews, but the Jews chose God—or the Ten Command-ments or a humane morality.) To move on, a Jew may do *mitzvot* without accepting the *metzavve* ("the One who commands"). He may certainly obey the *mitzvah* to study, and also—indeed above all—obey the *mitzvah* to behave like a *mensch*. A Jew could go along with all these aspects of the life of Judaism without ever quite reaching the climax to which the first part of this book has pointed: that the "faith" to which he is to "hold himself open" includes the possibility of an incursion of the Divine, not only into the world of man in general, or even the covenantal community in general, but into his own life. Thinkers may demonstrate that this possibility exists for the modern as well as the premodern Jew. (See above, chapters 1, section 2 and 4, sections 1 and 5.) But they can do no more. Hence unless *amcha* can be committed to the belief that prayer is "heard," Judaism, as it has existed ever since its origins, will come to an end. Such is the pivotal point at which we in this book have now arrived.

THE ORIGIN OF JEWISH PRAYER IN THE SACRIFICIAL CULT

"Modern man" at his most radical disposes of prayer. Even at his least radical he knows how to dispose of animal sacrifices. Primi-tive man was afraid of the unknown. He populated the unknown with angry deities. Whether angry with or without reason, these deities needed to be appeased. Primitive man did appease them, by sacrificing the produce of the fields, cheap animals such as hens, expensive animals such as rams and bullocks, and, if the fear of the divine anger was extreme, even his own children. Such was the practice of the worshipers of Moloch. Such would have been the practice of Abraham with Isaac, if the angel had not stayed his hand at the last moment. Or, rather, such would have been his practice had there ever been such a person and such an incident. For in fact the story merely symbolizes an "evolutionary process" that ends by making irrelevant not only human sacrifice but sacrifice as a whole.

For, of course, we moderns stand in no fear of angry deities that need to be appeased. An unknown there may remain, even "the Unknowable." But the former we try to understand, and the latter—if an Unknowable there is—we simply ignore: We do not populate it with deities. A bad but once widely popular philosopher, Herbert Spencer, called the unknowable "God"; indeed, he performed the remarkable feat of writing ninety pages about the unknowable. A better philosopher, F. H. Bradley, remarked acidly that Spencer's sole reason for calling it God was that he did not know what the devil it was.

In this manner modern man disposes of the whole subject of sacrifices: The entire practice was nothing but superstitious appeasement of gods or demons, done away with by modern enlightenment—both the gods themselves and the fear of them. But is this the end of the matter? Is it even the beginning? Once it struck me especially forcefully that this whole approach to the subject is based on nothing but a shallow modernistic prejudice, projected on ancient realities beyond "modern man's" ken. (I spell out what I hope has been evident from the start—that modern man need not be "modern man," and that he need not be either prejudiced or shallow.)

My family and I were climbing Mount Sinai. On each of the other four occasions we had done so our guides had rushed us to the top so as to reach it at sunrise. This guide stopped at every little holy place and explained what there was to explain. Partway up we came upon a small but lovely oasis, with a building in the midst of it. It was called, the guide informed us, "the monastery of the forty martyrs." Then he told us the story. Once a band of marauding Bedouins had attacked the monastery and killed thirty-nine of the monks. A survivor said to himself: "What is my duty now? Thirty-nine is not a holy number, but forty is!" So he committed holy suicide, for the greater glory of God. "What a perversion!" was my first reaction. "And this at the very mountain from which issued the commandment, 'Thou shalt choose life!' "

But gradually further thoughts came to my mind. What if, as explained above with reference to the Twenty-ninth Psalm (chapter 4, section 2), a divine presence reduced all to nothingness, and induced in those experiencing that presence an awareness of their own nothingness; what if, as stark terror turned into awe, the awareness of nothingness turned into a yearning for pious self-surrender? What more radical, more serious expression could such self-surrender have than holy suicide? "Modern man" has made all sacrifice into an attempt to appease the deities, motivated by fear. The purpose of such appeasement presumably must have been to save one's own—one's property, one's family, or at any rate one's own life. If so, the holy suicide of that monk partway up to Mount Sinai was a strange way indeed of appeasing the gods! In fact, of course, it cannot be understood in terms such as these at all. His shocking behavior appears rather as an extreme—nay, unsurpassable—form of self-surrender, or self-sacrifice. In these *genuinely religious* terms its inner logic is obvious; and it is the commandment to choose life that now seems to become unobvious! For "modern man" that particular commandment is obvious, and he may even be fond of quoting it. But this is so only because he has reduced a premodern religious profundity to a modern humanistic, if nice, platitude.

But whether holy or not, the Tenach forbids suicide. We therefore withdraw one step, to the sacrifice of one's children. This too, of course, is forbidden in the Tenach. The condemnation of it would hardly have been so vehement, however, had nothing more serious been at stake than fear and appeasement of angry deities. Franz Rosenzweig rightly observes that many a "Carthaginian father must have shed a tear as he led his son to the sacrifice of Moloch." Might such a father not have loved his son more than his own life and, if appeasement was needed, offered his own life

so that his son might live? Such would certainly have been the
case with Abraham, for when eventually he died it was "in good
old age, an old man, and full of years" (Gen. 25:8), fulfilled in
the knowledge that Isaac lived; yet when the word came, "Take
now thy son, thine only son, whom thou lovest," he was prepared
to do what he was told. Through the ages a Jew has had to struggle with the awesome story of the *Akeda*, the sacrifice of Isaac
(Gen. 22:1–19). God commands Abraham to sacrifice Isaac, the
very son through whose descendants the nations were to be blessed;
the father is ready to obey without a murmur of protest, but is
stopped by divine intervention at the last moment: The whole
matter was only a test of his faith, the supreme test in his whole
life. How could the God of Abraham demand such a thing? How
could Abraham be willing to obey? Jews have always had to struggle with the fearsome story of the *Akeda* ("the binding"), calling
it by that name so as forever to remind themselves that there was
no sacrifice but a reprieve. Many Midrashim grapple with the story.
And then there were times when no reprieve came: the Crusades,
the Inquisition, and—a catastrophe as yet hardly confronted by the
religious consciousness—the Holocaust. New Midrashim may be
required for the *Akeda*. One thing, however, is clear: This text is
the traditional Torah reading for Rosh Hashanah, and that place it
must continue to occupy.

We withdraw a further step, to *olah*, the "burnt offering" (see
Lev. 1:3–17; 6:1–6). An anthropomorphic aspect attaches to this
in that the burning of the bullock or sheep or hen produces a
"pleasant smell" for God. But—the main point—God does not
consume the sacrifice: It is consumed by fire. The sacrifice is still
for its own sake, or, more precisely, it is a form of surrender to
God. This fact must be borne in mind when we seek a transition
from the sacrificial cult to prayer, the "sacrifice of the lips." A
bullock can be sacrificed with the mere stab of a knife and the
maintenance of fire by the priests. The "sacrifice of the lips" consists of empty words unless given, along with the words, is the
heart. We have above quoted the rabbis of Yavneh, to the effect
that it matters not what a person does as long as he directs his
heart to heaven. Perhaps we have quoted the rabbis too lightly:

How is such a thing possible, that a human, being merely human, directs his heart, itself merely human, to no less than heaven? As will be seen, in all Jewish prayer this question continues to be present, and prayer degenerates whenever the question vanishes.

Is there a transition from animal sacrifices to prayer? Perhaps this can be found if we turn from the *olah* to its radical opposite, the sacrifice of the paschal lamb. At the beginning of the Pesach festival the people would flock to Jerusalem. According to the Talmud they were "dense throngs." (For the year 65 C.E., the historian Josephus gives the nearly incredible figure of three million! Yet Josephus is usually reliable.) In groups they would sacrifice the paschal lamb—and then eat it themselves! How is such a thing possible? "Modern man" has a ready answer: Sacrifice is appeasement of angry deities by ignorant, fearful primitives; when these primitives begin to lose their fears, then, instead of giving animals to gods, they eat them themselves; and soon thereafter the sacrifice aspect vanishes altogether, making the Pesach Seder into a folk festival; and that is what a "modern" Seder ought to be. But if the surviving accounts can be trusted, all this wholly fails to do justice to the spirit, and even the numbers, of those once assembled for Pesach in Jerusalem. However strange the ancient rituals may seem to moderns, the throngs would truly sacrifice the paschal lambs as they were offering them to God—and could eat them themselves only because what had been *humanly given* to the Divine was *divinely restored* to humans. A supernatural joy, as it were, must have filled the hearts of those assembled throngs as they filled their bodies with the food returned to them; the same joy fills Jewish hearts still wherever the Seder is truly celebrated. It is no wonder that Christianity took over, for its own central symbol, the Jewish paschal lamb. Nor is it surprising that the sole physical part of the ancient sacrificial cult that survives in the Jewish liturgy of today is a shankbone of the Seder plate, reminiscent of the paschal sacrifice. I yield for a moment to hyperbole: If in the Messianic age the Jerusalem Temple were to be rebuilt, the one sacrifice, if no other, that could meaningfully be restored is that of the paschal lamb. At least unless we were all to become vegetarians, the throngs of all humanity would join in the celebration of a liberty that is not *from* God but rather is endowed with that, as it were, supernatural quality that can only be *given by* God, yet is a *self*-liberation in that what is divinely given is humanly received.

THE DIALECTIC OF JEWISH PRAYER

That prayer in Judaism precedes the Temple and its sacrificial cult was already seen in the example of Hannah. Hers, however, was the spontaneous expression of a heart filled, first with anguish and subsequently, with joy. More striking still for the case of "prayer independent of the Temple cult" is the prayer with which Solomon inaugurates the edifice just completed. Centuries had passed since Israel had entered the land. War had alternated with peace. Kings had at last consolidated the state, but Saul had been rejected altogether, and even the great David had not been privileged to build the Temple, for the blood of warfare was on his hands. And now at last Solomon had built it—the sole and central sanctuary of the God of Israel! Gripped by the solemnity of the moment, he utters a prayer containing these words:

> But will God in very truth dwell on the earth? Behold, the heaven of heavens cannot contain Him; how much less this house that I have builded! (I Kings 8:27)

What a contrast between the one and only house for the God of Israel and the God—the same God!—who cannot be contained by the heaven of heavens! This contrast enters into all aspects of Judaism. Here it raises a very specific question: If the heaven of heavens cannot contain Him, then how can there be anything humanly offered—*anything whatsoever*—that is divinely acceptable? Indeed, must not all sacrifice, however radical and genuine, be beneath the notice of Divinity? Perhaps there is no other passage in the Tenach that highlights so clearly the problem of all sacrifice, be it that of animals or that of the lips.

The problem of prayer, however, comes fully into its own only when the Temple is destroyed, and prayer, now become central, is institutionalized. The process of institutionalization harks back to the days of the Mishnah and finds its completed expression in the *Siddur* (the prayer book for daily and Shabbat worship) and the several *Mahzorim* (the prayer books for the three festivals of pilgrimage, Pesach, Shavuot, and Succot, for Rosh Hashanah, and for Yom Kippur.) The first complete *Siddur* was composed by the tenth-century Gaon Saadia, already mentioned. The *Siddur* and the three *Mahzorim* now in our possession differ according to several traditions, but in no important respects.

Of each and every service, the central prayer is the *Amidah* ("the standing"). It is given that title because a Jew stands as he recites this prayer. More precisely, he takes three steps in order to take his stand before God. I have heard my friend and rabbi, Emanuel Forman, say that these are the three hardest steps a Jew can take. This is recognized in the prayer that introduces the *Amidah*: "O Lord, open Thou my lips, and my mouth shall declare Thy praise!" This seems paradoxical and absurd. That view was expressed by Immanuel Kant (1724–1804), a son of pietist parents but perhaps the most distinguished and certainly the most profound representative of the Age of Enlightenment. In a little-known essay on prayer he takes those to task who denigrate their own will, their own reason, all their own powers to such a degree as to pray to God not only for the gift of all these, but for the ability even to pray. Kant understood much about religion; prayer he did not understand. And when as rector of the University of Koenigsberg he would lead his students to church on Sunday, he would perform this act as part of a rector's duty. He would lead them to the door, but remained outside himself.

What Kant rejects as self-denigrating and absurd is in fact at the heart of all Jewish (and presumably also Christian) prayer. A Jew takes the three steps so as to stand before God: No power above will move him like a marionette. Yet how on his own dare he—*can* he—take not this step or that, but step before Him whom the heaven of heavens cannot contain? Hence he prays that God may open his lips so that his mouth may declare His praise: Yet for God to hear this prayer, and to open his lips, a Jew must *already* have opened them and prayed! Sounding paradoxical—

absurd and to be rejected by reason—this contradiction is in fact part and parcel of the dialectic of prayer, and while "dialectic" signifies tensions and contradictions, it is not without a reason of its own. Only because of a unique dialectic was it possible for Solomon to know God to be beyond the heaven of heavens, yet build Him a house on earth. And only because of this same dialectic is it possible for a Jew today to take his stand before God in prayer.

Deep thinkers have often failed to understand this dialectic. An ordinary Jew shows an implicit understanding whenever he genuinely takes those three steps and opens his lips for the *Amidah*. The implicit understanding became explicit when in olden times pious Jews would spend an hour each morning in silence before venturing to begin their morning prayers. And the explicit understanding is unmistakable in the custom of a certain Hasidic rabbi who would preface his prayers with the prayer that God might enable him to pray.

THE *AMIDAH:* THANKSGIVING, PETITIONS, AND PRAISE

A Jew has taken the three steps that place him before God in prayer. Having done so, he recites eighteen *berachot*. (The meaning of "*beracha*" will become clear shortly.) This is in daily worship. On Shabbat and festivals only the first three and the last three are the same, or nearly so. The place of the intermediate twelve is taken by just one (except for three on Rosh Hashanah), fitting the occasion. "A Jew" recites the *berachot:* More correctly, it is the covenantal community that does the reciting. Not once does the word *I* replace the omnipresent "we." A *minyan*, ten males past bar mitzvah age, needs to be assembled for the cantor to recite the *Amidah* aloud on behalf of them, and if fewer are in attendance each recites the *Amidah* silently, on his own. (Seeking to overcome the traditional male chauvinism, Reform and some Conservative synagogues count women also.) However, a silent, private recitation precedes the one that is public and aloud, recognizing the individual as such, within the community. For

Halachic reasons, at evening prayer the *Amidah* is generally recited silently only.

Appropriately enough, the first of the *berachot* recited by the covenantal community addresses the God of Abraham, Isaac, and Jacob, the God of the covenant. No less appropriately, the last is a prayer for the—ultimately Messianic—peace that is the goal of the covenant. Of the eighteen as a whole in the daily *Amidah* one may say what Rosenzweig said of the *Siddur* as a whole, that they add up to a theology of Judaism. A Jew today, even if "open to faith," may well find this or that aspect of the theology questionable or even altogether unacceptable. He may wish to make changes. But events in our time warn him against making such changes either quickly or irreverently. The second *beracha* addresses God as Him who "sends wind and rain" in winter and "dew" in summer. This must have seemed hopelessly irrelevant in nearly all places where Jews once lived. It is not so to me in Jerusalem when in winter the wind and the rain on Mount Scopus nearly knock me off my feet and when, in the present hot, water-starved summer, I walk out in the early morning and find the grass wet with dew.

The *Amidah*, then, contains the basic prayers of Judaism. It also discloses what, in Judaism, prayer as such is. Each of the eighteen ends with a *beracha*, a benediction. "Praised be Thou, O God . . ." is *the* basic prayer in Judaism: There is no prayer in which, implicitly or explicitly, praise is not an essential element. A Jew recites a *beracha* over bread, wine, other kinds of food; on first seeing a tree or animal of a species previously unknown to him; on seeing the ocean and a rainbow. He recites one *beracha* when he sees a great Jewish sage, and another when he sees a great Gentile one; one on hearing good news and another on hearing bad news. And a series of early morning *berachot* ends with one that discloses the root of praise and hence of prayer itself. "Praised be Thou, Lord our God, King of the world, who removest sleep from my eyes and slumber from my eyelids." A Jew awakens and is astonished and grateful: He is both because sleep has not been death. The Creation is renewed, every day.

Praise is implicit or explicit in all Jewish prayer. In each of the eighteen it is explicit, for they all end with a *beracha*. But praise is

not all they are: This is true only of three of them. Another includes thanksgiving also, and no fewer than fifteen are petitionary.
Thanksgiving is possible only on the grounds of a more ultimate
praise. In good fortune a Jew, like Job, thanks God. In ill fortune
he again follows Job, who neither "curses God and dies" (Job 2:9)
nor demeans himself by actually thanking God for sending the
storm that killed his three daughters and seven sons. He does, however, accept what has happened, saying, "Naked I came out of my
mother's womb, and naked shall I return. The Lord gave and the
Lord has taken away. Praised be the name of the Lord." (Job 1:21)
Even in extremity praise still remains.

The petitions in the *Amidah* take us a step further. Insofar as
they are petitions, they are for what now is not but eventually—so
the covenantal community pleads and hopes—will be. But insofar
as they end with *berachot* they are for what already is. Thus in the
eighth *beracha* God is implored to heal the sick of His people—
and praised as "faithful and merciful Physician." And in the six-
teenth he is beseeched to hear prayer—and praised as "He who
hears prayer." This means nothing less than that the petitionary
prayers of the *Amidah* are bound up with hope; and the synthesis
of the two makes the hope ultimate and unshakable. This is why a
Jew who only a week earlier prayed in the *Amidah* for health for
his sick mother can now say at her graveside, "Praised is the true
Judge."

IS PRAYER "HEARD"?

> The Lord is my shepherd; I shall not want. . . .
> Yea, even though I walk through the valley of the shadow of death,
> I will fear no evil, for Thou art with me;
> Thy rod and Thy staff, they comfort me . . . (Ps. 23:1, 4)

We need quote only briefly from this most famous and beloved of
all psalms, for it is still known nearly universally: It is recited at
Christian and Jewish funerals, those of a good many agnostics or
even atheists included. The *Amidah* of course presupposes the faith

that prayer is "heard," and we have argued that this faith is irre-
futable. Our argument, however, has only been negative. No better
positive proof that prayer is "heard" can be found than the Twenty-
third Psalm. This is of course no proof at all. But it expresses to
perfection an experience trusted by the believer; and so universal
is that particular psalm that even those who lack the experience,
and would not trust it if they had it, can still understand the meaning of its words.

God "hears" even in the valley of the shadow of death. That His
"hearing" is not confined to that extremity is expressed in another
psalm that, somewhat less widely known, should be cited somewhat more fully:

> Whither shall I go from Thy spirit? Or whither shall I flee from
> Thy presence? If I ascend into heaven Thou art there. If I make
> my bed in the netherworld, behold, Thou art there. If I take the
> wings of the morning and dwell in the uttermost parts of the
> sea, even there would Thy hand lead me and Thy right hand
> hold me. And if I say, "surely darkness shall envelop me, and the
> light about me shall be night," even the darkness is not too dark
> for Thee, but the night shineth as the day, the darkness is even
> as the light. (Ps. 139:7–12)

What is it that distinguishes the praise in psalms such as these
from the praise that might well up in the heart of one filled with
wonder at the order of the universe, at its beauty, at the sheer fact
that something exists rather than nothing at all? The wonder at
these, but nothing more? In the psalms cited, the valley of death
is not removed, neither is the netherworld, which is why we cannot
speak here of "hearing" without the use of quotation marks. The
praise is at nothing but this: the presence of God. It makes the
darkness shine like the light. Or, to allude to the title of one of
Abraham J. Heschel's books, what is praised is the fact that man is
not alone.

In May 1940 the British government did what should have been
done at the beginning of the war: When the Germans invaded the
Lowlands, they interned the hundred thousand or so German and
Austrian nationals in the country, refugees from Nazi Germany in-

cluded. Who could tell in that dark hour who was a bona fide refugee, and who a spy or fifth columnist? I was one of those interned, and when a few weeks later we were sent by ship away from the embattled island I found myself in a new position. I had preached quite a few sermons before: Now suddenly, together with my friend Henry Fischel (one of the three to whom this book is dedicated), I was rabbi of a congregation. An emergency congregation in a crisis situation, for not only did we not know where we were going, the rumor had also reached us that another ship filled with refugees had been torpedoed by the Germans and sunk.

On Shabbat evening on board ship we conducted a service. I was the one who preached the sermon. Some twenty-five years or so later I ran into a man who remembered that service. He told me that he also remembered my sermon, which I myself had completely forgotten. "What did I say?" I asked him. He replied: "You said that we did not know where we were going and to what fate or destiny, but that wherever and whatever it was, God would be with us."

IS PRAYER ANSWERED?

To one open to faith, then, prayer is "heard." But is it answered? That this is so in certain cases we have already seen in the classical case of Hannah. In my first year at the *Hochschule* I took some private tutoring since my Hebrew was inadequate. We came upon some passage in Genesis in which parents thank God for the gift of a child. (I forget which passage it was.) My tutor asked me, "Why did they thank God?" I was puzzled by the question. "Because," my tutor said, "they were too ignorant to know how children are born." I thought that I had never heard anything so silly, and I think so still. Moreover, I know physicians, by no means all Orthodox or even religious, who would fully agree. In the presence of their newly born baby, uttering healthy cries, any parent with a heart gives thanks, even if it be with the silent proviso "to whom it may concern."

Hannah's prayer is by an individual. A classical case of an answered communal prayer is that of the exiles in Babylon. As well-known and beloved as the 23rd Psalm is the 137th:

> By the rivers of Babylon we sat and wept as we remembered Zion. We hung our harps on poplars. We were asked to sing by our captors, to entertain those who had carried us off. "Sing," they said, "some hymns of Zion!" How could we sing one of the Lord's hymns in an alien land? If I forget thee, O Jerusalem, may my right hand wither! May my tongue cleave to the roof of my mouth, If I do not count Jerusalem my chiefest joy! (Ps. 137:1–5)

They would not forget Jerusalem, yet were too dejected even to pray for a return. Hence when return they did they were like dreamers:

> When the Lord brought back those that returned to Zion
> We were like unto them that dream.
> Then was our mouth filled with laughter,
> And our tongue with singing.
> Then said they among the nations:
> "The Lord hath done great things with these."
> The Lord hath done great things with us;
> We are rejoiced. (Ps. 126:1–3)

Why did they say that the Lord had brought them back? Because they were too ignorant of the Mideast politics of the time, Babylon, Persia, Cyrus, and the rest? I would think such an answer as silly as that of my tutor of over fifty years ago. So would many professors of history—all those who observe the *mitzvah* of prayers after meals. On Shabbat and festivals these begin with the 126th Psalm. For the Jew of the Tenach God was present in history. For a Jew "holding himself open to faith" today, His presence in history has not come to an end.

But even in the Tenach history is not *Heilsgechichte* alone but includes flesh-and-blood fact with no meaning beyond itself. (See above, chapter 3, section 9.) Flesh-and-blood history has been inescapable ever since, and remains so today. Hence the fact had always to be faced that even the worthiest and most heartfelt of prayers remain often unanswered: The prayer of Hannah was heard;

those of countless other barren women have remained unanswered, as have been those of the sick, the naked, the hungry. This is true of individuals. As for the covenantal community, the prayers of those in the first exile were answered, after a mere fifty years. The prayers for the end of the second exile were not answered for nearly two millennia, in one sense, and in another are unanswered still. How, then, can one thank God for the blessings given to oneself when one sees others, equally or more worthy, cry unto their God in vain? In the psalms we read: "O give thanks unto the Lord, for His mercy endureth forever" (Ps. 118:1).

A Jew today may well ask whether such a prayer can still be said. How could it *ever* have been said, including and above all by those to whom mercy had indeed been shown: What of others in whose lives no signs of divine mercy were in evidence? One English saying I have never been able to understand: "There, but for the grace of God, go I." What kind of grace is this, that saves one but abandons another? More to the point, what kind of *person* is this, who sees the disaster of another, sees himself spared, and understands his escape from disaster as an act of grace?

To the question raised, when all is said and done, there is only one answer in Judaism. A Jew at prayer finds himself situated between revelation and Redemption, in an unredeemed world. How can he react when a prayer of his is unanswered? Or when, though his own prayer is answered, he sees unanswered the prayers of others, no less worthy than his own? Only with the hope for an end in which all worthy prayers are answered and no tear will remain unstilled.

Even with this hope, however, prayer becomes often precarious, even in that greatest repository of Jewish prayer, the book of Psalms. The same book that affirms the presence of God in the valley of death and the netherworld also contains the following:

Thou hast laid me in the nethermost pit, in dark places, in the deeps. Thy wrath lies hard upon me . . . I am shut up and cannot come forth. (Ps. 81:7–9)

The terrors of death are fallen upon me, and horror has overwhelmed me. (Ps. 55:5–6)

God is ever-present? Then why has He "forgotten," "hidden His face," "forsaken," "cast off," "abandoned"? (Pss. 13, 22, 42, 55, 74, 79, 88). Biblical critics may rightly attribute such differences in attitude to differences in authorship. Yet a religious (if not a literary critical) truth attaches to the tradition which ascribes most if not all of the psalms to the one author, King David. Theologians may take the author (or authors) to task for his (or their) "bumptious" lack of the proper meekness or even a "blasphemous" attitude toward God. I could quote chapter and verse of such views as expressed by theologians, sitting safely in their seminary studies. But I prefer to throw in my lot with *amcha* when they view David as the author of most of the psalms, and David himself, not as a remote and unreal saint, but as one of his people. In the popular song already cited it will be Moses who will teach the people Torah at the Messianic feast; but it will be David who will play the harp, not by way of performing a concert appreciated by a few connoiseurs, but by way of leading the whole people in song.

In the Psalms the lament that God has forsaken and abandoned and hidden His face is still addressed to God. In the depth of national catastrophe some rabbis were forced to go further. "Ever since the destruction of the Temple," the early second-century Rabbi Eleazar lamented, "the gates of prayer are closed, and only the gates of tears are still open." Moreover, according to him the weeping that accompanies the tears does not seem to be heard in heaven, for he goes on: "Since the day of the destruction of the Temple, a wall of iron separates Israel from her Father in heaven." The rabbi remained certain that one day the wall would be removed; but when this would be he was unable to say.

Then what remains if the gates of prayer are closed? The third-century Rabbi Samuel ben Nahman replied: "The gates of prayer are sometimes open and sometimes closed, but the gates of *teshuvah* are always open."

We have already identified *teshuvah* as the deepest source of Jewish life. Much more will have to be said on this subject. Here only one point needs to be made. *Teshuvah* and prayer are not the same, but they manifest the same dialectic. This is evident in a text already cited:

Turn Thou us unto Thee, O Lord, and we shall be turned;
Renew our days as of old. (Lam. 5:21)

EPILOGUE

On reciting the central prayers a Jew stands, having taken the steps
that make him stand before God. On reciting the *aleynu* prayer on
Yom Kippur he kneels, but only to rise and stand again as he continues his prayer. So crucial is the *aleynu* that it is recited also at
every service, just before the end.

The first part of the *aleynu* declares the kingship of God, and
the praise that is due to Him for having called Israel to His service.
The second part takes recognition of the fact that the kingship of
God is not universally recognized, and ends up by quoting the
Tenach to the effect that the very oneness of God's name will be
complete only when the kingship of God will be an accomplished
fact: "The Lord shall be King over all the earth; on that day the
Lord shall be One and his name One" (Zech. 14:9). On that day
the "abomination" of the "false gods" will be removed. What will
have occurred will be *tikkun olam.*

I have mentioned several of my teachers at the *Hochschule.* I
owe much to those mentioned as teachers. Leo Baeck impressed
me as a person. An awe-inspiring figure, he understood better than
most others the catastrophe that had befallen German Jewry, yet
he stayed with his people to the end. Leo Baeck will remain unforgettable to me. He ought to remain unforgettable.

As unforgettable is a sermon I once heard him preach during
that great if short-lived religious renaissance in the 1930s whose
center was Berlin. The subject of his sermon was the *aleynu* prayer.
He preached about the abomination of the false gods, and everyone present knew what he had in mind. He ended up with the subject of *tikkun olam.* This can be translated in several ways. The
standard translation is "perfection of the world," leaping forward,
as it were, to the Messianic age. In his time in Berlin, Baeck gave
the more sober translation of "preparing the world for the kingship
of God." Fifty years later one must give yet a different—but equally

correct—translation. For twelve years an idolatry without precedent ruled a large part of the world. It very nearly destroyed it, and it and its consequences will continue to haunt the world. Today the foremost and immediate task of a Jew in prayer and *teshuvah* is to mend what has been broken. As I remember that unforgettable sermon of Baeck's, I translate *tikkun olam* as "to mend the world."

10. THE CYCLE
OF THE JEWISH
YEAR

THE WORKADAY WEEK

"The earth is the Lord's . . ." (Ps. 24:1). Abraham J. Heschel had a way with titles for his books. As title of a book about Shabbat, the opening words of Psalm Twenty-four were a stroke of genius. Shabbat is the mainstay of *The Life of Judaism* (the title of the part of this book to be concluded with this chapter). But whereas the *havdala* "separates" between the "holy" and the "profane" (see chapter 4, section 3), in the *beracha* by that name with which Shabbat ends, it is God who is praised as doing the separating: He does not confine His sovereignty to one day out of seven, or to sacred spots on earth of which the Temple once was, and the synagogue now is, the most obvious example. In the life of Judaism, *the earth* is the Lord's: the *whole* earth, not only some sacred part of it.

We must therefore begin not with Shabbat but with the workaday week. In the Tenach human labor first appears after the expulsion from the Garden of Eden. This occurs because of the first couple's sin of disobedience. Adam is told:

In the sweat of thy face shalt thou eat bread, till thou return
unto the ground; for out of it wast thou taken; for dust thou art,
and unto dust shalt thou return. (Gen. 3:19)

This text disposes one to assume that in Judaism work is a curse.
But against this must be set the fact that God Himself precedes
man in working, for He has created the world, and there can be no
higher vocation for man than to imitate God. In its very first verse
the Tenach teaches the dignity of divine labor, and therefore the
dignity also of the labor of man. To be sure, after the expulsion
from the Garden a curse mixes with the dignity. However, the importance of human labor is now further enhanced by its urgency:
The world is henceforth in need of redemption, and human labor
has a share in filling the need. With each sole he nailed to a shoe,
a certain Hasidic shoemaker was fond of telling his customers, he
was trying to repair not only shoes but also the relationship between God and the world.

All this would have seemed strange, not to say scandalous, to the
profoundest among the pagans with whom ancient Jews could intermingle—the Greek thinkers and their followers. God *working?*
God *dirtying His hands* by creating a material world? The inhabitants of the city of Plato and Aristotle were divided into slaves who
labored, and free men who (if they were wealthy enough to own
slaves) were engaged exclusively in leisure. The distinction between labor and leisure is not identical with that between strenuous activity and a life of ease, but rather between activities engaged
in as means to ends, and such as are ends in themselves. A free
man's leisure includes political activity, military service in defense
of the city, and, above all, philosophical thought. All these, including the last, are strenuous, for whereas God is not tired by thought,
philosophy does tire man. The free man, therefore, needs relaxation, the third great part of life in Aristotle's city; moreover, if prudent, he will grant relaxation to his slaves also, if only in order that
they may resume their labor efficiently and be refreshed. But neither labor nor relaxation can be ascribed to the God of Aristotle;
His life is leisure in its purest form, eternal self-contemplation. As
for man, what meaning there is in his life is found only in leisure,

for this alone is an end in itself. So it was for the wisest among the pagans, and thus alone it could have been. For to them this world, as it now is, was all there was. Its redemption was either unnecessary, impossible, or both.

The Greek idea entered into Christendom as well. Marcion was an early Christian bishop who presented his ideas in Rome in 144 C.E. Excommunicated, he went on to form a church of his own. God working? God dirtying His hands by creating a material world? As a Christian, however heretical, Marcion could not reject the "Old Testament" outright. But his chief idea was that there were two Gods, the higher, purely spiritual "New Testament" God, and the lower God of the "Old Testament," this latter materialistic enough to create a material world. Marcion himself was excommunicated, yet Marcionite ideas have kept reappearing within Christianity, invariably accompanied by anti-Jewish animosity. For Christians too it has sometimes been difficult to connect labor with dignity, to say nothing of connecting it with God.

Whatever the difficulties a Jew may have with this connection, they are removed in the life of Judaism, in which not only God Himself labors but Redemption is necessary and possible, and in which human work is required if the Redemption is to be realized. The problem here is not labor but rather leisure. Does Judaism leave room for leisure, in anything like the sense understood by Aristotle? Presumably a Jew needs relaxation, for like all humans he gets tired and needs to be refreshed. But how can he engage in activities that are ends in themselves, when *all* should be means to the *one* end of the Redemption? Presumably God's rest on the seventh day was leisure, for He stands in need of no relaxation, and He created the world good. But the world is no longer what once it was: How then can a Jew take a day off from work for anything beyond necessities, when the all-encompassing task is *tikkun olam?*

SHABBAT

Shabbat anticipates the Redemption: This is the answer in Judaism. It is the ultimate answer, for without this "foretaste" of Redemption a Jew could not survive in an unredeemed world. But it is not all of the answer.

> Remember the Sabbath day to keep it holy. Six days shalt thou labor and do all thy work. But the seventh day is a Sabbath unto the Lord thy God. In it thou shalt not do any manner of work, not thou, nor thy son, nor thy daughter, nor thy man-servant, nor thy maid-servant, nor thy cattle, nor the stranger that is in thy gates. For in six days the Lord made heaven and earth, the sea and all that is in them, and rested on the seventh day; wherefore the Lord blessed the Sabbath day and hallowed it. (Exod. 20:8–11)

For a Jew, what does "hallowing" the Sabbath day mean? It includes relaxation. The free man of Athens, if prudent, would allow his slaves to relax: A Jew is *commanded* to do so, for whereas a Greek could consider a slave an "animated tool," to a Jew he is created in the divine image like himself. To go further, even the cattle must be allowed to rest, to say nothing of the stranger: Not unless *total* rest permeates the world of a Jew is it possible for the holiness of Shabbat to descend into it.

What will the world to come be like? In the Midrash Israel begs God for an example and is given the holiness of Shabbat. As the shadows of evening fall, an air of expectancy descends, today nowhere more so than at the Western Wall in Jerusalem. (One has to experience this expectancy in order to believe it.) A Jew has put on festive garments. He has got himself ready to live differently, even to walk and speak differently. According to a tradition a "higher soul" is entering into him, to depart again only when Shabbat comes to an end. To what end all this expectancy? In *kabbalat shabbat* ("receiving Shabbat"), the opening liturgy already referred to above (chapter 4, section 2), there is a hymn, composed in Safed by the sixteenth-century mystic Solomon Alkabets, "Come, my friend, to meet the bride; let us welcome Shabbat." The sixteenth-century mystics in Safed were descendants of refugees from Spain. Having come to the Holy Land, they would welcome Shabbat by walking to the end of the town, in order to receive the "Shabbat bride," and then lead her to synagogue where they would complete their prayers. At the Western Wall today it is much like what it must have been at the edge of the town of Safred, and this for mystics and nonmystics alike. The expectancy, the excitement, the last-minute rush until Shabbat begins: How often can one be expectant and excited about receiving the same bride? Perhaps thus it will be between grooms and brides in the world to come: With the Shabbat bride it is so already here and now.

After Shabbat evening services a Jew goes to his home. There could be no real home without Shabbat, and also no real Shabbat without a home. Hence the *kiddush* ("sanctification") is recited in the synagogue only for those who have no home, or are away from it. It is in the home that the essential *kiddush* is recited, prior to the Shabbat meal, ending with the *beracha:* "Praised art Thou, O Lord, who hallowest Shabbat."

The holiness of Shabbat reaches its climax with the Torah reading during the morning service. As was already seen (chapter 4, section 2), Shabbat is the feast of Creation. A "foretaste" of the world to come, it also anticipates Redemption. And it is a feast of Revelation as well because, week by week, a portion of the Torah is read until on Simhat Tora the cycle is completed, only to be immediately resumed.

A note of melancholy begins to mingle with the holiness of the day with the *se'uda sh'lishit*, the third of the three festive meals ordained for the day. The sun is beginning to set, and it is as if the meal, as well as the songs and discourses accompanying it, were meant to delay the departure of the day. Yet depart it must and does. And when Shabbat ends and its end is recognized, a sense of poignancy and even apprehension can no longer be shut out. (Of this mention has already been made in chapter 4, section 3.) This is less because the workaday week is about to begin than because Shabbat is about to end, and because the workaday world into which a Jew returns is unredeemed. The *havdala* is recited, which recognizes the end of the Shabbat even as it praises God. And with it goes what is perhaps the most moving—and in our time certainly the most heart-rending—of all Jewish prayers:

O Guardian of Israel, guard Thy people Israel, lest those perish who say, "Hear, O Israel [the Lord, our God, the Lord is one]."

SACRED HISTORY: PESACH, SHAVUOT, SUCCOT

On Shabbat, Creation, Redemption, and revelation are all in one. This is of course far from the case during the workaday week. Neither is it the case in history. In what may well be the sharpest and most necessary polemic in this whole book, we have above stressed against the apostle Paul that within Judaism all Israel is Israel, a flesh-and-blood people, and that the Jewish Tenach, unlike the Christian Old Testament, is not sacred history only, but rather sacred history intermingled with plain flesh-and-blood history that does not pretend to a higher meaning. (See chapter 3, section 9.) Consequently a Jew who lives with the Tenach finds himself in a history that is between revelation and Redemption, and is himself a witness to both that in-betweenness and the Redemption beyond it. It is this witnessing that constitutes his participation in sacred history, and this is done on the three festivals of pilgrimage, Pesach ("Passover"), Shavuot ("Feast of Weeks") and Succot ("Feast of Booths").

Not that these festivals celebrate sacred history only. Pesach is a spring festival (Exod. 23:15). Shavuot celebrates the wheat harvest (Exod. 23:16, 34:22). Succot is an ancient festival of vintage connected with dwelling in booths (Exod. 23:16).

A German proverb has it that "this is so long ago it is no longer true." Is this proverb itself true of either the natural or the sacred-historical aspects of the three festivals of pilgrimage? That it is false at least in part I once experienced powerfully on an occasion I shall never forget. In 1935 I enrolled at the Berlin *Hochschule*. At the same time I also attempted to enroll at Berlin University, as was prescribed for all rabbinical students prior to 1933. In 1935, however, I was rejected: Jewish students, though not yet quite eliminated, were strictly limited in number. But as I still wanted what good was left of a German university education, I tried to to enroll at my home University of Halle in 1937, succeeded, and attended for three semesters until the *Krystallnacht* made an end to this as to everything else. I was the last Jewish student enrolled at Halle University.

There I attended classes given by Otto Eissfeld. Eissfeld was a famous biblical scholar. He was also a brave anti-Nazi. One class consisted of only three students, and he conducted it in his home, aware, I am sure, that inviting a Jew to his home was not without risk. Another of his courses was on the Book of Isaiah. This class was large, yet when he lectured on chapter 1:8 he made me feel that this was for none of the "Aryans" but just for me. He explained the symbol "booth in the vineyard" as used by the prophet. The ancient Israelites would build booths in the vineyards at harvest time, so as to be able to work from early morning till late at night without wasting time going to and from home; but since these booths were meant to last for but a few days they were frail. The Isaiah passage reads as follows:

> The country is desolate. Your cities are burned with fire. . . . And the daughter of Zion is left as a booth in the vineyard, as a lodge in a garden of cucumbers, as a besieged city. Except the Lord of hosts had left unto us a very small remnant, we should have been as Sodom, we should have been like unto Gomorrah.

Nothing was truer, to me then, than this passage as expounded by that man at that time and that place. And nothing was truer for the Jew through the ages than a prayer in the same vein recited during the Succot festival. The festival expresses the hope for and faith in the ultimate Redemption; yet it contains this prayer: "May He who is merciful raise up for us the booth of David that is on the point of collapse."

That the agricultural aspects of the three festivals have been renewed in Israeli kibbutzim is a well-known fact. In alluding to that renewal previously (chapter 6, section 7), I have implied my belief that even in secular kibbutzim this renewal has a religious significance. Whether or not this be so, and if so how universally and lastingly, is a question for the future. This much is clear, however: Had these festivals not retained their religious significance through the ages of dispersion, their revival in any form, however secular, would have been impossible in Israel. Pesach celebrates the Exodus from Egypt; Shavuot, the gift of the Torah at Sinai; Succot, the forty years of wandering in the desert, the preservation during these years by God, and the end of the wandering with the arrival in the promised land. One mentions these facts, and the proverb cited above comes back to mind: How could these events of "so long ago" remain "true"? Perhaps to achieve this end was the purpose behind the *mitzvah* of a pilgrimage to Jerusalem on these occasions: This would help bring the past back to life. But then, this *mitzvah* could not be obeyed in the time of dispersion, yet even so what had happened so long ago continued to remain true. A Jew was not merely to remember the ancient events but to relive them, and relive them he did through the ages.

During the week-long Pesach ("the time of our liberation") a Jew eats *matzah* (unleavened bread), the poor bread of affliction of slavery. At the Seder meal that initiates the festival he also eats *moror* (bitter herbs) in memory of the bitterness of a slave's life, and the Haggada is read, which relates the story of the Exodus at length. The Seder celebrates the liberation of a Jew's ancestors— and of their descendants today. The text contains the following passage: "In every generation each Jew is obliged to regard himself as though he personally had gone forth from Egypt."

Jews persisted in celebrating the Seder during the Crusades, the Inquisition, when wandering from country to country in search of a haven. They stubbornly continued to celebrate their freedom, and to praise God for its gift. Was the Exodus "still true" in those times, no less bitter than that of the ancient Egyptian slavery? I venture this bold statement: Jews have been slandered, persecuted, and murdered, but in their long history no enemy has succeeded in forcing them back into slavery. I say this because no one, I think, is a slave until the oppressor has robbed him of his religion, whether or not he has imposed on the oppressed his own instead.

The Pesach Haggada also contains the following passage:

> Not only one arose against us to exterminate us, but in every generation some arise to exterminate us; but the Holy One, praised be He, saves us from their hands.

This is one statement in the Haggada few Jews could continue to believe during the Holocaust. That the enemy quite consciously intended to refute it is demonstrated by the fact that the final assault on the Warsaw Ghetto began on the first day of Pesach, 1943. Then also began the historic Ghetto Uprising. The fighters knew that it was Pesach. They celebrated the Seder as they could in the circumstances. Having no *matzah*, they ate a bread poorer than *matzah*. And then they began their hopeless armed struggle. Inevitably the uprising was crushed. Few survived, and most of the survivors were murdered. The uprising was hopeless except in one respect: The fighters died not as slaves but as free men and women.

Shavuot is the second of the three festivals of pilgrimage. It is the "time of the giving of the Torah." For a long time it was of the three the one least "true still," probably because few symbols are connected with it that speak to the family. Only few Orthodox groups would still practice the traditional all-night study of Torah. But in recent years the practice has received a new lease on life. It has spread, and there is hardly a congregation in which some Torah study is not done during Shavuot night. "Still true," after all, seems to be the ancient saying that the Torah is given whenever a Jew receives it.

Unless I am mistaken, Succot is the one of the three that currently is most ambiguous. For centuries Jews spent the week-long festival sitting in booths, reliving a wandering supposedly ended when in fact a Jew had been made into a wanderer once more. They defied the facts, celebrated the "time of rejoicing," and did so in places where the autumn climate is inclement or even harsh. The rejoicing should be the greater, now that for many the wandering is ended again, that a Jewish state has been restored, and that a Jew, in Israel at least, could sit in his succah in fine weather: He could even live in it for the week. But precisely in Israel Jews have little time to take off for rejoicing. Their apartments are small. There are no backyards with room for a succah. Their lives are rushed and tense. "Israel" may no longer be a "booth on the point of collapse." But it is still a "besieged city," and the siege shows few signs of coming to an end.

ETERNITY: THE "DAYS OF AWE"

Now O Lord our God, put the awe of Thee upon all Thy works, and let all that Thou hast created come to revere Thee. May all Thy works fear Thee, and all Thy creatures worship Thee: so that they may all become one brotherhood to do Thy will with a perfect heart. For we know, O Lord our God, that Thine is the dominion, the power and the might, and Thy name is awesome above all that Thou hast made.

There can be no prayer or poem or other form of affirmation anywhere more explicitly and convincingly universal than this prayer, contained in the liturgy of the climactic festivals of the Jewish year, the "Days of Awe"—Rosh Hashanah and Yom Kippur. One point distinguishing this affirmation of human brotherhood from most others should be noticed at once: Here a universal human brotherhood is seen possible only in the fear of God and under His kingship.

One looks at the contemporary world and wonders whether this might not be true. Liberal affirmations of human brotherhood are mostly without much reality. Marxism may begin with ideas of brotherhood but ends up with the Gulag. And whatever else may be said of the Ayatollah Khomeini's relation to God, certain is that he does not fear Him. It was because the midwives of Egypt "feared God" that they refused to obey Pharaoh's order to murder the male babies of the Israelites (Exod. 1:17).

So awesome are the days that many a Jew would spend the whole preceding month of Elul in preparation. Once in Elul an itinerant shoemaker passed the house of the eighteenth-century Hasidic Rabbi Levi Yitzhak of Berdiczev, crying, "Anything to mend?" Upon which the rabbi wept bitterly, saying, "Woe is me and alas for my soul, for the Day of Judgment is almost at hand, and I have not yet mended myself!" The required mending is assisted by the sound of the *shofar* (a ram's horn), the chief symbol of Rosh Hashanah but not confined to that day. In the district of Jerusalem in which we live the *shofar* is heard during all of Elul, from very early on in the day. The *shofar* is meant to arouse or, as the Rambam in a rare flight into poetry put it, it is to awaken the sleepers from their sleep. In Elul and on Rosh Hashanah the *shofar* arouses a Jew to the mending of himself, and when the period is ended with the end of Yom Kippur the *shofar* is blown once more. But at other times it may arouse to a different purpose. For nineteen years Syrian troops had shelled Israeli kibbutzim in the valley below, from the Golan Heights. They could do so without fear of retaliation, for the heights are steep, and the fortifications built by the Syrian army were formidable. To capture them was said to be impossible. Yet on the last day of the 1967 Six-Day War Israeli troops stormed the heights. With them was Shlomo Goren, then chief rabbi of the state, blowing the *shofar*.

Rosh Hashanah is called the Day of Judgment. Taking the three steps that place him before God with every *amidah*, a Jew on Rosh Hashanah takes his stand before eternity. Anyone who ever wonders at the order of the universe, at its beauty, at the fact that something exists rather than nothing at all—any such person can confront eternity, for, though a fleck of dust, he can *know* himself to be one. He can therefore stand in judgment on the way he is spending—or wasting—the brief days allotted to him. A Jew does not know who he is until he finds himself judged.

The Rosh Hashanah *amidah* contains three *berachot* specific for the day: *malchuyot* ("kingship"), *zichronot* ("memory"), and *shofarot* ("arousal through the shofar"). Divine kingship is—and is yet to be. Divine memory is of God's promises—when it often seems that they are long forgotten. Arousal through the *shofar* refers both to what has already been—and to what is yet to be. In a Midrash all parts of the ram that Abraham sacrificed in Isaac's stead were preserved for future use. Of special use were the two horns. One was blown at Sinai when the Torah was given (Exod. 19:16, 19). The other, somewhat larger, will be blown in the end of days, to fulfill the words of Isaiah, "And it shall come to pass in that day that a great horn shall be blown" (Isa. 27:13).

In all three *berachot* a radical universalism is intertwined with an equally radical particularism. The *malchuyot* contain the plea that God may shine forth in His majesty on all inhabitants of the world, yet end with a *beracha* addressing Him Who sanctifies Israel and the day. When in the *zichronot* God is reminded of human merit, the merit of Noah is not forgotten, yet the *beracha* with which they end refers to the covenant with Israel. The *shofarot* call on all who dwell on earth to hark when the last *shofar* will be sounded, yet end with a *beracha* praising Him who hears the *shofar* blown by His people Israel.

The number of days from the beginning of Rosh Hashanah to the end of Yom Kippur is ten. They are called the ten days of *teshuvah*, and, according to a book published in the Polish town of Piotrkov, these days "are a process of drawing upward from earth to heaven; on Yom Kippur the Holy One, blessed be He, draws down from heaven nearer to Israel." The book was published in 1932. Seven years later the Germans came to Piotrokov at just about that time of the year, murdering Jews right and left, and on October 28, five days after Yom Kippur, they set up the first ghetto in that city in the Poland they had occupied. It is fair to assume that their intended timetable had been delayed by five days.

Teshuvah is the ultimate source of Jewish life and renewal. (See chapter 2, sections 4–5.) In Yom Kippur *teshuvah* finds its deepest expression and most profound confirmation. Even an Orthodox worshiper, however, may be put off by the medieval-style litanies, repeated seemingly endlessly and containing confessions for sins one has never committed. (Reform congregations have reduced the repetitions greatly, thus disposing of the litany style, but show good sense when they fill the time gained with other forms of religious expression, so as to make Reform Jews, like their Orthodox and Conservative brethren, remain in the synagogue for all of the day.) A Hasidic rabbi expressed much the same feeling in a sermon. Formerly, he said, Jews would speak the truth in the marketplace but lie on Yom Kippur in the synagogue, whereas now they do the opposite. The prayer he had in mind was "for the sin we have committed in Thy sight by fraud and falsehood . . . , forgive us, O God of forgiveness, and grant atonement." What is the core of the Yom Kippur *teshuvah*?

First, according to clear, unanimous, and uncompromising Jewish teaching, Yom Kippur may atone for sins between a person and God; it does not atone for sins between a person and others until steps have been taken toward reconciliation. Second, the spirit behind all those litanies is expressed in three words of the liturgy: *eyn banu ma'assim*, "no deeds are with us." As a Jew stands before eternity on this day of days, he stands not in possession of this or that merit but nakedly: He has not little merit but none at all. His deeds are as nothing. What is *not* nothing, however, is his *recognition* of their nothingness. Not nothing, too, is the *teshuvah* that flows from that recognition, and through the forgiveness of God it is everything. The Day of Atonement is therefore the Day of Reconciliation also. It begins with the utmost solemnity. The solemnity is maintained throughout the long day and indeed reaches a climax when the sun begins to set, when the "gate" of the day is about to close, and when therefore a prayer ascends heavenward that "the gate of prayer" may yet be open. However, when the day is ended and the last blast of the *shofar* has been heard, a certain lightheartedness manifests itself: The reconciliation so earnestly sought has been achieved. Such is the teaching of the tradition. Such is the experience of *amcha* to this day.

It is instructive to consider what was made of the experience of *amcha* by the two greatest Jewish philosophers of this century, Hermann Cohen and Franz Rosenzweig. We have already identified Cohen as the deepest thinker yet to emerge from liberal Judaism, and Rosenzweig could be called neo-Orthodox. (He moved ever closer toward the traditional observance of the *mitzvot*, and had his life not been so tragically short, might have moved closer still.) Although Rosenzweig had been Cohen's disciple, the two were therefore far apart. Yet their two great works, Cohen's *Religion of Reason* and Rosenzweig's *Star of Redemption*, have one thing in common: The core of both is the Yom Kippur experience.

Nothing is more essential in a liberal's creed than autonomy, freedom, and the right and the duty of a person to self-determination. No thinker affirms that doctrine more radically than Cohen; and no one else even approaches him in his attempt to relate it to Judaism. The consequence of the attempt is that, if there is such a thing as *teshuvah*, man alone must do it: No one else can do it on his behalf. And if there is such a thing as the radical Yom Kippur *teshuvah*, this too can be done only by man alone: Not even God can do the turning for him. Cohen therefore quotes with

approval a passage from Jeremiah, but it is in a passage from Ezekiel that his Yom Kippur finds its true essence. The Jeremiah passage reads in part as follows:

> Behold, the days come, saith the Lord, that I will make a new
> covenant with the house of Israel, and with the house of Judah
> . . . I will put My law into their inward parts, and into their
> hearts will I write it . . . (Jer. 31:31,33)

This passage is much-beloved and -cited, by Christians more so
than by Jews, for obvious reasons. Cohen loves it also. But it is an
Ezekiel passage that is the apex for him of both the Yom Kippur
experience and the Tenach itself:

> Therefore I will judge you, O house of Israel, everyone according
> to his ways, saith the Lord God. Return ye, and turn yourselves
> from all your transgressions; so that they may not be a stumbling
> block of iniquity unto you. Cast away from you all your trans-
> gressions, wherein ye have transgressed; and make you a new
> heart and a new spirit; for why will ye die, O house of Israel?
> (Ez. 18:30–31)

"Make you a new heart and a new spirit!" Done away with is the
dialectic of teshuvah in which God is implored to turn a Jew so
that he may turn on his part. Superseded is Jeremiah for whom it
is God who will make the heart new, and even this only in the end
of days: On Cohen's Yom Kippur each Jew is to make himself a
new heart. The limitations of his being human are shown in the
fact that he must do the making of a new heart again and again,
on each Yom Kippur. But there are no limitations to a Jew's autonomous freedom to turn absolutely on that day of days, to make
himself new.

Then what, if anything, is left in Cohen's Yom Kippur for God?
A person can achieve reconciliation with his neighbor. He can
make his heart new. What he cannot do is undo or wipe out the
sinful self of the past year. Hence for man on his own the reconciliation sought on Yom Kippur would be a goal ever sought yet
ever elusive. What on Cohen's Yom Kippur is left for God? A Jew
on his own turns and makes himself a new heart; it is God that

forgives the sins of the old. In Cohen's Yom Kippur a liberal's autonomy is pushed to an extremity. Yet in this very extremity, however, the Yom Kippur of *amcha* is regained.

We have described Rosenzweig as neo-Orthodox. The source of his neo-orthodoxy lies in his assault on the modern liberal doctrine of autonomy, in behalf of a reaffirmation of revelation. This occurs in his very first essay on Judaism in which revelation is affirmed, and defined as "the incursion of a higher reality into an unworthy human vessel." This incursion is an "insult" in the eyes of paganism both ancient and modern. And the modern paganism to be taken most seriously rests on the doctrine of human autonomy vis-à-vis all things, divine as well as human.

Cohen and Rosenzweig are modern philosophers; yet they recover the Yom Kippur's traditional eternity. For Cohen, the Yom Kippur's human *teshuvah* and divine forgiveness are, as it were, an eternal moment in time. For Rosenzweig Yom Kippur quite literally carries a Jew to an eternal reality beyond time. Paganism culminates in the tragic wisdom that time devours all because death devours all. Against this Christianity pits its good news of an eternal life beyond time. The Jew Rosenzweig supports that Christian message, and goes so far as to consider the spreading of it to be the world historical function of Christianity. By itself, however, it is rootless and groundless, for the Christian eternal life is a news only hoped for. It is only because on Yom Kippur a Jew *already lives in* eternity that an *ultimate* ground exists not only for Judaism but for Christianity as well. A Jew alone, and he only on Yom Kippur, experiences eternity in the midst of time.

> Death meant to mow down all life lest it live on to eternal life. He had presumed that no end could be reached except by dying. But the eternal people is held up to him as a triumphant proof that the end can also be experienced by living. With that the scythe of the grim reaper breaks.

THE RETURN INTO HISTORY

The first thing a Jew does on returning home after Yom Kippur ends is to drive a few nails into the boards of his *succah:* He returns into history. This latter is both sacred history and flesh-and-blood history. That the two may intermingle, however, is in our time shown dramatically by the change that has come upon observances as yet unmentioned. (See, however, above, chapter 3, section 9.) Purim once celebrated the God who saved the Jewish people from Haman; today a Jew cannot remember Haman, who failed, without also remembering Hitler, who succeeded. Hanukkah once celebrated a divine miracle rather than the valor of the Maccabees. (In a story known to most Jewish children, the Maccabees, having reconquered the Temple from the Syrians and cleansed it of idolatrous abomination, wanted to rekindle the eternal light, a symbol of God's eternity. They found only enough oil to last for one day, required eight days to find more—but the light miraculously kept burning, proof that God Himself had done the saving.) But at a time in which a Jewish state needs the valor of its soldiers the valor of the Maccabees cannot be ignored or belittled. Sacred and "secular" history cannot be, for a Jew, two things wholly apart.

Perhaps not much of religious relevance has happened for a Jew in secular history for centuries. That much of relevance has happened in our time is shown most dramatically in the change that has come over the ninth of Av. On Yom Kippur a Jew fasts because he is beyond things temporal, including eating and drinking. (At one time the most observant of Jews would refrain even from sleeping, and spend the night as well as the day in the synagogue.) On the ninth day of the month of Av a Jew fasts because he mourns. It is the day of collective Jewish mourning par excellence. We put it this way because, as already mentioned, the rabbis decided, wisely, that all great Jewish catastrophes be mourned on this one day—the destruction of both Temples, the Crusade massacres, the expulsion from Spain and the numerous others. A wise decision indeed: A Jew could not spend a day on each catastrophe separately, yet live a life the core of which is meant to be joy and hope. Tradition has it that all these catastrophes literally occurred on the ninth of Av.

Through the ages a Jew has mourned on the ninth of Av. If this is the time of mourning par excellence, the place par excellence is the Western Wall in Jerusalem, the only part left of the second

Temple. It used to be called Wailing Wall, yet one hardly hears this expression anymore. What has happened?

In June 1968 Rose and I first visited Israel. We went to the Wall, making our way through the narrow streets of the Old City. The crowds were immense, but there was no pushing or shoving. Jews had no place to shove or push to: They were already there. And so it has been on every ninth of Av that we have gone to the Wall. Right in front of the Wall are the black-robed Jews of pre-modern orthodoxy, engaged in intense prayer and study, but even these, if they still mourn, do not wail anymore. And then, behind them are those immense crowds. It seems that, caught up as they are in the midsts of the momentous events of contemporary Jewish history, they could not say why they are there. But they do know that there they must be.

Momentous events: Traditionally no *mitzvot* are to be dropped from the 613 commandments of the Torah, and none are to be added; but sooner or later all except the most die-hard Orthodox among Jews committed to Judaism will have to recognize two observances to be added to the cycle of the Jewish year. Both are in response to events of this century. One is Yom Ha-Shoah, the day of mourning for the victims of the Holocaust. The other is Yom Ha-Atzmaut, the Day of Independence, in celebration of the foundation of the State of Israel.

Why not mourn the Holocaust on the ninth of Av? The idea of following the example of the wise rabbis of old is natural, yet to merge Yom Ha-Shoah with the ninth of Av is impossible. On the ninth of Av a Jew mourns but seeks a meaning in the catastrophes mourned. Jews were punished for their sins, and the punishment is "sufferings of love" since it leads to *teshuvah*. They have suffered vicariously for the sins of others, a suffering not without meaning and purpose. Jews implore God to let go of His fierce anger, an anger that punished them doubly for their sins. All these are ways of connecting Jewish suffering with the will of the God. In the case of the Holocaust such a connection is impossible. A possibility may still exist in the case of the martyrs who died in the Holocaust with the *Sh'ma Yisrael* on their lips, and in that of the fighters who died with weapons in their hands; and it is these that we know how to mourn in the already-existing Yom Ha-Shoah observances. But what of the children thrown into the flames alive? What of those murdered in spirit even before, skin and bones, they dropped to the ground? What of all those who were murdered in the twinkling of an eye before they knew what was happening? Theirs is an innocence that cries to heaven: It is a cry that can never be stilled. We cannot without blasphemy connect that innocence with the will of God, and must revere it on a day of its own. But how? The thinkers and rabbis do not yet know how to observe Yom Ha-Shoah. But the people know that observed it must be. In downtown Jerusalem only religious restaurants are closed on the ninth of Av. On Yom Ha-Shoah, however, all are closed: On that day downtown Jerusalem resembles a ghost town.

As little do we yet know how to celebrate Yom Ha-Atzmaut. At one extreme are those many who take the State of Israel for granted and hence have little to celebrate. (No reason for celebration exists at all for those among the religious fanatics who reject the state, but live in it and accept its benefits.) At the other extreme are those who take for granted, not the state, but its future survival, growth and material and spiritual prosperity: For them the Jewish state is the "beginning of the growth of the redemption" of the Jewish people and the world. Between these extremes is the great majority of Israelis, as well as of Diaspora Jews who celebrate Yom Ha-Atzmaut. The day arrives, and a Jew of this kind knows that another year has gone in which the state has mastered some crises and failed to master others, has suffered attacks from without and dissension within, yet has somehow managed, but that with all that it has succeeded in adding a few lines to a new page in Jewish history. That page was opened when, after the greatest Jewish catastrophe ever, the Jewish people decided to make an end to Jewish homelessness and helplessness, and to reestablish a Jewish state. A Jew on Yom Ha-Atzmaut knows all this and knows one thing more: The State of Israel cannot be taken for granted. If he is a secularist counting only on man, he knows that the state and its power are small, and its enemies numerous. If he is a religious Jew counting on God, he knows that a God who did not or could not prevent the Holocaust cannot be counted on to prevent a catastrophe for the State of Israel. A Jew knows all this, knows that he must celebrate, but does not quite yet know how.

On our first Yom Ha-Atzmaut in Jerusalem, we decided that we must go downtown. "Have you got your hammer?" a neighbor asked. We were puzzled. We had listened to speeches and eaten falafel at Yom Ha-Atzmaut celebrations in a large Toronto synagogue, but had never heard anything about hammers. "Never mind," the neighbor went on, "they sell them downtown." And so it proved to be. There they were, hawkers of toylike plastic hammers, with a whistle at one end, a hammer that squeaks if you bop someone on the head. (It squeaks but does not hurt.) So we bought our hammers and joined the crowds. Who is one of us celebrants? Why, anyone with a hammer, young or old, religious or secularist, students who look like hippies and dignified bearded figures whom you normally might hesitate to speak to. But if he carries a hammer, he is one of *amcha* on Yom Ha-Atzmaut, and as one bops him on the head (and is bopped in turn) one shares in a community that has just passed through another difficult, often nerve-wracking year but is determined to carry on.

EPILOGUE

The Yom Kippur liturgy ends in an unexpected way. One would expect it to end with the *Sh'ma Yisrael*, and this, the watchword of the Jewish faith, is in fact recited three times. What comes last, however, is the recitation, seven times, of a confession the people of Israel made on a notable occasion, "The Lord, He is God."

The occasion, reported in the first Book of Kings, was as follows. The condition of Judaism was low. King Ahab had taken a foreign wife and turned to the worship of Ba'al. There were no fewer than 450 priests of Ba'al. On the side of the God of Israel there remained just one man, the prophet Elijah. Then Elijah challenged the priests of Ba'al to a desperate test in the sight of the people, on Mount Carmel. They were to slaughter a bullock and place it on wood, and so was he. Neither side was to set fire to its sacrifice but pray for the necessary fire, the one side to Ba'al, the other,

Elijah alone, to the God of Abraham, Isaac, and Jacob. So the priests of Ba'al prayed for hours on end, and nothing happened. But when Elijah prayed, the fire of the Lord fell from heaven and consumed not only the sacrifice but also the wood and the stones and a trench filled with water that Elijah had built as an altar. It is then that the people made the confession with which the Yom Kippur liturgy ends.

A few decades ago several English philosophers reflected on Elijah's action on Mount Carmel. They decided, to quote one of them, that it had been an "experiment to test the hypothesis that Jehovah and not Ba'al control[s] the physical world." It had been, that is, a precursor of modern scientific practice—needless to say, a primitive and even superstitious one, long left behind by enlightenment. In the view of these philosophers, therefore, had the heavenly fire consumed the sacrifice offered to Ba'al, not only the people would have gone over to Ba'al; Elijah would have done so as well. The professors did not understand Elijah.

If the Jewish people were able to understand him, it is because their collective situation so often was like that of the ancient prophet: Like him, the people were often alone. Who "controls" the historical world? Had this people gone by the evidence of history alone, they would long have let go of their age-old fidelity and thrown in their lot with the Hellenistic world, the Christian world, the Muslim world, or the Communist world. What would Elijah have done had the fire consumed the sacrifice, not of his God but of that of the priests of Ba'al? He would have cried unto his God, saying, "Till now I was only almost alone. Now I am quite alone, for You have abandoned me too. But I will not abandon You. I will remain at my post."

PART III

FUTURE

JUDAISM IN AN AGE OF RENEWED JEWISH STATEHOOD

11. JUDAISM AND
A NEW JEWISH
STATE

TEL AVIV, MAY 14, 1948: THE STATE

The place was Tel Aviv; the date, May 14, 1948, in the Jewish calendar the fifth day of the month of Iyyar, 5708. The partition of Palestine into Arab and Jewish states had been voted for by the newly founded United Nations Organization on October 29, 1947. To me, at the time rabbi of a Reform congregation in Hamilton, Canada, the latter was the great date, the time to celebrate, to celebrate the fact that after the horror of the Holocaust the Jewish people had been granted a state of their own by the world; what happened afterward more or less passed me by at the time. The plain fact is, however, that the October date would have been a nondate had David ben Gurion and his colleagues not taken their courage into their hands and, on that fateful day in May, proclaimed the first Jewish state since Hadrian's Roman legions had smashed that of Bar Kochba, 1813 years earlier. Of course, May 14, 1948, too, would have been a nondate had the soldiers of the newly proclaimed state not succeeded in warding off six Arab

armies that invaded it, with the intention to strangle it at birth—
and had the Israeli Defense Forces not repeated that first success
in 1967, 1973, and to this day. Nor was military valor alone enough.
Civilian valor was also required: May 14, 1948, would have shriv-
eled into a nondate had Israelis left their state in droves, discouraged by the enmity of their neighbors and tired of being under
siege. Many did leave. Others, however, have kept coming, the
most dramatic recent case being that of the Beta Yisrael, the black
Jews of Ethiopia. May 14, 1948, then, is a date—a historic date in
Jewish history—because it was made so by courage and decisive-
ness, by faith and hope. The national anthem of the State of Israel
bears the title "The Hope."

To this day, however, the historic date also has the hallmark of
risk and danger. After the United Nations vote Isaac Herzog, chief
rabbi of Palestinian Jewry, declared that after two millennia of
darkness the dawn of Redemption had broken for the Jewish people. Judah Magnes, president of the Hebrew University and foremost advocate of a binational Arab-Jewish state, said, "It looks like
trouble." If Herzog was right, so was Magnes. Consider what happened between October 29, 1947, and May 14, 1948:

1. Arab attacks on Jews increased in Palestine, and irregulars in-
   filtrated the country from the surrounding countries: In all but
   name, full war existed even before the withdrawal of the British
   forces and the proclamation of Jewish statehood.
2. On March 18, 1948, Warren Austin, United States delegate at
   the United Nations, rose in the General Assembly to declare
   that the partition vote could not be implemented peacefully;
   and he went on to propose that it should temporarily be replaced by a United Nations trusteeship over all of Palestine.
3. Just prior to that date in May, Ben Gurion and his colleagues
   were urgently advised by George Marshall, then United States
   secretary of state, to accept the trusteeship proposal. Marshall
   was no particular friend, but, a great World War II general, he
   was no amateur in military matters, and he expressed the fear
   that a Jewish state, were it declared, would be crushed by the
   Arab armies. Undersecretary of State Robert Lowett added a

political point. If the Jews were to accept the trusteeship proposal and still were attacked, U.S. military forces could intervene on humanitarian grounds. But were the Jews to turn that proposal down, such an intervention would mean taking sides in a political conflict and was therefore impossible. If they went ahead and proclaimed a Jewish state, the Jews of that state would be on their own.

There was general jubilation among Jews on both October 29, 1947, and May 14, 1948. (I myself shared in this at the time for, like most Jews among whom I lived, I was politically quite naive.) Ben Gurion did not share in the jubilation but, as he later confessed, was filled with a sense of foreboding on both occasions: He and his colleagues were aware of the risk and of the danger. If, nevertheless, they went ahead with the proclamation of statehood, it was because in their heart of hearts they knew what historians were to understand only decades later in hindsight: It was either then or not at all. That supposedly indecisive Zionist statesman, Chaim Weizmann, telephoned from his sickbed in New York this crisp advice: "Proclaim the state, now or never!"

Weizmann was right. When if not in the wake of the Holocaust would the world allow a Jewish state? When if not then would Jews themselves muster the courage and determination to proclaim it, defend it, build it? Perhaps the world would allow a Jewish state in the Messianic age as prophesied by such as Isaiah—when states, and certainly the defense of them, would no longer be needed. Ours, however, is not the Messianic age.

The Jewish state proclaimed on May 14, 1948, has altered the Jewish condition. Some, non-Jews as well as Jews, welcome the fact. Others, Jews as well as non-Jews, deplore it. No one can deny it. But has it altered the condition of Judaism also? That is the question of the present chapter, and the answer will leave its mark on the remainder of this book.

BASEL, PETACH TIKVAH, AND RISH'ON L'ZION, AUGUST 1903–AUGUST 1905: THE LAND

The date was not precise, for it was of a decision made, not by an emerging government but rather arising from debates by a congress far from being a government. On the agenda of the Sixth Zionist Congress, meeting in Basel in August 1903, was a momentous item. A territory in Uganda was being offered to it for Jewish settlement by the British government. The excitement generated by the offer was great, but so was the controversy. In 1897 the first Zionist congress had established Palestine as the goal, and the sixth congress was of no mind to abandon it. However, as Palestine was ruled at the time by the tyrannical, arbitrary Ottoman Sultanate, it was a faraway dream. To Uganda, in contrast, Jews were actually invited, and this by a civilized government. In hindsight a white Jewish colony in black Africa may seem quite as problematic as a Jewish homeland in the Arab Near East—in many respects more so. This, however, was not how matters seemed at the time. Moreover, the timing of the British offer could not have been more appropriate. A pogrom had been staged in the Russian city of Kishinev during Easter 1903. Forty-nine Jews had been murdered. A world still capable of being shocked by mass murder had been shocked. The event dramatized to any Jewish leadership, the Zionist included, the need for a place of refuge for many thousands of Jews, not in some dreamed-of future, but not a day later than was humanly possible. No wonder the delegates assembled in Basel were both excited and torn. A delegate from Russia, Yechiel Chlevov, exclaimed, "*Wir sind keine Hascher nach schnellen Erfolgen; wir werden warten und lange warten.*" ("We are not running after quick successes; we shall wait, and wait for a long time.") But the real *cri de coeur* of the whole conference came from a German delegate, Heinrich Loewe: "*Das ist nicht Zionismus, aber es ist notwendig.*" ("This is not Zionism, but it is necessary.")

At the time no one symbolized Zionism quite as much as Theo-

dor Herzl. Yet, because of what Kishinev symbolized, Herzl himself proposed at least an investigation of the Uganda proposal. The
debate that followed was acrimonious. Herzl's proposal was nar-
rowly accepted. But when the Seventh Zionist Congress met in
1905, again in Basel, the Uganda idea was rejected. (Herzl had
died in 1904.) On July 30 a resolution was passed reaffirming the
"fundamental principle" of a "publicly recognized home for the
Jewish people in Palestine" and rejecting as harmful diversions all
"colonizing activity outside Palestine and its adjacent lands," and
this not merely as alternative "ends" but also as temporary
"means." The Jewish people were in desperate need of land, but
it seems that there was no substitute for *the* Land: Among the
delegates firmly opposed to the Uganda scheme were those from
Kishinev.

Still, congresses and their resolutions are only that and nothing
more. Let us shift attention to a Russian Jew, Aharon David Gordon. As a young man he had been rejected by the czarist military
authorities as unfit for military service. In subsequent years and
until the age of forty-eight, he had been a desk worker. Yet then,
in 1904 and just between the two congresses, he set out for Palestine in order to till its soil with his own hands. Prior to that Gordon,
a major Zionist thinker and widely considered the spiritual father
of the kibbutz movement, had written that a Jew needed more
than a physical haven from persecution. It was not enough even to
revitalize Hebrew, to create a new Hebrew literature, to renew the
Jewish mind. Redemption of Jewish *existence* was what was
needed, and a Jew could redeem his existence only by redeeming
the Land through his labor. Gordon's ideas are sometimes viewed
as derivative to those of such as Leon Tolstoy, and derivative they
perhaps are. But there is one difference between Tolstoy and Gordon, and on this Gordon's fame and influence entirely rest: Tolstoy did little more than preach, Gordon practiced, with back-
breaking labor in the vineyards and orange groves of Petach Tikvah
and Rishon l'Zion, suffering in the process unemployment, hunger,
and malaria. I confess that in my youth Gordon overwhelmed me,
and I love him still. My family background is anti-Zionist. I ceased

to be anti-Zionist in 1933 but was non-Zionist still in my *Hochschule* days, with little use for political Zionism. The thinker who then almost converted me to Zionism was Gordon.

Gordon's appeal was not to man in general, land in general, or labor in general. All these would have been to him empty abstractions, and the same is true of like-minded Jews, many of them his followers, then and now. Just about at the time of the first Zionist congresses attempts were initiated to "normalize" the Jewish condition by settling Jews on the land, in Canada, Brazil, and particularly Argentina. Nearly everywhere, those settled there sooner or later drifted back into the cities. Only in *the* Land did Jews return to the land.

Because for Gordon the bond between Jew and Land through labor was to be redemptive, his views have been dubbed a "religion of labor." For him the ultimate test of the religion was Jewish behavior toward the local Arab population. What if they are hostile? "Their hostility is all the more a reason for our humanity." How to respond to hostility with humanity when the land is not empty? Gordon and his comrades and followers managed to solve this problem by moving to the no-man's land of swamps and desert, and making it bloom. They could have performed this man-made miracle in no other land.

Without this bond between the people and the Land the Jewish state could never have been founded on May 14, 1948; or, if founded, it would have been against even greater odds than was in fact the case. (Could it have survived?) How to understand that bond, and hence the state itself? As the long-delayed fulfilment of a divine promise? As the resumption of a mystical relation between people and Land? Even minimally it can be understood only as a reactivation of a claim that had never been renounced.

One must go back in history. Having crushed the Bar Kochba rebellion in 135 C.E., the Roman Emperor Hadrian made an unprecedented attempt to cut the bond between people and Land once and for all. He renamed Judaea "Palestina" ("land of the Philistines"), an act of verbal delegitimation the effects of which reverberate to this day. The land was devastated by three years of war: Hadrian resettled it with Roman ex-servicemen and other foreigners, knowing full well it is more difficult for a people to retain its claim on a land populated by others than on an empty one. Hadrian took additional measures, harsher still, in his attempt to wipe out the Jewish religion. It was in pursuit of that larger goal that he sought to break the bond between the people and the Land. He never succeeded:

> Whoever lives in the Land of Israel is considered a believer in God. Whoever lives outside the Land is considered to be in the category of idol worshippers.

> Living in the Land of Israel equals in importance the performance of all the other *mitzvot* of the Torah.

Statements such as these, made after the edicts of Hadrian, are to be found in rabbinic literature. They are surely hyperbolic, for it was the schools in Babylonia that in the end produced the more authoritative Talmud. (See chapter 3, section 5.) Yet their very hyperbole is indicative of an awareness on the part of the rabbis of the need to resist the assault on the bond between people and Land—to resist it despite their powerlessness.

The rabbis were not entirely powerless: They could enact laws that the faithful at least would observe.

> All can be compelled to move to the Land of Israel, but no one can be compelled to move away from it . . . , whether it be a man or a woman.

This rabbinic ordinance refers to marriage and divorce. If a wife refuses to "ascend" to the Land with a husband wishing to do so, the latter may divorce her and keep the dowry. If a husband refuses to "ascend" with a wife wishing to do so, she may divorce him and get back her dowry. So strong is the rabbinic resolve to resist the breaking of the bond between people and Land that here, for once, male chauvinism is overcome.

Doubtless the ordinance just cited was rarely if ever enacted. The spirit behind it, however, kept on living in the consciousness of the whole people. After each meal observant Jews thank God for the gift of the "lovely, good and spacious land." They have

done so in ages when they *could not* live in it, and are doing so
today even if they *will not* live in it. This is because the Land is
bound up with the Messianic expectation. (See below, chapter 13.)
The Ramban, already cited, was a rabbinic scholar of mystical
bent. The general rabbinic attitude toward the Messianic expectation was cautious: The Messiah was sure to come, but no one
knew when, and, since there had been so many false hopes, it was
too hazardous to fathom signs of his coming. Being of mystical
bent, the Ramban ventured a step beyond this caution. When will
the Redemption come?

> Many nations have devastated the Land, but none have rebuilt
> and replanted it. When you see trees growing in Galilee, then
> you may gather hope.

The traveler today sees the trees in Galilee, planted by such as
Gordon, and is astonished.

JERUSALEM, JUNE 7, 1967: THE CITY

The date, this time, was quite precise, for it was of a military
operation. Only a week before had there been reason to fear that
the state would be destroyed. Now, on June 7, 1967, for the first
time since the collapse of the Bar Kochba rebellion, the old city of
Jerusalem was in Jewish hands. An officer involved in the operation
was to remark subsequently that he could explain every military
move that had taken him and his men to the Wall, but that this
only served to deepen his wonder. Just so, in a book published
some twenty years earlier, Martin Buber had written of the event
with which Jewish history began—and almost ended before beginning in earnest. Ordinarily, Buber had written, one stops wonder-
ing at an event once the latter is explained. When the Red Sea
split just when catastrophe threatened, the people were filled with
"abiding wonder"—a wonder that abides in the Jewish consciousness to this day. (See Exod. 14:5–31, 15:1–21; also above, chapter
2, section 5.) And if the wonder has kept abiding, it has been not

because the people could not explain the event but rather because, the more it was explained, the more wondrous it became.

The experience of that Six-Day War officer was the experience of many Jews everywhere and of nearly all Israelis. Jerusalem had been divided for nineteen years. Barely three weeks after the city was reunited under Jewish rule the Israeli government assumed sovereignty over it. In Israel nearly every governmental act is subject to controversy. Except at insignificant fringes, there was no controversy over this governmental act. Jerusalem had been lost for so long: The city would not be lost again.

For how long had Jerusalem been lost? Once again we must hark back to Hadrian. Jerusalem and its Temple had of course been destroyed long before Hadrian, by the Roman Emperor Titus in 70 C.E. Hadrian knew that an empty land can be regained: He also knew that a destroyed city can be rebuilt. Going beyond Titus, in 135 C.E. he renamed the city Aelia Capitolina, built a temple to Jupiter where the Temple once stood, and—most telling of all— forbade Jewish residence in the city on pain of death.

The last-named act was also of the greatest consequence. Only scholars today still know of Aelia Capitolina, and even these do not seem to know what became of Hadrian's temple to Jupiter. But it was otherwise with Hadrian's decree forbidding Jewish residence in Jerusalem. To be sure, it was revoked after barely four years, upon Hadrian's death. But the secular pagan Roman Empire had hardly become holy Christian when, in 335 C.E., Hadrian's law was reenacted. The ground for this particular action had been well prepared by such Christian writers as the second-century Justin Martyr, who had declared that

circumcision was given to the Jews as a sign, not of divine favor but rather of future reprobation, so that they might be recognized by those presently occupying the city and prevented from re-entering it.

To such as Justin Martyr Jewish reentry into Jerusalem was absolutely unacceptable. Traces of this were to remain in various forms through the ages. When in 1903 Herzl visited Pope Pius X the latter declared that whereas the Church could not prevent a Jewish return to Jerusalem, it could never sanction it. When in 1967 the old city returned to Jewish control, the Vatican began to issue a series of calls for its internationalization: This had never happened during the nineteen years that the city was under Jordanian control. Nor are the long-term effects of Hadrian's ancient acts confined to Christendom. The late King Saud of Saudi Arabia used to complain that he could not worship in the al-Aqsa Mosque in Jerusalem (the third-holiest shrine in Islam, next to the Ka'aba in Mecca and Muhammed's tomb in Medina) since it was in Jewish hands: He never bothered to visit the mosque in the nineteen years that it was in Jordanian (Muslim) hands. In short, whatever the differences in theological rationale and political purpose, Christians and Muslims alike have had difficulty all along with a Jewish presence in Jerusalem; and these merely rose to the surface when in 1967 the city came under Jewish sovereignty. Krister Stendahl, former dean of Harvard Divinity School, has said that whereas Christians and Muslims have holy sites in Jerusalem, to Jews Jerusalem itself is holy. After a long history beginning with Hadrian, one cannot reasonably expect that this profoundly true statement will soon be widely shared, so that true peace may come to Jerusalem.

But can stones be holy? When King Solomon inaugurated the first Temple, he addressed a prayer to Him Whom the heaven of heavens cannot contain, much less the house that he had built. After the second Temple was destroyed, the rabbinic imagination discovered a *Yerushalayim shel Ma'alah*, a heavenly Jerusalem "above." They never abandoned, however, the *Yerushalayim shel Mata*—the earthly Jerusalem "below." Indeed, in a Midrash that reads as if written against Hadrian and all his followers, God refuses to enter the heavenly Jerusalem until it is possible for Him to reenter the earthly one as well.

Can stones be holy? Not by themselves. In a Midrash the *schechinah* leaves the deserted and desolate Land because the people have been driven from it. There is one place, however, where the *schechinah* remains: at the Wall. But how can the *schechinah* remain when its very nature is to dwell *between* people, *among* them, and the people are gone? The *shechinah* remains at the Wall, waiting: She is waiting for her people to return.

JUDAISM AND THE STATE OF ISRAEL

It took the advent of Nazism, the Holocaust, and the total Arab rejection of the national home [of the Jewish people in Palestine] to convert the Zionist movement to the belief in [Jewish] statehood.

I go back to that fateful and risky decision of May 14, 1948, and it appears in retrospect as the grasping of a historic moment that would never return. Amazing in its boldness, it becomes all the more so in the light of the above-cited statement by Walter Laqueur. The facts referred to by the well-known historian are briefly as follows. Under the impact of the Dreyfus trial Theodor Herzl had called for a *Judenstaat* in a pamphlet of that title. (The word can be translated both as "Jewish state" or "state of Jews"; which is chosen makes a big difference.) However, the Zionist movement had been far from committed to Jewish statehood until the events referred to by Laqueur, and this for several reasons.

The most obvious was that Jewish statehood seemed beyond reach. It was wholly so until the Turks were driven out of Palestine by the British in World War I. The British Balfour Declaration of 1917 "viewed with favor" a Jewish "home" in Palestine but said nothing about Jewish statehood. Nor did the advent of Nazism in 1933 change the British mind in this respect. On the contrary, as the Jewish need for a home escalated so did Arab opposition; and precisely when in 1939 Jewish need—and political weakness—became desperate the British yielded to Arab pressure and virtually closed the gates of Palestine to Jews. (Arabs from neighboring countries, attracted by economic opportunities, were never kept out.) Only as the facts of the Holocaust began to become known did the Zionist leadership commit itself to a Jewish state, implying as it would Jewish control over immigration. And even then this commitment might have been derailed had the postwar British government—or the Palestinian Arab leadership—accepted U.S. President Harry Truman's request for the admission of one hundred thousand Jewish Holocaust survivors, with the tacit understanding that these would be the last. But both the Arabs and British Foreign Secretary Ernest Bevin rejected Truman's request.

But unattainability was only one of several reasons for Zionist reluctance to embrace Jewish statehood. We have cited Gordon to the effect that Arab "hostility" ought to be "all the more reason" for Zionist "humanity," and this Gordonian principle was practiced not only by like-minded kibbutzniks but also by other immigrants who paid exorbitant prices for Arab land, went out of their way to make friends with Arab neighbors, and in general followed Achad Ha-am (1856–1927), Herzl's great ideological rival. Achad Ha-Am taught that the essence of Zionism was the renewal of Jewish culture, and that the essence of that was a humane, prophetic morality. These were the teachings of Gordon and Achad Ha-Am. However, as to what Jews ought to do if Arab "hostility" took the form of murdering children, or—as promised by then P.L.O. chief Shukairi in 1967, "pushing the Jews into the sea"— Gordon had nothing to say. Nor, so far as I can discover, did Achad Ha-Am.

What little either man may have said here or there on this subject must have amounted to this: Rely on world conscience. This certainly was the case with those of their followers who believed that the British would honor the Balfour Declaration; after all, the British post–World War I rule of Palestine was a mandate of the League of Nations, the only political embodiment of world conscience then in existence. Subsequent developments were cruelly disappointing. Yet Zionist belief in a world conscience was revived with the advent of the United Nations, and this is why I, like so many others, were naive enough at the time to celebrate on October 29, 1947, far more than on May 14, 1948.

The belief in world conscience was not confined to the politically naive. It was shared by a good many political leaders one should have thought would have been far removed from political naivety. In the days just prior to May 14, 1948, Ben Gurion's Council of Nine, having rejected the United Nations trusteeship proposal and decided to risk proclaiming a Jewish state, were drafting the Proclamation of the State of Israel. One of the nine suggested that a reference to the boundaries of the state as "laid down in the [October 29, 1947] United Nations resolution" should be included in the document. Ben Gurion pointed out that the United States Declaration of Independence contained no reference to future boundaries; that in rejecting the United Nations partition proposal (which the Jews had reluctantly accepted) the Arabs had forfeited their rights to its benefits; and that in any case in the midst of warfare future boundaries were unpredictable. Had the proposal opposed by Ben Gurion been accepted Israel would have been the first state in history to hand a weapon to those sworn to destroy it in its own most basic document. Even with Ben Gurion's forceful opposition, this piece of political folly was defeated only by a vote of five to four.

At work here was something deeper than naivety born of two millennia of political inexperience. About a decade after the Kishinev pogrom Hermann Cohen in Germany and Kaufmann Kohler in America, Jewish thinkers of substance both, had taught that Judaism had been "denationalized," and that this was a blessing since it made Jews freer to pursue their universal Messianic mission. There is a story about the first-century Rabbi Yohanan ben Zakkai that is known to every educated Jewish child. The destruction of Jerusalem by the Romans in 70 C.E. was preceded by a long siege. Opposed to surrender, the militants were holding out and, lest morale crumble, were preventing those they considered fainthearted from leaving the city: Only the dead could be carried outside the city walls. It was then that ben Zakkai saw his chance to save Judaism if not the Jewish state. Foreseeing that Jerusalem would be destroyed, he had himself carried outside in a coffin. Then he asked to be taken to Vespasian, the Roman general, made the not-too-difficult prophecy that he would soon sit on Caesar's throne, and the general, superstitious in his belief that rabbis could prophesy and pleased by what he had heard, granted ben Zakkai's small request—a school in Yavne. And thus Judaism was saved. It is a beautiful story. But at religious school in Germany I was taught something the story does not contain: The destruction of the state was a blessing in disguise, as it liberated Judaism from the burden of statehood. I believed it too. The antistate version of Judaism was not just taught by thinkers such as Cohen and Kohler. It was widely, sincerely accepted.

Those accepting it did not deny that the destruction of the ancient Jewish state had been followed by a long, miserable exile. Nor did they deny that in dark places such as Kishinev the Jewish condition was one of exile still. They affirmed, however, that in some places "exile" had become Diaspora, and that these were the places that counted: Czarist Russia would not long be able to resist the power of modern enlightenment. To this day I cannot wholly fault this view, for a modern Jew had two hopes for liberation from exile, a democratic state and a Jewish state. But where would a Jewish state be today were there no democratic states? However, during the twelve years of the thousand-year-Reich that were equal to a thousand, Jews were in an exile more horrible than any ever dreamed of: not only those trapped and murdered in Nazi-occupied Europe, but also those who were safe in decent countries. They were safe themselves but impotent. They implored the decent countries in which they lived to do what they could to come to the aid of their brethren. But what could have been done was not done.

That exile has become Diaspora is characteristic of liberal Judaism. At least in theory Orthodox Judaism has never abandoned the view that what in 70 C.E. became exile is exile still. The traditional prayer book contains the following passage:

> Because of our sins we were exiled from our country and banished from our land. We cannot go up as pilgrims to worship Thee, to perform our duties in Thy chosen house, the great and holy Temple which was called by Thy name, on account of the hand that was let loose on Thy sanctuary. May it be Thy will, Lord our God and God of our fathers, merciful King, in Thy abundant love again to have mercy on us and on Thy sanctuary; rebuild it speedily and magnify its glory.

The Hebrew for "exile" is *galut*, and a Judaism that is committed to the view expressed in the passage just cited may be called Galut Judaism. This is characterized by the following beliefs:

1. Exile, though painful, is bearable because it is meaningful.
2. Its meaning is not altogether negative, for though punishment for Jewish sins, a God who punishes is, at any rate, not a God that has abandoned or rejected. On the contrary, the punishment is "sufferings of love" intended to induce *teshuvah*.
3. Punishment for Jewish sins, exile is at times viewed also as vicarious atonement for the sins of others.
4. Climactically, exile will not last forever. Whether or not either the suffering or the *teshuvah* is capable of hastening the messianic end, some future Jewish generation will live to see the ultimate Redemption of Israel and all mankind.

Galut Judaism is given a profound expression in a Midrash in which, following the destruction of the Temple, God is pictured as exacting three oaths, one from the Gentiles and two from the Jews. Now that the Jews are defenseless, the Gentiles will not always resist the temptation to persecute them: They are made to swear not to persecute them excessively. The Jews are made to swear, first, not to resist the Gentiles when they persecute them, and, second, not to "climb the walls" [of Jerusalem], (attempt to rebuild their state until the ordained time of exile is complete) and God will send the Messiah. The great *mitzvah* of Galut Judaism, then, is to wait in hope, and through *teshuvah* and in no other way to hasten the end.

But the same Midrash that expresses perfectly the nature of Galut Judaism also expresses with the same perfection that the Holocaust has made an end to Galut Judaism. To be sure, there are those among the ultra-Orthodox who reject this opinion, and continue to hold fast to Galut Judaism even if (as many of them do) they live in Jerusalem. In their view it is because some Jews broke the Jewish oath not to "climb the wall"—embraced Zionism and returned to Jerusalem before the appointed time—that God released the Gentiles from their oath and let them do what they wished to other Jews, to the victims of the Holocaust. But how can they be serious? The children thrown into the flames alive; their mothers; the *Muselmaenner*; all those murdered before they knew what was happening; the pious ones who died with the *Sh'ma Yisrael* on their lips to the sound of Nazi Viennese waltzes: How is it possible to connect all this with the will of a God permitting or even ordering it? Is this not blasphemy toward the victims? Is it not blasphemy toward God—unwitting blasphemy, to be sure, but blasphemy all the same? I know that the view I am assailing is seriously held, and this by some learned rabbis and many pious folk. But in charity I can view it only as the product of desperation: Events have shattered a venerable tradition, and there are those among the pious who cannot or dare not confront the fact.

For my part, I see no choice but to give the opposite interpretation to the Midrash of the three oaths in our time. It is the Gentiles who broke their oath at Auschwitz, for if Auschwitz is not excessive persecution, one could not say what excessive persecution is; and in consequence of this breach of the one oath by the Gentiles the Jews are released from the two oaths exacted from them. To resist their persecutors is no longer forbidden, neither is the climbing of the walls of Jerusalem.

I find myself compelled to go one step further still. The Holocaust has much in common with other catastrophes, Jewish and non-Jewish, past and present. What makes it—thus far—uniquely unbearable is an unprecedented togetherness of helplessness in the victims with wickedness in their persecutors. It is necessary to make an end to this togetherness, and since the victims cannot make an end to the wickedness they must make an end to the helplessness. In May 1943 the remnants of the Warsaw Ghetto took to arms when their enemies came to cart them off for murder. To do so was not merely religiously unobjectionable. It was a *mitzvah*. And it was equally a *mitzvah* for those nine in Tel Aviv in 1947 to decide, whatever the risks, to declare the State of Israel. Once founded, moreover, the state soon initiated two further *mitzvot* the day-to-day performance of which has become part and parcel of Jewish life. One is the 1950 Law of Return that grants automatic Israeli citizenship to all Jews asking for it: With this law the new state does whatever it can to make an end to *galut*, and it makes an end altogether to Galut Judaism, the submission to exile as meaningful. The full significance of this new *mitzvah* is still unfolding, as is shown by the condition of Soviet Jewry. Still more is this true of the other new *mitzvah*, this one begun in earnest on June 7, 1967. This is the rebuilding of Jewish Jerusalem.

Has the condition of Judaism been altered by that fateful act in Tel Aviv on May 14, 1948? In my view, the answer is clear: *Had a Jewish state not been founded then, it would be a* mitzvah *to do it now.* One ponders this fact. One also ponders the fact that what would be a religious necessity now would no longer be a political possibility. One ponders all this, and stands in awe and wonder before the decision made on that day.

EPILOGUE

> O Guardian of Israel,
> Guard Thy people Israel,
> Those who proclaim,
> Hear, O Israel [the Lord our God, the Lord is One]

I recently heard this song sung at a military ceremony in Jerusalem. The words, of course, are those recited at the *havdalah* service that ends Shabbat and ushers in the workaday week in an unredeemed world. (See above, chapters 4, section 3; and 10, section 2.) The reader will notice, however, that three words are omitted in the military song: "Lest Israel perish." The omission, of course, is deliberate.

It is absurd to assume that the Israeli Defense Forces are unaware of the possibility that Israel might perish. That possibility is their whole *raison d'être*. "Lest Israel perish?" Israel knows the possibility but refuses to countenance it. Taking up arms against it, she calls on the Guardian of Israel, even as she does whatever she can to do the guarding herself.

12. ISRAEL AND THE NATIONS

WHO IS ON TRIAL?

Israel und die Voelker ("Israel and the Nations"): This is the title of a tome, heavy as well as authoritative, on the subject of the present chapter. It is a great work. If it falls short of being a classic—a book that could speak as directly to our time as to its own—it is due not to some fault in its author but to the place and time of its publication: Vienna, 1922. The city has been left nine years earlier by a vagabond named Adolf Hitler and was not ready yet for his return. But it had long been rife with proto-Nazi anti-semitism. Karl Lueger, its vastly popular mayor from 1897 to his death in 1910, had declared that capitalism and Marxism, evils both, were equally products of the Jewish mind. The Weltanschauung of Georg Ritter von Schoenerer, repeatedly a member of the Austrian Parliament, contained a good summary of "racist" anti-semitism: *"Was der Jude glaubt ist einerlei; in der Rasse liegt die Schweinerei."* ("Jewish faith is irrelevant; the swinishness lies in the race.") It was on foundations such as these that the young Hitler built his own Weltanschauung; and his armies and storm troopers no sooner returned to Vienna in March 1938 than they put it into practice.

Von Schoenerer's epigram notwithstanding, stock-in-trade parts of "racist" as well as religious antisemitism were always attacks on Judaism. A special object of attack was the Talmud. Since the assailants lacked all knowledge of the subject they all relied, directly or indirectly, on a few semischolarly books, the most important of which was Johann Andreas Eisenmenger's *Entdecktes Judentum* ("Judaism Discovered," [1700]). Eisenmenger did have some knowledge. The use to which he put it, however, was not exposition but vilification, and this was inspired by the fear that here and there some benighted Christian might find Judaism attractive, even after Christianity had superseded it.

Among the tracts based on Eisenmenger was *Herr Professor* August Rohling's *Der Talmudjude* ("The Talmud Jew"). First published in 1871, it was republished again and again over the next half-century, in other European languages as well as German itself. The French edition was introduced by Edouard Drumont, the chief instigator of antisemitism in France during the Dreyfus affair (1894–1906). In Vienna itself, a certain Franz Hobulek, sued in 1883 for inciting mob violence against Jews, pleaded in court that he had acted in good faith on the authority of Rohling, after all, a full professor at the German University of Prague. Hobulek was acquitted, an act that encouraged the antisemites to carry on with their defamation and their street violence. Such was Vienna, or a significant though usually ignored part of it, way back before the mentors of young Hitler, to say nothing of Hitler himself.

Rohling himself did not rest on his laurels of 1871. When in 1883 the Jews of a small Hungarian town were accused of ritual murder he volunteered to testify on oath that the Talmud demanded Christian blood for Jewish religious purposes. This time, however, a Jew struck back. Jewish militancy toward the antisemites was not encouraged by the conditions of the time, but a distinguished Viennese rabbi and Talmudic scholar, Joseph Samuel Bloch (1850–1923) was a pioneer. He publicly denounced Rohling as an ignoramus and a liar, and offered to pay three thousand florins if he could translate so much as a single page of the Talmud—any page at all of his own choosing. Rohling had no choice but to sue Bloch for libel. Two years went by, during which both sides prepared for the trial. Then, thirteen days before the scheduled date, Rohling withdrew his action. Bloch had won a battle. But as subsequent history was to show, he had not won the war. And now, when once one hoped that at least this is all over, there exists in the Soviet Union a book entitled *Judaism Without Embellishment*. It is Eisenmenger's *Judaism Discovered* all over again.

It is to the described circumstances that Bloch's *Israel and the Nations* owes its origin. A vast compendium on the subject of its title, it places the facts of rabbinic teaching before the civilized world, asking the gentile reader to judge Judaism for himself. But in the process it also reproduces the lies and half-truths of the antisemites, even as it goes to great lengths to refute them. Bloch's work, in short, is scholarship mixed with apologetics—apologetics at its grandest. However, whether puny or grand, apologetics no longer has a place in an exposition of Judaism. After what has occurred since the appearance of Bloch's work, no self-respecting Jew can place Judaism for judgment before the world. If anything is under judgment today, it is the world, its civilized part included. After the Holocaust, so far as the relation between Jews and Gentiles is concerned, it is not *Israel* that is on trial; if anything, it is *die Voelker*.

DISPOSING OF APOLOGETICS IN AN ACCOUNT OF JUDAISM TODAY

The Talmud is a vast work composed of numerous heavy tomes. Even after a lifetime of study few ever master it whole. Naturally, to anyone except a total devotee it contains quite a bit of unattractive material, including that about Jewish-Gentile relations: In an unapologetic account of Judaism this frank statement should be made as a matter of course. But then, unattractive material is found in the Jewish Bible also—and in the Christian. "Let the

dead bury the dead," said the Nazarene to a young man who
wished to follow him but asked just this before doing so, time to
bury his father (Matthew 8:22, Luke 9:60). Yet no one ever seems
to accuse Jesus of callousness. And when he gets angry, or speaks
of bringing the sword rather than peace (Matthew 10:34), this is
said to prove only that he is human. Then why should the same
allowance not be made for such as Rabbi Shim'on Bar Yochai? A
second-century disciple of Rabbi Akiba, he had seen what Hadrian
had done following the defeat of the Bar Kochba uprising. Some
of the Roman emperor's actions have already been mentioned.
(See chapter 11, sections 2 and 3.) Yet unmentioned is the climactic one: He had forbidden the practice of the Jewish religion
on pain of death, and when his edict had been defied by ten rabbis,
Bar Yochai's own teacher Akiba included, he had had them captured and tortured to death. Hounded by the Romans himself, Bar
Yochai had lived in a cave in hiding, as the story has it, for no less
than thirteen years. It was then that the rabbi exclaimed in a moment of despair, "Even the best of the Gentiles should be slain."

Needless to say, passages such as these are pounced on gleefully
by the Eisenmengers, the Rohlings, and the Soviet authors of
Judaism Without Embellishment. On his part, Bloch maintains
that the best manuscripts of this particular text add "in time of
war," and that the exclamation expresses the scruples of a rabbi
trying to understand when the killing of a fellow human being is
permitted. For all that is known to me, no Talmud scholar, Bloch
may be right. My point is that what in 1922 had a place in an account of Judaism has no such place today. In the 1930s the Gold-
schmidt German translation of the Talmud appeared in a popular
edition in Berlin. It is safe to assume that Hitler never heard of it,
and the idea of Hitler reading a few pages in it in order to check
his views is ludicrous. (More ludicrous still is the assertion of
Werner Maser, a postwar German Hitler biographer, to the effect
that Hitler had a "remarkable knowledge" of the Talmud.)
Rohling-type trash is all Hitler knew and all he needed to know.
And what was true of Hitler then is true today of neo-Nazis on
the Right, neo-Stalinists on the Left, and such as the Ayatollah
Khomeini and Louis Farakhan.

THE NOACHIDIC COVENANT

What causes hatred of Judaism? The subject is vast and quite beyond the scope of this book. Well within its scope is at least one cause: the doctrine of the chosenness of the Jewish people. Even as self-described a "purely racist" and "nonreligious" Jew-hater as Hitler declared on at least one occasion that there could only be one chosen people. As to who that people was he was far from clear, for the Japanese were honorary "Aryans," and the "Semitic" Arab Mufti of Jerusalem was an honored guest in war-time Berlin, lending a hand in the Nazi anti-Jewish program. However, Hitler *was* clear as to who the chosen people was *not*, and he did all he could to destroy both that people and its claim to chosenness. The Christian theologian Roy Eckardt has written: "In the Holocaust the holy nation is turned into excrement. That was the program's entire purpose."

The doctrine of the chosen people is difficult for Jews as well as Gentiles, yet difficult to dispense with even in an age of pluralism and dialogue. (See above, chapter 5.) The difficulty is diminished greatly, however, by the fact that in Judaism God's covenant with Israel is not the only one nor the first. That distinction belongs to a divine covenant with Noah and his offspring, the entire human race. Relying on Gen. 9:1–17, the Talmud formulates seven laws as contained in the "Noachidic covenant." All mankind is bidden to practice justice, as well as to abstain from blasphemy, idolatry, incest, bloodshed, robbery, and the eating of flesh torn from a living animal. Except for the momentous case of idolatry, these might be called the basic laws of morality, with a fine touch added by the last-named law, suggesting as it does that one cannot be covenanted to God and behave like a savage. What goes beyond basic morality, however, is that the seven laws are part of a relation between mankind on earth and the God that dwells beyond the heaven of heavens. Moreover, this particular covenant has one feature at least that is unique. As the facts show all too painfully, neither covenant guarantees that its human partners will abide by its terms. The fear ought therefore to be ever-present that since the human partner often betrays the covenant the divine partner may one day terminate it. And indeed, in the case of God's covenant with Israel that fear *is* present, for on one occasion reported in the Tenach, following the sin of the golden calf, God almost did terminate that covenant, and would have done so but for Moses' intercession (Exod. 32:9–14). In contrast, the Noachidic covenant is permeated by no fear of divine termination. God has already destroyed a sinful generation in a flood, and in the covenant with Noah vows not to do so again. He now accepts the fact that "the imagination of man's heart is evil from his youth" but "will not again curse the ground for man's sake . . . neither smite any more every living thing" (Gen. 8:21).

REASON AND REVELATION

> Rabbi Akiba used to say, "Beloved is Man, for he was created in the image of God; but it was with special love that it was made known to him that he was created in the image of God, as it is said, 'For in the image of God made He Man' (Gen. 9:6). Beloved are Israel, for they are called children of the Omnipresent; but it was with a special love that it was made known to them that they are called children of the Omnipresent, as it is said, 'Ye are children unto the Lord, your God.'" (Deut. 14:1) (*Abot* 3:18)

No rabbinic text is as widely read as *Pirke Abot*. No rabbi is more authoritative than Akiba. And the statement of his just cited was made by him not casually or on just one occasion but again and again. It therefore deserves close scrutiny. To be scrutinized in particular is, first, the conjuncture of "Man" and "Israel"—that both are beloved of God; and, second, that it is made known to both that they are beloved of God. Yet precisely these conjunctions give rise to a question. "Ye are children of the Lord, your God," Israel learns from its own Torah: How does Man learn "In the image of God made He Man," when this is written in the Torah given only to Israel?

To this altogether fundamental question the tradition has two main answers. A Talmudic passage distinguishes between those ordinances (such as against the eating of pork) "to which Satan and the Gentiles object" and those (such as against idolatry, incest, murder, robbery, and blasphemy) "which would have had to be written if they were not already written." Again, one Midrash has it that six of the seven Noachidic commandments (all except that against the eating of living flesh) were already given to Adam. These two texts may be cited together, for what matters in the second is that the Adamites have no Scripture, and in the first, that they must be able to write the required laws in case they are not found in written form before them. These texts (as well as others one could cite) imply that there are what the Greeks call *agraphoi nomoi*, "unwritten laws" that have universal validity because they are part of "nature," and which man is capable of recognizing by virtue of his own nature. The Jewish idea of the divine image in man, then, is much like the "rational animal" of the Greeks, the principal characteristic of Greek "rationality" being the ability to know the true, the beautiful and—for the Jews above all—the good.

But the assimilation of the Noachidic covenant to the "natural law" tradition harking back to the Greeks cannot be pushed within Judaism beyond a certain point. Nothing in the Greek idea suggests a divine covenant with all humanity, to say nothing of a divine promise not to destroy it; the gods of Greek myth never made any such promise, and the God of the Greek philosophers is indifferent to humanity and its fate. Moreover, whereas in the texts cited by Akiba, Adam is made in the divine image, the knowledge of this fact is given only to Noah. This may well be why the Rambam, Greek-inspired though he is, distinguishes between "wise Gentiles" who observe moral laws on the basis of "reason," and "righteous Gentiles" who observe these same laws "because the Holy One, blessed be He, commanded them in the Torah." In short, what according to the Rambam it is necessary for righteous Gentiles to know, but not possible to know on the basis of reason alone, is that they are part of a covenant with the God who created them in His own image. But how is the required knowledge available to Gentiles when the Torah was given to Israel and not to mankind in general? In the relevant passage the Rambam refers to "resident aliens," citing Num. 15:6, "One law and one ordinance shall be both for you and the resident alien." But what of Noachides in distant China, Africa, or Labrador?

JUDAISM AND ITS "DAUGHTER RELIGIONS" CHRISTIANITY AND ISLAM

In Christianity and Islam, the "daughter religions" of Judaism, the problem just posed was to explode into tremendous missionizing activities. In Judaism (in which converts have always been accepted but rarely been actively sought and then, as it were, by mistake) the problem has resulted in a very special attitude toward these two religions. Maimonides is a good example. The all-too amiable nineteenth-century expression "daughter religion" would never have crossed the lips of the Rambam, who had to flee twice from Muslim persecution and might have suffered Christian persecution had he ever lived in a Christian land. Tough-mindedly he writes that

> whereas all the prophets affirmed that the Messiah would redeem Israel, . . . gather their dispersed and confirm the commandments, . . . [Jesus, whether directly or through his followers] caused Israel to be destroyed by the sword, and their remnant to be dispersed and humiliated . . .

Even so he acknowledges that Jews share with Christians and Muslims the beliefs in Creation, miracles, and, of course above all, the One God. Then, having stressed that God's ways are not ours, that His thoughts not our thoughts, and that therefore "it is beyond the human mind to fathom the designs of the Creator," he goes on as follows:

> All these matters relating to Jesus of Nazareth and the Ishmaelite [Muhammed] who came after him only serve to clear the way for King Messiah, and to prepare the whole world to worship God with one accord, as it is written, "For then will I turn the peoples into a pure language, that they may call upon the name of the Lord to serve Him with one consent." (Zeph. 3:9)

This was written in the "dark" Middle Ages. Can Judaism go further in the "light" modern age, and especially in one in which "pluralism is the will of God"? In idea, Abraham J. Heschel's above-cited dictum has made sense ever since modern theology discovered that it could no longer say honestly "this is God's way" but at most only "I am *committed to* this, *as being* God's way" (see chapter 1, section 2). Ever since then the possibility could have been recognized that the different or even conflicting commitment of another may be equally honest—nay, partake of truth—and that one's own commitment might be enriched by learning from it. This is in theory. In practice, however, the idea is being put seriously explored only in our time, and this after world-shaking events. Western empires have collapsed. White attitudes toward nonwhites are being revolutionized. Fairly or unfairly, past Christian missionizing of non-Christians is being tarred with the brush of colonialism. And, whether or not as a result of all this, Western Christians are now widely engaged in an activity called "dialogue," with Muslims, Buddhists, Hindus—and Jews.

Interreligious dialogue in general is one thing. Christian dialogue with Jews in particular is another. Of Islam, Buddhism, and Hinduism the ordinary Christian has yet to learn. Judaism, he has been taught through the ages, he has known all along—and superseded. "Dialogue" is defined as an activity in which each partner is listening to the other even as he speaks to him. In 1982 I went to Germany for a Jewish-Christian dialogue. (It was, as I told those present, the first time in forty-four years that I spoke on German soil, and the last time had been on Yom Kippur in the synagogue of Baden-Baden, just before they burned it to the ground.) The words I heard there included the most relevant to Jewish-Christian dialogue I ever heard anywhere. The Protestant theologian Martin Stoehr began as follows: "We Christians have lived with Jews for nearly two millennia. But never once have we listened to them, and our Christian faith has not helped us in this regard. Then why are we eager to listen to them now? Not because of our Christian faith, but because six million Jews were murdered." The Catholic theologian Hans Hermann Henrix, speaking elsewhere, took it up from there: "Christian anti-Judaism will not come to an end until

Christians develop a positive attitude toward Jews, not despite their nonacceptance of Christ but because of it." On the part of Christians, how can there be an honest dialogue with Jews so long as they are sure in advance that the Jewish truth about to be heard has already been heard and superseded? Christians often act as if Jews had spent the Christian centuries rejecting their Christ. They are mistaken: Except in relations with Christians, the Christ of Christianity is not a Jewish issue. There simply can be no dialogue worthy of the name unless Christians accept—nay, treasure—the fact that Jews through the two millennia of Christianity have had an agenda of their own. To come to the crux: There can be no Jewish-Christian dialogue worthy of the name unless one Christian activity is abandoned, missions to the Jews. It must be abandoned, moreover, not as a temporary strategy but in principle, as a bimillennial theological mistake. The cost of that mistake in Christian love and Jewish blood one hesitates to contemplate.

So much about Jewish-Christian dialogue from the Christian side. A point must be added from the Jewish side. Fruitful Jewish-Christian relations have existed all along. In the Middle Ages the Christian Thomas Aquinas learned from the Jew Maimonides. In modern times Jews such as Buber and Rosenzweig have learned from Christians such as Lessing and Kierkegaard. The two religions share much, and much was always to be gained in many spheres from Jewish-Christian cooperation. Even Christian missions to the Jews could be accepted by Jews, as misguided, to be sure, and this as a matter of course, but at any rate as sincere and well intended. In this respect, however, events have produced a change. A post-Holocaust Jew can still view Christian attempts to convert Jews as sincere and well intended. But even as such they are no longer acceptable: They have become attempts to do in one way what Hitler did in another.

This post-Holocaust Jewish necessity ought to have implications for Christianity as well. That this is so in relation to Jews and Judaism is implicit in the above-cited statements of Stoehr and Henrix. That it goes beyond these relations is suspected by some. As I write these lines I have before me an issue of the *Jerusalem Post*, dated September 5, 1986. In a letter published in that issue

Elie Wiesel is reported as remarking to the Christian theologian Claire Hutchet-Bishop that Christianity died at Auschwitz. The Christian author of the letter reports this statement but does not report Hutchet-Bishop as protesting. Instead he proceeds to cite a statement by Irving Greenberg, and with this he evidently agrees. Greenberg writes: "In the light of the Holocaust, classical Christianity dies to be reborn to a new life; or it lives unaffected, to die to God and man."

THE RIGHTEOUS AMONG THE NATIONS

In a large number of rabbinic texts much that we have said in the preceding pages seems simply swept aside. This applies to the Noachidic covenant and the problem of how the Gentiles can know of their share in it. It applies to premodern Jewish views of Christianity and Islam. It applies to "dialogue," at least insofar as this latter is confined to the religious. The texts, as I say, are large in number, but the following few samples will suffice:

> A Gentile who occupies himself with the Torah is equal to the high priest.

> The righteous among all nations have a share in the world to come.

> I call heaven and earth as witnesses: whether a person be Jew or Gentile, man or woman, man-servant or maid-servant, according to their deeds does the holy Spirit dwell upon them.

First, why does a Gentile who occupies himself with the Torah attain to a rank equal to the high priest? Even by the strict standards of the Rambam he need occupy himself only with its first nine chapters, up to and including the Noachidic covenant; his occupation with the whole of the Torah is therefore motivated by the pure love of it.

Next, how does a Gentile come to know righteousness, and what motivates him to pursue it? The rabbis do not say and do not seem to know. They know but two things about Gentile righteousness.

The first, the unwavering recognition that it does exist, is striking enough. But more striking still is the second. The rabbis pretend to know but little of the world to come (see chapter 13, section 8). But they affirm without hesitation that righteous Gentiles do have a share in it.

The third above-cited text is climactic. Heaven and earth are cited as witnesses. The unnamed rabbi who calls on them does not go on to say what motivates Gentiles to their righteous deeds: He does not pretend to know. He does know that it is something so powerful and crucial as to smash all distinctions between Jews and Gentiles, men and women, masters and servants, and as to make them all one in the sight of God. This oneness and equality, moreover, is not merely in the nebulous future but here and now: What dwells upon them is the *shechina*, the holy spirit.

The cited rabbinic text bears a striking resemblance with one by the apostle Paul:

> All baptized in Christ, you have all clothed yourselves in Christ, and there are no more distinctions between Jew and Greek, slave and free, male and female, but all of you are one in Christ Jesus. (Gal. 3:27–28)

The similarity is great, but there is one difference. The Pauline text refers to the baptized only, and Christianity has generally taught that salvation lies only within the church. Of any such limitation the rabbinic text shows not a trace.

The rabbis combine certainty of Gentiles' righteousness with bafflement as to what motivates it. Both the certainty and the bafflement reached a climax without precedent during the Holocaust. For years an all-powerful propaganda machine had slandered the Jewish people, singled them out as vermin, devils, not of the human race: The very word "Jew" had been made into a hissing and a byword. Persecution in word had gone hand in hand with persecution in deed, robbing Jews of property and civil rights, isolating them from their fellowmen, and hunting down all those reachable with systematic thoroughness, for deportation and eventual murder. Many Gentiles who were not murderers were yet accomplices. Nearly all others were bystanders, and to adopt this stance was very nearly natural, since for a Gentile to hide or otherwise help a Jew was a capital crime. Then why were there Gentiles who risked their lives and those of their families by aiding, not only Jewish friends but total strangers? What motivated them to do what they did? Were they Christians? Were they secular humanists? Research into this question has led to no conclusion and does nothing to justify either Christian or secular humanist triumphalism. Jews are as baffled as the researchers. They know but this: Gentile righteousness did exist during the Holocaust; the number of the righteous was smaller than ever; but the righteousness of those few was of a quality never known before, a source of wonder for generations to come.

Why does the world still exist? According to an ancient Jewish tradition, it is because in every generation there are at least thirty-six righteous ones; without these the world would perish: But no one knows who they are. More important still, the righteous ones do not know it themselves. Over forty years have passed since the Holocaust. Yet every now and then a Jewish community still gathers to honor some Gentiles who saved Jewish lives at that time. The reaction of those honored is always the same. "Why all the fuss?" they protest. "We did nothing special."

EPILOGUE

In Rome stands the Ark of Titus, a monument commemorating Titus's 70 C.E. victory over the Jews and his destruction of Jerusalem. It is not the original ark, erected in 80 C.E. during Titus's reign as emperor. This is no longer extant. However, the original inscription was copied on the duplicate that was built in the Middle Ages. It refers to the exploits of Titus as unparalleled feats among the achievements of former kings and commanders. During the Middle Ages no Jew was allowed to pass under the ark or, if allowed, would agree to do so. (Instead Jews would pay a fee for being allowed to pass through an adjacent house.) Following the 1967 Six-Day War an unknown Jew scribbled these words on the ark: *am Yisrael chai*—"the people Israel lives."

What was in that unknown Jew's mind I do not know. That it was nothing better than a triumphalism countering that of Titus and those after him I cannot believe. I like to connect his intention with a Midrash according to which, if only the Gentiles understood, they would mourn the destruction of Jerusalem more than the Jews. That Midrashic author, were he alive today, would surely say that if only the Gentiles understood, they would rejoice in the rebuilding of Jerusalem more than the Jews.

Do the Gentiles understand? Some do, and in this lies hope not only for *Israel* but also *die Voelker*.

13. OF LAST THINGS:
THE MESSIANIC
DAYS AND THE WORLD
TO COME

SWORDS INTO PLOWSHARES?

"The state will wither away?" Nicolai Lenin once asked in an unguarded moment. "When has such a thing ever happened before?" Lenin is an unlikely person with whom to begin a chapter on Jewish Messianism; no more unlikely, however, than the question just cited coming from his lips. For the most powerful and influential dogma in all of Marxist-Leninism is precisely this, that what did not happen—nay, could not have happened—in all past history will happen in future history, and this with such inevitability as to be "scientifically" predictable: the end of warfare between ruling and ruled classes; the advent of the classless society; the "withering away" of the state, an instrument owned by the rulers to keep them ruling; and, along with all this, universal peace for a liberated humanity.

Much of what Marxist-Leninism predicts with scientific certainty was prophesied well over two millennia earlier by the prophet Isaiah, albeit on as unscientific a basis as divine authority:

> And they shall beat their swords into plowshares, and their spears into pruning-hooks. Nation shall not lift up sword against nation, neither shall they learn war any more. (Isa. 2:4)

Any such hope was unheard of in ancient times among the pagans: The wisest of them, the Greek philosophers, quite explicitly described history as a cycle in which nothing radically new ever did or could happen. Nor was this wisdom confined to the pagans.

> What was will be again. What has been done will be done again. And there is nothing new under the sun. (Eccl. 1:9)

These weary words are not in some pagan treatise but in the Tenach. Moreover, whereas tradition ascribes Ecclesiastes, the book in which they are found, to King Solomon, scholars believe it to have been composed much later, after Isaiah's prophecy just cited had been heard. Those first hearing it must have found it unheard of. As for the author of Ecclesiastes, he in effect replied, "Swords into plowshares? When has such a thing ever happened before?"

Through the millennia that followed, however, those addressed by Isaiah, the Jewish people, did hear and rehear Isaiah's prophecy, believed it, and kept on hoping for the Messianic days, often alone and against much if not most of the evidence. What is more, had they not done so they would, like most ancient peoples, have long disappeared. Who is a Jew? We have cited the Midrashic answer, "One who opposes the idols." Somewhere in the sources there has got to be a Midrash along lines such as these: "Who is a Jew? One who hopes."

A new thing seemed to begin to be happening in San Francisco in 1945. The most horrendous war in all history was coming to an end. The worst enemy of all mankind was going down to defeat, and the victors—and saviors of mankind—were assembling in the American city in order to unite. So conscious were they of the new thing they seemed to be inaugurating that when some years later they had built themselves a permanent home on the bank of the East River in New York City, they hewed into one of its walls the very prophecy of Isaiah that we have cited.

Another, not unrelated, thing happened in 1947. They, the United Nations, the victors over Nazism, voted for a state for the people that had been Nazism's most radically singled-out victim. The wretched Jewish survivors of Dachau and Belsen would have a home, as a matter not of charity but of right. The dispersed of Israel would be free, if they wished, to return to Zion, the very place from which Isaiah's prophecy had once come forth. Jews were no longer alone in their Messianic hope. Nor did the hope run all that much counter to the evidence any more.

Less than half a century later, things are other than they seemed at the time. In these brief years wars have probably been more numerous, and certainly more destructive, than in many previous centuries taken together; and the threat of a final, apocalyptic war now hangs over all humanity. This is recent history. As for United Nations history, a famous saying of Carl von Clausewitz comes to mind. The general (who was also a significant military philosopher) defined war as "policy carried on with different means." In the halls of the United Nations of today policy is war carried on with different means, and its most radically singled-out victim is the very people that had once supplied the organization with its motto. It is not just the State of Israel that is under constant attack; in the world of today, the United Nations is, for the present at least, the only reputable forum in the free world in which vile slander of Jews can be expressed with total impunity; to cite Roy Eckardt, that forum is "the effective world center of antisemitism." One can picture one fine day workmen erecting a scaffold at that wall on the banks of the East River, in order to climb up and remove the Isaiah passage, not so much because of what it says but because it was said by a Jew.

THE ORIGIN OF THE MESSIANIC HOPE

It is in this somber situation that the Messianic hope that has sustained the Jewish people at all times must be reexamined in our time. What caused so unprecedented a hope ever to arise to begin with? This is the first question to ask. Historians will ask about the when and where. We must ask about the why. The Christian version of the hope was dismissed by such as Karl Marx as the "sigh of the oppressed creature" and "opiate of the people," as an illusory escape from the world by those among the oppressed that are either too weak or else too cowardly to revolt against their oppressors. But whatever may be true of Christian Messianism (see below, section 4), Jewish Messianism (which was beneath Marx's notice) arose from the wish, not to flee *from* the world but rather to find fulfillment *in* it. It arose from the quest for something that had never yet happened but one day would happen.

It all begins with the divine covenant with Abraham. The Creator of heaven and earth who is beyond heaven and earth singles out one human family for the sake of all future humanity: He makes a covenant accompanied by a promise. Suspended for four centuries of slavery, the covenant is reactivated with the Exodus from Egypt, with Israel's entry into history. Like all history, however, this history is full of trouble and conflict, and this by no means ends when the promise is partly fulfilled with Israel's entrance into the promised land. Trouble and warfare do not end even when the promise seems wholly fulfilled with Solomon's Jerusalem Temple—the place in which the God whom the heaven of heavens cannot contain will, nevertheless, dwell among His people on earth. Trouble does not end without, between Israel and the surrounding nations. Neither does trouble within, between Israel and the God to whom she is covenanted. That covenant is likened by the prophet Hosea to a marriage:

> And I will betroth thee unto Me forever. Yea, I will betroth thee unto Me in righteousness and justice, And in lovingkindness and compassion. And I will betroth thee unto Me in faithfulness; And thou shalt know the Lord. (Hos. 2:21–22)

(Observant Jews reconfirm this vow daily as they put on their phylacteries for morning prayers.) Yet the marriage is troubled from the start, and troubled it continues to be. As for Israel, she forever wavers between fidelity, whoring after alien gods, and *teshuvah*. As for God, the psalmist testifies that "His mercy endureth forever" (Ps. 118:1)—and that the innocent sufferer cries to Him in vain! The new thing that has begun with Abraham, then, continues to be fragmentary, so much so as to warrant the weariness of Ecclesiastes—and the inclusion of his book in the Tenach by its editors. Was perhaps the whole new thing, way back to Abraham's exodus from Haran (Gen. 12:5), nothing but a long, costly mistake?

At this point the stubborn fidelity, described by us as the most basic Jewish characteristic (see chapter 2, section 2), produced what was to become its most influential result. If the new thing that began with Abraham was to be truly fulfilled, the wolf ought to dwell with the lamb, and the leopard with the kid (Isa. 11:6). The mountain of the Lord ought to be not Israel's alone, but all nations should flow unto it (Isa. 2:2). Out of Zion ought to go forth Torah, and the Word of God from Jerusalem (Isa. 2:3). Yet nothing like all that exists now or ever has been. Is the age-old, stubborn Jewish fidelity, then, to suffer collapse? On the contrary, reply the Messianic prophets. What now is not, "shall come to pass in the end of days" (Isa. 2:2). This reference to the future immediately precedes the passage about Zion and Jerusalem, which in turn immediately precedes the one that serves the United Nations as its motto.

Thus Messianism originated in Judaism. Whether (as in the religious view) a divine revelation, or (as in the secular humanist view) a product of human genius, it has had a colossal effect not only on Jewish but world history. Yet it was nearly destroyed by the catastrophe of exile. With Saul the tribes had been united in a state. After Solomon (tenth century B.C.E.) the state split in two. The northern kingdom of ten tribes, its capital Samaria, was destroyed in 711 B.C.E. by the Assyrians, who carried off its inhabitants into exile. The same fate befell the southern kingdom, its capital Jerusalem, at the hands of Babylon in 586 B.C.E. The tribes of the southern kingdom returned from exile, for they could not forget Jerusalem. If the ten northern tribes were "lost," it is not for some farfetched reason imagined by sundry odd sectarians. Rather, they assimilated, just as they were intended to by their conquerors. The reason for this is obvious enough: Can one imagine a psalm containing the words, "If I forget thee, O Samaria"? What the world of today would be like had the Jews assimilated in Babylon as well it is hard to imagine. Quite certain is that it would differ vastly from our world, had the longing for Jerusalem, and Jewish Messianism itself, been overwhelmed by the fleshpots of Babylon.

THE PERSISTENCE OF THE MESSIANIC HOPE THROUGH THE AGES

The Babylonian exile lasted for a mere fifty years. The second exile, begun in 70 C.E. with the destruction of Jerusalem by the Romans, lasted until May 14, 1948, and in several senses is not ended yet. Even during the first exile the question of how to persist in the Messianic hope must have been real enough. During the second exile it became inescapable: Just what is the right way for a Jew, stubborn enough in his fidelity not to give up, to persist in the Messianic hope?

In the Talmud we read:

> Rabbi Joshua ben Levi once met the prophet Elijah. He asked him: "When will the Messiah come? "Go ask him," Elijah replied. "He sits at the gate of Rome among the wretched, laden with sickness. Only whereas the others uncover their wounds all at once and then bind them up again, he uncovers and binds up each one separately, for he thinks, 'lest I be summoned and be detained.'" So Joshua ben Levi did as he was told, found the Messiah and asked him, "When will you come?" "Today," the Messiah replied. When the day was over, Joshua ben Levi went back to Elijah and complained, "The Messiah spoke falsely to me, for he said he would come, yet the day is over and he did not come." Then Elija said, "You did not hear him to the end. He was quoting Psalm 95:7, 'Today, if you hearken to My voice.'"

Like the others at the gate of Rome, the Messiah is wretched and sick, but unlike them he behaves so as to be available at a moment's notice. Why is he wretched and sick? Because unless humans prepare his coming he is impotent to come. Why is he ready to come at a moment's notice? Because the human deeds required need not include world historical processes, taking millennia to unfold. If (so the rabbis teach) all Jews were to observe but a single Shabbat in total purity the Messiah would come at once. How then must a Jew persist in the Messianic hope? He must wait praying and doing acts of lovingkindness as though these sufficed to make the Messiah come.

All Jews observing one Shabbat in *total* purity? Such a view, a skeptic might observe, if high-minded, is safe enough: To test it is impossible. For all Jews to behave with such perfection would require the prior existence of that very "new heart" which, for Jeremiah, is characteristic of the Messianic age (Jer. 31:31–34). To make the Messianic advent depend on the work of man *alone*, then, is to end in paradox.

Of this the rabbis are not unaware. Consider the following rabbinic text:

> Rabban Gamliel says, "During the period in which the son of David will come the school house will be used for debauchery; Galilee will be destroyed, and its inhabitants will go from town to town but be shown no favor, and the wisdom of scholars will vanish. Sin-fearing people will be despised. The people of that generation will be shameless as dogs. Truth will be lacking, and he that departs from evil will make himself a prey."

Other rabbinic texts are still more extreme. As one has it, "When you see an age in which suffering pours like a stream, then hope for him!" According to another the seven gates of Jerusalem will at that time have one thing in common: There will be an escape through none of them. Little wonder that one rabbi expressed the wish not to be present when the end was at hand. How then must a Jew persist in the Messianic hope? To be sure, with prayers and good works, but not in the belief that these can hasten the Messianic advent. The end is ushered in by catastrophe and is the work of God.

Historians concerned with the "when," the "where," and the "by whom" may argue that the two cited views, diametrically opposite as they are, express different schools of thought, the one "progressivist," the other, "apocalyptic"; and quite possibly they are right. Concerned as we are with the "why," however, we must consider the rabbinic mind as a whole and also, more importantly still, *amcha* who through the ages have lived by the rabbinic teaching. How must a Jew wait for the Messianic Redemption? He must both act as though all depended on him and pray as though all depended on God. Through the long centuries of exile *amcha* have lived by the belief that the Messiah will come when men have become good enough to make his coming possible—or wicked enough to make it necessary.

CHRISTIANITY: MESSIANISM WITHOUT MAN

Such is the tension in which Jewish hope has endured through the ages. From the standpoint of that tension, much of Christianity is best understood as premature Messianism, as the product of a wish once and for all to overcome the Jewish premessianic tension. In John 16:33 Jesus bids his followers gather strength, for while in the world they will have trouble he, Jesus, has "overcome the world."

In Judaism the Messianic advent is the shared work of God and man: In its Christian counterpart it is, as it were, the work of God alone. It is Messianism without man, or rather, a Messianism with one man only, and he is the "Son of Man." There is no more waiting, for He has arrived, and the difference now is only between those cognizant of the fact and those as yet ignorant. Moreover, His advent was not and could not have been humanly prepared, for the Son of Man is God's only begotten Son, sent by God as a pure, humanly unmerited gift of grace.

But have swords been beaten into plowshares? Has warfare vanished from the earth? To a Jew, questions such as these show Christian Messianism to be premature. A Christian response to the Jewish question may consist of abandoning the world to its unredeemed fate, and of finding Redemption solely in the soul within, a world beyond, or a togetherness of the two. A Christian move in this direction makes the gulf between Jew and Christian great. Never, perhaps, was it greater than when Martin Luther preached the freedom of a Christian; condemned the peasant serfs who sought freedom from their overlords in the name of his own teachings for seeking a freedom so worldly; and went so far as to denounce all attempts, good works included, to "seek help from man's own works" as being idolatrous. Not accidentally, perhaps, Luther ended up as a nasty antisemite.

But the Christian response to the Jewish question may also be quite the opposite. The advent of the Christ was only His first coming. Swords will be beaten into plowshares with His second coming. Meanwhile a Christian, like a Jew, must wait, and he works for the end even as he prays for it. That in this case the Jewish-Christian difference is not great is illustrated in an Israeli joke. The Messiah has arrived in Jerusalem. A Jew and a Christian, longtime friends, approach him to let him settle an argument. "Excuse me, sir," one of them asks, "have you been here before?" The Messiah's answer is not reported in the joke. But the question itself shows that, whatever the answer, the two can each remain who they are and continue to be friends.

MODERN PROGRESS-WORSHIP: MESSIANISM WITHOUT GOD

The traditional Hanukkah hymn praises God for redemption but contains no reference to the ultimate, Messianic Redemption. Slavery in Egypt, exile in Babylon, the threat posed by Haman, by the Syrians at the time of the Maccabees: Redemption from all these was interim only, that is, located *in* history; it was not the final Redemption *from* history and all its turmoil. In contrast, the last stanza of the American *Union Prayer Book* reads as follows:

> Children of the martyr-race, whether free or fettered,
> Wake the echoes of the songs, where you may be scattered.
> Yours the message cheering, that the time is nearing,
> Which will see all men free, tyrants disappearing.

The prayer book was in use until 1975 when it was replaced by the *New Union Prayer Book*. This latter, mercifully, replaces "children of the martyr race" with "children of the Maccabees." The rest of the stanza, however, remains unchanged. Even in the last part of the grim twentieth century, it seems, the Messianic age is progressively drawing nearer, so smoothly so that nothing radical needs to be done by either God or man about tyrants. They will simply "disappear."

Reform Judaism aims at contemporary relevance and often achieves its goal. In this particular case, however, the Orthodox Birnbaum *Siddur* comes far closer to the aim of up-to-date relevance. It adds a stanza in which God is implored to hasten the day of salvation, to avenge the blood of His servants shed by a wicked kingdom—all this because the hour is late and there is no end to the days of evil. This stanza could have been composed during the Holocaust. It could have been composed by Soviet prisoners of Zion. Perhaps it is because Birnbaum's courage fails him at the thought of augmenting the tradition that his note about the added stanza says only that it is a "comparatively late addition." But whether very or merely comparatively late, the stanza does fit the present age. In contrast, the nineteenth-century progress-worshiping belief that tyrants will "disappear" has itself disappeared.

Even in the halcyon days of the worship of human progress no form of Judaism embraced a Messianism without God. For this latter to be possible, the role of God must not merely be minimized or left open. It is necessary for man to *turn against* God, and in so doing to exalt himself. Ludwig Feuerbach (1804–1872), the thinker who started it all, replaced theology with anthropology. The madman in the famous tale of Friedrich Nietzsche (1844–1900), having declared that God is dead, exclaimed, "Now let the Overman live." And Karl Marx (1818–1883) let the role of God be taken by the revolutionary proletariat, embodied in the Communist party leadership. Nietzsche, the profoundest of the trio, showed his profundity by mourning the death of God and putting his words into the mouth of a madman. The most influential, however, has of course been Marx. To be sure, a great many of those who call themselves Marxists today embrace only this or that aspect of Marx's own thought and are indifferent to his Messianism. Others invoke it for cynical political purposes without believing it themselves. However, others still believe in Marxist Messianism to this day.

I do not know whether Leonid Brezhnev was among the cynics or believers when at the Twenty-fifth Communist Party Congress he claimed that Soviet communism had created "the New Man." I know only what Rose and I saw with our own eyes. Shortly after Brezhnev had made his claim, during our 1977 visit to refuseniks, we walked the streets of Riga and Leningrad, Minsk and Moscow. Here and there we stopped at a store or restaurant. Never before or after did we see people so alienated from their labor. In various forms, Marxism in power has had a chance, for the better part of this century, to produce the Messianic age. It has failed to bring it any nearer. Many would say it has made it more remote. Still, there are sundry maverick theories that assert that this or that version of Marxist action will yet realize the Messianism without God that has thus far eluded it. But as one considers these theories one is filled with new respect for the realism of the rabbis who asserted that the Messiah will come either when men have become good enough to make his coming possible—or wicked enough to make it necessary.

MESSIANISM AND THE HOLOCAUST

A time came when both these conditions were fulfilled, but he did not come.

Boundless was not only the number of the wicked but also the quality of their wickedness. Within prior Jewish experience, wicked ones had tortured Jewish martyrs, in so doing honoring their martyrdom. They had slaughtered Jewish fighters, in so doing honoring their heroism. They had raged in drunken pogroms against Jewish women and children, but then their thirst for Jewish blood was quenched as their drunkenness passed. The new wicked ones were coldly sober, and their thirst for Jewish blood was unquenchable. They did not honor either Jewish martyrdom or Jewish heroism but did what they could to destroy the opportunity for both. For to them Jews were not merely of a lower but still human race.

They were not of the human race at all, but rather "devils" to be tortured and "vermin" to be exterminated. And they, the wicked ones, knew no task holier than to verify—make true—these parts of their Weltanschauung. They would starve Jews so as to make brother steal bread from brother; they would forbid Jewish births on pain of death so as to make Jewish mothers kill their newborn babies: Thus Jews would be made, as much as possible, into devils. They would be made, as much as possible, into vermin as well: From the viewpoint of the wicked ones the ideal Jewish death was that of the *Muselmann* dropping dead from exhaustion, covered with filth and lice. During the Holocaust, then, human wickedness made the coming of the Messiah necessary. But he did not come.

He did not come even though, at the same time, human holiness made his coming possible. One thinks of the Gentiles who showed a righteousness without precedent. One thinks of the victims who chose how to die, though robbed of all choice of whether to die. One thinks of those who fought with sticks and revolvers against flamethrowers and tanks. One thinks of Jewish men, women, and children who managed to preserve fragments of humanity when everything was done to destroy it. One thinks of all these, and knows that one has not thought hard and deeply enough. Hard and deep thought has come all along from survivors when they speak of the *k'doshim*—the "holy ones." With this term they refer to all the victims, martyrs and fighters, men and women, adults and children, believers and unbelievers, saints and sinners. All these are called "holy ones," for of the "crime" for which they were "punished" they were all equally innocent. What human being is holy? If ever there is such a person, it is one who has either resisted sin or done total *teshuvah* for it. But Jewish birth, as all birth, is not sinful but innocent, yet the *k'doshim* of the Holocaust were tortured and murdered on account of it. The hell of the religious imagination cannot so much as touch the innocent. The Holocaust world, hell surpassed, touched *none but* the innocent. Their innocence made the coming of the Messiah possible. But he did not come.

What came instead were, so far as the Messianic hope is concerned, the most terrible words ever heard by Jewish ears. The

Polish poet Tadeusz Borowski was not a Jew, but he suffered the Jewish fate and survived. Subsequently he asked why he and his comrades in suffering did not club one of them to death to be gunned down by the hundreds themselves; or, if robbed even of this much of a chance, why they did not slash their own wrists or throats. He replies:

> It is . . . hope that keeps . . . [people] from risking a revolt, paralyzes them into numb inactivity. . . . It is hope that compels man to hold on to one more day of life, because that day may be the day of liberation. . . . Never before has [hope] . . . done so much harm as in this war, in this concentration camp. We were never taught to give up on hope, and this is why today we perish in the gas chambers.

Having survived, Borowski committed suicide in 1951, six years after it was over.

THE STATE OF ISRAEL AND JEWISH MESSIANISM TODAY

"Ha-Tikvah" ("The Hope"): This is the title of the national anthem of the Jewish state that was proclaimed on May 14, 1948. In the text of the prestate Zionist movement, the hope had been described as "age-old," and it was for "the return to the land of our fathers, Zion and Jerusalem." Now these words were changed: the hope now was "bimillennial," and it was for being a "free nation." The return was no longer a hope but an accomplished fact, and the hope that remained was only for being a "free nation," together, of course, with its precondition, survival.

It is reasonable to assume that this precondition did not overly worry those first singing the hymn with the new words. As for the future, no one would then have thought that two generations later the state founded in 1948 would still be besieged by its neighbor states, nor that the halls of the organization that had endorsed its existence would resound with "anti-Zionist" slander. As regards the immediate past, while the survivors were ready to speak, few others were willing or able to listen; and, as we have seen, even far-from-naive Jewish leaders trusted the conscience of the world. Two generations later the horror of the Holocaust has begun to sink in, as has the fact that the conscience of the world—such as it is—is not to be trusted. *The Abandonment of the Jews, The Jews Were Expendable*: Books with titles such as these did not exist two generations ago. Now they do, and they relate not the crime of the criminals but the extent to which their enemies—those then embodying world conscience—were indifferent to it. Has world conscience changed between then and now? Not so much as to assure the survival of the State of Israel. The state *could* be destroyed, and—so at least Jews universally feared in the weeks preceding the Six-Day War—in June 1967 it almost was.

The result is that Yom Ha-Atzmaut cannot be celebrated as Jews through the ages have celebrated Pesach, Purim, and Hanukkah. Each of these festivals celebrates a salvation that came in time—if only at the last moment—and hence implies that the salvation that always did come always will come, until the days of the Messiah are at hand. Yom Ha-Atzmaut does not have this implication. This time salvation, while coming too late, did come; while come it did, it came too late. This, as asserted in chapter 1, section 4, is the decisive characteristic of the Jewish religious situation today. This, as asserted in chapter 10, section 5, is why we do not yet know how to observe either Yom Ha-Shoah or Yom Ha-Atzmaut. We know only this, that observed they must be.

It is in the light of this situation that, I think, one must understand a prayer that was composed by the Israeli chief rabbinate soon after the foundation of the state, and that is recited in many synagogues in Israel and throughout the world. It refers to the state as "the beginning of the growth of the redemption" of the Jewish people. Many of those reciting it believe that, however slowly, the Messianic age is about to dawn and that the State of Israel, its survival assured, is the first manifestation of it. Nor can one deny all justice to this belief. The ninth *b'racha* of the *Amidah* reads as follows:

> Sound the great shofar for our freedom; lift up the banner to
> bring our exiles together, and assemble us from the four corners
> of the earth. Praised art Thou, O Lord, who gatherest the dis-
> persed of Thy people Israel.

One considers the history of Israel since the foundation of the
state, and it seems as if He that is praised, as One who will gather
the dispersed of Israel, had begun to do so in our time.

Still, I cannot understand the chief rabbinate's prayer in this
millennarian sense, and it seems at least doubtful that this was intended by those who composed it. Critics of the prayer describe
the phrase cited as a hasty mixture of two traditional images, "the
beginning of the Redemption" and "the growth of the redemption." But among those who had a share in composing the prayer
is said to have been S. J. Agnon, no mean Hebrew stylist. The
prayer, it would seem, looks with caution to an uncertain future,
endowing with Messianic significance no more than this, the survival of the state itself.

But if all Messianic politics is prone to dangerous illusions, is not
this in the present situation the most dangerous illusion of all? If
salvation came too late once, it could come too late again, and next
time it might be too late for the state. But it is precisely here that
the chief rabbinate's prayer, at least as I understand it, shows its
true significance. The state could be destroyed but never will be:
This is the commitment of every Israeli that does not leave the
country, of every Jew who moves to it, and of the vast majority of
Jews everywhere. All these vow to do all they can to prevent what
could happen from happening. They would be quite unable, however, to make any such commitment, or take any such vow, without that great quality that is essential to Messianism, namely, hope.

*Never did hope do as much harm as during the Holocaust; and
never has hope been as necessary for a Jew as thereafter.* This has
been so at least if the Jewish people is to go on living. No clearer
testimony to the nations of a continued Jewish will to live is possible today than a commitment to the State of Israel, and if salvation is to be never too late for that state, the hope that must ac-
company that commitment must have Messianic dimensions. *The*

Messianic hope died during the Holocaust. The post-Holocaust State of Israel has resurrected it.

But not the state alone. After a recent lecture at an American university I was asked by a listener what would be most important to do for such as she, who were committed to Judaism but not prepared to move to Israel. I thought for a moment. I thought of the Jews for whom salvation had come too late, and that salvation might come too late again. I thought of hope, of post-Holocaust Jewish hope, and of the world's need of a Jewish testimony to hope. Then I replied to the young woman: "Have one more child than you plan to have."

THE WORLD TO COME

> Rabbi Yose ben Hanina said: "Moses taught, 'Visiting the iniquity of the fathers upon the children and the children's children.' " (Exod. 20:5, 37:7; Deut. 5:9) Ezekiel annulled it by teaching, 'The soul that sinneth, it shall die.' " (Ez. 38:4)

An astounding passage! One can imagine moderns citing it, in support of their own view that prophetic ethics is a "higher stage" in the "evolution" of Judaism than the Mosaic. But the rabbis? The Rambam's seventh principle asserts that Moses is "the chief of the prophets," never to be surpassed. (See above, chapter 1, section 2.) In this he merely expresses the unanimous view of the rabbis. A later prophet may interpret Mosaic teaching. Possibly he may add to it. But actually *annul* something said by Moses and replace it with something else? A matter of the greatest import must have been at stake for the third-century rabbi to make him say what he did.

It was. Abraham died satisfied, knowing that Isaac would live. Moses could teach what he did about the fathers and the children because what mattered to him was history, what may be called man writ large. And if history itself was full of unjust suffering, the crooked would be made straight in the Messianic days. So much for man writ large. But what of man writ small, each and every individual? Would the crooked be made straight for him even in the

Messianic days, when he would not live to see them? This is the question that occupied the rabbis ever since the days of the Pharisees, and the prophet who more than any other made them attend to it was Ezekiel.

The result of this attention was a bitter conflict between them and the Sadducees, their conservative opponents. Sticking literally to the Tenach, these latter found little or no textual evidence indicating that death was not the individual's end. It was Pharisaic doctrine, however, that prevailed. It is authoritatively expressed in the second *b'racha* of the *Amidah:*

> Thou sustainest the living with kindness, and revivest the dead with great mercy . . . Thou canst be trusted to revive the dead. Praised be Thou, O God, who revivest the dead.

Death is not the end; it is the beginning:

> "Rabbi Jacob said: "This world is like an antechamber to the world to come; prepare yourself in the antechamber, in order that you may enter the hall." (*Abot* 4:21)

Why the rabbis came to affirm a world to come is clear enough: Given the belief in divine justice, the belief that justice is due to the individual, and the condition of this world, this affirmation is very nearly inevitable, and the tenth-century Gaon Saadia went so far as to demonstrate a world to come on these grounds. But how could the rabbis, as "orthodox" as the Sadducees, affirm this belief when it has little or no biblical foundation? The rabbinic response combines boldness with profundity. "There is not a single chapter in the Torah," says one text, "which does not contain the doctrine of the resurrection of the dead; only we cannot understand it." "The prophets prophecied only about the Messianic days," we find in another, "but no eye has seen the world to come." So all-important is the world to come that it simply *must* be contained in every single chapter of the Torah; and if we cannot find it there, it is because its mystery, this side of eternity, is impenetrable. The rabbis go far enough to affirm that the righteous of all nations have a share in the world to come; but rarely do they go further. Theirs is a total commitment to the resurrection of the dead—combined with a near-total agnosticism as to its nature.

This is a far cry from scholastic debates as to why, if 51 percent of good deeds are enough to get people into heaven, they should aim at 100 percent; from three-story universes with heaven "above" and hell "below"; from assertions that a last-minute conversion will get Eichmann into heaven while his victims are kept out; and from fantasies compensating sufferers on earth in heaven, according to taste, with food and drink or beautiful maidens. Given views such as these, one would have to support those who, in most liberal prayer books, have replaced, in the second b'racha of the Amidah, "who revivest the dead" with "who gives life to all." The view about Eichmann and the children is plainly revolting. That of God as a bookkeeper of good and bad deeds is picayune. And while three-story universes are at best outmoded science, the fantasies that compensate those wretched on earth in heaven are fair prey of Freudian or Marxist criticism. Whether their wretchedness is neurosis or poverty, those resorting to fantasies such as these simply flee from the world into other-worldliness.

But the believing agnosticism of the rabbis? There is nothing in science to refute impenetrable mysteries. And as for escapism, the same rabbi we have cited to the effect that this world is but an antechamber of the world to come goes on as follows:

> Better is one hour of teshuvah and good deeds in this world than the whole life of the world to come; and better is one hour of bliss in the world to come than the whole life of this world. (Abot 4:22)

This paradoxical statement is found not in some esoteric treatise but in the Sayings of the Fathers, a treatise studied reverently by ordinary Jews through the centuries. No more profound statement on the subject could be found in Jewish literature; yet ordinary Jews, it appears, were able to understand it.

What is time in the sight of eternity?

> A thousand years in Thy sight are but as yesterday when it is past, and as a watch in the night. . . . The days of our years

are three-score years and ten, or even by reason of strength four-
score years; yet is their pride but travail and vanity; for they are
speedily gone, and we fly away. (Ps. 90:4, 10)

Hence if there is a world to come for humans to have a share in,
one "hour" of its bliss is better than the whole life of this world.

Yet better is one hour of *teshuvah* and good deeds in this
world than the whole life of the world to come. Deliberately resorting to paradox, Rabbi Jacob exalts this one hour even in the sight
of eternity, for it is unique. It is unique because each person is
unique, and what makes him unique is the hour in which, as eternity holds its breath, he *makes himself* unique. The rabbinic world
to come is not a case of escapism but its diametrical opposite. If
anyone, guilty of escapism are those among the modern minded
who dissolve human life into "Life," deny the uniqueness of each
human life, and thus persuade themselves into denying the shock
of the uniqueness of each human death. In contrast, the rabbinic
affirmation of a world to come arises only on the grounds of a prior
commitment, with Ezekiel, to the uniqueness of each person's
life—and hence death—in this world.

I confess that I have never been able to understand—let alone
share—the modern liberal Jewish rejection of the rabbinic world
to come. Liberals, if anyone, ought to side with Rabbi Yose ben
Hanina's view that Ezekiel has "annulled" the teaching of Moses
about the fathers and the sons, and replaced it with one doing
justice to the individual. Surely there is "progress" in a view that
cherishes personality in its own right, not only as a link in the
generations. Admittedly modern secularism makes it difficult to believe in a world beyond the one inhabited by us and known to our
minds; but that this is progress, from a religious point of view is,
to say the least, dubious. One thing, to me at any rate, is clear:
Man reaches the highest view of human personality possible in
what to most of us is known as a personal experience when a person dear to us is taken from us: One moment he was still here, the
next he was gone, and the loss is irreplaceable.

THE WORLD TO COME AND
THE HOLOCAUST

I remember the occasion though not the exact date when I found myself compelled to suspend the world to come; and had I not at length found myself able to reaffirm it, the present chapter, and possibly the present book, might never have been written. It was after the Six-Day War. Faced in the three weeks preceding the war with the threat of a second Holocaust, Jews the world over, I myself included, were compelled to confront the first. Soon after there was a conference. At this one participant rose to say, "Nothing evil happened to the children at Auschwitz. They are happy with God in heaven." He had the grace to add that if he did not believe this he would shoot himself, and I am sure he meant it.

"Dear God," I said to myself and kept on saying for years to follow, "are Marxists, Freudians, and similar folk right after all when they say that the hereafter is mere escapism?" If so, one should have no part of it. There is no decent escape from the sorrows of this world. There is no decent way of stilling the screams of the children that were thrown into the fire alive. Their screams, a Polish witness testified at the Nuremberg trials, could be heard in the camp. They must be heard still, and reheard.

I go back to Rabbi Jacob and his paradoxical statement: One hour of *teshuvah* and good works is better than eternity, for it makes a person worthy of eternity. But the children of Auschwitz were robbed of that hour. "Do *teshuvah* one day before your death," says another source. But robbed of that day were not only the children but also all those who were murdered before they knew what was happening, and especially those skin-and-bones men and women, dead in spirit as they already were before their bodies, covered with filth and lice, dropped to the ground. The human spirit can reach no higher peak than in the recognition that persons are unique, that death leaves them irreplaceable. In the Holocaust a nadir was reached that was hitherto inconceivable. As the philosopher Theodor Adorno has said, "In the camps it was no longer the individual that died; the individual was made into a specimen."

After this, is it possible to affirm the world to come? Over the years I have reached this conclusion: *Only if we share in the anguish of the victims dare we affirm their resurrection.* Only then dare we affirm the resurrection of anyone. For if the world to come does not exist for them, it does not exist at all.

EPILOGUE

A curious Midrash exists about the world to come. It asks what festivals will continue to observe in it. Shabbat? It will be *all* Shabbat. Pesach? Liberty will be universal and complete. Shavuot? Torah will be in the inward parts of all. Succot? Wandering will no longer be even a memory, as well be a booth so frail as to threaten to collapse. Rosh Hashanah and Yom Kippur? All judgment will have been accomplished, and reconciliation will be complete. Are all festivals, then, abolished? Not quite. Purim, and Purim only, will continue to be celebrated. A curious Midrash indeed.

Even in this world Purim has always had a Kafkaesque aspect. The defeat of Haman was being celebrated, even as other Hamans, more successful than Haman himself, had arisen. This Kafkaesque aspect was always manifest in the fact that, as the celebration went on, the celebrants came to confuse shouts of "hurray for Mordecai" with shouts of "down with Haman." No Jew can make this confusion unless he is somewhat intoxicated. On Purim, and on Purim alone, a Jew is *supposed* to be somewhat intoxicated. In the world to come there is no intoxication. But the knowledge that something was wrong with this world in some way survives.

Never was the Midrash about Purim and the world to come as meaningful as to the Jew of today. If indeed there is a world to come, why did there have to be this world with its unspeakable agonies? Perhaps this question will not be answered even in the world to come. Perhaps this is why Purim will continue to be celebrated. Perhaps this is why the victims of a Haman that did not fail will even then be remembered.

14. GOD IN THE AGE
OF AUSCHWITZ
AND THE REBUILT
JERUSALEM

HOW TO END

"In the beginning, God . . ." Thus begins the Jewish book, *the* Book. A book on Judaism for a Jew today, however, cannot begin but only end with God.

For our time, but not for every time:

> Now the Lord said unto Abram, "Get thee out of thy country and from thy kindred, and from thy father's house, unto the land that I will show thee." (Gen. 12:1)

One ponders this beginning of the history of Abraham and all the generations that descended from him. One keeps on pondering it, and cannot but conclude: For him and many generations that were to follow, in the beginning was God, even if one is skeptical enough to regard not a few of the earliest generations as merely legendary.

Consider Abram himself. He after whom all of them were to be named was born in Ur of the Chaldees. His parents had taken him

and his wife Sarai unto Haran to dwell there, presumably because
for them, nomads all, to move from one place to another was entirely natural. Both places were familiar. Both were Abram's country. There he had lived with his kindred. There he had lived with
its gods. And now he heard an unfamiliar voice. It bade him go to
a land that would be shown to him but of which he knew nothing.
Yet he whose name was to be changed into Abraham went. Had
he not done so there would have been no "Israel" and no "Torah."
When in this book we asked, "How to Begin" (chapter 2, section
1), we cited a much-quoted saying from the Zohar, "God, Torah
and Israel are one." Clearly, when the history of "Israel" began,
the beginning was God.

God remained the beginning throughout the entire history of
ancient Israel. The beginning He was for Moses and all the prophets. The beginning He was for the people as a whole. When they
came into the land they were surrounded by pagans who worshiped
the gods of this or that place, as familiar to them as the land itself.
The descendants of Abraham were tempted by both, and often
yielded to temptation. Had they forgotten the God of Abraham
that was not of this or that place but the Creator of heaven and
earth, they would have forgotten "Torah" also, and themselves
ceased to be "Israel." They almost did forget both God and Torah,
and ceased to be Israel. At Mount Carmel Elijah was alone against
450 priests of Ba'al (I Kings 18:20–40). If what almost happened
did not happen, it was because the God who was in the beginning
continued to be in the beginning again and again.

> I was no prophet, neither was I a prophet's son, but I was a
> herdsman, and a dresser of sycamore-trees; and the Lord took me
> from following the flock, and the Lord said unto me, "Go,
> prophesy unto My people Israel . . ." (Amos 7:14–15)

This is the confession of the prophet Amos. At his time there were
schools of prophecy in which pupils were taught how to work
themselves up into a frenzy that was to result in prophesying; and
Amos seems to be saying that professional prophets of this kind
would sometimes make their children follow in their profession.

But such were not the prophets of Israel. For them the God that would cause a person to prophesy was not familiar in advance and subject to manipulation. Beginning again, He took Amos, a herdsman, from following his flock. He took Isaiah, "a man of unclean lips and . . . [dwelling] in the midst of a people of unclean lips," and made him who felt "undone" on this account see "the King, the Lord of hosts" (Isa. 6:5). He knew Jeremiah before He "formed" him "in the belly" and made him prophesy when he was a "child." And when the future prophet protested that, being a child, he could not speak, the reply was as follows:

> Say not: I am a child. For to whomsoever I shall send thee thou shalt go. And whatsoever I shall command thee thou shalt speak. Be not afraid of them, for I am with thee to deliver thee . . . (Jer. 1:4–8)

In ancient times "Israel" was tempted again and again by the pagans, and then the beginning was "God" who kept "Torah" and "Israel" from vanishing from the earth. In medieval times, however, "Israel" was in the midst not of pagans but of Christians and Muslims. "Daughters" of Judaism both, they worshiped not gods but the One God who was also the God of Israel. Ungrateful daughters both, however, they viewed the "mother" as an anachronism when they did not actually declare her—or even tried to *make* her—dead and buried. A new temptation therefore arose for "Israel." It was to abandon "Torah," and it may have been because the Rambam recognized the danger, that in the ninth of his thirteen articles he went out of his way to emphasize that the Torah of Moses is final. What would have happened to "God" if "Israel" had yielded to the medieval temptation we do not know. We do know that it would have been the end of both "Torah" and "Israel." During that period, then, it was "Torah" that was the beginning, and Gaon Saadia spoke well when he said that Israel is a nation only on account of it.

How is it for a Jew today? We have seen from the start (chapter 1) that the modern world split Jews of fidelity into those faithful to "God" but not to Israel and those faithful to "Israel" but not to

God. Soon after (chapter 2) we saw Jews of fidelity split also into those for whom "Torah" continued to be *the* Book, and those for whom it could only be the Jewish book.

So it has been for a Jew of modernity. For a Jew today these splits have not merely increased. There has been—the image is inadequate—a quantum leap. The State of Israel exists, and Jews living in it are Jews of fidelity if only insofar as they are there by choice: Yet they oppose each other as "religious" and "nonreligious," clashing over both "Torah" and "God." This is one cause of the quantum leap. The other is the Holocaust. That unprecedented catastrophe has occurred: Yet though survivors have suffered a common fate this too splits them over "Torah" and "God." Above all over God, and this for reasons too obvious to need spelling out.

"God, Torah and Israel are one": Because a beginning with "God" or "Torah" would split even Israel's oneness in our time, we have had to begin with "Israel." But a book on Judaism cannot end there. "Torah" has had to be brought in soon after the beginning, and of the fact that "God" could not be left out the subject of prayer has been the most striking example. (What would Judaism be without prayer? And prayer without God?) Still, God has thus far come in only indirectly, with the possibility left open that even prayer can mean something to a Jew unable to believe in Him. But a book about Judaism in which God came in indirectly only would be a book without an end. God must come in as a theme in His own right: as the ultimate theme of Judaism, as the theme of themes.

DIVINE INFINITY

For us in this book God must come at the end. For the deepest thought and in the deepest experience it is so for the tradition as well. Consider this curious story from the Talmud. A young boy was once in the study of his *melammed*, his Hebrew teacher. The teacher had told him to wait for him there, that he, the teacher, would be a little late. The *melammed* was later than he had anticipated, and the boy got bored. So he picked up a Tenach and opened it at random. The book fell open at the first chapter of Ezekiel, and the boy's eye glanced at the word *hashmal* in the fourth verse. (This word appears in the Tenach only three times, all in Ezekiel, and two of the three are in the first chapter.) Its meaning is mysterious, but the boy understood it at once. Whereupon a fire shot forth from the printed word and killed him. Thereafter the rabbis sought to conceal the book of Ezekiel, containing as it does the first chapter, from all except the wise, the learned, the old. It was too dangerous to leave it lying about.

What is the verse in Ezekiel that the boy glanced at, the verse containing the word that he understood at once? I am almost scared to quote it:

> And I looked, and behold, a stormy wind came out of the north,
> a great cloud, with a fire flashing up, so that a brightness was
> round about it; and out of the midst thereof as the color of
> *hashmal*, out of the midst of the fire. (Ez. 1:4)

The Vulgate, the Catholic fourth-century translation, renders *hashmal* as "electrum." Most modern translations follow the Vulgate. Nothing better is offered even by Wilhelm Gesenius's scholarly dictionary to the Old Testament, an admirable product of a century of modern scholarship, the seventeenth edition of which, acquired by me in my *Hochschule* days, lies in front of me as I write these words. In modern Hebrew *hashmal* means "electricity," this too, I suspect, indirectly on the authority of the Vulgate. But what the word actually means in Ezekiel no one seems to know for sure. Yet in the Talmudic story the boy understood it at once.

What is the chapter about in which this dangerous passage appears? The whole chapter is dangerous. Having stated with precision an exact date, Ezekiel begins as follows:

"The heavens were opened, and I saw visions of God." (Ez. 1:1) Moses himself, to whom "the Lord spoke face to face . . . , as a man speaketh unto his friend" was told, "thou canst not see My face, for man shall not see Me and live" (Exod. 33:11, 20). Yet Ezekiel starts out as he does, and his whole first chapter describes what he saw when the heavens were opened. The rabbis could not

forbid the reading of this chapter outright, for after all it is in the
Tenach. But they made as sure as they could that it would be read
only by those for whom it represented the least danger: the pious,
the learned and, perhaps above all, the aged. Perhaps these would
be least prone to be carried away by a dangerous enthusiasm. Or
if what happened to them were what happened to that boy, they
would at least have lived a long life. This last notion is my own
but in line, I think, with traditional thinking. It is, as it were, a
Midrash on Midrash.

There is one other chapter in the Tenach that the rabbis urge
for the study only of the pious, the learned, the old—the first chapter of Genesis. "In the beginning God . . ." The complete verse
is, of course, "In the beginning God created the heaven and the
earth." One can read that verse. One can also believe what it says.
But who can understand it? "In the beginning": when? "God":
who? "Created": how? In the whole of the first verse of the Tenach
only "the heaven and the earth" can be readily understood and,
whether in simple experience, mythology or complicated modern
science, the human race has tried to do so since time immemorial.
But heaven and earth are with us. God as Creator of both is not.
To understand Him *as* Creator *could* lead into dangerous error,
and if anyone is safe, it is only the pious, the learned, the old. Even
in the Book, then, God is in the beginning in one sense only; in
another He is in the end. Perhaps He is only in the ultimate end.
As regards human existence this side of eternity, Isaiah wrote the
following:

> My thoughts are not your thoughts, neither are My ways your
> ways, saith the Lord. For as the heavens are higher than the
> earth, so are My ways higher than your ways, and My thoughts
> than your thoughts. (Isa. 55:8–9)

One wonders what the dangers posed by the first chapter of
Genesis might be, and the answer is not far to seek. The Homeric
gods are of an intimacy that breeds familiarity if not contempt.
Their heir is Thales, the first Greek philosopher, already cited by
us as saying that the world is full of gods: These gods are *in* the
world, not *beyond* it. Beyond the world is not even the God of

Aristotle: The "first cause" of the world, He can *be understood* as its cause, and is thus part of the world rather than beyond it. The dangers in that first chapter of the Tenach, as the rabbis knew them, then, were posed by Greek-type speculations, and they consisted of reducing the infinite Creator of heaven and earth to the finitude of heaven and earth. Hence in this instance we may perhaps go beyond the rabbis and affirm that the danger is posed by philosophy as a whole, modern as well as ancient, in case it constructs systems that seek to explain not only the world but God as well. Correspondingly we may perhaps say that modern science is closer to the rabbis than such philosophies, provided, that is, that while roaming the skies to explore them ever more deeply, it remains agnostic about ultimate realities. Even the most doctrinaire of sophisticated Western scientists laughed at the Russian astronaut who "refuted" the existence of God by failing to see Him in space. That an affinity is possible between modern agnosticism and traditional Judaism is illustrated by a remark attributed to Albert Einstein, a remark already cited by us previously but then left unexplained. "What will be different in the universe," he once was asked, "when man no longer exists in it?" He replied: "No one will be left to listen to the music of Mozart." The universe of modern science begins with indifference, has a brief moment of meaning in which the music of Mozart is composed, played, heard, and returns to indifference. On a cosmic scale one can hardly think of a more profound tragedy. Yet it is somehow elevating, for even after it is gone, Mozart's moment will have been, as it were, a moment of eternity.

This tragic yet elevating stance bears a certain resemblance to one of two popular hymns with which a synagogue service is customarily ended. The other, the *Yigdal*, was referred to close to the beginning of this book. (See chapter 1, section 2.) From this one, the *Adon Olam*, it is apt to cite when we are near the book's end:

Eternal Lord who ruled before any creature was created. When everything was made according to His will His name was called King. And when all will have ceased to be He alone will rule, awesome. He was, is, will be, ever-glorious.

Eternity begins with God, has a brief moment in which God is King of a created world (and is called by that name by those who recognize Him) and ends—if one may speak of an end of eternity—with God and Him alone. The resemblance is obvious. There are, however, differences as well. Whether in Einstein's eternity the universe *itself* may vanish remains unclear. For the *Adon Olam* it clearly can and will. And that for it He who is eternal is "Lord" even when there is nothing to be Lord *over*—an eternity "before any creature was created," and an eternity "when all will have ceased to be"—is, to be sure, a metaphor, but one of unique significance. For Einstein, man's moment of eternity consists of the composing, performing, hearing the music of Mozart. For the *Adon Olam* it consists of praise. It too is but a moment, but it is beyond tragedy. For the metaphor "Lord," applied to the eternal God even when there is nothing to be Lord over, implies that during the brief moment when praise was uttered the praise was heard.

DIVINE INFINITY AND DIVINE INTIMACY

Praise is heard:

> The idol is near, and is yet far. God is far [for is He not in the heaven of heavens?] and yet He is near. . . . For a man enters a synagogue, and stands behind a pillar, and prays in a whisper, and God hears his prayer, and so it is with all His creatures. Can there be a nearer God than this? He is as near to His creatures as the ear to the mouth.

> Rabbi Judah ben Simon said: "An idol is near and far; God is far and near." "How?" "An idolater makes an idol, and sets it up in his house. So the idol is near. But one may cry unto the idol, and it will not answer, therefore the idol is far. But God is far and near." "How?" Rabbi Judah ben Simon said: "From here to heaven is a journey of five hundred years: therefore God is far; but He is also near, for if a man prays and meditates in his heart, God is near to answer his prayers."

These two Midrashim contain as straightforward a statement as can be found of the ultimate principle of Judaism: *the intimacy of the divine infinity*. There is no doubt about the intimacy: God is as near to all His creatures as is the ear to the mouth. Nor is there doubt about the infinity: The finite god is an idol that cannot answer. He is an idol if made by a person who sets it up in his house; he would be an idol still if it were nature, history, or a universe that includes both. The intimacy of the infinite: We have already come upon that principle several times, especially when considering the idea of the covenant. (See chapters 5 and 12, sections 3–5.) But then we considered it, as it were, from the human side. Now the task is, as it were, to consider that same principle from the side of God.

One wonders to what extent this is possible. Possible at least is a marking off of Judaism from certain theologies. That God is "far" is not unique to Judaism. There have been thinkers for whom God is unknowable, and for whom knowable is only that He is unknowable. There is even a Latin term for that God: He is the *deus absconditus*, the hidden God, and not every pagan worshiper of the Divine has worshiped idols. However, the *deus absconditus* hears and answers not. He is "far," and far only. That He is not the God we seek, Christianity and Islam haved learned from Judaism, for the *deus absconditus* is not the God of Israel. To this latter for all His infinity belongs intimacy also, and this is manifest in that He hears prayer and also answers it.

His intimacy, moreover, is not confined to the hearing of prayer.

If two sit together, and words of Torah are between them, the *shechina* dwells between them.

When three sit and judge [in accordance with the Halacha] the *shechina* is in their midst.

The intimacy of the Divine may be manifest in prayer, in acts of judgment, and indeed through the length and breadth of the covenantal life. It may be manifest when a Jew recites a *beracha* on seeing a Gentile sage, and in the life of that sage itself; in a Gentile doing righteous deeds, and in a Jew recognizing their righteousness. And that it may be manifest in the low as well as the high is stated in a Midrash that asks why God spoke to Moses through a bush.

"In order to teach," is the reply, "that there is no place so lowly that God cannot dwell in it."

A God that is "far" and far only, then, is not the God of Judaism. Neither is a God that is "near" and near alone. That this is so in the case of gods that a person makes unto himself and sets up in his home we have already learned from the Midrash; and we have expanded the ancient insight so as to include nature, history, the universe. But it is so also with a God of modernity that the Midrash never knew of, and that I for my part would not dismiss as an idol. "God did not create the world; He created, is creating, will continue to create *Himself through* the world": this is the basic religious thesis of many a modern, whether or not he considers himself religious. God creates Himself in a Nature that "evolves *creatively*," ever upward. He creates Himself in a History that is *infinite* progress, whether manifest in the urge toward the truth, goodness, beauty, or the self-liberation of the oppressed masses. If the nonreligious holding such views are religious despite themselves, it is because in each case the evolution believed in is limitless. And if the familiarity of the intimacy with this God does not breed contempt, it is because, after all, an infinity is immanent in the intimacy. But precisely because of this immanence, the intimacy *exhausts* the infinity, resulting in the loss of the eternity of the God of Israel as expressed in the *Adon Olam*. The God that creates Himself in creating the world, then, may not be an idol. However, since He too is "near" and near *alone*, He is not the God of Israel.

To mark the God of Israel off from other Gods, then, is a possibility for our thought; and it serves to show that to embrace either a God "far" and far alone, or else one "near" and near alone, is a grave departure from Jewish tradition that requires the most serious justification and risks the most serious consequences. *But can our thought grasp the basic principle of Judaism, the intimacy of the infinite, not only from the human side but also, as it were, from the side of God?* With this question my lifelong love affair with Midrash, evident on nearly every page of this book, reaches its ultimate expression, even as it compels me to confess to a lifelong prejudice. It is against the Kabbala. It is not the kind of prejudice, however, that the late Gershom Scholem used to criticize. I heard him tell with relish several times an anecdote that illustrates the prejudice criticized by him. As a young man in Berlin he once visited a wealthy Jewish bibliophile who owned a large library. There was what amounted to a library within the library on the Kabbala alone. Awestruck by so large a library on so obscure a subject, young Scholem asked its owner: "And you read all these books?" The bibliophile replied: "*Was*, I should read that *Quatsch!*" Mine is not the Enlightenment-type prejudice against the Kabbala as *Quatsch* (nonsense). It is rather a lifelong feeling that the Kabbala rushes in where Midrash fears to tread. I was never sufficiently involved to discover whether my feeling is justified. Only in recent years did Kabbala arouse a deeper interest in me, and this on the grounds that sometimes, perhaps, rush in one must. But for the in-depth study that the subject requires it is, for me at least, too late.

So I am left with what may be a mere prejudice, and here is an example. Being infinite, God had to exercise a *tzimtzum*—make Himself small—so as to leave room for the world created by Him. This is a well-known kabbalistic thesis. My criticism is this. If this is meant as a mere metaphor, it is well within the realm of Midrashic thinking. But if, rushing in, it is meant to break the bounds of Midrashic metaphor, so as to penetrate to Divinity itself, then the thesis implies that God *cannot* enter the world He has created, lest in doing so He destroy it. Yet a Jew knows that God *has* entered into the world. He led Israel out of Egypt. He gave the Torah on Mount Sinai. Moreover, these two events are not the sole events of salvation and revelation. The God who saved once has saved again and again, in events celebrated on Purim, Hanukkah, and on other occasions; and the Torah that was given at Sinai is given also whenever a person receives it.

Our thought must link, then, infinity and intimacy, but cannot rush in so as to comprehend their relation in some sort of system. Then how can Midrashic thought link them at all? The crucial Midrashic term is *k'b'yachol* ("as it were"), and it means that the statement it qualifies is true, falls short of the ultimate form of truth, and that the ultimate form is beyond our finite understanding and in the keeping of God alone.

> "Ye are My witnesses, saith the Lord, and I am God." (Isa. 43:12) That is, when ye are My witnesses, I am God, and when ye are not My witnesses, I am, as it were, not God.

> When the Israelites do God's will they add to the power of God on high. When the Israelites do not do God's will, they, as it were, weaken the great power of God.

> When I praise God, He is lovely; and when I do not praise Him He is, as it were, lovely in Himself.

Without the key Midrashic term *k'b'yachol*, the intimacy of the infinite would be destroyed in each of these texts: In the first, since a God needing witnesses in order to *be* God would possess intimacy but lack infinity; in the third because a God that is lovely whether or not human praise makes Him so would dispense with the praise, so that His intimacy would be lost. Only in the second of the three texts cited would the intimacy of the infinite somehow survive, and even here it would be closer to the modern God that, in creating, creates Himself than to the God of Israel.

In the three cited texts it is the *k'b'yachol* that enables Midrashic thought to hold fast to the ultimate principle of Judaism, the intimacy of the divine infinity. Within this way of thought the second of the cited Midrashim is the weakest of the three, while the first and the third are the strongest; and between them these latter two express "the ultimate principle of Judaism" to perfection. So involved with His witnesses is God in His intimacy as to make Him, as it were, "not God" if He is adandoned by His witnesses. And so independent is He in His infinity of all human praise as to be, if not praised by them, as it were, "lovely in Himself."

GOD'S PRESENCE IN HISTORY

> Eternal God who ruled
> Before any creature was created
> And when all will have ceased to be
> He was, is, will be, ever-glorious.

God is the eternal before and after. Between the two eternities, as it were, He in the beginning creates and in the end redeems the world. But He also enters *into* the world, and without this we humans would know nothing of the Creation of the world, its future Redemption, not to mention the divine eternity.

Of God's entering into the world the paradigmatic examples in Judaism are the Exodus from Egypt and the Revelation at Sinai: There has been salvation in history, albeit not yet one redemptive of history; and a Torah was given in history even though it is not yet, as Jeremiah prophesied would once be the case, written into the heart (Jer. 31:31–34). These two events are paradigmatic in that they are not alone. On festivals such as Purim and Hanuka a Jew celebrates the fact that the God who saved at the Red Sea saved again and again; and the Torah was given not only at Sinai, but is given whenever a Jew receives it.

But as God enters *into* history an ominous threat makes its appearance—the fact that men can frustrate the divine purpose. "When ye are not My people, I am, as it were, not God." What if His people, *every one* of them, were to *refuse* to be His people? The possibility would then still exist that some Gentiles would recognize their share in the Noachidic covenant and rise to righteousness. But a Jew would have no right to rely on Gentiles in such an extremity. The prophets already have the image of a remnant. A Jew would have to stay at his post even if he were a remnant of one. He would have to stay at His post lest God, left by His people, become "as it were, not be God."

Great, then, is the threat to divine revelation in history. Greater still is the threat to salvation, if only because it comes, for the most part, from a source over which a Jew in his fidelity has no control, from Gentile wickedness. Never was a bolder image conceived in Judaism than when Jeremiah described Nebuchadnezzar, the idol-worshiping Babylonian destroyer of God's own Temple, as God's own instrument. He served God's purpose of punishing Israel for her sins, though he would not escape punishment himself for his own wickedness. But the image of Jeremiah could not be strained beyond certain limits. When Nebuchadnezzar destroyed the First Temple it was because of the Jewish sin of idolatry. When Titus destroyed the Second Temple some rabbis, to be sure, concluded that once again Israel was punished for her sins. But others protested that there had been no idolatry this time, and no rabbinic source that I know of describes Titus as God's instrument: He is simply "the wicked one," and nothing more. And then after Titus came Hadrian, who tried to make an end, not only to a Jewish state, but to Judaism as well.

It is in this new extremity that Midrashic thought showed the fullness of its power. "Whenever Israel went into exile, God, as it were, went with them," Rabbi Akiba is reported as saying during the time of the Hadrianic persecutions. "Where is God's power now?" asks the second-century Rabbi Joshua ben Levi. "He has turned it against Himself so as to exercise self-restraint. He wants to send the final Redemption on account of the sufferings of the age, yet restrains himself since the time is not yet ripe." Akiba gives a startling new turn to the divine intimacy with his people, but a more startling turn still to the divine infinity. Joshua ben Levi confronts head-on the threat to divine infinity as it enters into the realm of history. Yet both hold fast to the fundamental principle of Judaism, the intimacy of the divine infinity. In His love Akiba's God goes with His people into exile; but the exile will not last forever. For all His power, the God of Joshua ben Levi cannot bring the final Redemption now, desperately needed though it is. But it is sure to come in the end.

GOD IN THE AGE OF AUSCHWITZ AND THE REBUILT JERUSALEM

"When ye are not My witnesses, I am, as it were not God." At Auschwitz Jews were not His witnesses—not because of infidelity but because they were murdered. The memory of those is holy who witnessed to Him even then, and this to their dying moment. But that memory may not be piously exploited, as a means of forgetting that few could be witnesses, that most were not witnesses but victims. Elie Wiesel writes about three Auschwitz prisoners about to be hanged for some trifling offense, with the rest of the camp forced to watch what was a regular ceremony. There was one unusual fact about this particular ceremonial murder: One of the three was a child. Just prior to the hanging Wiesel heard someone behind him ask, "Where is God? Where is He now?" As they tipped the chairs over and the three were strangled, he heard a voice within himself answer, "Where is He? Here He is—He is hanging on this gallows." Wiesel never says that God is dying: As a Jew he could not say it, and during a walk on New York's Fifth Avenue he once told me that He could not respect a God lacking power. The God that hangs with that boy on the Auschwitz gallows, however, does lack power. He lacks it absolutely, and this because He persists in His intimacy with His people. Is the price paid for that intimacy, then and there, not a *total* loss of the infinity? We have cited Roy Eckhardt as saying that the whole purpose of the program was to reduce Israel to excrement. That program included the God of Israel.

"When I praise God He is lovely; when I do not praise God He is, as it were, lovely in Himself." At Auschwitz many did praise God to the end. But again pious exploitation is illicit. Again it is forbidden to forget those who failed to give praise because they were not yet able to speak, or because they could speak no more—the babies thrown into the flames, and the *Muselmaenner* already dead in spirit before they dropped to the ground. Did God remain "lovely in Himself" at Auschwitz? But He could remain so only if He failed to hear the screams of the children, and the no less terrible silence of the *Muselmaenner*. Such a God might preserve His infinity, but would He not have lost every trace of His intimacy?

"The intimacy of the infinite": Jewish faith has held fast to this principle ever since the Creator of heaven and earth became the God also of Abraham. It has held fast to it against every temptation and through every vicissitude. Has the Holocaust, at long last, destroyed it? Has it fragmented the God of Israel, into an intimacy of absolute impotence, and an infinity of absolute indifference?

We do not know what the murdered millions thought of this question: Their thoughts were murdered with them. We do not even know the thoughts of those who tried to communicate them to us: Doubtless many put them on paper, but most of the papers were lost or destroyed.

Among the few that survived is a collection of Shabbat and festival discourses given between 1939 and 1942 by Rabbi Kalonymos Shapiro in the Warsaw Ghetto. The mere fact that he put them to paper *after* having delivered them, and not before, is proof that they were meant to be not lecture notes but a document for posterity. But there is further proof: Having carefully recorded and dated them, the rabbi buried his notes, together with a letter addressed to someone who, he hoped, would find them. The work, published as *Esh Kodesh* ("The Fire of Holiness") in Israel in 1960, is the last great document of Polish Hasidism.

Even in his earlier discourses the rabbi has little recourse to the conventional wisdom that once more Jews are punished for their sins: Unlike some among the pious today, he knew that the disaster was too vast. But until the summer of 1942 he still tried to cling to the view that vast but meaningless catastrophes had befallen the Jewish people before, that they had always survived them and always would. An entry dated November 27, 1942, however, reads as follows:

> Only until the end of 1942 was it the case that such sufferings were experienced before. However, as for the monstrous torments, the terrible and freakish deaths which the malevolent murderers invented against us, the house of Israel, from that time on—according to my knowledge of rabbinic literature and Jewish history in general, there has never been anything like them. May God have mercy and deliver us from their hands in the twinkling of an eye.

More than forty years later, when all is known, what Rabbi Shapiro said in 1942 is still widely denied. Though the worst was unknown to him then, the rabbi did not shrink from the terrible truth.

In a discourse delivered on March 14, 1942, Rabbi Shapiro expounds a Talmudic passage that tries to reconcile two biblical passages. In the first (Jer. 13:17) God weeps in secret because His flock is carried away captive, while the second reads as follows: "Honor and majesty are before Him; strength and gladness are in His place" (I Chron. 16:27). How can both be in His place, asks the Talmud, weeping and gladness? One is in the outer chamber, the other is in the inner, is the reply. But which is where? On this the Talmudic text is ambiguous, and conventional piety would lead one to assume that earthly sorrow, if reaching the place of God at all, reaches only the outer chamber, that in the inner all sorrow is transcended by gladness. Rashi reverses the imagery; I do not know why but am astonished. Rabbi Shapiro seizes on Rashi and goes beyond him. There is gladness in the outer chamber: God hides. Does He hide in wrath against, or punishment of, His people? God forbid that He should do so at such a time! Does He hide for reasons unknown? God forbid that He should, in this of all times, be a *deus absconditus!* Then why does He hide? He hides His weeping in the inner chamber, for *just as God is infinite so His pain is infinite, and this, were it to touch the world, would destroy it.* Is it still possible for a Jew to break through to the divine hiddenness, so as to share His pain? Rabbi Shapiro does not seem sure.

In Israel today what once was a children's song has become akin to a hymn: *am yisrael chai,* "the Jewish people lives." How is it possible to sing this song-become-hymn, to sing it joyfully? How is it possible to go on to the next line, *od avinus chai,* "our Father still lives"? *It is possible and actual because, even then, the bond between the divine intimacy and the divine infinity was not completely broken; because God so loved the world that He hid the infinity of His pain from it lest it be destroyed; and because Rabbi Shapiro so loved God as to seek to penetrate to the inner chamber, so as to share in the divine pain, even at the risk that in the sharing he would be destroyed.*

EPILOGUE

A Midrash asks why the Divine covenant with Abraham was required. "This," is the answer, "may be compared to a house on fire. People ask, Does the house have no owner? Through the children of Abraham God says, 'I am the owner of the house.'"

A Jew today still willing to convey this message has a question of his own: If the house has an owner, why does He not put the fire out? Perhaps He can and yet will. Perhaps He cannot or will not. But if He cannot or will not, a Jew today must do what he can to put the fire out himself. A kabbalistic saying is to the effect that the effort from below calls forth a response from above.

ANNOTATED BIBLIOGRAPHY

Part of the purpose of this bibliography is to inspire the reader to start his own library of Judaica. (A good first step would be membership in the Jewish Publication Society of America; it is listed below as JSP.) For this reason, I have selected, wherever possible, books that are inexpensive and available. The books listed below are of two kinds: introductory ones for the novice, and ones valuable even for the most expert.

The reader ought to own at least two Jewish books: the Tenach and the *Siddur*, the traditional prayer book for Shabbat and weekday services. This latter also contains *Pirke Abot* ("The Sayings of the Fathers"), the most popular of all rabbinic texts.

If I were to choose just one additional book I would wish the reader to own, my choice would be *The Rabbinic Anthology*, C. G. Montefiore and H. Loewe, eds. (New York: Schocken, 1970). This is by far the best and most comprehensive Midrash collection available in English.

CHAPTER 1
1. Borrowitz, Eugene B. *A Layman's Introduction to Religious Existentialism*. Philadelphia: Westminster, 1965.

A readable introduction to existentialism: Catholic, Protestant, and Jewish. Out of print, but widely available in libraries.

2. Buber, Martin. *Tales of the Hasidim.* 2 vols. New York: Schocken, 1961.
Although critics have maintained that this masterpiece, and other books by the same author on the same subject, fail to portray Hasidism objectively, I would not hesitate to recommend this as a first book to a reader who wishes to learn about, as well as be inspired by, Hasidism and indeed Judaism as a whole.

3. Cohen, Arthur A. and Paul Mendes-Flohr, eds. *Contemporary Jewish Religious Thought.* New York: Scribner, 1987.
A massive and comprehensive collection of original essays on almost every relevant topic, literally from A to Z, by reputable scholars.

4. Epstein, Isidore. *Judaism.* Baltimore: Penguin, 1968.
A readable and inexpensive introduction.

5. Glatzer, Nahum N., ed. *The Judaic Tradition.* New York: Behrman, 1982.
Probably the best overall anthology, by the master Jewish anthologist.

6. Himmelfarb, Milton, ed. *The Condition of Jewish Belief.* New York: Macmillan, 1966.
Responses by 38 Jewish thinkers, representing Orthodox, Conservative, and Reform Judaism, to five questions basic to Judaism. This symposium was conducted just prior to the Six-Day War, which caused major changes of view among many, including participants in this symposium.

7. Mendes-Flohr, Paul R. and Jehuda Reinharz, eds. *The Jew in the Modern World.* New York: Oxford, 1980.
An authoritative and comprehensive collection of documents, introducing the reader to the modern and contemporary Jewish condition.

8. Meyer, Michael A. *The Origins of the Modern Jew.* Detroit: Wayne State, 1967.
An absorbing account of the origin of the modern Jewish identity in early modern Germany.

9. Millgram, Abraham E., ed. *Great Jewish Ideas.* vol 5. B'nai B'rith Great Books Series, 1974.
Popular essays on God, Torah, Israel, and ideas relating to them, written by experts.

10. Noveck, Simon, ed. *Contemporary Jewish Thought.* B'nai B'rith Great Books Series, 1973.
Popular essays on religious and secular Jewish thinkers, written by experts.

11. Steinberg, Milton. *Basic Judaism*. New York: Harcourt, Brace, 1965.
A classic of its kind that has helped many to find their way to Judaism. Written, however, before either the Holocaust or the State of Israel.

12. Wiesel, Elie. *Night*. New York: Bantam, 1982.
A moving account of the effect of the Holocaust on a deeply religious boy, given by the celebrated author who has made it his life's work to be a witness.

CHAPTER 2

13. Avi-Yonah, Michael. *The Jews of Palestine*. Oxford: Blackwell, 1976.
A history, by now recognized as a classic, of the survival of the Jewish political will after the Bar Kochba war, until the Arab conquest in the seventh century.

14. Bauer, Yehuda. *Flight and Rescue: Bricha*. New York: Random House, 1970.
The authoritative history of the determined effort of Holocaust survivors to make their way to the land of Israel, great obstacles notwithstanding.

15. Curtis, Michael, ed. *Antisemitism in the Contemporary World*. Boulder, Col.: Westview Press, 1986.
The most recent collection of essays on a nasty but unavoidable subject, by distinguished and perceptive contributors.

16. Fain, Benjamin and Mervin F. Verbit. *Jewishness in the Soviet Union: Report of an Empirical Survey*. Jerusalem Center for Public Affairs, 1984.
An account of the extraordinary fidelity of many Soviet Jews to whatever remnants of a Jewish heritage survive, government-inspired hostility notwithstanding.

17. Grayzel, Solomon. *A History of the Jews*. JPS, 1967.
A readable, inexpensive, and readily available one-volume history.

18. Schwarz-Bart, Andre. *The Last of the Just*. New York: Bantam, 1973.
An epic, unforgettable novel of Jewish fidelity through the ages and in our time.

19. Spiegel, Shalom. *The Last Trial*. New York: Pantheon, 1963.
An account of traditions concerning martyrdom, based on the biblical account of the "binding" of Isaac by Abraham (Gen. 22:1–19). (The traditional Jewish term is "binding" rather than "sacrifice," as a perpetual reminder of the fact that the awesome act was not consummated.) A classic.

20. Syrkin, Marie. *Blessed Is the Match.* JPS, 1976.
An account of the Jewish resistance during the Holocaust. Although published originally as early as 1947, and superseded in
some respects by subsequent research, this book remains required reading, not only because of the author's deep humanity
but also, and indeed especially, because it is totally free of the
tendency, marring many other accounts of this and related subjects, to divert attention from the Nazi criminals by laying blame
on others, the victims included.

CHAPTER 3

21. *Tanakh: A New Translation.* JPS, 1982.
While any translation of the Tenach will do, this most recent of
Jewish translations, the work of decades of scholarship, is recommended. The much cheaper 1917 JPS translation, reprinted numerous times, still serves.

22. Bickerman, Elias. *Four Strange Books of the Bible.* New York:
Schocken, 1967.
Fresh questions asked about the books of Jonah, Daniel, Kohelet,
and Esther by one of the most penetrating, yet readable, scholars
of the last generation.

23. Childs, Brevard S. *Introduction to the Old Testament as Scripture.* Philadelphia: Fortress, 1980.
A monumental attempt to understand the Tenach in three ways:
from the standpoint of biblical criticism, as Jewish Scripture, and
as Christian Scripture. An admirable, if controversial, tour-de-
force.

24. Hertz, J. H., ed. *The Pentateuch and Haftorahs.* London: Son-
cino, 1976.
This edition and translation, accompanied by essays and commentaries by the late Chief Rabbi of Great Britain, has been
found indispensable by generations of traditional worshipers and
will presumably remain so, even though recent events in Jewish
history have overtaken some of the rabbi's comments.

25. Kaufmann, Yehezkel. *The Religion of Israel.* Chicago: University of Chicago Press, 1960.
The well-known classic about Judaism in biblical times, expertly
translated and abridged by Moshe Greenberg.

26. Levenson, John D. *Sinai and Zion.* Minneapolis: Winston, 1985.
An excellent introduction to the Tenach that combines critical
scholarship with a Jewish perspective, by a highly promising
younger scholar.

27. Montefiore, C. G. and H. Loewe, eds. *A Rabbinic Anthology*. New York: Schocken, 1970.
By far the best anthology of Midrashic material available in English. A classic.

28. Pinchas, Peli H. *Torah Today*. Washington: B'nai B'rith Books, 1987.
The sages advise us to read the Torah as though it had been given today. The reader of the weekly Torah portion will find this book a great aid.

29. Plaut, W. Gunther and Bernard Bamberger. *The Torah: A Modern Commentary*. New York: Union of American Hebrew Congregations, 1981.
An impressive achievement, sponsored by the Reform movement.

30. Schechter, Solomon. *Some Aspects of Rabbinic Theology*. New York: Schocken, 1961.
A solid study by the famous figure in American Conservative Judaism.

31. Steinsaltz, Adin. *The Essential Talmud*. New York: Basic Books, 1976.
An excellent introduction, by an outstanding scholar and pedagogue.

32. Werblowsky, R. J. Zwi. *Joseph Karo*. JPS, 1977.
A definitive study of the fascinating figure who was both the author of the Shulchan Aruch, the authoritative code of traditional Jewish law, and a mystic.

CHAPTER 4

33. Buber, Martin. *Israel and the World*. New York: Schocken, 1965.
For a modest library, this, next to his *Tales of the Hasidim*, is the book of Buber's to acquire. A well-balanced presentation of the major aspects of his Jewish thought, it also contains "The Man of Today and the Jewish Bible." See also below, nos. 40, 41, 42, 108, 109.

34. Fackenheim, Emil L. *Quest For Past and Future*. Westport, Conn.: Greenwood, 1983.
Chapters 2, 4, and 6 are my first reflections on the subject of revelation. For my mature work, see below, nos. 101, 111, 112.

35. Herberg, Will. *Judaism and Modern Man*. JPS, 1961.
In some ways dated, this account of the Judaism of the God of revelation by a former Marxist still deserves respect and attention.

36. Heschel, Abraham J. *The Prophets.* JPS, 1955.
This work by one of the great Jewish religious thinkers of our age is modern-critical, yet takes the "Thus sayth the Lord" of the prophets seriously. See also nos. 74, 114.

37. Lauterbach, Jacob Z., ed. and tr. *Mekilta de Rabbi Ishmael.* JPS, 1949.
Inexpensive and available. A reader who would venture beyond the Midrash selections in no. 26 to a complete Midrash text is advised to begin with this one, in connection with the theme of this chapter. A series of commentaries on the Book of Exodus, the Mekilta includes in its treatment two Jewish root experiences: the Exodus and the Sinaitic Revelation.

38. Rosenzweig, Franz. *On Jewish Learning.* 2 vols. New York: Schocken, 1955.
These two volumes, edited with masterly skill by Nahum N. Glatzer, give a good first access to one who is becoming increasingly viewed as the greatest modern Jewish religious thinker. See also no. 117.

39. Rosenzweig, Franz. *Franz Rosenzweig: His Life and Thought.* New York: Schocken, 1967.

CHAPTER 5

40. Brenner, Reeve R. *The Faith and Doubt of Holocaust Survivors.* New York: Free Press, 1980.
An empirically base study of the religious feelings and reactions of Jewish victims—those who have a greater reason and greater right than any previous Jewish generation to reject the idea of divine chosenness.

41. Buber, Martin. *The Prophetic Faith.* New York: MacMillan, 1949.

42. Buber, Martin. *Moses.* New York: Harper Torchbooks, 1958.

43. Buber, Martin. *Kingship of God.* New York: Harper Torchbooks, 1973.
Perhaps the most lasting achievement of this great and many-sided Jewish thinker is his work with the Bible. For a modern Jew the best approach to the difficult concepts of a divine–Jewish covenant and the chosenness of Israel may well be via Buber's interpretations of biblical books and themes. Though scholarly, his interpretations are never without contemporary relevance.

44. Edelheit, Joseph A., ed. *The Life of the Covenant.* Chicago: Spertus College of Judaica Press, 1986.
In the early sixties, Herman Schaalman (in whose honor this

book was written) was active in rallying for regular meetings "covenant theologians," Reform, Conservative, and Orthodox. This theme provides the title of this book, written by his friends and colleagues, even though not all their essays deal with it.

45. Kaplan, Mordecai M. *Judaism as a Civilization.* JPS, 1981.
The magnum opus of the Jewish religious thinker who was the first openly to repudiate the traditional doctrine of the chosenness of Israel.

CHAPTER 6

46. Chill, Abraham. *The Mitzvot: The Commandments and Their Rationale.* New York: Bloch, 1974.
A traditional interpretation of the 613 commandments, reinforced by traditional commentaries.

47. Davis, Moshe. *The Emergence of Conservative Judaism.* JPS, 1963.
An authoritative account by a distinguished scholar.

48. Freehof, Solomon B. *Current Reform Responsa.* Cincinnati: Hebrew Union College, 1969.

49. Freehof, Solomon B. *Contemporary Reform Responsa.* Cincinnati: H.U.C., 1974.

50. Freehof, Solomon B. *New Reform Responsa.* Cincinnati: H.U.C., 1980.
This distinguished scholar is living proof that a Reform rabbi may have great respect for, and expertise in, Halachic matters.

51. Greenberg, Blu. *How to Run a Traditional Jewish Household.* New York: Simon and Schuster, 1983.
Those wishing to make their households traditionally Jewish may well be intimidated by the task. This sensitive book will inform them, inspire them, and relieve their fears.

52. Jacob, Walter, ed. *American Reform Response.* Central Conference of American Rabbis, 1983.
Collected Responsa to Halachic questions given by Reform rabbis, 1889–1983: an impressive document showing that as a group, Reform rabbis do not have the supercilious attitude toward Halacha often ascribed to them.

53. Klein, Isaac. *A Guide to Jewish Religious Practice.* New York: Jewish Theological Seminary, 1979.
Probably the best guide to Conservative Jewish practice.

54. Plaut, W. Gunther. *The Rise of Reform Judaism.* World Union of Progressive Judaism, 1963.

55. Plaut, W. Gunther. *The Growth of Reform Judaism.* World Union of Progressive Judaism, 1965.

The most up-to-date and comprehensive history of the Reform movement.

56. Rosenbaum, Irving. *The Holocaust and Halacha*. New York: Ktav, 1976.
A deeply moving account of Jewish fidelity in an unprecedented extremity. This book will arouse respect for Halacha even among those unable to subscribe to it.

57. Soloveitchik, Joseph B. *Halakhic Man*. JPS, 1983.
A brief but profound account by the unchallenged leader of Orthodox Judaism in North America.

58. Stendhal, Krister. *Paul Among Jews and Gentiles*. Philadelphia: Fortress, 1976.
An account of the apostle's study with Rabban Gamliel—quite at odds with mine, yet written by a noted scholar familiar with, and sympathetic to, the sources of Judaism.

CHAPTER 7

59. Holtz, Barry W., ed. *Back to the Sources: Reading the Classic Jewish Texts*. New York: Summit, 1985.
A guide, written by leading scholars, that fills a great lacuna. Warmly recommended.

60. Kadushin, Max. *The Rabbinic Mind*. New York: The Jewish Theological Seminary, 1952.
A highly original and widely respected interpretation.

61. Urbach, Ephraim. *The Sages: Their Concepts and Beliefs*. Jerusalem: Magnes Press, 1975.
A comprehensive study of the rabbinic sages, for advanced students. See also nos. 30, 31, 39 and especially 38. Rosenzweig's idea of "the new Jewish learning" is as compelling today as it was more than half a century ago.

CHAPTER 8

62. Bernfeld, Simon, ed. *The Foundations of Jewish Ethics*. New York: Ktav, 1968.
This sourcebook of rabbinic texts, published originally in German in 1922, is still highly serviceable. So are the introductions to the various topics, whose authors include my own teachers, Leo Baeck and Ismar Elbogen.

63. Fox, Marvin, ed. *Modern Jewish Ethics*. Columbus: Ohio State University Press, 1975.
A volume of significant legal and philosophical essays. Especially

significant are two essays by Orthodox authors about the relation between Halacha and other ethical systems.

64. Herford, R. Travers, ed. and tr. *The Ethics of the Talmud: Sayings of the Fathers.* New York: Schocken, 1969.
Even though the reader will find the text of *Pirke Abot* in his *Siddur*, there are good reasons for acquiring one of the numerous separate editions whose editors all provide commentaries. The late Travers Herford was a distinguished Christian scholar of Pharisaic and Rabbinic Judaism.

65. Kellner, Menachem Marc, ed. *Contemporary Jewish Ethics.* New York: Sanhedrin, 1978.
This is probably the best recent volume on the ethics of Judaism. Particularly valuable are the sections on contemporary issues, such as business ethics, sexual ethics, political ethics, medical ethics, and the Holocaust. The authors are serious scholars, rooted in the tradition.

66. Silver, Daniel Jeremy, ed. *Judaism and Ethics.* New York: Ktav, 1970.
Another valuable collection of essays, mostly written by Reform Jewish scholars. See also nos. 5, 29, 30, 31.

CHAPTER 9

67. The *Siddur* (the traditional prayer book for weekdays and Shabbat) and the High Holiday *Machzor* (the traditional prayer book for Rosh Hashanah and Yom Kippur).
Any edition will do, but because of its notes the Birnbaum editions, published by the Hebrew Publishing Company, are recommended. Rosenzweig described the *Siddur* as being not only a prayer book, but also a compendium of Jewish theology.

68. The *New Union Prayer Book* and *The Gates of Repentance.* New York: Central Conference of American Rabbis, 1975, 1978.
The official prayer books of the American Reform Movement. These have virtually replaced the Union Prayer Book, vols. 1 and 2, which had long been in use, almost without revision. Marked changes noticeable in the new volumes include a more positive attitude toward the tradition, an identification with Israel, and a facing up to the Holocaust.

69. *Machzor for Rosh Hashanah and Yom Kippur.* New York: Rabbinical Assembly, 1975.
The High Holy Days prayer book of the American Conservative Movement.

70. Glatzer, Nahum N., ed. *The Language of Faith.* New York: Schocken, 1975.

Yet another masterly anthology by the master Jewish anthologist.

71. Harlow, Jules, ed. and tr. *Siddur Sim Shalom.* New York: Rabbinical Assembly and United Synagogue, 1985.
Probably the most widely used, though not official, *Siddur* of American Conservative Judaism.

72. Millgram, Abraham. *Jewish Worship.* JPS, 1971.
A lucid and comprehensive exposition, inexpensive and available.

73. *The Rosh Hashanah Anthology.* JPS, 1970.

74. *The Yom Kippur Anthology.* JPS, 1971.

75. *The Hanukkah Anthology.* JPS, 1976.

76. *The Purim Anthology.* JPS, 1949.

77. *The Passover Anthology.* JPS, 1961.

78. *The Shavuot Anthology.* JPS, 1974.

79. *The Succot and Simchat Torah Anthology.* JPS, 1973.
Volumes 76–82 are all edited by Philip Goodman. They, and no. 75, are all excellent aids to a more meaningful celebration of Shabbat and the festivals.

CHAPTER 10

80. Agnon, S. Y., ed. *Days of Awe.* New York: Schocken, 1965.
An anthology of traditions, legends, and commentaries relating to Rosh Hashanah and Yom Kippur. A classic by the renowned writer.

81. Heschel, Abraham J. *The Earth Is the Lord's* and *The Sabbath.* Cleveland: World, 1963.
A profound and moving meditation on the celebration of Shabbat.

82. Kasher, Menachem M., ed. *Israel Passover Haggadah.* New York: American Biblical Encyclopedia Society, 1950.
There are numerous editions of the Passover Haggadah: traditional, Reform, Reconstructionist, Israeli-secular. (The Haggadah has also given much inspiration to artists.) What makes Rabbi Kasher's edition remarkable is his recourse to traditional sources in relation to the momentous events of our time: the Holocaust and the birth of the State of Israel. Many will find any such recourse religiously unacceptable and perhaps politically dangerous to boot. Even so, they should ponder the traditional texts cited or referred to by Rabbi Kasher.

83. Millgram, Abraham E., ed. *Sabbath: The Day of Delight.* JPS, 1944.

84. Newman, A., ed. *Mayanot: Yom Ha-atzmaut.* World Zionist Organization, 1967.

Articles and texts in aid of Israel Independence Day celebration.

CHAPTER 11

85. Ben Gurion, David. *Rebirth and Destiny of Israel*. New York: Philosophical Library, 1954.
Reflections by the chief architect of the State of Israel.

86. Collins, Larry and Dominique Lapierre. *O Jerusalem*. New York: Pocket Books, 1973.
An absorbing, although violently evenhanded, account of the major events that led to the foundation of the State of Israel. Not always accurate. A onetime best-seller.

87. Gilbert, Martin. *The Holocaust*. JPS, 1987.
For those who want but one book on this grim subject, this is the one to read. It documents not only the crimes of the criminals but also the suffering, martyrdom, and resistance of the victims. Of special merit is the heavy reliance on survivors' testimonies. No one who has read this book can doubt the moral necessity of Holocaust study, if only because remembrance is a duty owed to the murdered millions. In this connection, it should be mentioned that Claude Lanzmann's masterly film *Shoah* is a "must."

88. Holtz, Avraham, ed. *The Holy City: Jews on Jerusalem*. New York: W. W. Norton, 1971.
A popular account of the attachment of Jews to Jerusalem, through the ages up to the Six-Day War.

89. Kasher, Menachem M., ed. *The Western Wall*. New York: Judaica Press, 1972.
A collection of traditional text relating to the Western Wall in Jerusalem, the most sacred place in the Jewish religious consciousness.

90. Laqueur, Walter. *A History of Zionism*. London: Weidenfeld & Nicolson, 1972.
The most authoritative history of the subject. A bonus is the author's thought-provoking concluding "Thirteen Theses on Zionism."

91. Postal, Bernard and Henry W. Levy. *And the Hills Shouted*. JPS, 1973.
A history of the events that culminated in the proclamation of the State of Israel. Readable, inexpensive, available.

92. Rabinovich, Abraham. *The Battle for Jerusalem*. JPS, 1972.
A thorough history of the Six-Day War, with emphasis on the historic and consequence-laden battle for Jerusalem. Readable, inexpensive, available.

CHAPTER 12

93. Bloch, Joseph Samuel. *Israel and the Nations.* Berlin/Vienna: Harz, 1927.
   Important as an historical document, but presumably available only in specialized libraries.

94. Borowitz, Eugene B. *Contemporary Christologies: A Jewish Response.* New York: Paulist Press, 1980.
   Virtually a "first" in Jewish–Christian dialogue, a direct Jewish confrontation with leading Christian thinkers on the doctrine that sets Jews and Christians most obviously apart.

95. Eckardt, A. Roy. *Your People, My People: The Meeting of Jews and Christians.* New York: Quadrangle, 1974.
   Perhaps the most readily intelligible work of this prolific and masterly Christian theologian, who has been bolder than virtually all his colleagues in fighting traditional Christian anti-Jewish attitudes and doctrines, and in aiming at a positive Jewish–Christian relationship.

96. Eisenberg, Azriel, ed. *Witness to the Holocaust.* New York: Pilgrim Press, 1981.
   This volume includes chapters on the "righteous among the nations," and on *kiddush hashem* (martyrdom) and *kiddush hachayim* (sanctification of life).

97. Lichtenstein, Aaron. *The Seven Laws of Noah.* New York: The Rabbi Jacob Joseph School Press, 1981.
   An exploration of this neglected but crucially important topic by an outstanding rabbinic authority.

98. Littell, Franklin H. *The Crucifixion of the Jews.* New York: Harper & Row, 1975.
   A brief but powerful statement by a leading Christian thinker for whom the Holocaust is a "watershed" not only for Jews but for Christians as well, and who has done much to put this teaching into practice.

99. Parkes, James. *The Conflict of the Church and the Synagogue: A Study in the Origins of Antisemitism.* New York: Atheneum, 1969.
   An important study by the great Christian pioneer in the search for a positive Jewish–Christian relationship.

100. Talmage, Frank, ed. *Disputation and Dialogue.* New York: Ktav, 1975.
   By far the best, least sermonic, and most realistic anthology of the Jewish–Christian encounter through the ages and at the present time.

CHAPTER 13

101. Fackenheim, Emil L. *The Jewish Return into History*. New York: Schocken, 1978.

The last chapter of this book is an attempt to explore the relationship between the Holocaust and the State of Israel in the light of the prayer composed by the Israeli chief rabbinate which refers to the state as "the beginning of the growth of the redemption" of the Jewish people. See also nos. 34, 111, 112.

102. Klausner, Joseph. *The Messianic Idea in Israel*. New York: Macmillan, 1955.

A standard work on the history of the idea, from its origins to the completion of the Mishnah.

103. Maimonides, Moses. *Treatise on Resurrection*. Translated and annotated by Fred Rosner. New York: Ktav, 1982.

In view of the rabbinic thesis that the world-to-come is real but unintelligible in this world, it is not surprising that few works exist on this subject. The Rambam's treatise is a great exception and not surprisingly aroused much controversy in his time. Rosner's edition includes Daniel Jeremy Silver's authoritative account of that controversy.

104. Scholem, Gershom. *Major Trends in Jewish Mysticism*. New York: Schocken, 1941.

A classic, by the greatest authority on the subject. Of special relevance for the subject of this and the following chapter.

105. Scholem. Gershom. *The Messianic Idea in Judaism*. New York: Schocken, 1972.

An authoritative treatment by one of the great scholars of this generation.

106. Silver, Abba Hillel. *A History of Messianic Speculation in Israel from the First through the Seventeenth Century*. Boston: Beacon, 1959.

Though first published in 1929, still serviceable, especially since not much has been written on the subject more recently. See also nos. 29, 30, 31, 110, 117.

CHAPTER 14

107. Berkowitz, Eliezer. *Faith After the Holocaust*. New York: Ktav, 1973.

Combines traditional piety with profound honesty, in an attempt to grapple with the unprecedented problem.

108. Buber, Martin. *I and Thou*. Translated by Walter Kaufmann. New York: Scribner, 1970.

For all its brevity, Buber's ground-breaking work in his teaching about God and His relation to man. Despite the absence of technical terms, a difficult book.

109. Buber, Martin. *Eclipse of God*. New York: Humanities, 1979.
In *I and Thou*, Buber asserted that God "speaks" constantly, the implication being that in case we do not "hear," the cause is to be found in man and his world alone. In this work, written thirty years later, he withdraws that assertion and considers the possibility that there may be times of divine silence.

110. Cohen, Hermann. *Religion of Reason from the Sources of Judaism*. Translated by Simon Kaplan. New York: Ungar, 1972.
The major, massive work of one of the great Jewish philosophers of this century. Focused on two concepts, God and the messianic idea. Requires philosophical background.

111. Fackenheim, Emil L. *God's Presence in History*. New York: Harper Torchbooks, 1972.
In book form, my first and fairly popular attempt to grapple with the question of Jewish faith after the Holocaust.

112. Fackenheim, Emil L. *To Mend the World: Foundations of Future Jewish Thought*. New York: Schocken, 1982.
My major and (as far as I can foresee) definitive work in the field of Jewish thought. Requires philosophical background.

113. Halevi, Yehuda. *The Kuzari*. New York: Schocken, 1964.
One of the major works of medieval Jewish thought. Still compelling for the most part and, though written by a philosophically trained and sophisticated thinker, not beyond the scope of the intelligent layman. A classic.

114. Heschel, Abraham J. *God in Search of Man*. New York: Farrar, Straus, 1955.
Heschel's magnum opus on the subject of this chapter.

115. Maimonides. *The Guide of the Perplexed*. Translated by S. Pines. Chicago: University of Chicago Press, 1964.
The definitive English translation. Generally recognized as the greatest work in Jewish philosophy, the *Guide* is a classic which continues to be relevant. The reader without philosophical background will find the going difficult.

116. Polen, Nehemia. *Esh Kodesh: The Teachings of Rabbi Kalonymos Shapiro in the Warsaw Ghetto, 1939–43*. Ann Arbor: University Microfilms International, 1983.
Until Rabbi Shapiro's *Esh Kodesh* is available in English, those unable to read Hebrew are referred to this masterly doctoral dissertation.

117. Rosenzweig, Franz. *The Star of Redemption*. Translated by William W. Hallo. New York: Holt, Rinehart, 1971.
Widely considered the greatest Jewish philosophical work of

modern times, this book is also the most difficult. It was published just after World War I, and some of its crucial affirmations were overrun by the events of World War II. Even so, the book's impact seems destined to grow with the passage of time.

118. Rubenstein, Richard. *After Auschwitz*. Indianapolis: Bobbs-Merrill, 1966.
The book that shook the comfortable piety of the religious in all denominations of American Judaism.

119. Wiesel, Elie. *The Gates of the Forest*. New York: Holt, Rinehart, 1966.
The author's profoundly Jewish grappling with God after the Holocaust permeates nearly all his works. In this novel it is particularly direct.

SUBJECT INDEX

Abot, 974, 157–58, 270, 271
Adon Olam, 21, 281–82, 284
Aggada, 73
agnosticism, 271, 281
Akeda, 186
Aleynu prayer, 198
Aliyah, 83, 128
Also Sprach Zarathustra (Nietzsche), 182
Alt-neuland (Herzl), 56
Amcha:
    defined, 15
    fidelity of, 57
    Messianic hope and, 261
    Seder celebrations by, 164
    Shabbat experienced by, 94
    Torah study by, 101, 164–66
    Yom Kippur of, 212–14
Amidah, 189–93, 210, 267–68, 270
Amos, Book of, 20, 113, 276
animal sacrifice, 141, 181–84, 187, 218–19
Antisemite and Jew (Sartre), 53–54
antisemitism:
    Christian, 79
    Jewish reactions to, 50–51, 53–57
    literature of, 240–42, 243
    national, 86, 240–42, 256
anti-Zionism, 33, 55, 227–28
assimilation, 38, 50–53, 258–59
atheism, 72, 119
Auschwitz, 33, 34, 124–25, 288–289
Av, ninth day of, 215, 216

Babylonian Talmud, 69, 174, 229
Balfour Declaration (1917), 233, 234
Bar Kochba rebellion (135 C.E.), 15, 35, 71, 228, 230, 243
bar mitzvah, 29
Berachot, 190–92, 200, 204, 210–211
Beta Yisrael, 224
biblical criticism, 77–82
B'richa immigration movement, 55–56

Catholicism, 28–29, 45, 65, 77, 159
chosen people doctrine, 111–14, 120–25, 244
Christianity:
    canon of, 63–67, 82–83, 168
    conversion to, 54, 131–32, 249
    as descendant of Judaism, 63–64, 79, 114–15, 159, 187, 247–49
    Jewish universalist-particularist tension and, 110–12
    Judaism opposed by, 32, 51, 52, 57, 76, 174, 231–32, 248–50
    medieval literacy and, 150, 159
    practice of, 24–26, 29
    salvation in, 130, 214, 251
Chronicles, second Book of, 63
church services, 66, 82–83, 159
Conservative Judaism, 70, 122, 143–45, 147, 189

NAME INDEX

317